LEONARDO
DA VINCI

LEONARDO DA VINCI

An Untraceable Life

STEPHEN J. CAMPBELL

PRINCETON UNIVERSITY PRESS

Princeton and Oxford

Published by Princeton University Press, 41 William Street, Princeton, New Jersey 08540

In the United Kingdom: Princeton University Press, 99 Banbury Road, Oxford OX2 6JX

press.princeton.edu

Jacket image: Leonardo da Vinci, *The head of an old bearded man* (detail), c. 1517–18. Black chalk on paper, 21.3 × 15.5 cm. © Royal Collection Enterprises Limited 2024 | Royal Collection Trust.

Library of Congress Cataloging-in-Publication Data

Names: Campbell, Stephen J. (Stephen John), 1963– author.
Title: Leonardo Da Vinci : the anti-biography / Stephen J. Campbell.
Description: Princeton : Princeton University Press, [2025] | Includes
    bibliographical references and index.
Identifiers: LCCN 2024023693 (print) | LCCN 2024023694 (ebook) |
    ISBN 9780691193687 (hardback) | ISBN 9780691266220 (ebook)
Subjects: LCSH: Leonardo, da Vinci, 1452–1519. | Artists—Italy—Biography. |
    Artists in popular culture. | Art and society. | BISAC: ART / History /
    Renaissance | ART / Individual Artists / General
Classification: LCC N6923.L33 C36 2025 (print) | LCC N6923.L33 (ebook) |
    DDC 709.2 [B]—dc23/eng/20240719
LC record available at https://lccn.loc.gov/2024023693
LC ebook record available at https://lccn.loc.gov/2024023694

British Library Cataloging-in-Publication Data is available

Editorial: Michelle Komie and Annie Miller
Production Editorial: Karen Carter
Text Design: Lauren Smith
Jacket/Cover Design: Lauren Smith
Production: Steven Sears
Publicity: Jodi Price and Kathryn Stevens

This book has been composed in Garamond Premier Pro
Printed in the United States of America

1 3 5 7 9 10 8 6 4 2

CONTENTS

LEONARDO DA VINCI

INTRODUCTION

If you were looking for a book to read on Leonardo da Vinci, and you picked this one, you are probably aware that there are numerous other possibilities. More than two hundred fifty books on the artist have been published, across the globe and in multiple languages, during and in the aftermath of his quincentennial in 2019. Not that there weren't already hundreds of Leonardo titles available: books for children, books by and for specialists, books by nonspecialists promising sensational new revelations, books that offer self-help, or the refinement of your mental prowess, or of your effectiveness as a corporate strategist. Many of these books promise a unique access to the mind of a genius, to the man as he really was, a supreme achiever despite a career thwarted by misunderstanding and adversity, a timeless example.

Most of these books are biographical in their approach. That is, they assess the meaning of a life as a whole: from Leonardo's illegitimate birth in an obscure village, to a long and hard ascent to growing recognition and fame, despite painful failure; to breakthroughs in knowledge that were centuries ahead of their time. The human-interest character Da Vinci is so well-known that he has become over-familiar, just like his works. Yet somehow this story needs to be told over and over again. Why?

The obvious answer is that his legacy of drawings, writings, and paintings seems so rich that it rewards repeated examination. The copious but scattered archives of Leonardo manuscripts reveal his involvement in multiple fields of knowledge in the decades on either side of the year

1500—optics, anatomy, engineering, hydrodynamics, natural history (including geology, zoology, and paleontology); the reception of the Greek philosopher Aristotle and his teachings on the mind; the theory and practice of painting; recodified according to scientific principles; sculpture and technologies of bronze casting; the culture of books and libraries. As a window into the history of ideas about the nature of human beings, their relation to non-human animals and to a volatile and fragile natural world, these writings—fraught by both wonder and pessimism—have much to say to us today, although the challenges to editing and circulating them remain immense.

Somehow, these achievements need to be framed by a life story. I'd go further: we need the works and the writings to *become* that life story. We want a character somehow like ourselves, still living and breathing at the heart of that complicated legacy. An individual who can reconcile that legacy of achievement, to make sense of it all.

The character or personality of Leonardo, then, serves a purpose—even if that character is largely a fiction, a made-up person created by highly partisan interests after his death, elaborated into a timeless genius in the nineteenth and twentieth centuries, and increasingly made to resemble ourselves in the twenty-first.

Be reassured, this is a book about Leonardo da Vinci. As an art historian, I am invested in what my profession—in all its technical and critical and archival subfields—can say about his extraordinary legacy and the fascination it continues to exert. It considers Leonardo according to what we are still learning about the lifeworld of a Renaissance artist and its transformation around 1480–1520. I am interested in how questions of selfhood and identity, as we would now call them, were conceived by premodern individuals, especially artists—and in the radical differences from our own conceptions. Precisely for this reason, I began above with the Leonardo books—I now own tottering piles of them—because their very quantity, and the version of the artist and writer that they offer their readers, can shape new historical questions: namely that their version of Leonardo seems to be compensating for a sense of lack, or a loss.

Hence this is also a book about biography, a distinctively modern form of life-writing that seeks to interpret a subject's inner and public worlds, to see life and works in terms of each other, and to assign significance to the life as a whole. While modern forms of biography may succeed as entertainment, I will show how they often fail as history with regard to individuals like Leonardo da Vinci. I also maintain that the failures of biography are useful for getting to grips with Leonardo as a historical phenomenon. Lack, or absence, will be a major focus of the chapters that follow.

In contrast with the biographical optimism of much recent writing, the present book is about Leonardo's resistance to becoming a subject of biography, as well as the gaps in the historical record that have invited projection and fictionalization. We thereby gain an understanding of a Leonardo who is not like ourselves, who refuses our attempts to make him so. Because the Leonardo who emerges here manifests a distinctly nonmodern way of being a person, of having what we call a "self." And, in making Leonardo strange, we also gain an understanding of ourselves, or the historical contingency of our notions of personhood. We were not always as we are now, and there were always other possibilities. And we will also learn from our own desire for a fully realized Leonardo in the twenty-first century, as well as the various interests that are served (and ill-served) by the ubiquity of this largely made-up "character" in our time.

I will be returning to the documents to address what they actually warrant us to say about the professional life and the personal life of Leonardo da Vinci. Despite an abundance of records by contemporaries about Leonardo, and despite thousands of pages of notes and longer drafts in Leonardo's own hand, there is remarkably little that can be said with confidence about his life, let alone about his "character" and "personality." We know the circumstances of his illegitimate birth in Anchiano near Vinci in 1452, we have very sketchy knowledge of his childhood and apprenticeship, and we know more or less about whom he worked for as an artist and engineer, and where—Florence, Milan, Florence again, Rome, France. For much of his surviving artistic production, however, dates and documents are a problem: about one-third of Leonardo's surviving paintings lack records confirming his authorship or indicating for whom the work was made. Accounts of Leonardo's works by contemporaries often worryingly differ from the surviving works that we connect them to. While a few contemporaries refer to Leonardo's charisma and sociable nature, there is almost nothing in Leonardo's own words about Leonardo himself. In stark contrast, we have abundant poetry and letters by his contemporary Michelangelo that dramatically (though no less fictively) stage the challenges and vexations of being an artist, his sense of betrayal and disappointment with patrons and family members, his professions of affection and of love, his state of physical health.

What is most egregiously at stake is the nature of our relation to the past—to the art of the past, to the past as record of human experience and accomplishment. Leonardo represents an extraordinary convergence of invention, imagination, skill, and curiosity that takes us into a premodern world discontinuous from ours, into a spectrum of relations with other makers and thinkers, that demands an adjustment of our twenty-first-century perspective on the past. How do we understand and build on the evidence while respecting the remoteness, the unknowability of past lives? How should we rise above the deadening presumption of the *claim to know*?

DA VINCI: NEW, IMPROVED, REANIMATED

Why am I doing this? And, is there not a tension between my desire to undermine the cult of Leonardo with yet another book that seeks to bring us closer to understanding him? What I hope to do here is not invalidate centuries of curiosity about the man and his works but push that curiosity in directions that undermine the myth and give us something better.

As a university-based art historian (and occasional curator), I have taught several courses on Leonardo over a thirty-year period. This book is shaped by the questions and interests that several generations of students brought to class. Such questions were not shaped by their desire to be or to impress an art historian but from their vocations as engineers and scientists, or their interest in science fiction and gaming, or their skepticism about a historical phenomenon, "the Renaissance," centered on dead white male celebrities like "Da Vinci." I thus began to think of multiple images of Leonardo, shaped by cultures far broader than the historical study of art and science. This proliferation of images, in publishing, in electronic media, in tourism and museums, in the art market and its journalistic echo chamber, seemed to be a distinctly twenty-first-century symptom—but of what?

Most obviously, the constant spotlighting of Leonardo "discoveries" in popular media shows how "Da Vinci" has become a historical legitimation of our obsessions with art, genius, and technological innovation as a means of obtaining celebrity and wealth. Let's pursue this a little further.

"Leonardo" is manifest in a series of different platforms, fields of inquiry, realms of spectacle—let's call them "Da Vinci Worlds." Think of the image of Leonardo in TV and electronic media, commercial publishing, online gaming, tech branding, mass tourism, the art market, museums and pseudo-museums. Our Da Vinci has been refashioned to fit the profile of twenty-first-century celebrity: a wayward nonconforming painter; a pioneering technical innovator and problem-solver; an athlete, even, and a fashion influencer. A type whose idealisms and *personal struggles* draw as much attention as his achievements—gay, vegetarian, pro–animal rights, a religious agnostic. We seemingly cannot get enough of this phantom celebrity, this Da Vinci. But what does this Da Vinci have to do with the artist known in his lifetime as Leonardo da Vinci, or Leonardo of Florence, Léonard de Florence, and in occasional literary contexts as "Vincius" or "Vinci"? He was never called "Da Vinci" until the 1800s.[1]

And "Da Vinci Worlds" are also a way of containing and exploiting our boredom with the personality cult and its ubiquity. Exasperation with the overhyped portrait, and with the Leonardo cult in general, is nothing new—more than a century ago, it caused the art connoisseur Bernard Berenson to celebrate the 1911 theft of the *Mona Lisa* from the Louvre. His most famous portrait has long symbolized "old master," "masterpiece," and "European canon" and been a focus for modernist iconoclasm—a series of defaced Giocondas from Kasimir Malevich to Marcel Duchamp to Andy Warhol (fig. 1). If you're an influencer in the art world, *Mona Lisa* can stand for everything you dislike or resist: Robert Hughes's 2008 BBC documentary *The Mona Lisa Curse* opens with a chilling screen blend of the face of the *Mona Lisa* with *For the Love of God*, a diamond-encrusted skull by Damien Hirst—epitomizing the twenty-first-century art world as a hoax-ridden ritual squandering of wealth. If you've been to the Louvre you'll know that it is of very little interest to anyone that you're

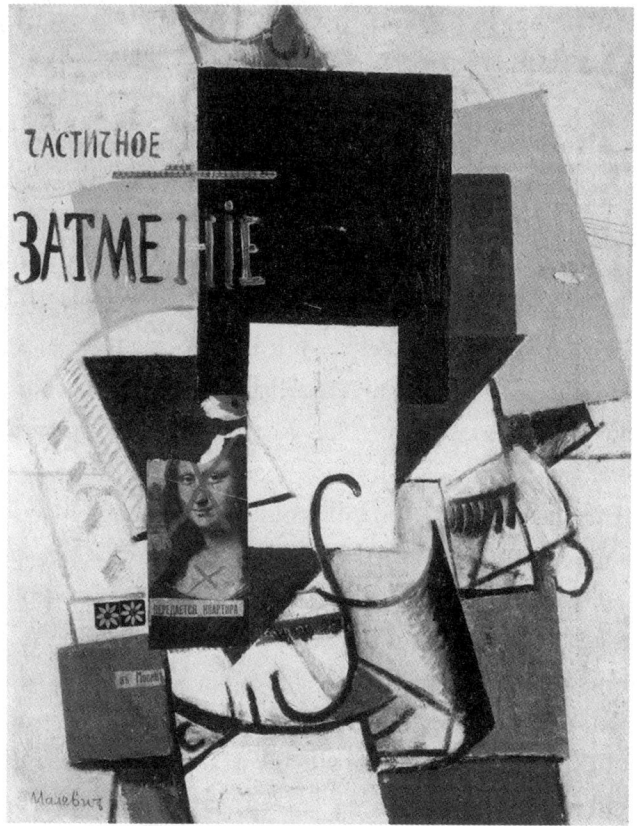

1. Kasimir Malevich, *Composition with Mona Lisa*. 1914. Oil, collage, and graphite on canvas, 62.5 × 49.3 cm. St. Petersburg, State Russian Museum.

underwhelmed with the painting in its bullet-proof shrine-like enclosure, that you can't see what all the hype is about.[2] And yet, while what lies at its center seems pointless and dead, the cult is real: as we will see, it is one facet of a globalizing network of capital and expertise that binds in its mesh museums, fine art publishing, tourism, social media and big tech, and an unregulated and seemingly unstoppable art market that funnels billions of dollars annually to an elite corps of dealers and investors.

What distinguishes most of these worlds from the college classroom or specialist seminar is the phenomenon of complete visibility, the claim to know, to crack codes and dispel mysteries. One of the compulsions that animates Da Vinci Worlds is the desire to *give a face* to the artist from

Vinci. Classical and Renaissance experts on persuasion—rhetoricians—called this *prosopopoeia*, from the Greek word for mask, *prosopon*. So too, the constant claims to have identified a new portrait, or a new personal glimpse, are part of an elaborate apparatus of persuasion. We need our Da Vinci to have a face, a body, and a biography, and we need to resurrect it in his physical traces, his fingerprints, even his DNA. We want a reembodied Da Vinci to guarantee the existence of a genealogy of male genius (including Albert Einstein and Steve Jobs); we need this Da Vinci to prove to us that the Renaissance really existed, that artistic genius and "the creative brain" are problems to be solved by science. Since the documents don't give us what we need, we have fabricated a series of pseudo Da Vincis that finally mostly resemble ourselves.

What is at stake, for instance, in claims that "traces of DNA" have been found on his manuscripts, or that there are fingerprints detectable in his paintings, or that locating the bones of Lisa Gherardini (aka Mona Lisa) might solve a "Leonardo mystery"? It is as if we would clone him if we could. Many of those engaged in studying and teaching his work see him as increasingly lost and dispersed in the fog of overexposure, like an abraded and overpainted presence in a damaged and overvalued old painting. As the hype intensifies, might there be less actually "there" to see?

Da Vinci, we are constantly told, is one of us. He has more to do with our world of technological entrepreneurism than the premodern world of superstition and prejudice in which he made his untimely appearance. Professional Leonardo scholars have been far from blameless in reinforcing this image of the artist's untimeliness, his precocious individualism, his scientific ability to see through the benightedness and superstition of his age. Either they have cheerfully jumped on the bandwagon or they've tried to maintain a dignified distance from all the Da Vinci media noise.

What, though, if that noise were placing expertise itself at risk? This was the publicity, for instance, for an exhibition of Leonardo manuscripts and alleged new "scientific" discoveries about the artist in Madrid: "Curated by one of the big da Vinci experts, the Spanish actor, television presenter and writer Christian Gálvez, it is the only exhibition in the world endorsed by the Leonardo DNA Project. It is an international project involving Gálvez together with a team of geneticists, historians, archaeologists and other experts that wish to reveal da Vinci mystery using his DNA in the year of his 500th anniversary."[3]

With the backing of a media corporation, a powerful auction house, a private art foundation, or even their own self-created institute, anyone can be a *Da Vinci expert*. Going by the roster of contributors to a 2021 publication from a reputable scholarly press, a dead-in-the-water Leonardo attribution can be given credibility by experts with credentials in "cultural heritage," directing a national Academy of Food and Wine, or being the director of documentaries for the History Channel.[4]

Fair enough. Academics and curators don't own Leonardo. National and local economies benefit from marketing the past. But there's a problem if, increasingly, scholars find that they have to jump on the Da Vinci bandwagon in order not to have their voices drowned out in the hype and the noise. From what is now held to constitute "expertise" in a Da Vinci World platform, you might think that a traditional enclave of specialists had lost control of their Leonardo. A certain media-friendly version of the Leonardo expert—like the genial Oxford emeritus Martin Kemp, or Lord Kenneth Clark, the once-anointed guide to *Civilisation* for a deferential television audience in the late 1960s—no longer controls the discussion. Nor, it seems, do his present-day counterparts, the art historian or curator. These only appear in the media to the degree that they can keep the whole circus going, and the circus is run by journalists, commercial publishing, and the art market. Is that such a bad thing? For me, it's a question of who benefits. While *Da Vinci* might seem to be "the people's Leonardo," something between a celebrity brand and an inspirational role model, that is very far from the case.

As specialist voices caution skepticism, freelancers, dealers, amateur art sleuths, and outlier scientists, many with a new explanation of an eternal mystery or a new one no one had noticed, are guaranteed a journalistic echo chamber. "Outsider" scholarship has long proliferated on the fringes of the visual arts in particular, and was generally regarded as the domain of amateurs and cranks. "Surfacing unexpectedly, often characterized by a tone of near-fanatical urgency, and typically accompanied by a lengthy and disputatious footnote apparatus," it almost never bypassed the academic policing operation of peer review.[5] In the age of the internet, it is the peer-reviewed experts who have begun to look like the outsiders. Wielding the word "science" is always helpful (and medical journals in particular have long provided a haven for eccentric scholarship offering pathological diagnostics of figures in Renaissance masterpieces). The promise, explicitly or implicitly, is that the true Da Vinci is being *revealed*, that we are finally making contact with the genius in his untimely and subversive wisdom, despite denials by an elite cabal of academics and tradition-bound experts. Such anti-specialists can pronounce on his thought, his character, and his sexual life with seemingly undeterred confidence. And, what Leonardo does not reveal in his often fragmentary and mostly impersonal writings can be gleaned through signals and clues, enigmas that he supposedly bequeathed to true disciples of later times.

I have characterized this book as concerned with art history's Leonardo, which means that it is also concerned with the role of expertise in historical scholarship. Expertise, in a field like Leonardo studies, increasingly has to take account of questions of cultural capital and market value in the objects that it claims to study. This means that this book is also concerned with that precarious and contentious thing we call "the public interest," toward which scholarship in the academy and the museum is (or was) nominally devoted. It addresses the erasure between a research- and education-oriented paradigm of public interest and one better described as a consumer market for entertainment. It also addresses the responsibility attending on such expertise and on its complicity in propagating the Da Vinci phenomenon. While this erasure has deeper historical roots, it has escalated in recent years.

SALVATOR MUNDI

"In the increasingly high-stakes world of multimillion-dollar fine art sales, science is becoming ever more important. The purpose, ultimately, is to 'get inside the head of the artist.'"[6]

Let's take a notorious recent example. The painting known as the *Salvator Mundi* is emblematic of how the artist *has become a problem*. It was first sold as an authentic Leonardo in 2008, exhibited in a public museum in 2011, underwent conservation and consolidation for several years, and then obtained its present incessant notoriety when it was sold for $450 million in 2017 and then sequestered at an unknown location. A gift to some sectors of the art world, perhaps—but otherwise the frenzy around the hapless painting has become a blight to art historical scholarship, to art museums with a commitment to creating informative public conversations through exhibitions and acquisitions, and to the principle of a public culture independent of market forces. On the other hand, the *Salvator Mundi* has become a triumph of branding and of marketing, of how to generate profit from cultural artifacts and keep the public avid for wilder rumors and allegations. Any aesthetic or historical aura that might still accrue to the artifact is beside the point. Aura was generated instead from a bundling together of intoxicating cultural fetishes: the "last Leonardo," the "lost Leonardo," the "male Mona Lisa," as well as the unimaginable wealth of super-elites, shady oligarchies, conspiracy theorists, entrepreneurial dealers, whistleblowers of art fraud.

Above all, this painting of the face of Christ raises the specter of the fake, a hunger for a denouement where the artifact is revealed to be not what it was claimed to be, where the "expert elites" were deceived or deceived themselves and the public, or perhaps betrayed science through the allure of fame and wealth.

The point is not that art world elites should be exempt from public scrutiny, or that experts should not be called out by watchdog media for self-deception or opportunistic self-publicity. The persona of the journalist as skeptic and as sleuth is in many ways more appealing. And yet, in such coverage the outlier characters are often afforded sympathy and respect, a pat on the back: the traditional expert elites are "exposed" as fallible, weak, or mendacious. The anti-establishment posturing of such popularizing accounts is palpable. In one such exposé, the dealer Alexander Parish is quoted regarding "some of these museum people": "They're really woeful in terms of their practical application of looking at pictures. People in the trade, they look at five thousand pictures a year, if you add all the auctions together and all the pictures they're shown. Somebody who's an associate curator, he's looked at the same two hundred pictures in his collection over and over again, but they're not getting out there. . . . This is the truth. They don't have the practical experience to be in the field, as it were, on their feet, judging pictures as they come in."[7] Parish was a stakeholder in the 2008 sale of the *Salvator Mundi*.

Such exposé narratives, with their webs of subterfuge and cast of characters both dubious and duped, have the ring of the crime thriller about them. When the *Salvator* is referred to as "the Holy Grail" of art history, you begin to realize the hold that Dan Brown's lucrative "Da Vinci" bestseller has over the journalistic presentation of "true stories." "There was no formal process by which the attribution of the painting was conducted. The National Gallery did not ask to have the painting left with it to be examined by its own restorers in its own restoration studios. . . . For all the outside world knows, incense may have been shaken and incantations uttered in Latin, along with Knights Templar oaths."[8] (There was in fact a vetting of the picture at the National Gallery by a team of Leonardo experts, although several later stated that they never supported the attribution.)

Given what is at stake, the *Salvator Mundi* seems less like a Holy Grail than a poisoned chalice: with such vast profits to be made, assessments of authenticity can risk appearing compromised. No major museum sought to acquire the work, and the response by Leonardo experts was for the most part noncommittal or skeptical.[9] To weigh in with an opinion, or to produce new historical and technical scholarship, could have effects on the work's highly disruptive market value. The work is by no means a "fake," as some journalists insinuate, but has been heavily damaged by shifts in the wooden panel and old restorations; it required retouching over areas of damaged but intact original paint layer, the refilling of the background, and reconstruction of lost areas of the face and hair.[10]

There is little consensus about whether the original portions reveal the hand of Leonardo, or Leonardo and assistants, or a Leonardo follower like Giovanni Antonio Boltraffio or Bernardino Luini, and even the painting's provenance—that is, the history of its past ownership—is much debated.[11] With its off-the-charts valuation, the *Salvator Mundi* has been placed off-limits for scholarship—and not just because art historians have had little opportunity to see the work. Whether in a Swiss free port or on a billionaire's yacht, the painting has acquired a tainted status, resembling illegally trafficked cultural artifacts (although its repeated resales are legal), removing it from the purview of responsible scholarship.

In the buildup to the Louvre's great quincentennial exhibition of 2019–20, the museum's director, Jean-Luc Martinez, stated in a radio interview that the *Salvator Mundi* was expected to make a star appearance.[12] The painting was certainly topical, and one of the goals of the exhibition was to bring together the greatest number of Leonardos ever displayed. Since it was widely reported in 2017 that the *Salvator* had been acquired for the Louvre Abu Dhabi, there was a clear dimension of co-branding of "Louvre" with "Leonardo." The actual political ramifications, including diplomatic overtures between President Macron and the Saudi Crown Prince Mohammed bin Salman, were less widely known. An agreement was reached, a catalog entry was written, and exhibition designers included the work in the maquette for the final room of the show. And yet an alternative version of the catalog without the entry was printed, just in case.

It was the prospective appearance by the "last Leonardo"—however justifiable in art historical terms—that turned a scholarly and didactic exhibition into a Da Vinci World. And yet for reasons variously explained, the loan was canceled shortly before the opening (one account suggests that the prince wanted the painting displayed next to the *Mona Lisa*, which was never intended to be part of the exhibition but to remain on display in the permanent collection).[13] The alternative catalog was placed on sale, and a workshop version known as the Ganay *Salvator Mundi* stood in for the absent painting. The exact whereabouts of the *Salvator Mundi* remain a mystery at the time of writing, although certain Louvre staff may have had access to it in the run-up to the exhibition. More than that, the Center for Research and Restoration of the Museums of France (C2RMF) had conducted a technical examination of the painting, and the museum had even produced a forty-eight-page book, *Léonard de Vinci: Le Salvator Mundi*.[14] The publication presented diagnostic analyses of the paint layers and panel support using the most up-to-date repertoire of non-invasive techniques: x-radiography, multispectral imaging, infrared reflectography, thermoluminescence mapping, and optical coherence tomography, complementing evidence published by the painting's conservator, Dianne Dwyer Modestini, in 2011. X-rays of the Louvre's own Leonardos—the *Mona Lisa*, the *St. John*—presented similar characteristics to the radiography of the *Salvator Mundi*—a ghostly indistinctness resulting from the artist's characteristic use of opaque white lead underpainting in his late works, and not found in versions of the *Salvator Mundi* by Leonardo followers.

When the loan was withdrawn, the book—its existence still a secret—was suppressed. As a national museum the Louvre is prevented by law from providing expert assessment on the authenticity of works in private hands: the only exception is where the work in question is displayed by the museum. In other words, there was a clear policy in place to safeguard the balance of public and private interests. While the Louvre's technical study would have been of benefit to scholarship (usually considered a public good), its advantage to the work's owner, its past and future vendors, outweighed the case for the public interest served by making it available.

And yet the publication went on sale. Or at least one copy did, on December 18, 2019, when after an early morning visit to the Louvre exhibition I added it to a bundle of Leonardo-related titles that I purchased at the museum's bookstore: it had been placed on a table along with stacks of the catalog for the show. I barely looked through it over the following weeks, until—as part of the research for this book—I met with Dianne Modestini, the conservator who had restored the painting and who had published the most thorough case for its authenticity.[15] I asked for her opinion and was surprised when she told me she had known nothing of the book's existence. Failing to find it for sale online, Modestini contacted the Louvre and was informed that no such book existed.

In late February 2021 I received an admonishing email from a colleague at the Louvre stating that "the book doesn't exist anymore and it is forbidden to mention it or use it." By that time, news of the book had reached the *Art Newspaper*, which ran a story on March 31, describing the contents and detailing the book's suppression. Modestini was quoted as saying that the withdrawal of valuable information was "unfortunate."

"I would, of course, like to study high-resolution digital files of the new images," she told the *Art Newspaper*, appealing to the principle of sharing information with the larger community of scholars. "Scientific and chemical imaging can change or greatly add to our understanding of how a work of art was created. Due to the expense of the equipment and the computational power required to process the data, only a few museums and conservation institutes are able to study paintings with these new methods and when this information is shared it benefits the entire community." By April 2021 *Art Newspaper* reported that scans of the publication had been released to the media to counter the claims of a documentary broadcast on French TV purporting that the painting had been withdrawn because the Louvre's technical studies had caused the museum to *question* its autograph status—exactly the contrary of what the little "non-book" claimed to reveal.[16]

Like many students of Leonardo, I am agnostic as to whether the *Salvator Mundi* is by "Leonardo" or "Leonardo and . . ." The painting's historical interest and importance do not ride on its status as a 100 percent autograph work, nor even on its aesthetic qualities, and are utterly independent of its market value. As we will see further in chapter 5, much of Leonardo's pictorial production after 1500 was created in collaboration with if not delegated to assistants; contemporaries were aware that he had trained a group of followers who could replicate his manner of painting and that the degree of his commitment to various artistic projects was inconsistent and unpredictable.

Some of my own research over the past ten years has concerned followers of Leonardo working during the span of his lifetime (1452–1519), in the geographical region in which he worked and traveled (northern Italy from Florence to Milan to Venice). One of the most distinctive aspects of Leonardo as a shaping force in the history of art is the way his style and his methods came to be transmitted and extended in the work of others, and in ways that we are still learning about. As with the *Salvator Mundi*, so it is the case for many of Leonardo's works—the *Mona Lisa*, the *Leda and the Swan*, the *Virgin and Child with St. Anne*, the Louvre *St. John*—a copious level of production of replicas and variants. Present-day expertise, on the other hand, has tended to limit the Leonardo corpus to the strictly autograph, solo performances of the artist, perpetrating the aura of absolute rarity and inestimable value. Every author of such a catalog has to determine the cutoff between "Leonardo" and "Leonardo and . . ." in the penumbra of workshop collaborations. It is likely that the difference mattered little, if at all, to Leonardo's original clients.

Today's art market seeks to have it both ways. On one hand, it demands a loosening of criteria for distinguishing between the artist and his followers. On the other, it seeks to capitalize on the rarity of every alleged Leonardo discovery, with the stoking of market value to sensational levels. The chapters that follow do not offer a way out of this complicated entanglement of specialist research and the market cult of authenticity. Nor am I attempting a critique of connoisseurship—the art historical practice, really an essential skill acquired only with time and patience, of discriminating between the hands of particular artists. Rather, I would argue for the necessity of connoisseurship *and* technical analysis as a means of curtailing the seemingly endless market supply of Leonardesque paintings that Leonardo did not paint.

At the same time, I will argue that such criteria for determining the limits of an artist's work existed only loosely, if at all, in the lifetime of Leonardo. The notion of the artist as solitary author acting alone is challenged first of all by the conditions of workshop production. Second, the idea of individual artist-as-author is called into question by radically different notions of selfhood, of personal history and identity in the premodern world. We will see that the history of Leonardo, too often taken to be the story of a solitary, misunderstood genius, is far more meaningful as a history of his encounters and entanglements with a collective of colleagues, followers, and assistants.

This book is also an exploration of the critical demands of art history, the potential and limits of art history as a discipline, and its capacity to challenge cultural myths. Most commonly, mass culture's "Da Vinci" is a guarantee of one of Western culture's most cherished myths, that of the "Renaissance Man," and of European cultural supremacy. Academics have largely given up on those tarnished stereotypes, no less old-fashioned than ethnocentric and sexist, and in recent years the core of a racist identity politics. However, the myth of multitalented intellectual daring and innovation sits well with the twenty-first-century image of the *creative class*, the technological entrepreneur, those whose facility in "making connections" marks them out as supreme achievers.

The image of Leonardo in more rigorous historical scholarship might seem rather faceless by comparison: a manifestation of social displacement, even of political disintegration, rather than a solitary genius, less an independent voice than a point of convergence for different currents of thought, both classical worldviews and artisanal wisdom, some of it not especially progressive or forward-looking. With this book, which you can think of as an anti-biography, the goal is not to produce a fussy academic critique of popular stereotypes but a Leonardo that can be less easily instrumentalized by the forces that shape our twenty-first-century mental ecology, a description that might resist the banalities of the Da Vinci Industry. It seeks to make Leonardo unfamiliar, in ways that will allow the sometimes shocking character of the writings and images to resonate in their own historical moment as well as ours.

Chapter 1 explores how traditional cultural spaces like the museum have been transformed by the twenty-first-century emergence of what I call Da Vinci Worlds—spectacular worlds of simulation, of enhanced sensation, where the historical and the fragmentary are transformed into "experience." For most people, the museum, or the historical site turned into a museum, serves as the primary interface between Da Vinci Worlds and the historical traces of Leonardo. The Louvre in Paris and Santa Maria delle Grazie in Milan are the point of contact for several million visitors every year, many of whom will probably never see another painting by Leonardo. At the same time museums, as notionally public spaces, have become theaters for spectacular interventions of various kinds—not only the thrills of the blockbuster exhibition but highly mediated demonstrations against a cultural establishment constantly upbraided for cultural complacency and resistance to progress. While the focus is on "Da Vinci" spectacles of the past quarter century, the chapter also describes how various practices of art history—despite pressure from the realm of media spectacle—offer a redress to misinformation, cliché, and myth.

Chapter 2 will closely examine some highly debatable "facts" and received ideas that structure the modern Leonardo biography—the stereotype of the flamboyant social and sexual outsider, the religious agnostic, the vegetarian, the humanitarian. We will look at the instability and ambiguity of the evidence on which it is based, at the same time demonstrating that the fragmentary nature of such evidence is of rich historical significance in itself. Again, the counternarrative in this chapter shows how historical disciplines including art history and literary studies have responded or might respond to the received ideas of the Leonardo biography.

The Leonardo biography is considered historically in chapter 3, which traces the artist's conflicted afterlife over the past two centuries, focusing in particular on the combined impact of the writings of Walter Pater, Paul Valéry, Sigmund Freud, and Bernard Berenson on the various Leonardos of the twentieth century. Returning to some of the concerns laid out in this introduction, it will then examine some of the motivations at work in the twenty-first-century production of Leonardo biographies.

Chapter 4 gets to grips with the conditions of life-writing in the premodern era, exploring who got to have written lives and why, as well as the practices of writing that emerged among artists and craftsmen in the 1400s. It reveals some governing preoccupations of the world in which Leonardo lived, of how people conceived personhood or "identity" in relation to groups and individuals. A key question to be confronted is why artists like Ghiberti, Alberti, Michelangelo, and Cellini could become authors of autobiographical texts—the last three with conspicuous attention to the physical life of the author. Leonardo seems to have pointedly refrained—except very partially and obliquely—not only from narrating his own biography but from references to his own body in his writing. This brings us to the question of writing and literary persona in the case of a figure like Leonardo and the ways in which writing came to be a form of surrogate embodiment.

The final chapter will be devoted to Leonardo as a premodern thinker and maker. Less as a solitary, beleaguered voice, an echo chamber of modern existential selfhood, Leonardo will appear more as a point of relay within a collective production of knowledge, manifesting conceptions of social and personal identity very different from our own. Grounded in an analysis of Leonardo's works and in their reception by other artists, it will advance some new conclusions about the radical aesthetics of Leonardo's painting and the curious ways in which it seeks to challenge notions of a boundaried selfhood.

Chapter 1

DA VINCI WORLDS

A museum is a not-for-profit, permanent institution in the service of society that researches, collects, conserves, interprets and exhibits tangible and intangible heritage. Open to the public, accessible and inclusive, museums foster diversity and sustainability. They operate and communicate ethically, professionally and with the participation of communities, offering varied experiences for education, enjoyment, reflection and knowledge sharing.

—STATEMENT OF INTERNATIONAL COUNCIL
OF MUSEUMS (ICOM), AUGUST 2023

By "Da Vinci Worlds" I mean environments in which the legacy of the Florentine artist polymath is put on show for a mass public of spectators, who at the time I'm writing might be habitual museum goers, tourists, children, students of art history and museum studies, tech enthusiasts, gaming aficionados, fans of historical fiction, and so forth. Increasingly in the twenty-first century these are real and virtual spaces of consumption, organized for the delivery of an experience as much as for the divulgation of knowledge, and in ways that have transformed the operations of the traditional museum. While answering a demand for an encounter with Da Vinci, Da Vinci Worlds serve as much to produce that demand. Both real and virtual Da Vinci Worlds are at the end of a historical process, as old as the museum itself, of making Leonardo visible and intelligible for a public. At the same time, they reflect some distinctly twenty-first-century preoccupations, the breadth and diversity of the public now being addressed by the museum being one of them.

Increasingly, in the twenty-first century, the experience offered by museums seeks to keep pace with the uncanny spaces of virtual reality. The idea of "Da Vinci Worlds" first occurred to me while watching a documentary released during the 2019 Leonardo quincentennial, and in particular a sequence at the beginning with a voiceover: "To show the full extent of his work, we need an approach. An imaginary space, an immense gallery that would allow us to travel to see, to make everything he studied concrete, the works and the machines that he imagined and sometimes designed." On screen appears a vast digital simulation of the Grand Palais in Paris, furnished with realizations of *The Last Supper*, wrested from its architectural context, *The Adoration of the Magi*, the Sforza horse, and other paintings, alongside huge fresco-like enlargements of the drawings for machines and three-dimensional reconstructions of the flying machines, giant crossbow, and other devices never built. The crossing of the virtual gallery is occupied by a colossal model of the tribune of Florence cathedral, if only because Leonardo's teacher Verrocchio constructed and installed its crowning gilded sphere when Leonardo was in his workshop.

A few frames later, the cameras pan through the recently reinstalled High Renaissance galleries at the Uffizi in Florence, where we see a similar digital sensibility at work, but now in real space. Since 2018 the galleries have been streamlined to facilitate the efficient passage of thousands of tourists per day and with perfectly lit fiber-optic visibility. Paintings like Michelangelo's *Doni Tondo* and Botticelli's *Primavera* are sunk behind glass into a white wall, while Raphael's Doni portraits are suspended as if weightless in a vitrine. The display strips the works of their objecthood and turns them into screen-like simulations of their own electronic reproductions. More recently, Leonardo's stunningly renewed post-conservation *Adoration of the Magi* and *Annunciation* have been given the same treatment.

While multiple "Da Vinci Worlds" take virtual form in electronic media, they often and increasingly embed themselves in real spaces:

primarily the private "museums," the for-profit exhibitions featuring inter-active models based on Leonardo's machines, and reproductions of draw-ings and paintings, that have sprung up in several locations in Italy. The primary purpose of these Da Vinci Worlds is to generate the sensations of contact, of empathy, of identification with the undead and universal per-sona of the genius artist, to convince us that this simulacrum is a mirror of our times, perhaps also that our times can have no other possible mirror.

I certainly do not discount the possibility that there is something to be gained from these environments: Leonardo's machine designs lend themselves well to reconstruction. Entertainment can be educational, it can enrich more traditional museum practices of conveying technical and historical dimensions to art objects, and address larger publics. (However, when the entertainment imperative is introduced as an argument against traditional museum practice, as a seemingly progressive alternative, then we need to ask, whose conception of "entertainment™" are we talking about? In other words, who are we outsourcing to?)

And I certainly don't want to foreclose the possibility of alternative environments where Leonardo can be engaged with, less prescriptively and according to program, with our body as much as with our eyes: land-scapes, for instance, in which we can reenact the artist's physical movement through space, choosing what to look at without curatorial cues. If you make the short trip from Bergamo to Vaprio on the river Adda, and walk upriver to the castle of Trezzo, you can explore a landscape well-known to the artist, where he lived and worked as a guest of the Melzi family in 1511. The Ecomuseo Adda di Leonardo is devoted to the historical preservation of a natural environment, from the time when Leonardo supervised an extension to the Martesana canal to the development of pioneering hy-droelectric plants in the 1900s. Committed to "slow tourism" and commu-nity engagement in the broadest sense, it offers a very different realization of what a museum might be. And venturing even further off the grid of organized tourism, there are other sites across the Italian peninsula where the well-traveled artist's footsteps can be followed. Terracina is an ancient resort town between Rome and Naples, where the Appian Way meets the sea at the edge of the Pontine Marshes. At the behest of his employer Gi-uliano de'Medici, Leonardo in the winter of 1513 devised a scheme to drain the noxious malarial swamp. In his detailed map of the region, annotated by his disciple Francesco Melzi, he included an exquisite miniature of two of the ancient city's wonders: the dramatic landscape intervention by Emperor Antoninus Pius, for whom masses of enslaved laborers cut through the jagged cliff to allow the extension of the Appian Way, carving the new face with Roman yard markers, and—high above—the elaborately vaulted basement of the temple of Jupiter Anxur (plate 1).[1]

Such green Leonardo worlds stand in contrast to the spaces described in this chapter. Our account begins in Milan, in what would be the first Leonardo "museum." Perhaps *The Last Supper* is the work that most fully epitomizes "Da Vinci" for our time, his fugitive and always seemingly falsifiable nature, the remaining fragments of paint standing for his near-loss, even his future possible total loss. The fate of *The Last Supper* is emblematic of the fate of Leonardo as it is considered in this book: a phenomenon where partial and fragile evidence is fashioned into a provisional whole, where reinvention proceeds with the magical blessing of science, where the pursuit of visibility over obscurity leads to a mirage.

We will then look at another site of encounter, the Louvre in Paris, and at a portrait that for not much more than a century has been the pivot of Leonardo mythology. I will focus in particular on how the obsessive and repetitive fixation on the *Mona Lisa* and its "mysteries" has to do with its apparent promise to compensate for the absence of Leonardo himself and—since no one painting can ever adequately do this—on how the Mona Lisa phenomenon has been repeated and extended through the art market, commercial media (which in the twenty-first century includes exhibitions), and the "magic" of technology.

The chapter concludes with a look at technology and its impact on the presentation of Leonardo, during the recent past, in London, Milan, and Boston. The technical study of past works of art has been enriched in the twenty-first century by an array of new tools enabling the imaging of paint layers and nondestructive material analysis. However, in the case of Leonardo's battle painting for the town hall in Florence, which may never have existed beyond a large design on paper, highly speculative claims grounded in the capacity of technological instruments have turned a historic space without Leonardo into a Da Vinci World.

I had initially planned this chapter as a straightforward primer on Leonardo's art through his best-known works, for a reader who seeks an up-to-date account of recent discoveries and the role of exhibitions. However, it soon became apparent how volatile the conditions of encounter with these works have become since the turn of the century, that more than ever these had turned into heavily mediated experiences fraught by indecision over the role or even relevance of the historical past. In particular, the pressure to monetize cultural heritage, a term which has increasingly morphed into "cultural assets." That became my focus: where Da Vinci Worlds are concerned, you have to follow the money.

MILAN: *THE LAST SUPPER* AND ITS LEFTOVERS

The *Cenacolo*, as it is called in Italian—Leonardo's great mural of *The Last Supper*—was painted for the refectory of the main Dominican friary in Milan, Santa Maria delle Grazie, between 1495 and 1498 (plate 2).[2] It was Leonardo's breakthrough work, one of the very few that the forty-five-year-old artist had completed, and it had the widest fame during his lifetime. By the time of his death in 1519, the work was in a seriously deteriorated condition.

Despite its catastrophic subsequent history, it is among the most visited of all works by Leonardo. With a four-month waiting list for admissions in 2023, it was—according to social media posts—easier to get tickets to a Bruce Springsteen or Taylor Swift concert. And yet, that was not always the case. When I first saw *The Last Supper* in 1985, there were no reservations, no long lines, and while there was plenty of visitor traffic, the space was not crowded. We need to consider how this escalation in demand has come about and whether *The Last Supper* might not be a victim of its own success.

The drama of the painting itself is inseparable from the circumstances of its production: the patron Ludovico Sforza, known as Il Moro, was a usurping ruler, the uncle and probable poisoner of the young Duke of Milan, whom he succeeded in 1494. Despite the emperor's confirmation of his ducal title within days of the death of his nephew, the ensuing years saw Il Moro's political and personal fortunes taking a turn for the worse. His decision to back the invasion of the peninsula by King Charles VIII

of France in October 1494 nearly cost him his state and plunged Italy into
a state of catastrophic warfare that would continue for nearly forty years.
Some of his chief associates plotted with the French, and the duchy would
fall to another French king, Louis XII, in 1499.

The Milanese state of the Sforza was at a turning point, with Ludovico
at one moment overreaching in his anxious attempts to legitimate his new
ducal title and at another trying not to overplay his hand. Within a month
of the death of the young duke, in November 1494, Ludovico canceled a
major project by Leonardo: the colossal bronze equestrian monument
of the founder of the Sforza dynasty, Duke Francesco Sforza, which was
supposed to outdo everything yet accomplished in the art of sculpture.
The raw bronze was sent to the Duke of Ferrara, Ludovico's father-in-law,
for the founding of cannons. Years of work by Leonardo—modeling a
colossal clay horse, designing and building a set of furnaces and a casting
pit of stupendous daring and complexity—had come to nothing. The clay
horse, already one of the marvels of Milan, would be pulverized when the
invading French—in an act of political iconoclasm—used it for target
practice in 1499.

Leonardo, bereft of the great commission, was given some routine
decorative work in the Sforza castle, and made a short trip to Florence.
In 1495, having nearly lost his state during the French invasion of Italy,
Ludovico charged Leonardo with a new project more in keeping with
the public image of a pious Christian prince, and one worthy of his court
artist's ability to work on a monumental scale. It was an episode from
Christ's passion, the Passover supper that inaugurated the Mass, the revelation of his sacrificial victimhood in the announcement of his betrayal
and death. Leonardo's convulsive treatment of the event, which focuses
on the Apostles' spectrum of reactions to Christ's "One of you will betray
me," is often seen as having an emotional and spiritual resonance for the
beleaguered duke, whose coat of arms and ducal title, along with those of
his wife and son, are relayed in the heraldic imagery overhead.

The mural, executed in a slow and piecemeal fashion in an oil-based
medium suited to panel painting but not for painting on walls, had begun to
deteriorate within a decade or two of its completion; rising damp prevented
the paint from adhering to the plaster. Although he was inexperienced in

painting in fresco, where paint is applied to wet plaster, forming a durable bond with the wall, it seems extraordinary that Leonardo could have been so unaware that his painting would decay, and that the gains of oil painting for the refined rendering of hair, soft shadows on faces, metal dishes, and crystal glasses would be short-lived. I have often wondered if awareness of the work's fragility after completion was the reason for the rapid production of full-scale replicas and versions in fresco and portable media—numbering at least a dozen by 1520, and several by Milanese artists trained by or in contact with Leonardo.[3]

Antonio de'Beatis, a cardinal's secretary who wrote of his visit to Leonardo in France in 1517, recorded that his great work in Milan was already fading. By the 1600s, *The Last Supper* was barely legible, and its reputation rested entirely on reproductions. Cardinal Federico Borromeo, who established the Milanese art academy and museum known as the Biblioteca Ambrosiana in 1618, commissioned a copy from the painter Il Vespino as a kind of official or canonical record: "I cherish this [copy of the] *Last Supper*, one of the masterpieces of my Museum. Leonardo's original work, which has always been considered a kind of treasure, is already ruined and utterly lost, so the copy will be more valuable with every passing day."[4]

There are signs that the painter's reputation was dwindling along with the remains of his most famous work. This was increasingly the case following the first publication in 1651 of Leonardo's *Treatise on Painting*—a highly selective abridgment from various manuscript drafts, edited to correspond with the classicizing tastes of the seventeenth-century art academies. Leonardo's works, it now seemed, failed to live up to the artistic standards of his own writings. In 1657 the critic Francesco Scannelli wrote of his excitement at the prospect of seeing the legendary original, and the expectation that he would be "restored" by the artistic fare in the Dominican refectory. However, "I can attest, that owing to what I there encountered, I was left with an extremely disagreeable taste, coming upon a work of which nothing was left but a few vestiges of the figures, now so confused that only with great difficulty was I able to make out the painting that it had once been." The figures he found "almost completely annihilated," in some cases separating from the wall. "The good remains of the work rendered almost wholly useless," he concluded, "there is nothing left for the beholder but its past fame."[5] Leonardo, he decided, had overthought things and produced an overwrought work in an unsuitable medium.

The painting was thus often passed over by foreign artists and elite tourists during the 1700s, the age of the Grand Tour, when antiquity and the Italian Renaissance were increasingly regarded as the pinnacle of European artistic achievement. For instance, the painter and tastemaker Anton Raphael Mengs (1728–1779), the friend of the pioneering art historian Johann Winckelmann and one of the proponents of the movement in the arts later known as Neoclassicism, comes across as an early example of a Leonardo skeptic: a partisan of Raphael, the preeminent "classical" role model, Mengs declared that he wouldn't go to see the *Cenacolo* even though he visited Santa Maria delle Grazie to see Titian's *Christ Crowned with Thorns.*[6] In his notes on the church, the French academician Charles de Brosses (1709–1777) appreciated the composition of Leonardo's *Last Supper* but found the faces of all the figures to be "really ugly."[7]

It may have been a 1722 guidebook report on the mural's ruined condition by two English connoisseurs that motivated the Milanese to finally take steps to conserve the painting.[8] However, conservation in the 1700s tended to be less a case of preserving what remained than of replacing what was lost. Restorers sought to make the work conform to later copies and to drawings in Milanese collections often dubiously regarded as Leonardo originals. And, in a scenario that has many echoes in more recent times, a succession of experts presented themselves, each laying claim to an advanced and innovative scientific and technical expertise that would enable them to "resurrect" Leonardo's ruined picture. Michelangelo Bellotti declared in 1726 that he had a "secret" way of reviving the painting, which consisted of washing the surface with caustic soda and then repainting it.

In the late 1700s the painter Giuseppe Mazza undertook a second highly invasive and controversial campaign. The prior of the convent, who published a "true history" of the painting in 1796, sought to justify the recent restorations: "In my opinion, it is better to have a retouched painting than to have none at all. Our *Cenacolo* was so ruined that the learned men who saw it in various occasions, gave it up for lost, as if it no longer existed. If we had done nothing, we would hardly have anything now to point to so as to be able to say; here it was. And if in Rome it is allowed to put a restorer's hand to the works of the great Raphael, so in Milan we can do so to the great Leonardo."⁹ By the 1800s, following further attempted restorations sponsored by the Napoleonic government, including a proposal to detach it entirely from the wall, it seemed as if the painting itself had receded behind an outpouring of new engraved versions, replicas in paint and mosaic, and a "definitive" modern version by Giuseppe Bossi (which could be more accurately described as a surrogate or even a memorial) produced in tandem with a four-volume monograph on the picture.[10]

Traveling in Italy in 1850, the writer Théophile Gautier was surprised to be told—while examining an engraving of *The Last Supper* in his hotel in Milan—that the original "which we believed to be no longer in existence" was in fact extant and could be seen "in a convent transformed into an Austrian barracks." He wrote rhapsodically of the barely visible painting: "All trace of art has disappeared," he wrote: "it seems to float on the surface of the wall, which absorbs it as a light vapor. It is the ghost of a painting, the specter of a masterpiece returned to earth. The effect is more solemn and more religious even than if the picture were alive. The body has disappeared but the soul survives in its entirety."[11]

Paradoxically, by the 1900s the disappearing masterpiece had become, as the great art historian Heinrich Wölfflin recognized, "after Raphael's *Sistine Madonna*, the most popular picture in the whole of Italian art."[12] It was still far more famous than the *Mona Lisa*, with a self-propagating afterlife in the form of prints, painted copies, drawings, and photographs, many of which had introduced corrections or modifications to the image; thus, there were multiple *Last Supper*s connected with the name Leonardo. Mauro Pellicioli's campaign of restoration sought to deliver the "original" by stripping off areas of eighteenth-, nineteenth-, and twentieth-century overpainting, reinforcing patches of what were deemed to be Leonardo's original work with shellac, filling in areas of loss with removable pigments. His work on the mural was interrupted by the 1943 Allied bombings of Milan, which almost leveled the refectory of Santa Maria delle Grazie. Miraculously, the wall with *The Last Supper* and *The Crucifixion* on the facing wall survived. Pellicioli's *Last Supper*—which the art historian Cesare Brandi denounced as a "forgery" following its completion in the 1950s—was the main tourist attraction of postwar Milan. The *Cenacolo* was drawing 200,000 annual visitors by the mid-1980s, when I first saw it, by which time the conservator's scaffolding was rising once again.

The painting now looks very different than it did in the 1980s, owing to a radical and highly controversial cleaning that sought to strip away centuries of overpainting so that the "real" Leonardo could be revealed. Pellicioli's mid-twentieth-century conservation had sought to do pretty much the same thing. Yet Pellicioli had been guided by an idea of what "a Leonardo" was then understood to look like—somber spaces, bodies in smoky shadow, muted color.

The "definitive," and radical, conservation of 1976–99, which sought to strip away all later retouchings and repairs, yielded some alarming findings. By the exacting criteria employed by the conservation team—led by Pinin Brambilla Barcilon, a pupil of Pellicioli—only 20 percent of the painted surface could be identified as the original work of Leonardo (vastly different estimates, ranging from 18 to 50 percent, have also been given). The unrelenting scientific pursuit of the indisputable traces of Leonardo's hand displaced the aesthetic and art historical consensus of earlier campaigns and their tolerance for the conjectural "leonardism" of earlier interventions.

The ironic result of the pursuit of authenticity is the brightly colored haze that greets visitors today. Certainly, it could no longer be described as the ghost of a painting, but it might be more accurately thought of as an impressionistic postmodern simulation. Or you could see it as a kind of reliquary where patches of Leonardo's original pigments are unified by an infilling of watercolor, the entire surface a pale diluted version of the rich modeling and bold tonality that the original—as can be seen on early copies—possessed and that the early modern repaintings had sought to preserve. It was to achieve those effects, after all, that Leonardo used oil-based paints, not the lime water-based medium of fresco. As one commentator put it, philosophically: "Whether *The Last Supper* is Leonardo or not may, in the end, prove to be a side issue. After all, we find ways to be comfortable with what we are used to."[13]

Conservation can be a bitterly partisan matter in Europe, and high-profile projects often pit experts against each other. The team working on the mural was criticized for prioritizing "an archeological purity at the expense of a visual parity," while a conservator associated with ArtWatch International told the *New York Times* that "[the restorers] decided to proceed without even conducting the proper analyses to determine how much of the original painting remained. And now they show these remaining crumbs, these plates and glasses, and say it is Leonardo."[14] The controversy about the conservation of the mural, the question of how much original painting is required to make a Leonardo "authentic," and how this is to be determined, and by whom, has resurfaced in recent stormy exchanges around the *Salvator Mundi*. That, however, was a painting on the market: the Milan mural is a "public good," from which no fortunes can be made (apart from providing useful PR to the sponsoring Olivetti corporation, and more recently to Eataly).

Before 2019 annual visitor figures stood at about 450,000, although that number reflects limits imposed on the number of visitors in the interests of conservation. Because of the risks of airborne pollution, only twenty people can be present in the climate-conditioned room with the painting every fifteen minutes, which leads to long lines and would-be visitors being turned away. Clearly, the character of the encounter for visitors to the *Cenacolo* has changed substantially since the late twentieth century. The curatorial imperative in the 1980s had little concern with mediation or explanation or the manufacturing of *experience*—which is now the premier objective of cultural asset management, as important as (some would say more important than) an educational or scholarly mission. More recently, the imperative of conservation by limiting visitor numbers has given way to interventions—like the installation of an air-filtration system—to facilitate greater numbers of visitors, thus also "extending the life of the painting by Leonardo for another 500 years."[15] At Santa Maria delle Grazie the experience has been centered on the reanimating and reenchanting power of technology, its potential to give life to a nearly lost work of art and to bring us closer to the genius who made it. Technology reveals Leonardo's "secrets."

And of course, notoriously, the idea of the *secret* of *The Last Supper* has in the past twenty years taken on a life of its own, beyond any culture-manager's or curator's wildest dreams. A few have echoed the blatant silliness of Dan Brown's fictive "symbologist" character who unlocks the mystery of the Holy Grail—that is, secret marriage and blood descent of Jesus Christ and the Magdalene—by pointing to other supposed mysteries: Why are there no halos? (Actually, there probably were: gold paint is easily abraded.) Why are Christ and the Apostles eating eels with salt and lemon? And so on.

As regards what Leonardo actually sought to portray, there are far more interesting questions to consider. Renaissance commentators recognized that Leonardo was depicting the drama of Christ's impending betrayal, his announcement to the Apostles and their reaction: the earliest print after the painting bears the scriptural text *amen dico vobis unus vestrum me traditurus est* ("I say unto you that one of you will betray me" [Matt. 26:21]).

Earlier artists had sometimes alluded to the scriptural episode, showing Christ passing a morsel of bread to Judas, the agent of the betrayal. Other painters emphasized Christ's consecration of bread and wine, the institution of the Mass and the sacrament of the Eucharist. As the modern notion of Leonardo as the forebear of Francis Bacon and Isaac Newton took hold in the late 1700s, so too did the idea of a modern and secularist Leonardo focused not on the theological or sacramental meanings but on the "human drama" of Christ's announcement of his impending betrayal by Judas. This was the view of painter/author Giuseppe Bossi in 1810, and it was taken up most influentially by Johann Wolfgang von Goethe in his 1817 review of Bossi's book on *The Last Supper*. And yet Goethe by his own admission was looking not at the original work but at a print by Raphael Morghen after Bossi's replica, which omitted details such as halos visible in early copies and the bread and wine toward which Christ extends his hands in Leonardo's original painting.

Although the unfounded notion that Leonardo was uninterested in the religious meaning of the subject has not gone unchallenged, it is one that still prevails. The same notion has prompted some commentators to find it inconceivable that Leonardo would have painted a traditional Christian subject like the *Salvator Mundi*, and in such an archaizing, frontal arrangement, without the artist's defining interest in animation. Yet that icon-like tendency persists in *The Last Supper*, with Christ disposed frontally, hands extended, forming an equilateral triangle at the center of the composition. By comparison, the major precedents for Leonardo's composition—paintings in Tuscan refectories by Castagno, Ghirlandaio, and Perugino, all of which he would have known—tend to show an asymmetrically turned, blessing Christ, directing his attention to the prone figure of St. John dozing on the table to his immediate left. Leonardo may be focused on the instantaneous drama of Christ's prediction, but the arrangement suggests a deeper level of engagement with the significance of the episode.

One of the foremost authorities on the painting wrote in 1999 that "one must be cautious about imputing a religious motive to Leonardo in his narrative 'history' paintings. Every action and emotion he depicted had to be justified in scientific terms" and "everything centers on the 'scientific' and objective representation of reality. The scene appears to illustrate a law on the propagation of sound."[16]

It is easy for the religious resonances of Renaissance art, so much freighted with narratives of scientific discovery and progress, to fall into a kind of "modern oblivion." The phrase is that of the critic and art historian Leo Steinberg, who contested the modernist biographical myth of an agnostic or secularizing Leonardo. In the book *Leonardo's Incessant Last Supper* (2001), Steinberg refuted the common notion that the picture depicts a snapshot-like single moment. He argued that Leonardo structured his painting so that the event "diffuses into successiveness and duration." The subject is, in fact, manifold—"narrative, yes, but in equal measure symbolic, proleptic, and sacramental."[17] Steinberg marshalled exhaustive evidence—both artistic responses and the testimony of well-informed Renaissance viewers—to show that the picture was seen as a depiction *both* of Christ's announcement of the treachery among the Apostles *and* of the mystical sacrifice of Christ's body and blood, destined for incessant reenactment.[18] Leonardo has conceived the impassioned and pathos-laden gestures of Christ and his followers to sustain both the dramatic and theological meanings, and more in addition. The painting is a *historia* (depiction of action) that shows a series of actions described in scripture, but it also has an *iconic* and thus a theological and mystical aspect: Christ's frontality and triangular symmetry are invested with the human and divine nature of God; his hand gestures signify resignation to the passion, while also designating the bread and the wine, and directing our attention to

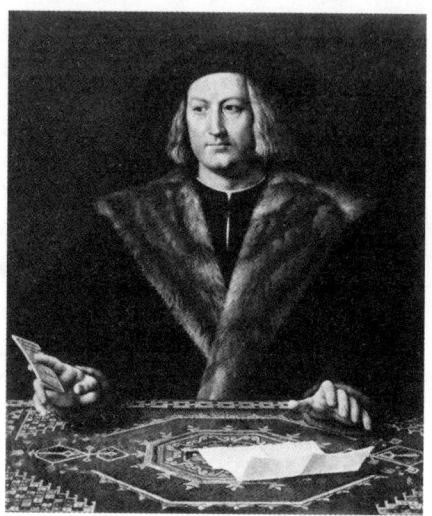

2. Andrea Solario, *Portrait of Chancellor Domenico Girolamo Morone*. Ca. 1515–24. On panel, 73 × 60 cm. Milan, Gallarati Scotti Collection.

Judas: no less importantly, they address the viewer, and would have had a particular impact when seen by a beholder entering the refectory from the original eastward entrance, now sealed, giving onto the convent's cloister cemetery. I would add that the richly determined gestures so fascinated the Milanese chancellor Girolamo Morone that around 1515 he had Andrea Solario portray him in the same Christ-like pose, a pious *imitatio Christi* that is also an address to the viewer, a gesture of command and conversion (fig. 2).

Steinberg's book does not set out to "solve" the painting as if it were a crossword puzzle, but to use historical inquiry to lay out a horizon of meanings that would have been intelligible to those who saw *The Last Supper* in Leonardo's lifetime and afterward. The book sought to start a conversation in which few enough of the anointed Leonardo authorities, with their pursuit of certain knowledge and scientific verification, have consented to engage.[19] At the same time, *Leonardo's Incessant Last Supper* signaled a general shift in Renaissance art history from production to reception, from the mystification of the artist genius to the ways historical beholders are likely to have adjusted to and make sense of complex and demanding works of art. Those historical beholders include the artists who produced what are conventionally called replicants and variants of the original but who, in the process of translation into a different medium, constantly modified and reinterpreted what Leonardo had left equivocal.

Correspondingly, we will throughout this book be contesting the assumption that meaning in a work of art is to be accounted for only in terms of the will or intention of its maker. The biography of an artist that determines our sense of his will or intention tends to simplify or reduce the question of meaning. But what if that biography is also a cultural artifact, a cluster of facts, false clues, and yawning gaps that biographers feel called upon to fill with varying degrees of fabulation?

PARIS: A TOO-FAMOUS PORTRAIT AND AN IDENTITY PERENNIALLY IN CRISIS

Perhaps you have been to the Salon des États at the Louvre and been part of the crowd all striving to see, and preventing you from seeing, the *Mona Lisa* in her concrete and bulletproof glass enclosure (plate 3). In the past few years you will also have seen the front of the crowd of visitors mostly with their backs to the painting, cell-phone cameras raised in the air, capturing the moment at which the urgent cultural imperative has been fulfilled. It's hard to blame them, and one certainly cannot blame the museum: six million or more viewers every year enable the vast museum to keep its numerous collections on view, but it can never withdraw the *Mona Lisa* from exhibition. Even if you had the gallery to yourself (on rare and terrible occasions, like in the aftermath of the terrorist mass murders of November 13, 2015, this has almost been possible), you probably would not see very much: the overfamiliar portrait can only be seen behind glass and from several feet away; you can have a better idea of the painting by looking at high-resolution digital images. You have probably turned to look at the other paintings by Leonardo on the wall to the right; you might have noticed that they exercise significantly less drawing power for the crowds in the room, many of whom are probably retreating with relief and getting back to a normal vacation. A few, usually younger college-age tourists, will gaze at them for a while; tourists in groups directed to pay attention to them for a second might honor them with a snapshot. The most important of these other Leonardos, *The Virgin and Child with St. Anne*, was cleaned some years ago, with the predictable controversies (plate 4); so, more recently, has the *St. John the Baptist*, at best something of a niche favorite, where conservation led to far more subtle changes in the picture's appearance (plate 5). However, this series of Leonardo paintings, unmatched in any other collection in the world, is mostly unlooked at; it is as if in reinforcing the cultural capital of *Mona Lisa*, their visual and historical interest has drained away. Because there is no script or master *narrative*, they seem strange. The dark-eyed woman known as *La Belle Ferronnière* differs from *Mona Lisa* in one crucial respect: not only is she anonymous, but there is no story, or romance, or mystery to connect her to Leonardo (plate 6). *Mona Lisa*, on the other hand, figures in the principal early biography of Leonardo, published as part of his collection of artists' lives by Giorgio Vasari in 1550 and 1568, which inadvertently set the legend of the *Mona Lisa* in motion: "Leonardo undertook to execute, for Francesco del Giocondo, the portrait of Mona Lisa, his wife, and after he had lingered over it for four years, he left it unfinished; and the work is today in the possession of King Francis of France, at Fontainebleau." Vasari extols the lifelikeness of the portrait, the moist and lustrous eyes, the subtlety of the flesh tints, and then "the eyebrows, through his having shown the manner in which the hairs spring from the flesh, here more close and here more scanty, and curve according to the pores of the flesh, could not be more natural." He goes on to praise the nose, the "rosy and tender" nostrils, the lips, and the pit of the throat, in which "if one gazed upon it intently, could be seen the beating of the pulse: and indeed it may be said that it was painted in such a manner as to make every brave artificer, be he who he may, tremble and lose courage."[20]

Yet Vasari had never been to Fontainebleau. That could explain why he is mistaken about the eyebrows; *Mona Lisa* clearly has none, as a later source notes (it is possible they were removed by a zealous overcleaning). Was he just following the poetical formulas for the head-to-toe description of beautiful women in vernacular poetry, where eyebrows are often complimented? Was he basing his account on an eyewitness description by someone else? Or—most likely—did he see a copy, perhaps even an alternative version, of the painting? It was the following passage, however, that decisively affected the afterlife of this portrait, and of its painter: Leonardo hired musicians and comedians to keep Mona Lisa entertained "in order to take away that melancholy which painters are often wont to give to their portraits. And in this work of Leonardo there was a smile so pleasing, that it was a thing more divine than human to behold, and it was held to be something marvelous, in that it was not other than alive."[21]

Here is the origin of the famous and kitsch legend of the Mona Lisa smile, a staple of Leonardo lore since the early nineteenth century. The smile, or rather half smile, is a signature effect of Leonardo, who wrote in his notebooks about the "motions of the mind," as volatile as the shadows on faces at twilight that he enjoined painters to capture.[22] For some reason, only the smile of the Mona Lisa is deemed mysterious. The other female portraits—the impassive *Ginevra de'Benci* in Washington, the half-smiling *Lady with an Ermine* (*Cecilia Gallerani*) (plate 7), or the brooding *La Belle Ferronnière*—seemingly cannot produce "Leonardo" for us in the same way (plate 6).

The painting has been given a quality of *personhood*—it is routinely referred to as "she." On "her" rare travels—back to Paris from Florence, across the Atlantic to Washington and New York in 1963, and to Japan in 1974—"she" is received by heads of state: Elena of Montenegro, Queen of Italy, in 1913; Jackie Kennedy and JFK in 1963; Crown Prince Naruhito in 1974.[23] In popular satires and in children's fiction the *Mona Lisa* repeatedly comes to life, sometimes escaping from the Louvre leaving only the background landscape in the frame. A century of popular fiction presents the figure in the painting as Leonardo's lover; more recent popular journalism speculates that she was his mother, or reports evidence (drawn from portraits that are probably not of Leonardo) that she is none other than Leonardo himself. The desire that ascribes person-like qualities to a painted woman might be seen as compensating for the absent personhood of the artist, the kind of longing that drives Da Vinci Worlds.

The painting, of course, cannot fulfill an imaginary promise to deliver Leonardo to us. Here perhaps lies the source of a recurring tendency to cast doubt on its very singularity, its originality, and hence its efficacy in revealing Leonardo. When the *Mona Lisa* was stolen from the Louvre in 1911—the first event that would prove its extraordinary power to boost newspaper sales—there was a wild proliferation of conspiracy theories about the motivation for the theft, which continued for years after the retrieval of the painting in Florence in 1913. For instance, it was widely believed that the crime was the work of Paris's artistic bohemia (the poet Guillaume Apollinaire, a friend of Picasso, was arrested and detained for several days). The actual thief, a museum worker named Vincenzo Peruggia, arrested in Italy in 1913, claimed to be an Italian patriot who wanted to repatriate the "stolen" work to its homeland. In 1932 one "Marquis de Valfiero" claimed that he had stolen the painting in order to propagate the hoax that the painting finally returned to the Louvre was a copy.

Scholars and collectors had long been aware of multiple versions of Leonardo paintings, made by pupils or followers, during and well beyond the artist's lifetime. On at least one occasion, in the midst of dire crisis, the Louvre did substitute one of these copies of the *Mona Lisa* for the original. A 1945 record concerning the Nazi repository for stolen art in the salt mines of Altaussee in Austria stated that the *Mona Lisa* was among "80 wagons of art and cultural objects" stored at the mines. But the version consigned by the Louvre and hidden at Altaussee was a copy; the original had left Paris secretly in 1939 and appears to have been stored at Chambord, Montauban, and other locations before being reinstalled in the Louvre in June 1945, well in advance of the release of works of art from the salt mine.

It was in the aftermath of the Louvre theft, and with the rise of mass circulation photography and newsprint, that copies in private hands were repeatedly deployed to contest the painting's originality and authenticity. In 1913, the art dealer Hugh Blaker claimed that a version of the painting that he saw in (and would subsequently acquire from) a private collection in Isleworth near London was an authentic autograph early version of the *Mona Lisa*. A 1926 monograph by John Eyre argued that the work was no less than the original *Mona Lisa* seen and described by Vasari, that in the Louvre being a later version. The Isleworth "discovery" was followed by extensively publicized alternative candidates or second autograph versions in subsequent decades—the Hekking *Mona Lisa* or *Joconde de Nice* in 1954, the Vernon *Mona Lisa* (formerly owned and declared to be the original by Sir Joshua Reynolds) in 1964, a version in the Hermitage in 2015.

The Isleworth version is part of a family of free copies of the *Mona Lisa* that show the sitter framed by a pair of columns; Leonardo included only slight indications of column bases in the Louvre portrait, just sufficient to indicate that his subject was seated at an open loggia. Although it is not clear why the copies show more of the columns, such an enhancement is not particularly anomalous or mysterious in the 1500s when notions of what constituted a copy or a replica were fluid and did not always imply literal reproduction. It is very possible that Leonardo sanctioned an early workshop version with just such variants, from which the numerous other versions derive, especially after the Louvre version had been taken to France. Perhaps, too, the copyist's revision appeared more complete to the eyes of clients, for whom Leonardo's vestigial slivers of column seemed disturbing. Nonetheless, there are reasons to doubt that the Isleworth version even came from Leonardo's studio: it is painted on canvas, which he never used, and in many particulars has the mechanical stiffness of a derivation, even a thirdhand modern one—in particular the opacity and dryness of texture of the veils, the hair, and the sleeves, and the perfunctory (impressionistic?) treatment of the landscape. The simpering expression suggests that the artist might have been beholden to the legend of the *Mona Lisa* smile and sought to enhance it.

A version in the Prado was cleaned in 2012 and proved to be of considerably more interest, especially because of the luminous landscape that resurfaced from under dark overpaint: it appears to be the work of a talented Leonardo assistant, painted in tandem with the original, and a reliable document of how the portrait was originally supposed to look (fig. 3).[24] Two additional replicas of the portrait—made long after the Prado version, and probably long after the death of Leonardo—were sold at auction in 2019 and in 2021, the latter—none other than the Hekking *Mona Lisa*—raised an "astonishing" 2.9 million euro.[25] Others will doubtless continue to surface.

GIOCONDA LAB: "SECRETS" OF
A FLORENTINE WIFE

In 2008, the Isleworth *Mona Lisa* resurfaced on the market and was acquired by a private foundation in Zurich that promotes research on the painting—especially research that strengthens the case that it is an autograph

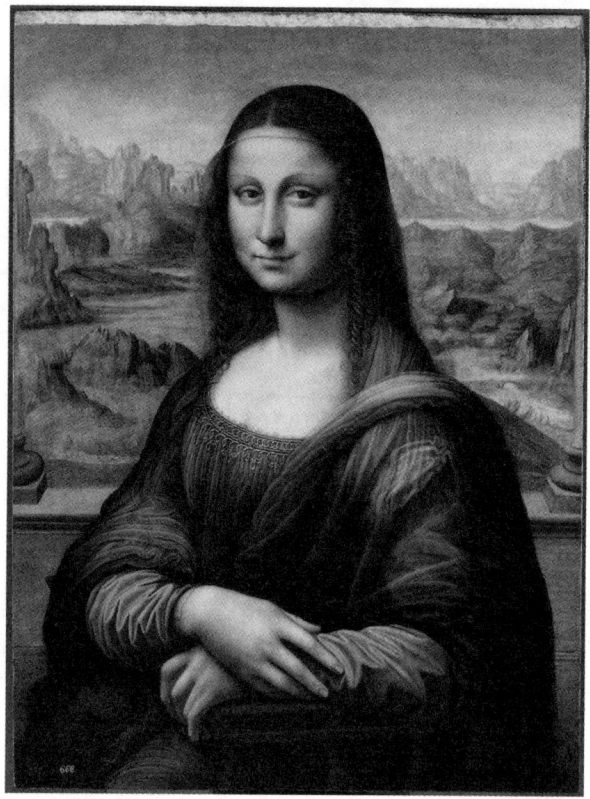

3. Follower of Leonardo da Vinci, *Portrait of Lisa Gherardini*. Ca. 1506–13. On panel, 76.3 × 57 cm. Madrid, Museo del Prado.

early version of the *Mona Lisa*. The painting has been exhibited around the world—in 2014 it was shown as a Leonardo in Singapore, in 2016 in Shanghai, in 2023 in Turin—but the field of art history in general and the leading Leonardo scholars in particular remain unpersuaded.

On their website, a Da Vinci World known as the Mona Lisa Foundation has claimed that the subject of both their painting and the Louvre portrait is Lisa Gherardini, one depicting her in her early twenties, and the other (the Louvre version) in her mid-thirties. It cited Forensic Facial Imaging analysis (used by police for criminal identification) to "prove" that the paintings depict the same woman at two different moments of her life, and further elaborate analysis to demonstrate an esoteric program of Pythagorean geometry and "binocular perspective" in the picture in Zurich. While the Isleworth version was alleged to have been executed in Florence ca. 1503–6 for Francesco del Giocondo—the cursory treatment of the landscape is declared to be characteristic of Leonardo's habit of leaving things unfinished, since he was in haste to leave for Milan—the Louvre version was supposedly painted in Rome ca. 1513–16 for Giuliano de'Medici. An ambiguous eyewitness source has served as the basis for the questionable theory of two original *Mona Lisa*s. A cardinal's secretary, Antonio de'Beatis, who visited Leonardo at home in Amboise in 1517, wrote in his journal about seeing "a portrait of a certain Florentine woman, the mistress of Duke Giuliano de'Medici."[26]

Since 2008 there has been no shortage of new theories about the *Mona Lisa*, many grounded in appeals to scientific analysis. It would take an entire book to describe even summarily the dense thicket of myth and wishful thinking that has accumulated around the *Mona Lisa*, where even a modest new observation seems not to uproot but to fertilize tendentious narratives. For that matter, entire books have been written seeking to establish that the sitter is *anyone* but the wife of Francesco del Giocondo. While the portrait of a woman seen by Antonio de'Beatis in Leonardo's French residence is usually identified as the *Mona Lisa*, it clearly has details inconsistent with Vasari's account. Documentation about any Renaissance portrait is rare, but this discrepancy has created untold difficulties for the many scholars who have labored to reconcile the two early testimonies with the painting in the Louvre. A reasonable explanation of the de'Beatis report might be that the secretary was close to elite circles of the Roman *curia*, then dominated by clients and relatives of the Medici pope Leo X. He would thus have been more interested in rumors about a Medici mistress than reliable information about an obscure Florentine merchant's wife. De'Beatis incorrectly reports that Leonardo was right-handed and his age as being seventy, so he is not in any case the most reliable of witnesses. There is also the possibility, raised by some, that the portrait in Leonardo's possession was *no longer* Mona Lisa—it was seemingly never delivered to the sitter's family, so Leonardo kept working on it over the years, to the point that it no longer resembled her.[27]

By now, a great deal is known about the fairly ordinary life of the sitter Lisa Gherardini—Vasari may have known her himself, in her old age.[28] Yet the relatively certain biography of the sitter, perhaps too mundane to suit the Da Vinci legend, has not prevented a torrent of more glamorous identifications. In the heyday of early Italian independence, Adolfo Venturi and Benedetto Croce saw her as the forty-year-old widow Costanza d'Avalos, the wife of Federico del Balzo who led the resistance to the French occupation of Naples. She has been several times identified as the Marchioness of Mantua, Isabella d'Este, even though she looks nothing like Leonardo's Louvre drawing of Isabella, and at least once as her sister Beatrice, the Duchess of Milan. In 2003, the independent scholar and blogger Maike Vogt-Luerssen revived an older identification of the portrait as Isabella of Aragon, the previous Duchess of Milan. Spurred by the reference to a Medici mistress, Carlo Pedretti identified her as Pacifica Brandano, an obscure woman from Urbino who bore a child to Giuliano. The Leonardo biographer Carlo Vecce maintained in 1998 that she was Isabella Gualanda, a Neapolitan woman whose portrait Giuliano may have commissioned from Leonardo; that identification was also endorsed by Carlo Pedretti.[29]

A new document published in 2005 looked like it might resolve the issue. A copy of a 1477 print edition of Cicero's *Epistulae Familiares* in Heidelberg University Library was found to contain Latin annotations by the Florentine Agostino di Matteo Vespucci, an acquaintance of Leonardo's. Cicero referred to an image of Venus by the great Greek painter Apelles, admired even though it was unfinished. Vespucci wrote in the margin: "The painter Apelles. In this way Leonardo da Vinci makes it in all his paintings, for example the head of Lisa del Giocondo and of Anne, the mother of the Virgin. We will see what he is going to do with regard to the hall of the Great Council about which he has just agreed with the Gonfaloniere. 1503. October."[30]

In 2008 the library issued a statement, widely reported in international media: "All doubts about the identity of the Mona Lisa have been eliminated by a discovery by Dr. Armin Schlechter." "Vasari, it turns out, was right," wrote James Fenton, in an op-ed vindicating the credibility of the much-maligned painter-historian.[31] The Louvre itself took a more cautious approach. "Leonardo da Vinci was painting, in 1503, the portrait of a Florentine lady by the name of Lisa del Giocondo," said the curator Vincent Delieuvin, interviewed on January 15, 2008. "About this we are now certain. Unfortunately, we cannot be absolutely certain that this portrait of Lisa del Giocondo is the painting from the Louvre."[32]

Such scholarly caution is justified, even if it allows the proliferation of unscholarly and reckless theories to continue, especially solutions to the "mystery of Da Vinci" that purport to decode the secret life of the master. These include the improbable yet widely publicized claims that *Mona Lisa* is a disguised self-portrait of Leonardo himself, or of Leonardo's mother (a Chinese slave, allegedly), or of his probable male lover, Salaì; these theories show no sign of going away.

Some scholars, drawing on the archival reconstruction of the life of Lisa Gherardini and less besotted with dynastic drama, have seen the painting in the context of Florentine marriage and the family. Needless to say, the painting resists such normalizing typologies. Portraits of wives in the Renaissance observed a decorum of gender and class: they depicted married women with the material tokens of family honor and property. Lisa wears none of the jewels or sumptuous clothing that we can find in contemporary or earlier spousal portraits like Ghirlandaio's *Giovanna Tornabuoni*, which preceded the *Mona Lisa*, or Raphael's *Maddalena Strozzi*, which derives from it (fig. 4). For pictures of wives, the intimate address of Lisa's gaze is seemingly unthinkable. In their departure from conventional formality, the only comparable portrayals are Leonardo's two earlier Milanese depictions of women, both identified as Sforza mistresses (plates 6 and 7).

Following a technical examination of the painting in 2006, there were further attempts to wring new biographical findings from previously overlooked details. The fine drapery on the figure's shoulder was deemed to be a *guarnello*, a veil worn by Florentine women when pregnant and after having given birth; flimsy evidence, so to speak, given that the identification of the garment seems less than certain, but there is a degree of probability given that Gherardini gave birth to her second son in 1502; the commission could have been given at that point for the work in process by Leonardo in 1503.

The effect of such investigation is at best to give a concreteness to the work, restoring it to a place and a time, an undramatic everyday realm from which the very odd painting constantly seems to break free, its ongoing life

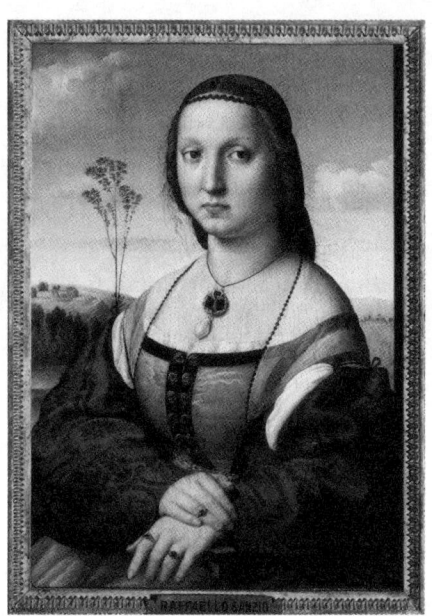

4. Raphael, *Portrait of Maddalena Strozzi*. Ca. 1504–7. On panel, 63.5 × 45 cm. Florence, Uffizi.

as a mythical archetype replenished. Yet even the more mundane approach can take a sensationalist leap. In 2011 Silvano Vinceti, an ex-politician, head of a private foundation with the momentous name National Committee for the Evaluation of Cultural and Environmental Heritage, and self-appointed specialist in the quest for the remains of illustrious Italians (including Petrarch, Pico, Poliziano, and Caravaggio), claimed to have found "the skull of the Mona Lisa" in the cemetery of the convent where Gherardini had died in 1542. The bones were unearthed before TV cameras and in the presence of some of Gherardini's living descendants. Now, finally, with the aid of forensic science, it was reported, the face of the real Mona Lisa could be reconstructed and compared with the Louvre portrait, and the mystery of her smile would finally be solved. (Vinceti had previously backed the theory that the Mona Lisa wasn't Gherardini at all but Leonardo's youthful lover Salaì—substantiated, supposedly, by his discovery that the initials L and V were to be found in Lisa's eyes.)[33]

When Vinceti's methods and assertions were called into question— there were, after all, a large number of women buried in the convent of Sant'Orsola—he proceeded, with financial support from the city of Florence and the usual squadron of cameramen and reporters, to exhume the remains of Francesco del Giocondo in Santissima Annunziata in order to obtain DNA from the remains of the two sons who had been buried with him. The art historian Tommaso Montanari, prominent as a whistle-blower against the abuse of cultural patrimony for revenue-generating and self-publicizing ends, denounced the enterprise as a hoax and lambasted Vinceti's fake science and lack of credentials.

For Montanari, the ascent of opportunistic pseudo-experts signals a wider conjunction of political corruption, journalistic irresponsibility, the discrediting of expertise, and a crisis of democracy itself: "If I were to claim I had seen the Higgs Boson in my living room with the naked eye, they would bring me to the mental hospital: but let anyone in the street claim to have discovered a Michelangelo, a Leonardo or a Caravaggio, and the media circus will immediately carry him in triumph. When it comes to the history of art, anything is possible. In Italy art-historical journalism is almost dead, and is now so used to thinking of itself as a megaphone proclaiming Big Discoveries that it is no longer able to distinguish a piece of news from a hoax."[34] By 2012, however, the problem was not just an Italian one.

Since the early 2000s new and credible information has been generated about the *Mona Lisa*, using state-of-the-art technology and usually with far more rigorous procedures and properly credentialed experts. There are better imperatives for costly and time-consuming studies. For the world's most famous painting, relatively little is known about Leonardo's working procedure and technique, or about the portrait's original appearance and physical history. The painting now appears almost monochrome, its original colors veiled in several centuries' reapplication of coats of varnish. Huge risks would attend on any attempt to restore the painting by detaching these from Leonardo's subtle glazes, applied in multiple layers.

A campaign of x-radiography in 2004–5 sought to build up an image of the inner structure of the paint layers: this was followed by an examination with X-ray fluorescence spectroscopy by the Centre de la Recherche et de Restauration. Even before these teams started their work, Pascal Cotte, an expert in high-resolution scanning, began an intensive campaign of multispectral photography generating thousands of images of the painting. Cotte's layer amplification method (LAM) uses thirteen different wavelengths of light bounced off the pigment, recording the painting's composite layered structure with unprecedented precision. Cotte's photography has resulted in perhaps the best reconstruction possible of how the *Mona Lisa* might have looked by the time Leonardo ceased working on it, its color palette a glowing harmony of amber, gold, and green, and quite different from the brownish apparition we see today.[35]

Cotte's scans detected early stages of the portrait quite different to what can now be seen on the surface. It is apparent that Leonardo, quite characteristically, had changed his mind at least once about the orientation and contours of the sitter's head, as well as the position of her eyes. Lisa's dress and veils proved to have been worked and reworked over time, to the point where their structural logic as garments is hard to grasp. Concerning the face and head in particular, much of the spectroscopic and x-radiographic evidence is difficult to interpret. Cotte, in a book from 2016 and in a sensationalizing BBC documentary by Andrew Graham-Dixon, was melodramatic about the meaning of his "150 brand new discoveries," claiming that his "scientific imagery technique . . . reveals secrets that have remained hidden for 500 years."[36] The *Mona Lisa*, according to Cotte, conceals three entirely different portraits of other women, and the "real" Lisa Gherardini is buried beneath the present portrait, which represents another person entirely. Inexplicable marks and smudges by Lisa's right temple coalesced in Cotte's explanation into a flamboyant headdress of pearl-studded pins worn by a "Madonna-like" figure also painted on top of the original.

With celebrity artists like Leonardo or Caravaggio, the significance of findings based on technological investigation and on newly patented techniques is often inflated. Whether they concern the identification of human remains or the meaning of preliminary marks in an underpainting, there is invariably a rhetoric of secrets being decoded, of a historical "cover-up" now being brought to the light of day. This tends to be far less the case with archival discoveries regarding a work of art, its maker, or its patron.

Ultimately, however, new discoveries—whether archival or technical—enrich our knowledge precisely by complicating it, by adding more tesserae to the mosaic: they seldom resolve long-standing problems or answer old questions. More often than not, they give rise to new ones. Already in 2014 the art historian Rab Hatfield, on the basis of X-ray images published by the Louvre in 2006, had argued that the painting is a palimpsest of three

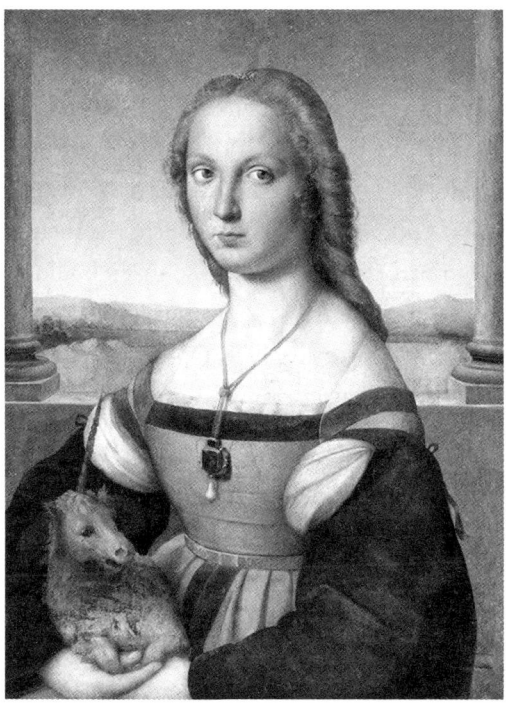

5. Raphael, *Lady with a Unicorn*. 1505–6. Originally on panel, remounted on canvas, 65 × 51 cm. Rome, Galleria Borghese.

separate portraits: originally a portrait of Lisa Gherardini in process in 1503, and noted in the Vespucci annotation as unfinished, the painting was supposedly reworked as a portrait of someone else by 1506—this is the version believed to have been seen by Raphael, the model for his painting of that date known as *Lady with a Unicorn* (fig. 5). The present painting, according to Hatfield, was made in Rome after 1513, and is the one attested by de'Beatis in Leonardo's studio as a mistress of Giuliano de'Medici.[37]

Rather than seeing the unreliable de'Beatis as merely making a mistake or reporting a kind of romantic folklore already accumulating around an enigmatic image, Hatfield sought to give the secretary's anomalous identification of the sitter a factual weight. To suggest, in other words, that Francesco del Giocondo's wife may actually have been Giuliano's mistress, or at least his ideal beloved. Hatfield's key piece of evidence was a scurrilous letter by Filippo Strozzi the Younger from 1515, which he had discovered in the Florence archives. Strozzi comments on the hearsay that he himself, in the company of Giuliano's nephew Lorenzo, had "tempted the honor" of (i.e., propositioned) Lisa and been rebuffed. Her husband, to Strozzi's amusement, was worried about the possible repercussions of rejecting one of the Medici. Through a web of inferences from other documents about the Giocondo family, the Strozzi, and the Medici, Hatfield proposes that Francesco del Giocondo had already by 1513 decided to offer the portrait of his wife as a gift to the Medici, or possibly that Giuliano had requisitioned the picture for his nephew or for himself, and returned it to Leonardo so that it could be "updated" to resemble Lisa as she looked in 1513. At some point, the boundary between historical interpretation and historical fiction has been crossed.

Filippo Strozzi's obnoxious behavior toward Lisa in 1515—even if he tried to mitigate it by declaring a preference for boys—is consistent with the well-known arrogance and sexual license of young elite males in Italian cities.[38] If Hatfield is correct, the *Mona Lisa* would be the idealized and poetical sanitization of historical toxic masculinity. Far from being the "portrait of an ambitious but insecure businessman's wife"—it doesn't display family wealth and status—it was probably not intended for Giocondo at all: "perhaps it was only meant to be a means by which the Magnificent Giuliano could worship Mon(n)a Lisa vicariously, as many men (especially in prison or the armed forces) did until just a few decades ago with pin-ups of movie stars."[39]

The considerable historical interest of the Strozzi letter aside, as evidence about the painting it offers, at best, a plot twist, or perhaps only a coincidence. It does not sanction Hatfield's interpretation of three separate portraits on one panel, nor of the connection of the sitter with a mistress of Giuliano de'Medici. Nor does the technical evidence: the "alternative" *Mona Lisa*s hidden beneath the layers reflect no more than Leonardo's improvisatory working method, a constant self-revision and experimentation over many years of work on the same portrait in Florence, Milan, Rome, and France. Martin Kemp's assessment of the evidence to date is levelheaded: "There is no such thing as a clearly definable layer that corresponds to the first version of a finished or even quasi-finished painting under the present one, to be succeeded by a comparably resolved composition, and so on. We should not at this stage read more into the techniques of scientific examination than they can safely give us."[40]

So, what can we finally say? That the *Mona Lisa* is best regarded as an ongoing pictorial experiment, an attempt to create a kind of ultimate or archetypal portrait of a beautiful human being, but not as the distant and abstract ideal that would become characteristic of Renaissance female portraiture in Florence and Rome. This was rather to be the fiction of a flesh-and-blood woman, instantiating a major theme of Leonardo's writings on art: the power of art to psychologically engage the beholder. The landscape with the massive, jagged geological formations and surging rivers was the last part of the picture to be completed, and was more than likely executed in Milan following Leonardo's return there in 1509. Such geological fantasy is not without precedent in Renaissance portraiture, especially at the courts of Northern Italy.[41] Leonardo, after his years in Milan, is elaborating on a theme associated with the courts, but he invests his landscape with an awesome and even an apocalyptic quality that sets his work apart. He was, in these years, engaged in drafting a treatise on geomorphology and the origins of the waters of the earth, which comes down to us as the Codex Leicester. The crucial point, however, is that this portrait has gone well beyond the point of recording a likeness. The contrast between a tender face and rugged mountains is setting up the conditions for making meaning, inviting the beholder to perceive poetic antithesis: the delicacy of a young wife versus the inhuman inhospitable vastness of nature; or metaphor, "Hers is the head upon which all the ends of the world are come" (Walter Pater, writing about this painting in 1873); or analogy, such as Leonardo's own "as bones and blood are to bodies, so rocks and streams are to the Earth." The long tradition of enraptured writing on the *Mona Lisa* is drawn forth by this structurally poetic aspect of the image itself.

What the portrait *does* is as important as *who it is*, or rather who it might originally have been; thus, many art historians find it most helpful to see the picture as a visualization of Leonardo's artistic principles. For others, the lacunose evidence is a spur to historical sleuthing and speculation; it bears the signs of an intrigue or a mystery, especially with the word "mistress" involved. Vasari's prosaic explanation of her blithe expression becomes insufficient—it is somehow instead to be seen as a *knowing* smile, the sign of a secret she shares with the painter. The novelist and art critic Théophile Gautier in 1855 wrote of *La Joconde* as "this sphinx of beauty who smiles so mysteriously in Leonardo da Vinci's painting and who seems to pose a yet unsolved riddle to the admiring centuries."[42] Later, in 1882, he elaborated: "Repressed desire and desperate hopes struggle painfully through a luminous shadow; and you discover that your melancholy springs from the fact that the Gioconda received, three hundred years ago, the confession of your love with the same sarcastic smile which she still wears today."[43]

SELL THE *MONA LISA*!

The *Mona Lisa*'s idol-like status as the repository of the ultimate in artistic and art historical value keeps it alive as the potential focus of extraordinary acts of iconoclasm, the attempted disruption of conventional values and received wisdom. Such disruptions, as we will see, are no longer the preserve of the likes of Duchamp or Warhol.

The central event in the celebration of the artist's quincentennial year in 2019 was without question the great exhibition at the Louvre, which brought together the museum's unrivaled cluster of Leonardo paintings and drawings with exceptional loans from museums and libraries in Milan, Florence, Venice, London, Windsor, Oxford, Berlin, New York, and elsewhere. Italy declined to loan the early *Annunciation* from the Uffizi, in a delicate state. It sent the *Vitruvian Man* drawing from Venice (plate 8), despite protests from heritage groups, and the monumental bronze *Christ and St. Thomas* by Andrea del Verrocchio, a key work by Leonardo's teacher. The bronze formed the centerpiece of the first gallery devoted to a celebrated series of drapery studies by Leonardo and other artists connected with the artist's workshop. A later gallery was devoted to the notebooks, where the generous holdings in France were shown alongside examples from the British Museum, the Royal Collection, and the Biblioteca Ambrosiana in Milan.

The exhibition—which sought to include more Leonardos than all previous ones—affirmed a long-standing narrative of France as the center of Leonardo's legacy. That story begins with several French military occupations of Milan after 1494, continues with Leonardo's emigration to France in 1516, and reached its climax with the stripping of Italy's art treasures for the Musée Napoléon in the 1800s. It had its cultural counterpart in the elaboration of a "French" Leonardo by art academies, critics, and curators in the 1600s and 1700s with the systematic study and publication of the artist's scattered manuscripts and reproductions of these. The joint efforts of the scholar Cassiano del Pozzo, the Rome-based French painter

Nicolas Poussin (who provided the illustrations), and the French man of letters Roland Fréart de Chambray culminated with the 1651 publication of the *Treatise on Painting* referred to earlier: a highly selective compilation of Leonardo's writings reflecting the normative and prescriptive approaches to theory and practice of French and Italian academicians. Poussin also copied several of Leonardo's optical drawings and circulated them in Paris.[44] By the 1800s French scholars could turn their attention to the Leonardo notebooks seized during the Napoleonic conquest of Italy and deposited in the Institut de France: this was an avowedly enlightenment project as well as an imperialistic one. By contrast, the Vatican-appointed custodians of the Leonardo manuscripts in the Ambrosiana in Milan, which included the vast compilation of scientific and engineering studies known as the Codex Atlanticus, restricted scholarly access, and withheld permission to publish the material.[45]

Within weeks of the closure of the record-breaking exhibition, the Louvre—along with every other museum across the globe—shut its doors for months. The loss of revenue to the French cultural sector—more heavily subsidized than elsewhere but dependent on high-volume tourist traffic through sites like the Louvre, and already debilitated by a long-running transport strike in the winter of 2019—was cataclysmic. The Louvre reported a 72 percent drop in visitor numbers for 2020, with only 2.7 million visitors by comparison with 9.6 million in 2019 (a figure boosted by the 2 million who came for the Leonardo exhibition). And yet before the consequences had made themselves felt, and as measures were being put in place to reopen the museums of France, prognostications and future outcomes were making the headlines, especially pronouncements by those we have enfranchised to be our "big thinkers"—digital entrepreneurs.

Stéphane Distinguin, the CEO of the digital innovation company Fabernovel, called for the sale of the *Mona Lisa*. The suggestion was inspired, he said, by the $450 million price tag for the *Salvator Mundi*. "I think it could be a good business move, from an economic and cultural point of view. Extraordinary times, uncharted solutions. The [heritage] sector is in pieces, the famous French cultural exceptionalism is likely to vanish."[46] The only cultural entities with the means to make a difference, he added, were giant media monopolies like Netflix.

Since when do digital entrepreneurs get to pronounce on national cultural policy? The answer, increasingly, is all the time. Among its clients,
Fabernovel counts leading newspaper and television companies, as well
as political operations like G7. There are no more sweepingly effective ways
of exerting influence in the twenty-first century.

The proposal, as Distinguin knew, was outrageous. He admitted that
his op-ed was an iconoclastic provocation, a kind of public-intellectual
thought experiment. Yet he knew that he would be taken literally, that
there was a dimension of reality and possibility to his outrageous idea.
Distinguin cited the "textbook case" of the collections of the Detroit Institute of Arts, valued by Christie's in 2014 with a view to a possible sale to
offset massive fiscal losses to an impoverished and debt-ridden city. And
2020 would turn out to be a year of controversial museum deaccessions,
motivated not only by the depletion of funds but by a worldwide out-
cry over the lack of diversity and inclusion in the audiences, staffing, and
governance of museums. Museums were taken to task for being beholden
to elite donors and audiences, hoarding the stolen heritage of colonized
peoples, and promoting a canon of white male European and American
artists. The Baltimore Museum of Art's attempt to sell off three signature works of twentieth-century American art—with the goal of making
its collection more diverse and availing of a loosening of deaccessioning
guidelines under the conditions of the pandemic—was called off following protests by trustees, local artists, art historians, and the public. Among
the works withdrawn from sale was Andy Warhol's *Last Supper* (1986)—a
monumental double-reproduction of Raphael Morghen's 1800 reproductive engraving (fig. 6). Part of a series based on the mural that Warhol
produced in the final years of his life, and the focus of a 1987 exhibition
in Milan at a site near Santa Maria delle Grazie, the *Last Supper* paintings
have been seen as the artist's final testament, as well as a memorial and
work of mourning for gay generations devastated by and stigmatized during the AIDS epidemic.[47]

By the time Distinguin gave an interview to *Corriere della Sera* a few
days later, there was no more "what-if?" Everything seemed a good deal
more concrete. "We can try to venture a price," he said. "Let's say at least
a hundred times that of the Leonardo *Salvator Mundi*? We weigh that

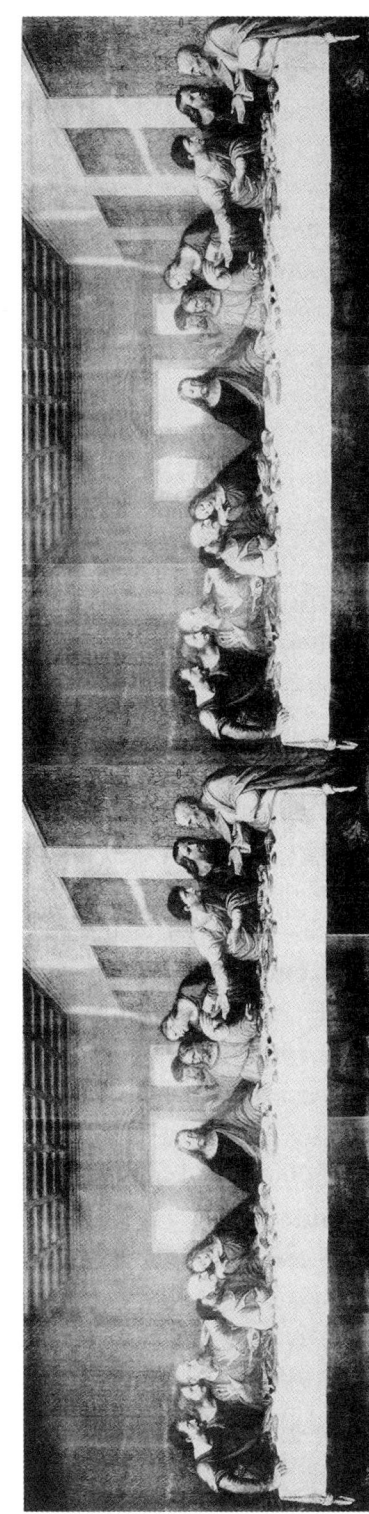

6. Andy Warhol, *The Last Supper*. 1986. Synthetic polymer paint and silkscreen ink on canvas. Baltimore Museum of Art.

against the fact that the *Vitruvian Man*, sent to Paris for the quincentennial show, has been insured for a billion. We can estimate that the *Mona
Lisa* generates for the Louvre and indirectly for the French economy (including merchandising, hotels and air tickets) roughly three billion euros a
year. Fifty billion seems reasonable to me; for the operation to make sense,
you have to ask for a huge amount."[48]

His embrace of the bottom-line logic of capital is nuanced with humanistic and intellectualizing qualifiers, which seem already contradicted
in advance by that same logic: "To pose the question of the sale of the
Mona Lisa opens the door to the transformation of two opposing a priori
aspects of our relationship to works of art. First, inalienability must be
universal. *Mona Lisa* belongs to humanity, no more to the French than to
the Italians. As with the protection of the planet and its animals, the next
generation would be well advised to rethink the governance of its inalien-
able resources." At the same time, Distinguin claimed that "the value of the
Mona Lisa is precisely its inalienability. If she sells, and leaves the Louvre,
she will lose her status."

On one hand, the French (especially the French intelligentsia) have
long had a healthily irreverent relationship with the *Mona Lisa* (think
once more of Duchamp's 1919 DADA version), and its cult status was in
large part the creation of those looking from beyond the shores of France—
Walter Pater, Dmitry Merezhkovsky, Nat King Cole. Yet France is also
proprietorial about a national public culture, vigilant about cultural assets
that belong to the people of France. Distinguin knows that it is irrelevant
whether the *Mona Lisa* is "worth" 800 million or 50 billion euros. His assertion of the painting's "universal inalienability" is both high-minded and
mischievous. It looks progressively post-nationalist. Yet he and most of his
readers must have known that for several years a nationalist organization
in Italy, the National Committee for the Evaluation of Cultural and Environmental Heritage, had already characterized the *Mona Lisa* as Italy's
Parthenon Marbles and were demanding its restitution, with endorsement
in 2014 from Hollywood star George Clooney.

Political tensions between France and Italy flared again with the ascent
of a right-wing coalition under Matteo Salvini in 2018. Because France
was hosting the prestigious quincentennial exhibition, and Italy had no

corresponding event of its own, the Uffizi's decision to withhold loan requests for the Louvre show, for solid conservation reasons, was inevitably framed in political terms. Leonardo was one flashpoint in series of clashes between the Salvini and Macron governments, which ultimately led to France recalling its ambassador. This is precisely why Distinguin was given a platform in a major Italian newspaper.

To state the obvious, the culture-capital of the portrait has escalated beyond its status as an autograph work by Leonardo, its art historical importance, its artistic merit. We have already referred to the painting's status as a cultural ambassador—a tool of political leverage—in 1963 and 1974. More than a cultural asset, it has reemerged as a spoil or a trophy, subjected to competing appropriations by ideologues of reactionary nationalism or technocratic elitism. The Frenchness of the *Mona Lisa*, its Tour Eiffel–like status, is real, but it is not a stolen object: it arrived in France centuries before the Imperialist looting of Italy by Napoleon, but it has become a strange symbolic restitution for some opportunistic populists. The very identity of Paris is indelibly associated with the portrait, which is why seeing it is *the* key ritual of mass tourism to Paris.

Something of the same status was being invested in the *Salvator Mundi* in 2019, where an exhibition loan was supposed to deliver a political concordat between the French nation and the Saudi royal family. The two paintings seem to have developed a political-economic codependency: we have just seen how the very market value of the *Salvator Mundi* was being used to express the worth of the *Mona Lisa* in "real" terms. The idea of the *Mona Lisa* possessing a real market value is an instance of the kind of think-outside-the-box sabotage of a fragile and fetishized past that we grow accustomed to in the age of "freakonomics" and disaster capitalism. It is also cannily aligned with liberal-progressive challenges to the elite culture of museums and their overseers.

Putting a price on it is as meaningful as asking "How much is Venice worth?" And yet, that very question has been asked, and answered with a similarly "visionary" managerial calculus, while being called into question by more far-sighted thinkers. In Italy, the Calderoli Act of 2010, drawn up by the minster for legislative reform under the prime minister Silvio Berlusconi, sought to put a precise euro value on every single Italian public heritage site, all listed and priced in two gigantic reports, with authorization to individual municipalities to realize their value through effective privatization. The Italian art historian and cultural activist Salvatore Settis (who was also chairman of the Louvre's Scientific Council) had already written a passionate polemic against treating cultural heritage as a fungible "natural resource" like petroleum, *Italia S.p.A.* In his 2014 book *If Venice Dies* Settis countered the "self-styled appraisers" of the Calderoli report with other ways of conceiving the value of cultural heritage. He cited a 2006 report commissioned by the Chirac government from the economists Maurice Lévy and Jean-Pierre Jouyet, which makes the case that the value of a nation's cultural heritage is precisely in the unquantifiable constellation of objects, spaces, cities, the lives of people, and their cultural memory.[49] This is a continuum worth far more—it generates jobs, ideas, and initiatives in its character as a totality—than if individual elements were to be aggregated and given a price tag. To do so, in any case, would go against French laws governing national patrimony: it is hard not to see in Distinguin's intervention the incipient bid by a technocrat to disestablish the entire legal and constitutional principle of a republic run on essentially social-democratic principles.

PERMANENT BLOCKBUSTER: THE MUSEUM AS SPECTACLE

One of the most startling works by Leonardo in a public collection is the so-called Burlington House Cartoon—a full-scale mixed-media drawing for a painting, depicting the Virgin and Child with St. Anne and St. John, executed in Milan around 1508 and now preserved in the National Gallery in London (plate 9). The work was acquired from the Royal Academy for what now seems the implausibly low sum of £800,000, with significant donations from members of the public following a campaign to keep the work in Britain. Visitors can now experience this work in conditions of extraordinary intimacy in an isolated shrine-like gallery of its own, with the reduced lighting necessary for the display of works on paper—precisely the opposite of the way the Gherardini portrait is encountered, at a distance and with minimal elbow room or breathing space. The cartoon is unencumbered by biographical anecdote (despite Freud's efforts to make it part of his case history of Leonardo), or controversy, or hype of any kind—even the National Gallery's other Leonardo, the later *Virgin of the Rocks*, has a press-friendly narrative (is this the real Leonardo, or is that the version in the Louvre?). If the *Virgin and Child with St. Anne and St. John* now has any notoriety, it is because it is one of the handful of iconic works that someone has tried to destroy. During its display at the gallery in 1962 a bottle of ink was hurled at the delicate surface; the glass broke and caused a small scratch, but the bottle remained intact. In 1987, in what he claimed was an act of protest against conditions in post-Thatcherite Britain, a man named Robert Cambridge fired a handgun at the drawing. The protective laminated glass shattered, tearing a six-inch hole in the robe of the Virgin, requiring a year's intensive conservation work to remove glass fragments and to replace some sixty tiny fragments of paper. Such a history of attempted assaults is one thing the cartoon shares with the *Mona Lisa*, in a bulletproof bunker since its return from Japan in 1974.

Following a second campaign of conservation, the cartoon was one of the key works in the gallery's 2011 exhibition *Leonardo da Vinci: Painter at the Court of Milan*. Tickets for this blockbuster sold out well before the opening, yet even with controlled admission just under a million visitors saw the exhibition during its six-month run. The number of Leonardos on display fell a few short of what the Louvre would manage to pull together in 2019 but included the debut of the *Salvator Mundi* and a robust complement of high-quality works by Leonardo followers. The gallery's own *Virgin of the Rocks* was displayed in the exhibition at the opposite end of a gallery from the earlier version, loaned by the Louvre (plates 10 and 11): the historic and unprecedented confrontation was the centerpiece of the show. The rationale for attributions in a few controversial cases, along with technical investigations of Leonardo's technique—including new data from the conservation of the London *Virgin of the Rocks*—were all accessibly and persuasively presented. Most notably, the exhibition presented Leonardo as part of a social, political, and artistic milieu, and—importantly—alongside Milanese contemporary artists who collaborated with and learned from him. The approach was strongly historicist and didactic but at the same time was able to appeal to the Leonardo of public imagination: "Particularly in the 1490s, Leonardo's painting of a world made perfect by analysis, discipline, and imagination could be understood as corresponding to the much-promoted notion of the prince as the per fected ruler of an ideal state."[50] The pathos of the exhibition's narrative was the catastrophic disintegration of that idealism.

The exhibition was a quiet turning point in a succession of events that have brought the afterlife of Leonardo da Vinci into a strange and often frenzied new phase. Around the turn of the millennium, the popularity and visibility of Leonardo seemed to take a quantum leap that shows no sign of lessening, as a convergence of circumstances turned a long-dead Renaissance artist and part-time engineer into a twenty-first-century media celebrity. The National Gallery's Leonardo commemoration dur- ing the 2019 quincentennial could not have been more different from the show eight years earlier, manifesting the degree to which traditional museum space had been permeated by Da Vinci Worlds. *Leonardo da Vinci: The Immersive Show* was centered on one work, the London *Virgin of the Rocks*. Visitors progressed through a series of four "multisensory rooms" with gigantic moving projections of the painting and simulations of the painter's studio and the original altarpiece in San Francesco Grande; the first was "a landscape populated by the thoughts and ideas of Leonardo as he sets about painting *The Virgin of the Rocks*."[51]

How could any five-hundred-year-old panel painting hope to compete with such technological magic? The rationale for such a display was to en- courage "slow looking," to prompt visitors to spend more time with a sin- gle work of art than an alleged fifteen seconds of attention in a traditional display. While the installation might not merit one reviewer's characteriza- tion of it as "the worst ever display of a major masterpiece in the UK," there are legitimate reservations: attention to a sequence of moving images by a moving beholder is hardly the same as focused attention on one object.[52] Whereas multimedia dazzle and surprise might make sense, for instance, in the Victoria and Albert Museum's 2012 *David Bowie Is* show, staged by the same design company, in a display devoted to a single Renaissance painting it mainly points to a lack of confidence in the object itself. Does technology enchant the object here, or is the enchantment of technol- ogy really about the displacement of the object—this fragile, obdurately material, old thing, which makes us uncomfortable? "Immersive"—which suggests engrossment and concentration—has now come to mean digital surrogacy and constant neural stimulation. The National Gallery was here following the lead not just of a neighboring museum devoted increasingly to fashion and style but the Museo Leonardiano in Vinci, a private museum without historical objects, which for the past few years has been touring its *Da Vinci Experience* to Beijing, Vancouver, Lima, and other cities around the globe: "a multi-sensory 360° immersive journey, with more than 10 replicas of his incredible machines as well as visual experiences in virtual reality of Leonardo Da Vinci's greatest inventions."

In 1997–98 a dispute about a traveling exhibition, with venues in Sweden, Germany, Austria, Boston, and Singapore, would be a harbinger of things to come. Billed in Boston as "the largest and most comprehensive exhibit ever mounted" on Leonardo, *Leonardo da Vinci: Scientist, Inventor, Artist* had been organized by the Institute for Cultural Exchange in Tübingen, Germany, with sponsorship from Mercedes-Benz and a Swiss watch company. At the Boston Museum of Science, visitors could see working models of Leonardo's inventions, including a modified (and functioning) version of his flying machine, as well as interactive displays on human and animal anatomy.

The show was a popular success and received generally positive reviews from journalists, less so from art historians. The section of the exhibition devoted to Leonardo as artist and his impact on his contemporaries consisted of several works implausibly attributed to Leonardo and other Renaissance artists, all in private hands. Among them was a supposed "third version" of *The Virgin of the Rocks* from a Swiss private collection, at best a weak copy by Giampietrino of the Louvre painting but now upgraded with the label "attributed to Leonardo and Pupils." A terracotta head of the young Christ and a plaster sculpture of a horse and rider were attributed to Leonardo, despite the complete lack of any surviving authenticated sculptures by the artist. The catalog also included the notorious so-called *Angelo Incarnato* ("Angel in the Flesh"), a black chalk drawing of a smiling nude youth based on a study for a lost *Angel of the Annunciation* by Leonardo. The drawing originates in Leonardo's circle but has been modified so as to endow the figure with a massive erection and a female breast. Despite its compromised status, it is regularly taken to be an autograph relic of Leonardo's supposed preoccupation with androgyny, even more specifically, as a testament to his homosexual relationship with his apprentice Gian Giacomo Caprotti, known as Salaì.

The Harvard art historian James Ackerman, who had been appointed as local advisor to the exhibition, questioned the attribution of these works to Leonardo. Their authenticity was defended by the exhibition's chief art historical consultant: Carlo Pedretti of the Armand Hammer Center for Leonardo Studies at the University of California, Los Angeles. The Boston museum's director for exhibitions maintained that given the museum's specific educational mission, none of this mattered: "it would if it were at the Museum of Fine Arts but not at the Museum of Science." Resigning as advisor, Ackerman declared that "a museum dedicated to the scientific method should know better," blaming the curators for creating public confusion about Leonardo as an artist: "It is not simply one person's opinion against another's. There are standards, and the public deserves to know the foundations on which to build an awareness of art."[53] Henry Zerner of the Harvard Art Museums echoed his colleague: "Some of the exhibits have practically no relation to him, and the captions leave one with the impression that art historical judgments are purely arbitrary. Excellent works are given the same attention as very poor ones, and the visitor comes away with no sense whatever of what distinguishes high skill from the work of a hack, and with little comprehension of Leonardo's supreme accomplishment as an artist, and of how it was understood and misunderstood by his contemporaries and his successors."[54]

It is hard to gauge the effect of such protests. Nearly two decades later in 2016 the Boston Science Museum held another exhibition, *Da Vinci—The Genius*. Instead of paintings and sculptures, there were "animated presentations" of *The Last Supper*, *The Virgin of the Rocks*, and *Vitruvian Man*. Although the exhibition included a number of "super-magnified, high-resolution sectional images" of the *Mona Lisa* by Pascal Cotte, art was included in an entertaining surrogate form bordering on parody, underscoring the earlier statement of educational priorities by the organizers. "Da Vinci had a remarkable, inquisitive mind, an insatiable curiosity about the world around him and the ability to conceptualize, design and construct tools and technologies. These essential

STEM (science, technology, engineering and math) skills are vital to today's students and tomorrow's innovators." This statement might be taken as the credo of the Da Vinci Worlds, the faith-based justification of the importance of science over history. It is a claim that has resounded in the past few years.

MANAGING DA VINCI WORLDS: CONSERVATORS, SCIENTISTS, ENTREPRENEURS

The years after 1997 have seen numerous instances of such a conflict of expertise, with controversial theories and opinions frequently grounded in appeals to scientific data and technologically innovative inquiry. Real discoveries make the news along with many more questionable ones. In 2001 the *New York Times* devoted a lengthy Sunday feature to Maurizio Seracini, a biomedical engineer with some bold new theories about the technical investigation of works of art. Seracini announced that there was something not quite right about *The Adoration of the Magi* (plate 12). The work had always been considered to be especially revealing about Leonardo's exploratory approach to pictorial composition, his attempt to keep several pictorial alternatives at play simultaneously. The near-monochrome surface with its shadowy mass of excited, gaping, and gesticulating figures around the Virgin and Child, the inner depths of the painting with its turmoil of rearing horses and strange ruins, was nothing less than a record of the artist's restless imagination, and it reinforced the image of a brilliant over-reacher falling victim to his own inventive powers. Supposedly unable to resolve the composition, or to put up with the demands of his clients for a timely completion, Leonardo stopped working; shortly afterward, he moved to Milan. Following an infrared examination of the painting commissioned by the Uffizi, Seracini told the journalist that the surface of the painting was a deliberately deceptive intervention by a later hand, that Leonardo's "true intentions" had been intentionally obscured by an obliterating layer of paint: "None of the paint we see on the *Adoration* today was put there by Leonardo. God knows who did, but it was not Leonardo."[55] The underdrawings revealed by infrared examination, he alleged, were stranger than we had thought.

Seracini claimed that his discoveries were not welcomed by the museum establishment: "there's a lot of interest in keeping the rules the way they are so you trust the experts and leave science out. . . . Technology is still left knocking at the door of the art world, and it's not so easy even to get your hands on a Leonardo."[56] He would subsequently argue that the painting was abandoned by Leonardo because his clients, the monks of San Donato a Scopeto, were unable to tolerate such a radically innovative approach to a traditional subject, and that its subsequent owners—the Benci family of Florence—had it "censored" by painting over its more unorthodox and distracting elements.[57]

There was another Leonardo that Seracini wanted to get his hands on, although it was one that most scholars believed had long perished: the colossal mural of *The Battle of Anghiari* for the Salone dei Cinquecento (Room of the 500), the grand hall of state in the Florence Town Hall, built following the expulsion of the Medici and dedicated to the city's short-lived new Republican government. Leonardo's mural was supposed to celebrate the fatherland by depicting a victory in the war against Milan in 1440 (soon Michelangelo would be commissioned to paint an earlier victory of the Florentine Republic for the same space). Yet the artist had once again abandoned the project, following the failure of another experimental painting method, in 1506. Some sketches and head studies survive (plates 13 and 14). His full-scale drawing showing battling warriors disappeared in the 1500s but is known from copies (which might be only partial copies) by other artists (plate 15). A few eyewitness reports, including a 1549 reference by Anton Francesco Doni to a "miraculous" *pezzo di battaglia* by Leonardo to be admired in the Sala Grande, had been taken as evidence that Leonardo at least began the painting of the wall of the Sala in 1506.

In the 1560s, at the behest of the Duke of Florence Cosimo de' Medici, Giorgio Vasari decorated the vast hall with huge murals of historical battles of the Florentine State, including the recent conquest of Siena (fig. 7). If Leonardo had painted anything on the wall, it would have been obliterated at that point: the erasure would suggest political motives, an obliteration of the Republic by the reinstated Medici. Carlo Pedretti in 1967 raised the possibility that Vasari might have preserved Leonardo's painting, or vestiges

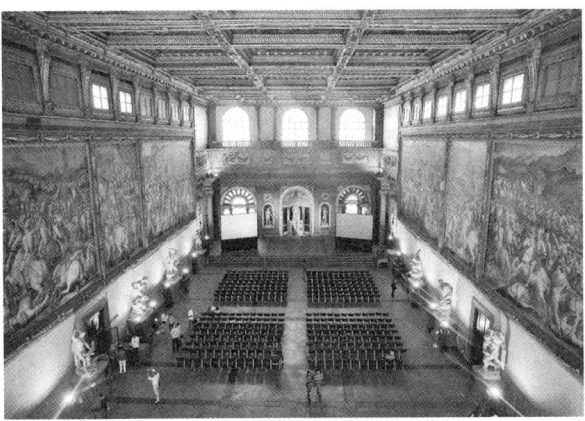

7. East wall of the Salone dei Cinquecento, Palazzo Vecchio, Florence, with frescoes by Giorgio Vasari and assistants. *The Battle of Marciano in Val di Chiana* (1570) is at the lower right.

of it, behind his own: he had, after all, done something similar with Masaccio's great fresco of *The Trinity* in the church of S. Maria Novella, when Duke Cosimo commanded a thorough renovation of the church.

An initial and inconclusive search for the lost mural had been undertaken in 1967, when plaster was removed from both long walls beneath Vasari's frescoes. Backed by Pedretti, a more radically invasive search was undertaken in 1976–80, when two American scholars, John R. Spencer and H. Travers Newton, believed they had determined the mural's original location. The investigation was supported by a $50,000 grant from the Kress Foundation with additional funds from Armand Hammer and the Smithsonian Institution. The team was additionally supported by Maurizio Seracini, who by means of ultrasonic scanning claimed to find a smooth plaster surface in the area pinpointed by Spencer, on the basis of his reading of Vasari's far-from-clear account. Pedretti demurred on the location, but he approved of the venture: "I'm prepared to say good luck to them—even a ghost of this lost masterpiece would be invaluable. May the best man win."[58] No less than ten square meters of Vasari's *Rout of the Pisans at the Tower of San Vincenzo* were removed before the search was abandoned.[59]

Seracini refused to give up. In 2002 he was permitted to scan the walls of the room with lasers, radar, thermographic survey devices, and a low-frequency sonogram. He also called on Massimiliano Pieraccini, a professor of engineering at the University of Florence and an expert in ground-penetrating radar technology, to investigate structural displacements in the building (he would subsequently examine the "Leaning Tower" of Pisa). Using a wide-spectrum geo-radar scanner, Pieraccini and his colleagues determined that Vasari had in fact raised a fifty-meter counterwall, some fifteen centimeters in thickness and a couple of centimeters away from the fifteenth-century wall of the Salone, beneath his frescoes of the *Battle of Scannagallo* and the *Taking of Siena*; the findings were published in 2005.[60]

In fact, historians had already established that Vasari, in his thorough renovation of the Sala, partly resurfaced the walls of the Salone to create a new surface for his own paintings. Contemporary documents refer to six *incrostature* (incrustations) of *mezzane*, a kind of large thin terracotta tile; the stacked *mezzane* constituted a counterwall, a smooth surface suitable for painting.[61] It was some of these *mezzane* that had already been temporarily removed during the 1980 search for the *Battle*. Attitudes to conservation had shifted, however, in the meantime, and the risk of collateral damage to Vasari's frescoes was no longer deemed acceptable.

Florence's cultural administration was initially enthusiastic, heralding a "second Renaissance" through Seracini's work, "bringing art and science together as the contemporary mission of this city."[62] With Florence poised to brand itself as a Da Vinci World, with Leonardo as the point of convergence for spectacular scientific discovery, prestigious grants, and even greater tourist revenues, Seracini's contract expired in 2005 and was not renewed. In a press statement, Seracini declared that he had actually pinpointed the location of the surviving Leonardo, that the next step was to drill through the "false wall" erected by Vasari. Making things altogether more gripping was a new thriller-plot element: Vasari himself had provided a clue with the words CERCA TROVA ("seek find," or "[he who] seeks finds"), words that appear on a banner in the fresco of *The Battle of Marciano in the Chiana Valley*.

Even though he had located private donors to fund further research, Seracini protested that his explorations had been annulled by the municipality of Florence while he was on the brink of success, even though that would mean the forfeiture of royalties from documentaries, reproduction rights, and further privately funded investigations. "We can't destroy one painting to find a few chips of old paint behind," said *assessore culturale* Simone Siliani, who had earlier supported Seracini's research.[63]

There is a strong sense of a latter-day Leonardo-like performance being conjured here: a great work broken off as the patron loses confidence, a heroic project destined to remain incomplete. But Seracini was allowed to resume his search in 2007, and by 2011 he was authorized to employ "minimally invasive" techniques—that is, microscopic drilling through Vasari's fresco—in order to undertake endoscopic photography of the original surface beyond Vasari's terracotta layer. He now had the backing of Matteo Renzi, mayor of Florence and subsequently Italian prime minister, and $250,000 from the National Geographic Foundation (in return for the rights to publish the results). Seracini was supervised by conservationists from the Opificio delle Pietre Dure (OPD), the old Medici workshop for decorative stone manufacture that now housed a state conservation laboratory, who ensured that drillings were made in areas of Vasari's fresco where no original paint remains (Seracini later claimed that this proviso would limit his ability to trace the *Battle*). Only one of the seven drill holes yielded results—traces of black and brown pigment, supposedly containing the same proportions of iron and manganese oxide that Leonardo had used in other paintings, but also quite commonly used by Florentine painters in the 1400s. None of the pigment analysis was conclusive: the Opificio, moreover, as a matter of policy, refused to pursue analysis on samples already manipulated by Seracini's lab.

These were not the only problems raised by art historians in a gathering murmur of protest against the disinterment of a phantom Leonardo. The heritage group Italia Nostra organized an international petition against the project. Cecilia Frosinini of the Opificio, an authority on mural paintings, refused to participate on ethical grounds, citing the dubious nature of the research. Tomaso Montanari of the University of Naples complained that art historical and scientific expertise had been set aside in favor of tourist and media revenue, the drift of heritage conservation toward "culture marketing."[64] Finally, the director of research at the National Center for Renaissance Studies in Tours, Stéphane Toussaint, published a devastating assessment in the *Tribune de l'art*: "In this whole affair, the principle of scholarly verification has once again been crushed under the pressure of the media, and scientific rigor has been flouted by the superficiality of journalists." Far more serious responsibility lay with politicians, ill educated in art history and ethics of conservation, "who should be, for the public good, excluded in the future from participating in cultural decision-making." As for the sponsors, "they would be better inspired to spread their financial balm on open wounds: while 250,000 euros have probably been wasted in Florence, we need to remember that there are historic villas collapsing and libraries that cannot afford to buy books in the city of Lorenzo the Magnificent."[65]

In September 2012 Cristina Acidini, superintendent for the Polo Museale Fiorentino, called off the investigation and ordered the filling of the holes in the fresco. In the meantime, Frosinini and her colleagues at the Opificio began the conservation of Leonardo's *Adoration of the Magi*, which had been found to be in a precarious condition, with paint lifting from the support. They began with a new campaign of noninvasive scanning techniques, which had achieved a degree of precision not possible during the investigation a decade previously. The cleaning of the panel would reveal visually stunning results, and a summary of the technical findings was published online with even-handed historical interpretation (plate 12). Since there was no fuel for Da Vinci World sensationalism and conspiracy theories, media coverage was relatively thin.[66] The team concluded that Leonardo had abandoned the painting at an advanced stage, prior to the application of color, for external reasons, and not because he had hit a crisis of indecision in bringing it to completion. The many elements now brought to light had been obscured by layers of varnish that had oxidized and darkened over time and by a series of attempted restorations documented in 1724, 1794, and 1914—the last of which involved an attempt to clarify the older varnish with solvents. Most importantly, the paint on the surface was Leonardo's: there was no basis to the claims that controversial elements of Leonardo's painting had been censored by a later hand.[67]

All too aware of the dangers that the name "Leonardo" had come to signal for the preservation of cultural heritage, Frosinini—along with the architectural historian Emanuela Ferretti, her Opificio colleague Roberto Bellucci, and several technical and archival specialists—organized a conference on the Sala Grande and its murals in 2017. A clear-eyed examination of documentary sources on the *Battle of Anghiari* commission allowed a reconstruction of Leonardo's working procedure—expenses are recorded for the making of the cartoon, and for a resinous substance ("Greek pitch") to prepare the wall for an oil-based medium, but not for any materials for painting on the wall. The startling conclusion is that the preparation failed, and thus the painting was never begun: what contemporaries saw in the Sala was nothing other than the cartoon itself, which had been provided with a wooden frame and was displayed there in the 1500s.[68]

There had been controversies before about the conservation of works of art, especially the way that advanced technical solutions were never fully detached from other incentives, like commercial revenues and publicity. Two in particular—the cleaning of Michelangelo's Sistine vault frescoes in the 1980s and, as we have seen, the removal of later overpainting from Leonardo's *Last Supper* in Milan, during the 1980s–1990s—had received extensive international press coverage. But the world was changing in the early years of the twenty-first century, largely because older news media could hardly keep pace with new means of transmitting information and misinformation. The increasing role of the world wide web changed the nature of journalism, as established news organizations responded to the demand for faster and more attention-grabbing stories. The stories of the *Adoration* and of the search for *The Battle of Anghiari* would have a long denouement of ten years or more, during which time the image of Leonardo was changed irrevocably.

THE ART MARKET AND THE DA VINCI SUPPLY LINE

Seracini had used state-of-the-art technology to probe a void in Leonardo's story, and the technology had produced the illusion of results, seeming vestiges of a painting where no painting existed. In 2003 he appeared as the only nonfictional character in a popular novel by Dan Brown, where he is identified as an "art diagnostician." The association probably did not harm his credibility. The impact of Brown's thriller on the Da Vinci phenomenon cannot be underestimated. Scoop Leonardo discoveries and controversies had made news headlines before, but the combination of the utterly fictive pop-cultural sensation Da Vinci with the emergence of the internet in all its truth-shaping and mind-altering ubiquity would completely transform the relation between art, art scholarship, and the public.

There were some legitimate discoveries, their historical significance usually overshadowed by their sale prices. In 2001, the sale of a horse and rider study for *The Adoration of the Magi* for $12 million, making it at the time the world's most expensive drawing, was something of a nine days' wonder. The record looked set to be broken by another drawing attributed to Leonardo, a *St. Sebastian*, which surfaced in France in March 2016. Following authentication by Carmen Bambach at the Metropolitan Museum, the drawing was valued at $15.8 million. Based on that valuation, in January 2017 the French government sought to reserve the drawing as a national treasure, offering 10 million euro as "fair international market value." Convinced that the drawing was worth far more, especially with the "success" of the *Salvator Mundi*, the custodians of the drawing have been trying to sell it on the open market since late 2018, with an anticipated sale price of $34–68 million. After a legal battle, an export license was finally granted in 2023.

The first decade of the twenty-first century saw one Da Vinci sensation after another. The most trivial "finding" about the artist, the most hopeless new attribution, the most lurid conspiracy theory, the most preposterous evaluation, kept the ghost of Da Vinci before the public. Now there were other elements at play, namely the conjoined forces of the art market with the unidirectional flow of global wealth into the hands of a corporate and fiscal elite. Itself transformed by the media revolution, the genteel and somewhat anachronistic world of collectors and dealers became an unregulated digital Leviathan, subordinating human expertise, fiscal constraint, and any semblance of ethical scruples. We had entered the era of international art fairs, internet auctions, and globalized "art busi-ness" firms, artists' reputations made and destroyed by stock market surges.

The impact was evident most immediately, and on a global scale, in contemporary art: artists in their twenties became famous through their entrepreneurial partnering with dealers and collectors, effectively form-ing price-fixing cartels; and their multimillion-selling "artworks" became investment stock.[69] Artists were co-branded with luxury products like designer jeans, handbags, and cell-phone cases (the Damien Hirst/Levi Strauss line was marketed in 2007, while the Jeff Koons/Louis Vuitton "Da Vinci" bag appeared in 2017). The Chinese art market, serving the world's highest per capita population of billionaires, became the world's largest, sending prices surging for premodern and contemporary Chinese art, as well as for Impressionist painting and a few select post-Impressionists such as Modigliani.[70] It was as if what the theorist of postmodernism Jean Bau-drillard had predicted in 1993 had come to pass: the whole world had be-come the art world, everything was aestheticized and turned into art, and in its utter mundanity art was unexceptional; it had lost any of the critical and oppositional possibilities it had claimed since the 1700s. Baudrillard called this *transaesthetics*: "It is often said that the West's great undertak-ing is the commercialization of the whole world, the hitching of the fate of everything to the fate of the commodity. That great undertaking will turn out rather to have been the aestheticization of the whole world— its cosmopolitan spectacularization, its transformation into images, its semiological organization."[71]

In addition, the unregulated global market has seen a rise in crimi-nal abuses—a hyping of fakes and dubious attributions and, even more worryingly, the trafficking in looted premodern artifacts from South and East Asia, the Mediterranean, and Central America. As Baudrillard im-plied, the art world is not a self-contained system—it is implicated with other forms of elite commerce including hedge funds, real estate, arma-ments, fashion, waste disposal and recycling, and cocaine. It is also thus responsive to fluctuations in the larger market, notably the world eco-nomic crash of 2008: the economist Clare McAndrew calculated that global art and antiques sales fell from $62 billion in 2008 to $30.5 billion in 2009, resulting in a massive sell-off of works by Hirst, Koons, Richard Prince, and numerous others. In 2017, at $63.7 billion, global sales were still 3.2 percent lower than the pre-recession $65.8 billion of 2007.[72] With an increase to $64.1 billion in 2019, sales of fine art and antiques dropped 22 percent to an estimated $50.1 billion in the pandemic year of 2020.[73]

The consequences of the pre-recession boom and the post-recession recovery have been far-reaching—and concerning—for cultural institutions in general, and especially for those where art scholarship happens: art museums and universities offering advanced degrees in the history of art. There had been significant, sometimes munificent investment in art museums before 2008, enabling acquisitions, exhibitions, and the expansion of specialized staff. In academia, there had been some growth in the humanities, manifest in the opening of overseas campuses with humanities programming by American universities. There were moves to fund partnerships between museums and advanced degree–granting institutions, a steady rise in demand for doctoral degrees in art history that led to the creation of new PhD programs, and the propagation of new fields of art historical inquiry through investment in faculty and graduate students. Whereas the upheavals of 2008 were followed by rapid recovery in banking and elite commercial sectors such as medical and communications technology, emergency conditions have been sustained in the cultural and educational area. Museums and universities, private as well as public, still operate at austerity budgets and staffing cuts have in large part not been restored: these circumstances were aggravated by the Covid-19 pandemic beginning in 2020.

With less public resources, museums are increasingly organized around the priorities of their boards of trustees, which include major donors who have effectively purchased their places on the board. Trustees steer the exhibition and collecting mission of a museum, which is often slanted toward the kinds of art that those trustee-collectors have a stake in. Museum expansion is motivated and often unbalanced by the intentions of investor-collectors who wish to boost the prestige and value of their collections.

Premodern painting—in fact, any work by nonliving artists—is regarded as a nonrenewable resource; preference goes to a living artist's work where an ongoing supply is guaranteed. Given this combined attrition on two fronts—the university and the museum—the general status and visibility of older art have been in crisis, a marginalization that has been reinforced, for instance, by the activist and often opportunistic rhetoric of the discourses of "Eurocentrism."[74] Museums, increasingly subject to the pressures of visitor numbers, struggle to maintain public interest in their premodern collections, or liquidate them altogether, as did Buffalo's Albright-Knox in 2007 and 2021.

Enter Da Vinci: a post-millennial branding that seemed to promise a solution but turned out to be part of the very economic mechanism that made our present into the only grounds for art, and living artists to become the oil wells and earth metal mines of our time. Thinking of Baudrillard again, it is as if art sustains the illusion of life with the saturation of reality by capital. Or, as if art—even the most oppositional and politically engaged, even the most contemptuous of the mechanisms of publicity and art world celebrity—makes present reality not only tangible but marketable and consumable. Da Vinci is like very few other past artists (maybe Rembrandt, Michelangelo, Picasso) in this respect. It is as if Da Vinci were very nearly alive, a figure of familiar living memory like the late celebrity designer Alexander McQueen.

In other words, just as it needed more Koons and more Hirst, the art world conglomerate of museums, dealers, and collectors and investors needed more Leonardos, and more Leonardo discoveries. And—as we saw with the multiple *Mona Lisa*s—they have been coming thick and fast.

Problem works from the exhibition in 1997—especially the terracotta head of Christ and the *Angelo Incarnato*—are still regularly promoted as autograph Leonardos. And they have been joined by many more. A *Mary Magdalene*, usually attributed to Giampietrino, in a Swiss private collection was attributed to Leonardo by Carlo Pedretti in 2004; the painting has been exhibited as a Leonardo in Europe and East Asia. A portrait on vellum in ink and colored chalks of a young woman in profile, wearing the dress and hairstyle characteristic of the Sforza court when Leonardo lived and worked in Milan, was identified as a German nineteenth-century Renaissance pastiche when it emerged in 1998. In 2008, the work's new owner began to solicit expert opinion regarding a possible attribution to

Leonardo da Vinci. Not unpredictably, Carlo Pedretti favored the attribution. So too, however, did normally more cautious and skeptical scholars like the master drawings specialist Nicholas Turner, as well as Martin
Kemp, a senior figure in Leonardo studies. Kemp proposed that the sitter
was a princess of the house of Sforza, Bianca Giovanna (1482–1496), the
illegitimate daughter of Ludovico Sforza and his mistress Bernardina de
Corradis. Little is known of Bianca beyond her marriage at the age of
seven to the Milanese general Galeazzo Sanseverino in 1489 and her death
in 1496: there are no known portraits of her.

The portrait has been the subject of three books endorsing the attribution, including one by the work's owner, much of it concerned with
undermining the scientific and scholarly "elites" who refuse to take the
"evidence" seriously. The most recent, by Simon Hewitt, presents Bianca
as the victim of a murder plot and is bracingly titled *Leonardo da Vinci
and the Book of Doom*. Alessandro Vezzosi included the work as an autograph Leonardo in his 2018 catalog of the complete works; Martin Kemp
and Pascal Cotte defended the attribution in a book published in 2010,
appealing to multispectral scanning imagery by Cotte.[75]

Others scholars were not so convinced: not Carmen Bambach at the
Met, nor Pietro C. Marani, a senior figure in Leonardo studies in Italy,
nor—needless to say—the art market experts who had sold the work
as "nineteenth-century German school." While often decried as a "forgery," and while it seems to emulate Leonardo's left-handed strokes in
the shadows, no emulator or forger from the sixteenth to the twentieth century could have imagined deceiving anyone by trying to pass this
off as a Leonardo. In terms of technique, its meticulous use of colored
chalk, it has nothing in common with any of Leonardo's surviving works,
and it has little in common with any other Italian artist working in Leonardo's lifetime.

The lack of reference to the portrait in any early source was answered
by claims for its function as a manuscript illumination. That would also explain why it has no known provenance prior to the twentieth century, when
it was first recorded in the collection of Giannino Marchig. Marchig, a
friend of Bernard Berenson and Roberto Longhi, was an artist and conser-

vator who had worked on at least one Leonardo painting, the Landsdowne *Madonna of the Yarn Winder* (see plate 33). Despite in-depth knowledge of the artist, Marchig never identified the portrait as a Leonardo, but he did regard it as a fifteenth-century Florentine work, probably by Ghirlandaio.

Given the lack of a provenance that could connect the drawing to Leonardo's Milan, there was considerable excitement when the vellum folio was matched with a manuscript produced at the Sforza court in the 1490s. Based on matching dimensions and a "close-enough" match of stitch holes, the art historian David Wright claimed that the sheet had been cut from the codex of the *Sforziada* in the Biblioteka Narodowa in Warsaw, which may have been decorated in 1496 as a gift to celebrate the marriage of Galeazzo da Sanseverino to Bianca Sforza.

All of these claims have been called into question, and the resulting dispute has been acrimonious.[76] Among the more obvious anomalies are the ink and chalk medium, which is unsuitable for book illumination—it tends to rub off on facing pages. Also anomalous is the lack of reference to the alleged subject of the portrait in the text of the book. In the case of two comparable examples of full-page portrait illuminations, those by Ambrogio de Predis of Ludovico il Moro and his son Massimiliano Sforza (ca. 1496–99) opening and concluding a luxurious manuscript of the *Grammaticus* of Donatus (Milan, Biblioteca Trivulziana), the two portraits illustrate the text in which they appear, and there is a sonnet glorifying Il Moro on the sheet facing his image.[77] It is also unheard of for an illumination to lack borders: artists conventionally preserved the sense of an image imposed on or "within" a page. Furthermore, although the image appears to have been trimmed on only one side, it is marginally smaller than the *Sforziada* leaves.[78]

The work falls into the category of problematic "quarantine" works, regarded by scholarship as off-limits not only because it is inaccessible in a Swiss free port but because objective assessment is compromised by its potential value, and because the evidence presented—including the results of "scientific investigation"—has proved too assailable.

There has been a particular compulsion to attribute sculptures to Leonardo—we know of course that Leonardo had been trained in the

workshop of an artist specializing in sculpture, that he had labored for
years to produce a colossal equestrian monument for the Sforza of Milan,
and that he had assisted the sculptor Giovan Francesco Rustici (see chapter 5)—but there are no documented works in three-dimensional media
that survive.

There is one sculpture ascribed to Leonardo that may actually be by
him: the Victoria and Albert Museum's exquisite *Virgin with the Laughing
Child*, otherwise attributed to Antonio Rossellino (plate 16). The connection was first made in 1899, and endorsed by several scholars, including
the authoritative Wilhelm Valentiner in 1932, before being taken up again
in 2004 and 2019.[79] This might be one case where stylistic evidence alone
allows the work to be associated with the young artist in Verrocchio's shop;
it has a clear affinity with a celebrated group of drapery studies on linen
mostly ascribed to him. However, while the Leonardesque character of
the drapery, and the face of the Virgin, can be persuasively argued, the
figure of the child and above all the child's hilarity have no counterpart
among the solemn and strangely self-conscious infants of Leonardo's drawings and paintings (plate 17): if this is Leonardo, it is Leonardo working
in collaboration, which would be entirely in character with the collective
production of the Verrocchio workshop.

TECHNOLOGY, SCHOLARSHIP, AND THE PUBLIC INTEREST

The future of art historical scholarship depends on an ongoing dialogue and cross-checking between its critical and historical practices
and its rapidly evolving technical side. The technical study of works of
art has been transformed by new nondestructive techniques of material analysis including high-resolution 3D imaging, X-ray, infrared reflectography and infrared photography, fluorescence mapping, electron
microscopy, Raman spectroscopy, and pigment microstratigraphy. These
technologies, all of which have been applied variously to Leonardo's
paintings and drawings, yield essential information about underdrawings, paint layers, and the composition of paints and varnishes. They can
help distinguish original work from later interventions, and they can
serve in identifying fakes.

For instance, a noninvasive imaging technique like macro X-ray fluorescence (MA-XRF) allows the mapping of pigments in the paint layer, since different non-organic materials used by painters have distinct fluorescence patterns. When applied to Jan and Hubert van Eyck's great altarpiece in St. Bavo in Ghent completed in 1436, conservators found that the surface had been painted over in the mid-1500s (consistent with a documented "washing" of the altarpiece in 1550) and the original paint layer was fully intact under the overpainting. Reflectography revealed traces of an original composition beneath the *Adoration of the Mystic Lamb*, which the conservators claim to be the unique surviving work of Hubert van Eyck, who had died in 1426, leaving the panel to be reworked by his brother Jan. Hubert's involvement, recorded in an inscription on the altarpiece, had long been disputed by scholars.[80]

Such advanced modes of technical imaging provide an objective complement to traditional modes of evaluation like connoisseurship, which primarily (but not exclusively) depends on the judgment of the eye. What they cannot do by themselves is *prove* the authorship of a work—at best, they can help disprove authorship: ultimately, the distinction between Hubert and Jan—that the difference is not just the result of early and late campaigns by Jan—will rely on the trained eye of the connoisseur. There are relatively few "eureka" moments in the conservation labs of museums. What is found can be sometimes surprising—an obliterated image of Cupid in Vermeer's *Girl Reading a Letter* in Dresden, the approach of grinning death in a scene of carousing cavaliers by Judith Leyster in Philadelphia—but more often this data constitutes a complicated enrichment of what we already know; as many new questions might be created as old ones answered.

The sciences of artificial intelligence (AI) and their claims to transform art history through data-based problem-solving have received considerable media attention and uncritical celebration: a study based on "distant looking" at 120,000 portraits from the thirteenth to the twentieth century claimed to show that the "canon of beauty" has changed over time. Another based on a sample of 77,000 paintings asserted that AI could track styles and art and arrange works in proper chronological order, thereby conforming to the principles of stylistic development proposed by Heinrich Wölfflin a century ago. And yet art historians have long given up on Wölfflin's principles, with their Eurocentric bias and their confidence in inner cyclical laws of history. Using Wölfflin's variables, the metric would be so schematic as to be useless for dating an actual work of art, for distinguishing, for instance, between a seventeenth-century landscape or still life and an eighteenth-century one, or a twenty-first-century copy of either.

"Digital art history has a fraught relationship to history and interpretation," writes the art historian Claire Bishop. "Does the data set exist in history before being sequenced digitally or is it only actualized once it has been laid out via the digital archive? Are the assembled historical 'facts' found or produced? What's the relation between what's empirically observable and what's true?"[81] While computational metrics can organize data and track patterns, they cannot determine causality or intentionality, which are among the goals of critical and historical interpretation in the humanities. Writing of the AI firm Oxia Palus, which creates reconstructions of "lost" works by Leonardo, Modigliani, Picasso, and other artists based on older X-ray and reflectographic scanning, some of them issued commercially as "Neomaster™ NFTs," Sonia Drimmer questions whether "outside of flexing the prowess of AI, is there any value—artistically, historically—to what the company is doing? These recreations don't teach us anything we didn't know about the artists and their methods." Drimmer argues that such sensational reconstructions serve as "soft diplomacy for AI, showcasing a 'cultured' application of the technology at a time when skepticism of its deceptions, biases and abuses is on the rise. When AI gets attention for recovering lost works of art, it makes the technology sound a lot less scary than when it garners headlines for creating deep fakes that falsify politicians' speech or for using facial recognition for authoritarian surveillance."[82]

Artificial intelligence and unsupervised machine learning can at best be used to create databases that track the relationships between multiple similar works of art or similar motifs within works.[83] If machines will ever be taught to recognize elements of an artist's style, or if facial recognition programs can serve to identify people in early modern portraits, that will always be based on stylistic and iconographic criteria identified by human beings, and the results will depend on human verification.[84]

We have seen that in the case of Leonardo we have constantly been presented with the spectacle of technological magic wielded against an inscrutable and resistant past, with sensational claims of discovery and problem-solving. So far, it is hard to see how such enterprises serve the interests of those not benefiting commercially: the community of researchers, educators, and the publics they are trying to reach. Digital products have been created that would allow the indistinguishable simulation of paintings like the *Mona Lisa*. However, it is ironic that a figure who has come to personify the reconnection of "science and the arts" has so far had such a small part to play in the so-called "digital humanities."

The level of technical investment that the study of Leonardo requires is far more modest. Some of the key problems and questions—including the problem of reading and making sense of the artist's written legacy, and the problem of public access to specialist scholarship—could benefit immeasurably from digitalization. I was able to write this book because I had access, through my university affiliation, to a comprehensive research library, with the essential added benefit of stack browsing. Independent scholars, professional authors, and the public at large often struggle to obtain this kind of access to key research materials, very little of which are on open access. The problem with Leonardo's manuscripts is considerably more complicated, and it is only recently that a single platform has promised access to the drawings and notebooks: the Codex Atlanticus in the Ambrosiana, the Codex Urbinas in the Vatican, the copious Leonardo sheets in Windsor Castle, the Codex Arundel in the British Museum, the Forster codices in the Victoria and Albert Museum, the Trivulziana notebook at Castello Sforzesco in Milan, and the Madrid codices in the Biblioteca Nacional de España. The e-Leo archive is a major initiative of the Biblioteca Vinciniana, theoretically searchable, with each digitally scanned sheet accompanied by a transcription of the original text. So far, the digital versions lack descriptions or the metadata available through the websites of the individual institutions, and users need to be adept in reading Leonardo's idiosyncratic Italian; the search function was not operational in the summer of 2023. To be truly useful, the digital editions require a full apparatus, with a description of every opening, a subject search option, a transcription, and a translation of the text. Without such features, the writings of Leonardo, while visible as aestheticized and auratic relics, remain inaccessible and impenetrable. These digital platforms so far are only a promising beginning.[85]

This kind of comprehensive digital access—not just the objects but the translation of the object—is the key obstacle in making a Leonardo available without the simplifications and sensationalizing of the Da Vinci Worlds. And such a reader-friendly platform does not call for significant technical resources to be a possibility—it requires the diligent traditional skills of a paleographer, a translator, and on occasion of a historian of science and an art historian. And perhaps therein lies the problem—what is still most urgently required is utterly lacking in the glamor and enchantment of commercial technology.

Chapter 2

"NOW UNMADE BY TIME . . ."

Toward an Anti-biography of Leonardo da Vinci

If the Leonardo biography could be said to have a self-inaugurating moment, it would be the exquisite landscape drawing inscribed from left to right in the artist's mirror-script: "Dì di s[an]ta Maria della neve / addj 5 daghossto 1473 [On the day of St. Mary of the Snows / on August 5 1473]" (plates 18a and 18b). In a career so lacking in autobiographical disclosures, this has been taken as the testimony of a young genius announcing himself to the world, and seemingly captivated by that world. The artist is a lover of nature and already in command of techniques of representing it, able to render the pulsing vitality of flickering light, flowing water, the movement of trees in the wind. The drawing might make us think of his celebration of the power of vision, some twenty years afterward: "What moves you, O man, to abandon your own houses in the cities and to leave relatives and friends and to go into the countryside through mountains and valley, if not the natural beauty of the world which, if you think about it, can only be appreciated by the sense of sight?"[1]

Here he's locating himself in a place and time—back home near Vinci, in late summer, on the day when a local parish celebrated the

miraculous August snowfall down in Rome through which the Virgin
had commanded the building of the great Roman basilica in her honor.
On the back, which contains more fragmentary sketches probably executed over an extended period of time (and mostly by different hands), an
enigmatic and probably incomplete phrase written in regular left-to-right
script, "Io, morando d'Antoni, sono chontento," has been interpreted as
referring to Antonio Buti, the husband of Leonardo's mother: "I, staying
with Antonio, am happy."

Some have claimed to locate the precise spot Leonardo made his
drawing: supposedly northwest of Vinci, looking toward the castle of
Montevettolini to the left, the plains known as the Padule de Fucecchio
in the distance, the conical hill of Monsummano right of center. The
drawing is considered a historical milestone in the history of European
art: "the first ever pure landscape" or, more cautiously, "the first dated
landscape drawing in the history of art,"[2] as well as "Leonardo's first art
drawing," "the shimmering start of a career of combining scientific observation with artistic sensibility," "depicting nature for its own sake."[3]
Others believe that Leonardo also represents here the beginnings of
scientific geological investigation, with his attention to the craggy rock
formations on the right.[4]

As usual, a closer study yields a more complicated and ambiguous scenario. Beyond a few similar topographical features, Leonardo's drawing
bears little resemblance to the corresponding view from the hill over Montevettolini. The usual conclusion is that the drawing is a clever composite
of multiple views with a strong element of the artist's imagination, with
motifs—like rock formations nonexistent in Tuscany—imported from
works of Netherlandish art well-known to Florentine artists. It is at best
an evocation of a landscape of mountains and plains that would convey
the idea of a countryside, or a wild place, to a Florentine audience. Ernst
Gombrich—who demonstrated Leonardo's debt to the panoramic landscape backgrounds of the Netherlandish painter Jan van Eyck—rejected
categorically the possibility that the drawing had anything to do with observations made on-site, but this is too extreme a view.[5] While there are
technical challenges to working outdoors with pen and ink, we have later
less elaborate *plein air* drawings made by Leonardo in this medium.

Yet recent examination of the drawing by the Opificio delle Pietre Dure has thrown the biographical significance of the drawing into question. Using advanced infrared and X-ray technology along with organic matter analysis, researchers have concluded that the drawing is the final stage of a process involving several phases and different media, including copying or tracing from other drawings, and very likely with reference to Netherlandish models. In the first phase Leonardo sketched and traced using a lead stylus. Then followed two phases of working up elements of the landscape with ink—two different kinds of ink can be identified. The back of the sheet is covered with landscape sketches worked up in carbon black now thought to be in pastel form (pigment mixed with animal glue); doodles of figures and a head in profile are rendered in red chalk or sinopia. However, pastel and sinopia are media that do not appear in Leonardo's drawings dated before the 1490s: their traces indicate the hand of someone else. Not for the first time, specialized scholarship in art history yields results that pose new problems of interpretation, and the biographer's Da Vinci recedes into the shadows.[6]

The drawing is not the on-the-spot record of a homecoming excursion by the twenty-one-year-old artist, and it is not concerned with the rendering of a specific topography. However virtuosic in its command of perspective, its feeling for the motion of light, its intuitive grasp of geology, it is a means to an end, part of a routine workshop process. The inscription "Io, morando d'Antoni, sono chontento" can be more plausibly rendered as a notarial formula for a draft agreement, "I, Morando d'Antonio, am content [that] . . ." Leonardo was reusing an old drawing as a writing surface, or it was reused by someone else in the busy *bottega* when he had finished with it.

While the sheet is a document of Leonardo's early activity, it locates him in a workshop—that of Andrea del Verrocchio—and as part of a collective of artisans of various specializations and levels of skill. Alessandro Nova has related the sheet to others from Verrocchio's workshop that combine sketches and drawing exercises, including head studies like the profile in the Uffizi sheet, and "prove di penna"—little calligraphic trial runs for a newly cut pen, which could often take the form of fragmentary bureaucratic or legal formulas.[7] The sheet in all likelihood began life as a

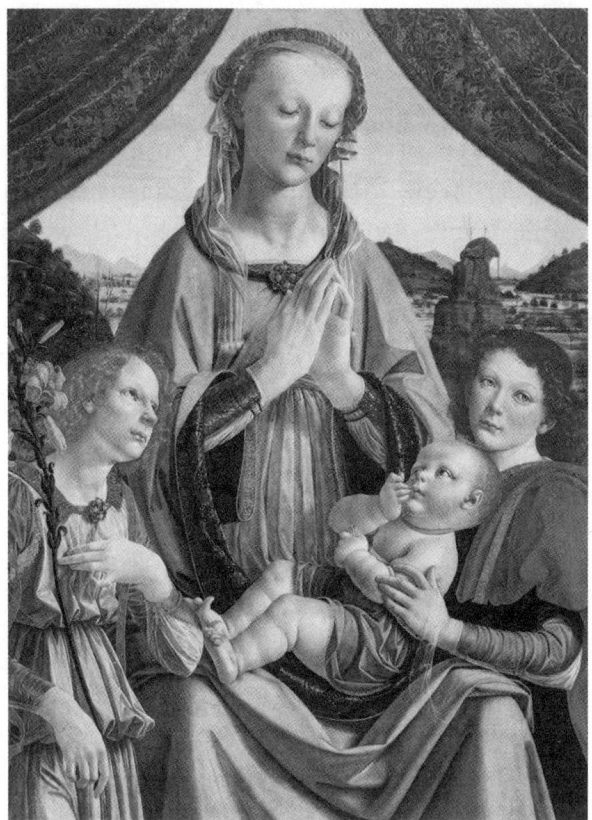

8. Andrea del Verrocchio and assistant (Lorenzo di Credi?),
Virgin and Child with Angels (Volterra Madonna).
Ca. 1476–78. On panel, 96.5 × 70.5 cm. London,
National Gallery.

study for a landscape background in a painting: it can be compared with
the landscape in the Verrocchio *Virgin and Child* of ca. 1476—known as
the Volterra Madonna—with its similar fantastic rock formations (fig. 8).

Claims about "firsts" in art history are always risky. The Uffizi sheet
may be the first *surviving* landscape drawing, but it is unlikely to be the first
of its kind from a Florentine workshop. It was preserved, probably among
Verrocchio's papers and not his protégé's, because someone later identified
it as a Leonardo. Some later hand, a century or more afterward, inscribed
the sheet with the artist's name. The rival workshop of Antonio Pollaiuolo

and his brother Piero had included panoramas of river valleys and soaring rock formations in their paintings already for more than a decade (and that could be the case with Verrocchio as well, but his paintings are notoriously hard to date). While it is true that "pure landscape" did not yet exist as a distinct kind of image, the rise of drawing on paper had already led to increasingly dramatic or expressive uses of expansive outdoor views by Italian artists. The Venetian Jacopo Bellini, by 1450, was using his drawing books to create panoramic urban and landscape spaces that often dwarf or overwhelm the ostensible religious subject and went vastly beyond any possible destination as the model for a finished painting. The possibilities of drawing, as a medium not solely beholden to the production of religious art, already a generation earlier contained the possibilities of independent exploration and invention.

"AHEAD OF HIS TIME"

That Leonardo was *ahead of his time* is a familiar claim, but one that presumes a great deal about Leonardo's time. The ever-contentious historical debates about art, society, religion, economics, and culture in Italy and Europe in the late 1400s and early 1500s might warn us to proceed more cautiously. At best, *ahead of his time* is a shorthand way of grasping Leonardo's singularity; more often than not, it's a harmful cliché, an expression of glib superiority toward the past.[8]

The claim that someone is *ahead of their time* supposes that time has a particular shape and that historical phenomena are predictable at every moment. Phenomena are "untimely" if we conceive of a steady evolutionary progression from "primitive" to "advanced," and that a way of painting, say, or a design for a machine could disrupt the sequence. Leonardo's conception of a flying machine or an underwater breathing apparatus, or his analysis of the pulsion of the blood through the valves of a beating heart, are taken as signs of a precocious modernity. They could just as logically be seen as symptoms of our own nonmodernity—our failure to be as modern as we thought, of the fragility of the assumptions by which we measure ourselves in time in relation to an imaginary past. "There is always a neuroticism to the present, which believes itself superior to the past but can't quite get over a nagging anxiety that it might not," writes the novelist and biographer Julian Barnes. "And the further the past recedes, the more attractive it becomes to simplify it. However gross our accusation, it never replies, it stays silent."[9]

I'm reminded of a passage in the notes on perspective, datable around 1510, which suggests that Leonardo, who seldom conveys a sense of being interested in history, had a relativist or "perspectival" understanding of time: "Our judgement does not reckon in their exact and proper order things which have come to pass at different periods of time; for many things which happened many years ago will seem nearly related to the present, and many things that are recent will seem ancient, extending back to the far-off period of our youth." The perception of time is subjective and anachronic: "And so it is with the eye, with regard to distant things, which when illumined by the sun seem near to the eye, while many things which are near seem far off."[10] Such relativism about the perception of past and present is Leonardo's own challenge to the progressivist "timeline" determinism of those who would consider Leonardo "ahead of his time." The vocal quality of his writing, which makes us feel almost as if we are being addressed in the present ("You . . . you . . ."), is like the light that makes distant things seem near: and it is an illusion.

This section of the book concerns Leonardo as a biographical subject. The practice of biographical writing since the nineteenth century works with categories of personhood, identity, and subjectivity (that is, the socially conditioned sense of being a distinct person) that have questionable applicability to premodern selves. For instance, the subjectivity of interest to a biographer tends to be conceived as an individual autonomous mind coterminous with a body, one capable of knowing and expressing itself distinctly from others, of having a "personality." For a premodern person, on the other hand, self-understanding might rely less on autonomous mind as distinct from social role and membership of a group, on a dichotomized body and soul each with its own purposes, and on an individuality defined, in relational terms, to other living and nonliving (or otherworldly) individuals. For Barbara Newman, writing about medieval Christian identity, "the essence of personhood is the capacity to be permeated by other selves, other persons, without being fractured by them."[11]

The challenges to a Leonardo biography lie not only in the insufficiency of the information basic to a written life of (for instance) Thomas Jefferson or Florence Nightingale but in the very different notions underlying what it meant to have a *self* or be a *person* a half millennium ago. It also lies in the limitations—revealed by forms of inquiry as different as psychoanalysis and neurobiology—to modern notions of the self as a coherent and boundaried consciousness.

There are no corresponding terms in Leonardo's lifetime for "self" or "identity" in the sense that it would be conceived in Western philosophical or political thought from the mid-1600s onward, with the increasing tendency, in the wake of Descartes, to identify selfhood with consciousness. By contrast, there was in Leonardo's epoch a word for "person"—*persona*—used to designate an embodied material existence distinct from the mind or soul. In *Purgatorio* II.110 Dante calls on the shade of Casella to sing of love in order to calm his soul, "which coming hither with its body [*persona*] is so wearied."[12] *Persona* is also the Latin word for mask—for a fictive exterior self. A portrait by one of Leonardo's Florentine contemporaries, with a cover adorned with a mask and the motto *Sua cuique persona* (to each their own mask), shows the currency of the notion.[13]

The body or persona is like the mask to the soul—a mutable and alterable outer appearance. The epoch once admired for the "discovery of the individual" is better considered the age of the mutable or socially fabricated self—which is why another of the artist's contemporaries, Giovanni Pico della Mirandola, thought of human nature as chameleon-like. So too the humanist polymath Leon Battista Alberti—a major role model for Leonardo—was described by an admiring colleague as "like a new chameleon [who] assumes the colors of what he writes about."[14]

The drawing (ca. 1515) of an old man with braided hair and a tapering nose is not, by any conventional understanding, a portrait of Leonardo da Vinci (plate 19). It is questionable that it is a portrait of anyone, and it probably belongs with the extravagant and grotesque fantasy likenesses the artist and his pupils drew throughout his career. However, if we take the generally recognized portrait of Leonardo by his pupil Francesco Melzi as evidence for how Leonardo looked in the final years of his life, the drawing, which is in Windsor, could be seen as Leonardo's parody or

travesty of his own features—a fictive self. The famous red-chalk drawing of an old man in Turin (plate 20) was long considered to be a "self-
portrait" of the artist. It still adorns the covers of numerous books about
Leonardo, since it fulfills many of our expectations of what a self-portrait
should look like. It has an existential and confessional quality, a dimension
of self-recognition in old age, that countless commentators have found in
the late self-portraits of Rembrandt, above all a "poignant psychological
grandeur. This is a man physically burdened by the power of his inner vision and intellect, as is indicated by his gaze of absorption."[15] Yet the same
scholar's authoritative dating of the drawing places it around 1500–1502,
when Leonardo was only in his forties. Melzi's portrait, dating from as
much as fifteen years afterward, clearly shows a less aged individual (plate
21). Such an anomaly can only be rationalized to a degree by different
concepts of aging in premodern Europe. The Turin and Windsor drawings
are character studies, portrait fictions. We can't rule out that Leonardo
might have glanced at his own features in a mirror (or a pair of mirrors)
while working on them, but we certainly can't claim them as an intentional
record of his appearance in 1500 or 1515.

IN HIS OWN WORDS

Isn't it the case, you might say, that we know more about Leonardo than we
do about any of his contemporaries? Yes, his written legacy vastly exceeds
the output of any other premodern artist, but assembling a "life" from
these thousands of sheets poses a challenge. Leonardo's own charting of
life events seems oddly sporadic and often pointless. It has been suggested
that he had acquired the habits of notarial recordkeeping from his father's
milieu, but it is hard to see how his personal recordkeeping squares with
the notary's legalistic attention to dates, names, and places. He will write
memos randomly on sheets of drawings, without the meticulous accounting of commitments and obligations typical of mercantile *libri di ricor-
danze*: "——ber 1478 [the date is partly canceled] I began the two Virgin
Marys." And on the same sheet: "Fioravante di Domenico at Florence is
my most beloved friend, as though he were my . . ." Or, near the drawing
of a castle: "St Mary's Day, the middle of August at Cesena 1502." Of the

hundreds of such memos, remarkably few have to do with identifiable artistic commissions, or any of the normal business of artists or engineers.

Notebook pages will on occasion be devoted to a haphazard keeping of accounts. The records of payments due and received become more systematic in the last ten years of his life, when he is in the service of the French, the Florentine state, and the pope's brother Giuliano de'Medici, handling larger sums of cash than he ever had before. There are multiple glimpses of craftsmen and people with useful expertise, or books that Leonardo planned to consult, lists of expenses related to boarders, toolmakers, and metalworkers. "Though he possessed, one might say, nothing," wrote Vasari in 1550, "and worked little, he always kept servants and horses, in which latter he took much delight, and particularly in all other animals."[16]

"On the 18th day of March, 1493, Giulio, a German, came to live with me—Antonio, Bartolomeo, Lucia, Piero, Leonardo."[17] The documents confirm that whatever Leonardo earned was expended on the least durable of goods, on human resources and their upkeep. Leonardo's papers refer to expenditures on meat, beans, bread, and bedding; luxury clothing for the teenager Gian Giacomo Caprotti, nicknamed Salaì or Salaino ("little Saladin"). In 1497: 4 braccia of silver cloth, green velvet for trimming, ribbons, and small rings, totaling 26 lire and 5 soldi (however, "Salaì spent the soldi"). In April 1503 Salaì receives money to buy "rose colored stockings and their trimmings" (*calze rosate co'sua fornimenti*) and "twenty-one braccia of cloth, for making shirts." A note without a date in the Codex Forster II (c. 60v) refers to two dark purple surcoats for Salaì. An inventory in the Codex Madrid 2 4b lists the contents of a chest, with specifications about items of clothing with foreign or exotic origins: "One velvet lining that can be used as a gown. One Arab burnouse. One gown of dusty rose. One rose-colored Catalan gown.... A cape in the French mode, once owned by Cesare Borgia, belonging to Salaì."[18] Glimpses, in other words, of lives intertwined through personal effects, of Leonardo with Salaì, of both with the notorious papal warlord.

There are multiple short paraphrases of classical authors—Vitruvius, Archimedes, Lucretius, Hippocrates, Ammianus Marcellinus. Occasionally he will record an authorial endeavor: "Book entitled Of Transformation, that is, of one body into another without diminution or increase of substance, begun by me, Leonardo da Vinci on the 12th day of July 1505."[19]

Some of these notes convey a sense of being in the moment, even if only in the moment of writing itself, since the event referred to seems fictive or chimeric. In 1504, "on the night of St. Andrew," we find him proudly claiming to solve the infamous problem of generating a square with an equal area to a given circle. Apparently he hadn't though, since on April 28, 1509, he reported the success of a second attempt: "Having for a long time sought to square the angle of two curved sides, that is the angle, which has two curved sides of equal curve, that is curve created by the same circle: now in the year 1509, on the eve of the calends of May, I have solved the proposition at ten o'clock on the evening of Sunday."[20]

In such notes there is very occasionally a sense of quotidian catastrophe, reported with uncomplaining patience: "On the 6th day of June, 1505, Friday, at the stroke of the 13th hour I began to paint in the palace. At that moment when [I] applied the brush the weather turned bad, and the bell tolled calling the men to assemble. The cartoon ripped, the water spilled and the vessel containing it broke. And suddenly the weather grew worse, and it rained so much that the waters were great. And the sky was dark as night."[21] This is probably the event that precipitated the termination of work on *The Battle of Anghiari*. Who was this written for? Is it a personal memo or *ricordanza*, a draft of a letter, or an accounting of a setback to his employer, the government of Florence? The artist's surviving personal correspondence—less than a dozen letters—consists of drafts and redrafts of reminders about his salary, or about disputed legacies, or concerning water rights in Milan. For the biographer, these provide essential but fairly humdrum data.

Leonardo's drafts for a treatise on painting have been mined for glimpses of an inner life. One passage is repeatedly cited as evidence of his solitary temperament, of a selfhood that seemingly holds itself together in contemplative isolation: "The painter or draughtsman should be solitary, especially when intent on those speculations and reflections which continually appear before his eyes to provide subjects for safekeeping in the memory. If you are alone you belong entirely to yourself [*E se tu sarai solo sarai tutto tuo*; more literally, "if you will be alone you will be entirely yours"]. If you are with just one companion you belong only half to your-self [*sarai mezzo tuo*: "you will be half yours"] and less so in proportion to the intrusiveness of his behavior. And the more of your companions there are, the more you will fall into the same trouble."[22]

The precept regarding solitary speculation is restated more than once but always with a sense of the risks of detachment: "If you should say 'I will go my own way, and draw apart—the better to be able to speculate upon the forms of natural objects,' then I would say that this would be harmful to you because you will not be able to prevent yourself from lending an ear to their idle chatter. And since you cannot serve two masters you will perform badly in the role of companion and there will be an even worse consequence for the speculative study of your art. And if you say I shall withdraw so far apart that their words will not reach me, and will cause me no disturbance, I for my part would say that you would be held to be mad. But consider: you would at least be alone."

Find your companionship within your (private) studies, he con-cludes. "All other company could be extremely detrimental [*dannosa*] to you." And yet a few notebook pages later in Melzi's transcription of the notes, we find: "To draw in company is much better than to draw on one's own for many reasons." The reasons include *shame* at the potential inad-equacy of one's drawing "and this disgrace must motivate you to profitable study," and "that you will learn something from the drawings of those who do better than you, and if you become better than them you will have the advantage of showing your disgust at their shortcomings and the praise of others will enhance your virtue."[23]

In a related note he proceeds to his famous injunction that the artist "must liken his mind to nature, giving it a surface like a mirror which is transformed into as many different colors as there are colored objects placed before it. And the company he keeps should be like-minded towards those studies."[24]

What emerges from these reflections on solitude is the image of an intensely social world, that of the workshop—a world of labor, contest, and chatter, of praising and shaming, from which the advantages of oc-casional detachment are called into question as soon as raised. What is also revealed is the *permeable* nature of the premodern self. The artist's being is precariously susceptible to whatever occurs around him—as much a chameleon as a mirror, it changes color in accordance with the forms it encounters, and working with a companion is reduced *to only half of itself*, being completed in the halved personhood of that other coworker. (Echoes here of the famous phrase by Horace on his friendship with Virgil, *animae dīmidium meae*, "half of my soul.") While the artist counsels vigilance against creative contamination by other selves, it is important to note that the risks of the workshop are also its seductions and its pleasures—an extension of mental and physical being among comrades.

And it is that highly social workshop life that pervades the notebooks. Sometimes this is evident in ways that seem to point to more fraught personal connections—as when he itemizes his apprentice Salaì's petty thieveries as a set of debits, possibly for a reckoning with the boy's father.

Other connections—such as those of family—are laconically and dispassionately signaled. On a sheet with pen portraits of three noteworthy horses, Leonardo recorded the arrival, in July 1493, of a woman named Catarina. A biographer here cannot but identify this Catarina as the woman named as Leonardo's mother in his grandfather Antonio da Vinci's 1457 tax return. Although Leonardo has never mentioned her, and gives us little to clarify her relationship to him, it seems a reasonable inference that she is now widowed and dependent on his support. A Milanese parish necrology of the following June records the death of "Chatarina de Florenzia," sixty years old, of quartan fever; in writing, Leonardo reacts to her death only by itemizing the expenses for her funeral.[25]

Might a document recently publicized by Carlo Vecce throw light on Leonardo's diffidence here? A notarial record by Leonardo's father, Piero, from November 1452—six months after his son's birth—records the emancipation of an enslaved woman belonging to a certain Ginevra, wife of the merchant Donato Nati. Her name was Catarina, "filia Jacobi eius schlava sue serva de partibus Circassie": daughter of Jacob, from the region of Circassia—that is, the region to the north shore of the Black Sea, where Circassians were captured and trafficked through the Genoese port of Tana.[26] The objection has been raised that the name "Catarina" was regularly bestowed on enslaved women in Tuscany. Even with this uncertainty, the absence of ultimate proof, a biographical approach must proceed now always with the *possibility* that Leonardo was the son of a slave, since this cannot be confirmed nor denied.

And such a possibility has rapidly given rise to others: that Catarina was a Jewish slave, given the name of her father and the substantial Khazar Jewish population of the Caucasus, and that Leonardo was therefore Jewish. This is history in the mode of conjecture, and it is of great interest that Vecce chose to present his documentary research in the form of a novel, *The Smile of Catarina*. Might it not be the case that fiction grounded in slender and ambiguous archival gleaning might offer a more solid means of exploring and visualizing the past than biographies reliant on hypothesis and fabulation that claim to be true?

By contrast with this dispassionate record of Catarina's arrival and death, Leonardo addressed one of his several stepmothers as "My dearest mother" in a letter of 1509.[27] His record of the death of his father in 1504 stands out in being written in a conventional left-to-right hand instead of in his idiosyncratic mirror-writing, as if he were at least momentarily taking on the persona of a Florentine patriarch: "On July 9th 1504, on Wednesday at the seventh hour, my father Piero da Vinci, notary, died in the Palazzo del Podesta, at the seventh hour. He was 80 years old and left 10 male children and two females."[28] Such neutrality is striking given the circumstances of the father's death and its implications for the son. Leonardo does not record the crucial fact that Ser Piero da Vinci died intestate: if there had been a will, Piero might have made provision for Leonardo, but his failure to do so meant that his illegitimate son would now be excluded from any rights of inheritance.

The few letters addressed to other members of his family display what commentators like Kenneth Clark have regarded as an unsympathetic degree of emotional detachment. A letter to his brother commiserates with him on the birth of his first son: "I received a letter from you from which I learnt that you have had an heir, which circumstance I understand has afforded you a great deal of pleasure. Now in so far as I had judged you to be possessed of prudence I am now entirely convinced that I am as far removed from having an accurate judgment as you are from prudence; seeing that you have been congratulating yourself in having created a watchful enemy, who will strive with all his energies after liberty, which can only come into being at your death."[29]

It seems caustic and sententious, but it may reflect less of a personal animus than Leonardo taking on one of his occasional *personae*: that of the prophet or the philosopher, expected to deliver maxims or portentous statements. The advice is a paraphrase of a passage in a book of stories by Francesco Sacchetti that Leonardo owned.

EYEWITNESSES AND EARLY BIOGRAPHIES

The few known facts of Leonardo's early career suggest multiple interpretations. For instance, in the 1460s and 1470s, following his apprenticeship, he had a professional association with his teacher Andrea del Verrocchio in Florence—but of what kind, and for how long? In all his writings, despite twenty years of association, he never mentions Verrocchio. The sole documentary evidence of their association is in the form of a record that the twenty-three-year-old painter was prosecuted in April 1476 for the crime of sodomy. While that charge was dismissed, the document, published in 1896, has become the cornerstone for the entire modern production of Leonardo.[30]

The master-pupil relationship leaves its trace in the collaborative painting *The Baptism of Christ* of 1472–75 but has come to assume an apocryphal embodied form in Verrocchio's bronze *David* (fig. 9). In 1998, David Alan Brown wrote that "the curly haired biblical hero is popularly believed to be a likeness of Leonardo."[31] While keeping his own distance from such a view, Brown then debunks the main commonsense objection to it—that the statue was completed shortly before its sale by the Medici to the government of Florence in 1476, when Leonardo would have been twenty-four. However, since many scholars now believe that the bronze was produced in the late 1460s, Leonardo *could have been* young enough to serve as model.[32] The attractive hypothesis has taken on a life of its own: the bronze has served both Charles Nicholl and Walter Isaacson as an image of the ephebic young artist, or rather—as Brown has it—"the first glimpse we catch of Leonardo in the shop is not as a practicing artist but as an object of appreciation."[33] Another writes rather cryptically that

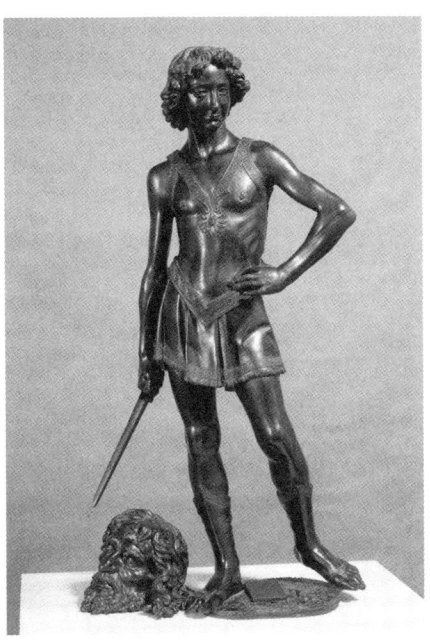

9. Andrea del Verrocchio, *David*. 1466–69 or 1473–75. Bronze, 125 cm. Florence, Bargello.

the bronze David is "a notional portrait, if not an actual one, of the young artist at that age."[34]

A hypothesis achieves semi-factual status and becomes the basis for further semi-facts. A drawing of a nude model posing in the attitude of the statue is hence sometimes been supposed to be a representation of the adolescent artist's naked body, gratifying the biographical craving for the intimate glimpse, for "fleshing out" when details are scarce (fig. 10).

Nearly everything else reported about his early life comes from sources that postdate the artist's death in 1519 by decades. Some scholars have made much of a statement in a compilation of anecdotes on Florentine artists from ca. 1540, known as the *Anonimo Gaddiano*, that Leonardo was taken into the household of Lorenzo de'Medici, "the Magnificent," and trained in the sculpture garden at San Marco. Vasari published his first edition of the *Lives* ten years later, and if he was aware of the *Anonimo* he ignored it. However, he was well-informed about the artistic world of Florence at the time of Il Magnifico. As a Medici partisan and propagandist, it seems

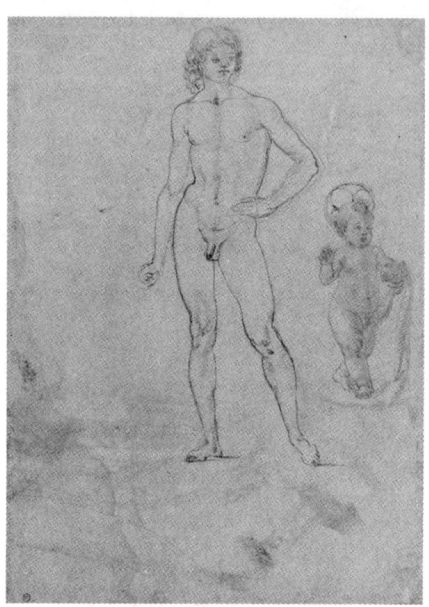

10. Francesco di Simone Ferrucci,
Standing nude male; Christ Child.
Metalpoint and brown ink on pink
prepared paper, 26 × 19 cm. Paris, Lou-
vre, Département des arts graphiques,
RF 451, recto.

unlikely that he would have sought to suppress Leonardo's early Medici
connections, had they actually existed.[35] Certainly, Leonardo would write
laconically, in 1515, "li medici mi crearono e distrussono" (The Medici created me and destroyed me). That date corresponds to the period when
Leonardo lived in Rome in the service of Giuliano de'Medici. Perhaps
he was expressing frustration at the conditions of employment under the
son of the Magnifico, but the line is not only laconic, it is deliberately
ambiguous; it flourishes the instability of language. The phrase can also
be translated as "the physicians have created me and destroyed me." Leonardo seems to have regarded doctors as a menace to health—elsewhere he
describes them as *destruttori di vite*. A rhyming memo of instructions for
healthy living he copied a year or so later included the injunction "He who
takes medicine is ill advised."

Nonetheless, the passage has served some biographers as the basis for
an entire missing chapter of Leonardo's early life, and it has provided re-
assuring grounds that Leonardo can be sited at the heart of the cultural
and political intelligentsia of late fifteenth-century Florence—the circle of
Lorenzo the Magnificent. Of course, everything in Florence can ultimately

be traced to the Medici network and to Lorenzo, the *maestro di bottega* (the "master of the workshop" or "big boss"), but the case of Leonardo might be a good point at which to recognize that not everything can or should be translated into Medici patronage. His teacher Verrocchio was in every sense a Medici protégé, but Leonardo himself seems to have obtained no clear advantage from the connection.[36] The desire to see Leonardo as a Medici artist reflects a common biographical imperative to fill gaps by "borrowing" details from other, better documented lives—in this case, that of Michelangelo, who was raised in the Medici household. It might be more valuable to speculate in the other direction, to think about the possibilities for professional survival of an artist on the outer fringes of the Medici network.

For reasons variously explained, Leonardo left Florence for Milan between 1481 and 1483, and stayed until 1499. Was this departure on his own initiative, to find work at the court of a prince who would recognize and support his talent and ambition, or was it at the behest of Lorenzo de'Medici, as the *Anonimo Gaddiano* reports? And why did it take him so long—possibly as much as ten years—to receive commissions from the Sforza rulers of Milan? An undated draft of a letter to Ludovico Sforza (Codex Atlanticus fol. 1082), in which Leonardo vaunts his ability to supply new military technology for the Milanese army and navy, ending with a claim to expertise in painting and sculpture, is routinely dated to 1482, but there are more compelling reasons to assign it to the end of the decade, when Leonardo had developed the necessary expertise among the munitions factories of Milan.[37]

This raises a broader problem with sources of information for an artist who is considered better documented than most.

In the controversy regarding the attribution of the *Salvator Mundi*, the lack of documents is often cited as a major stumbling block to the work's authenticity.[38] However, with the corpus of paintings accepted as authentic Leonardos (or those of most Renaissance artists, for that matter), there is often no documentary basis for the attribution. Such records as we have are sparse and often confusing. While we have a substantial paper trail for an altarpiece of the Immaculate Conception for San

Francesco Grande, commissioned from Leonardo in partnership with the Da Preda brothers in Milan in 1483, there is nothing that definitively explains why two versions of its central panel, known as *The Virgin of the Rocks*—one in the Louvre, one in the National Gallery in London—were then produced, and probably in tandem. (There is some consensus that the partnership sold the Louvre version for a higher price to another client, leaving the London version to be completed many years later in fulfillment of the contract, in 1505–8. To make things more complicated and more interesting, the London version seems to represent a return to Leonardo's first thoughts for the composition, which was modified and refined in the Louvre version.)[39]

In 1472 Leonardo joined the Company of St. Luke, the corporation of Florentine painters. However, he seems largely to have operated outside the normal structures of the art market, where works were produced according to contract and subject to evaluation, so the negotiations between the artist and his clients have left little trace. Records of payment are few before the last decade of his life. A verbal agreement with Isabella d'Este for a portrait did not seem to advance beyond a preparatory drawing (probably, but not certainly, the profile portrait in the Louvre); the exasperated correspondence culminated in the marchioness's compromise proposal that he send her a "young Christ" instead. While both Leonardo himself and an eyewitness account by an agent of Isabella d'Este refer to other younger painters in his household, and while his notes on painting prescribe a detailed regime of group training, we have no clear idea of how formal or organized his workshop practice was.[40]

In an age when artistic signatures were increasingly associated with artistic identity and what we now call intellectual property, Leonardo did not sign his works. His distinctive style may have served as its own "signature," even as it was transferable to and closely imitated by others. As we will see in the final chapter, the very few works that he completed tended to extend his authorship, to generate a proliferating corpus of pseudo-Leonardos by younger painters at varying degrees of remove from the artist himself. It is as if he recognized that by creating a few paintings he was setting something in motion, that the paintings would have a force or agency of their own that was no longer his to control.

We tend to think of having a self in terms of agency and our autonomous will. The notion of human rights is premised on such a notion of selfhood—rights involve a legal protection of the freedom to express what one considers oneself to be. Such notions of the self in turn presuppose the notion of consciousness and its continuity over time: a severe loss of memory is typically experienced as a catastrophic loss of identity. And yet such notions of the self are in large part culturally specific and historically relative. What if selfhood was primarily thought of in terms of the body, for instance? For a premodern Christian who believed in the doctrine of the resurrection of the body, there is no real afterlife without the organic, perishable, but finally renewable container of consciousness. Even the shades of the dead in Dante's afterlife, some of whom are subjected to graphic physical punishments, seem highly embodied.

And what if individuals thought of themselves in terms of relations of belonging, of ties to various groups—what historians of Leonardo's Florence have called *amici, parenti, vicini*—connections of kinship and neighborhood that can then be multiplied in terms of professional status, confraternity membership (ritual brotherhood and sisterhood), political faction, or the protection of a magnate?[41] In recent decades, social historians, anthropologists, and psychologists have converged in thinking about selfhood in *relational* terms. The self, in effect, is and was always a network: it is "relational through and through, consisting not only of social but also physical, genetic, psychological, emotional and biological relations that together form a network self. The self also changes over time, acquiring and losing traits in virtue of new social locations and relations, even as it continues as that one self."[42]

If an individual is described as gay, vegetarian, pro-animal rights, a religious agnostic, a "creative," a scientific innovator—all terms applied to Leonardo—this is because these are *categories* of personhood that we now recognize. It is meaningful to be gay, vegetarian, pro-animal rights because of a sense of common cause with others; they entail a politics of identity, a personal story that is also the story of a group. Leonardo has also been included in modern pathologies such as "attention deficit disorder," trauma, and PTSD, which in our networked age can also serve as the basis for community, of group support and activism.

If we lay out a set of terms that Leonardo's contemporaries and near-contemporaries used to characterize him, we get a rather different profile, one that does not answer to the chronological or psychological desiderata of modern biography. For more than two centuries after Vasari, "lives" of Leonardo amounted to amplifications or annotations of the 1568 *vita*, sometimes adding new information and challenging Vasari's biases, but mainly consisting of exemplary anecdotes and lists of works, and indifferent to basic questions of chronology. While Leonardo's life dates, the date of his arrival in Milan, and the fact of his illegitimacy were only established by the late 1700s, the increasingly abundant literature on Leonardo's works and manuscripts frequently omitted such particulars or got them wrong.

The first systematic and documentary-based account of his career was the *Essai* on Leonardo's mathematical and scientific thought published by Giovanni Battista Venturi in 1797. It has been described as lacking in literary pretensions, "organized like a scientific or mathematical thesis rather than a biography."[43] However, the modern genre of biography—centered on personality revealed through time and experience—had not yet fully emerged. That emergence would transform the understanding of several shadowy figures from the premodern world, Shakespeare among them, and not without a cost. In *Shakespeare without a Life* (2023), Margreta de Grazia shows the impact on Shakespeare criticism of his late-emerging biography, observing "that what we understand by biography was neither desired nor attempted until late into the eighteenth century" and that "by looking for faint intimations of what is now the norm, we efface the very different priorities once at work."[44]

Thus we restrict ourselves here to what can be gleaned from the handful of early sources on Leonardo's career—and let me say at once that few of these particulars are verifiable, some are founded in hearsay or prejudice, and even eyewitness accounts can be inconsistent with other evidence. We have a few statements by the artist about himself, the earliest life (1527) by Paolo Giovio (PG), notes by Antonio Billi (AB) and the so-called *Anonimo Gaddiano* (AG) from after Leonardo's death, eyewitness accounts by the cardinal's secretary Antonio de'Beatis (B), the Carmelite Fra Pietro da Novellara (PN), and the mathematician Luca Pacioli (LP), and finally the two versions of the life of Leonardo, from 1550 and 1568, by Giorgio Vasari (GV).[45]

FLORENTINE (AB, AG, PN, GV)
Born out of wedlock (PG, AG, GV)
Born in Vinci (PG: "an insignificant village")
"Lives with Verrocchio" (document of 1476)
Had a handsome appearance (PG, AG, GV)
Left-handed (LP, PG)
Studied optics/perspective (AB, LP, PG, AG, GV)
Skilled in music (PG, AG, GV)
Skilled in oratory (AG)
Practiced human dissection (PG, AG, GV; B: "dissected more than
    thirty bodies")
Has written several books (LP, PN, B)
Skilled in engineering (LP; also *Ingeniarus et pinctor*—an "engineer
    and painter"—in a Sforza court document of 1495)
Left many works unfinished (AB, PG, AG, GV)
Leads a life that is "haphazard and extremely unpredictable, so that
    he only seems to live from day to day" (PN)
"Caprice and changeable inconstancy" (PG)
Had numerous pupils (PG, AG)

Here are traits reported by Vasari that do not appear in earlier sources, as well as traits recorded by later sixteenth-century commentators—the physician Girolamo Cardano (C) and the painter and writer Gian Paolo Lomazzo (L).

Possesses bodily strength (GV)
Dresses elegantly (GV)
Practices generosity and liberality (GV)
A philosopher (GV)
Heretical ideas (GV version 1550)
Pleasing in conversation (GV)
Loves horses and other animals (GV)
Erat enim purus Pictor, non medicus nec philosophus (he was entirely a
    painter and neither a physician nor a philosopher; C)
Had sex with a fifteen-year-old apprentice (L)

The challenge to building a biographical portrait of Leonardo from such characteristics is that several derive formulaically one from the other.

Especially with Vasari, one or two positive traits produce additional compatible ones, thus supplementing the dearth of biographical particulars: one pleasant in conversation is probably also one who dressed pleasantly; a practitioner of mathematics as well as anatomy could be labeled a "philosopher"—literally, a lover of wisdom. According to the same principles of consistency or decorum, the various early writings on Leonardo's life tend to embellish and amplify each other.[46]

Decorum and consistency are particularly characteristic of humanist life-writing, exemplified by Giovio's terse life of the artist intended for his 1527 collection *Lives of Famous Men*. As a young medical student in Pavia, Giovio probably met Leonardo through his teacher Marcantonio della Torre, who collaborated with Leonardo in his anatomical researches. Two decades later, Giovio succinctly lays out what contemporaries saw as Leonardo's key achievements—the rendering of three-dimensional effects on a two-dimensional surface, his study of light and shade, and his devotion to "unpleasant and inhuman" research into human anatomy: "Thus he was able to depict, with wonderful skill, all the minute particulars of the body, down to the tiny veins and the bones beneath the skin, so that from this work of many years it would be possible to forge figures of bronze." On the downside, "while his works were sought by many, due to an unstable character and a natural tendency to tire of a work soon after having begun it, he brought few works to completion beyond the early stages."[47] *The Last Supper* and the Sforza horse are praised, despite deterioration or total destruction, because Giovio could have found them mentioned and duly praised with correct formulae in Luca Pacioli's *De divina proportione* of 1509. *The Battle of Anghiari* would have been "extraordinarily magnificent," but "came to an untimely end owing to the defective plaster which persistently rejected the colors ground in walnut oil. It seems as if the very natural regret caused by this unexpected injury and interruption of the work was instrumental in making it famous. Humanist lives sought to draw lessons from the apparent shortcomings of noteworthy individuals, and Leonardo's volatile work habits and his failure to complete works have been a staple of Leonardo narratives ever since: "he was able to complete few of his works through caprice and changeable inconstancy; his talent so strived for perfection and was so troublesome to himself that he began many things and then left them unfinished."[48]

Giovio offers no particulars about Leonardo's family, training, private life, or acquaintances—either because they were not known to him or, more likely, because he did not see them as important. He concludes with a brief portrait of the artist that makes him resemble the image of the ideal courtier in a celebrated bestseller published by the nobleman and diplomat Baldesar Castiglione the same year, *The Book of the Courtier*: "Leonardo was a man of great talent, mental lucidity, liberality, of handsome appearance; being a great creator and judge of all things elegant and pleasurable, especially theatre, music, and song, he was pleasing to the powerful for the whole of his life." And Castiglione himself mentions Leonardo, along with Michelangelo and Raphael and Giorgione, each of them "perfect in their own particular style."

And yet there may be another Leonardo in Castiglione's book, one that decisively colored his image for posterity. One of Castiglione's speakers chides those "who strive to do what they cannot and avoid things they understand." An example, not named, is "one of the world's finest painters [who] despises the art for which he has so rare a talent and has set himself to study philosophy; and in this he has strange notions and fanciful revelations that, if he tried to paint them, for all his skill he couldn't."[49]

On one hand, such a characterization might seem to anticipate the free-thinking, visionary, even Faustian genius that the nineteenth century fashioned and that survives in contemporary images of the transgressive, secretive, outsider artist. On the other, we might instead see the scorn of an aristocrat for low-ranking professionals who refused to know their place. Castiglione was in Rome at the time Leonardo was working on hydraulic projects, fortifications, and the design of armaments, probably in secret, for Giuliano de' Medici. He probably knew that Leonardo's anatomical research was denounced before the pope (as necromancy?) by a disgruntled assistant.[50] The spectacle of a painter who would do anything other than just paint, outlined here by Castiglione, would be elaborated by Vasari in his account of Leonardo in Rome, spending all his time "on philosophical studies and in particular on alchemy," and of Leo X's despair at an artist who distilled his varnishes before he'd begun to paint: "this man will never do anything, for he begins by thinking of the end of the work before the beginning." It is more likely that Leonardo was preparing his pigments with oil, a technique probably understood by few nonprofessional contemporaries in Rome.

Apart from some caviling on the part of Cardano and Castiglione about whether Leonardo could be considered a *real* physician or philosopher, and apart from some emphatic revisions regarding the artist's heterodox beliefs between the two versions of Vasari's life of Leonardo, there is a recurrent tendency toward consistency, and no interest in paradoxical traits, secrecy, or enigma.

There are other ways of plotting Leonardo's personhood: through the spectrum of his social relations. We have seen that his notebooks abound in short memos with proper names, many of them of persons who can be identified, to whom the artist has some kind of recourse—they possess a certain expertise in mathematics or artistic technique, or they are the owner of a book that Leonardo needs to consult, or they have a horse, or a servant, with a physical characteristic worth recording: such a network of usually mundane acquaintances connects multiple professional and social worlds. Many of Leonardo's scattered notes resemble the following:[51]

> The Algebra which is in the possession of the Marliani [physicians, astrologers], written by their father.
> A nun lives at The Dove in Cesena, who is a good maker of straw plaits, and a friar of San Francesco.
> Get Messer Fazio [Cardano; professor of medicine and law in Pavia, father of Girolamo] to show you about proportion.
> Get the Brera Friar [i.e., at the Humiliati monastery of Milan] to show you *De Ponderibus* [the thirteenth-century treatise on weights by Fra Giordano of Nemi].
> Get from Jean de Paris [the painter Jean Perréal] the method of coloring al secco, and how to prepare tinted paper, double folded, and his box of colors.
> [Talk to] Giannino, the Bombardier, re. the means by which the tower of Ferrara is walled without loopholes.

Ask Benedetto Portinari [Florentine merchant with family
  operation in Bruges] by what means they go on ice in
  Flanders.

Find a master of hydraulics and get him to tell you how to repair a
  lock, canal and mill in the Lombard manner.

The measurement of the sun promised me by Maestro Giovanni
  Francese.

Giuliano da Maria the physician has a steward without hands.

Giovanni Vespucci will give me a book on geometry.

Map of the world from Giovanni Benci. Giovanni Benci has my book
  and jaspers.

Learn the multiplication of roots from Maestro Luca [Pacioli].

Rosso's mirror—watch him make it.

Ask the wife of Biagino Crivelli [crossbowman] how the capon
  rears and hatches the eggs of the hen when he is in the mating
  season.

Master Battista dall'Aquilo [the pope's private chamberlain] has my
  book *De Vocie* in his hands.

These terse memos, recording links to fellow artists and engineers, to craftsmen with a range of specializations, to soldiers and military experts, to physicians, to clerical intellectuals like Luca Pacioli, and to members of distinguished Florentine families (Benci, Vespucci, Portinari), give a sense of the complex social identity of a figure like Leonardo beyond the narrow and elite perspective of Castiglione or Cardano, or beyond the constraints of decorum operating in humanist life-writing, like Paolo Giovio's. A recent multivolume monograph on Leonardo—referred to by its author as a "biographical-archeological" study—takes on the challenge of exploring Leonardo precisely through this web of connections named in his manuscripts. Emphasis falls on the artist's legacy on paper, in order "to reconstruct a general typology of his manuscripts" so as to grasp "his sense of process and sequence of ideas."[52] The "paper Leonardo" is a mosaic of written traces of social interactions. As the mosaic grows and extends, so do the gaps between the tesserae, and the serial momentum of life events, experiences, and achievements resists a predictable and orderly narrative arc.

LEONARDO PERSONAE AND
THE RHETORIC OF EXPERIENCE

And yet it would be misleading to suggest that early modern Europeans lacked the idea of a life defined through critical junctures and radical transformations that—with the hindsight of life-writing—can be seen not as random accidents of fortune but as providential, the very point or purpose of a life lived. There is even a sense that personhood is finally articulated in an abrupt departure from a given path, from a predictable social role. Diversions from one's lot in life, sometimes recognized as *conversions*, form the substance of one of the oldest forms of premodern life-writing: the life of the saint. The canonical life of St. Francis—the basis for the famous cycle of medieval frescoes in the basilica at Assisi—is particularly elaborate in its multistaged self-transformations, self-recognitions, and turning points of various kinds: his acclamation by the poor man of Assisi and vocation by a speaking crucifix, his stripping naked to transition from the worldly domain of his father to the spiritual domain of the Bishop of Assisi, and finally his miraculous stigmatization.

When Lorenzo Ghiberti began to collect and compose lives of the artists in the first half of the 1400s, several presented this character of diversion/conversion: "In a village near the city of Florence, called Vespignano, a boy of marvelous genius was born. He was drawing a sheep from life, and the painter Cimabue, passing on the road to Bologna, saw the boy sitting on the ground and drawing a sheep on a flat rock. He was seized with admiration for the boy, who was so young and could do so well. . . . He asked the father for the boy; the father was very poor. He handed the boy over to him and Cimabue took Giotto with him and he was Cimabue's pupil. . . . And Giotto grew great in the art of painting."[53]

(Leonardo, as we will see, would adapt Ghiberti's account of Giotto's beginnings in his own notebooks.) Ghiberti preceded the self-celebratory narrative of his own career with the cautionary one of the goldsmith Gusmin of Cologne, employed by the Duke of Anjou, whose conversion happens when he sees the works he had accomplished "with such love and skill [all] destroyed for the Duke's public requirements." Making a pious vow, he divides up all his possessions "for love of the creator of all things" and retires as a penitent to a hermitage—but not without consenting to teach younger artists who seek him out: "he received them very humbly, giving them wise instructions and showing them many measurements, and giving them many examples." Not so much a renunciation of art here as a renunciation of practice for theory, more valuable than gold.

Ghiberti, also active as an engineer and architect, would have been aware of a similar combination of memorialization and moral conversion in the work of the sculptor-mason and architect Giovanni Pisano, whom he included among the handful of outstanding sculptors of the generation before his own. Giovanni, who died ca. 1318, adorned the spectacular marble pulpit he carved for the cathedral of Pisa with two monumental inscriptions. The first reads: "I praise the true God, through whose agency the best of things exist, who has permitted a man to fashion these pure figures. The hands, alone in their skill, of Giovanni (the late and son of Nicola) carved this work here when thirteen hundred and eleven full years of our Lord had passed, while Federigo, count (at the time, I say) of Montefeltro ruled over the Pisans, of one accord and yet separate with Nello di Falcone assisting, concerned not only with this work but also with the rules of the craft. He was born at Pisa, like that Giovanni who is endowed above all others with command of the art of pure sculpture. Sculpting splendid things in stone, wood, and gold, he could not have carved base ones even if he had so wished. There are many sculptors: to him alone remain the honors of praise. He made celebrated sculptures and various figures. Whoever you are, when you have marveled [at them], then you will approve them rightly. Christ have mercy upon him who had such gifts. Amen."[54]

The inscription sets the artist's achievement in relation to a family lineage and to his "life and times" in Pisa, identifying the work as a collaboration with the cathedral official Nello di Falcone; of particular importance is the reference to the sculptor's craft as adhering to a set of rules or governing principles. Similarly, the writing of Ghiberti and of Leonardo, over the following two centuries, would be devoted to upholding the virtues of art as intellectual practice over material reward. Possession of such intellectual virtues, however normative or generic, constitutes a form of personal distinction.

The second inscription, written in the voice of the pulpit itself (another instance of the figure of *prosopopoeia*—"giving a face"), is far more concerned with the shape and meaning of a life, of a journey and a conversion: Giovanni is presented as a Dante-like nomad, the Stoical victim of envy and unspecified grievances. "Here Giovanni encircled the rivers and regions of the world, undertaking without hope of reward to learn many things, and preparing everything with heavy labor. He now cries out: 'I have not been on guard enough, since the more I have shown my [achievements] the more I have experienced hostile injuries in my heart.' But I [the pulpit] endure the penalty of an ignoble man with an embittered mind, so that I may take envy away from him and soften his sorrow. And let me entreat an honor [from you]: bedew these verses [with your tears]. He proves himself unworthy in reproving a man worthy of the crown. Thus he reproves himself and approves him."[55]

Giovanni's pulpit, a third-person externalization of Giovanni's own self, "bears witness," as does Ghiberti's Gusmin. Gusmin, Giotto, and Ghiberti himself all experience life-changing and life-defining turning points. Such a biographical self-consciousness is perhaps not surprising among great sculptor-engineers like Giovanni, Ghiberti, and Filippo Brunelleschi: part of their stock-in-trade involved the creation of memory, through the production of monumental structures and sculptures, commemorative effigies and inscriptions. There is a pattern of conformity, a decorum even, between a political community, a historical consciousness, and an individual ambition—and one that, as we will see, did not exist in Leonardo's case.

Leonardo is aware of the convention of bearing witness, of the exemplary turning point, but such episodes in his writings have an oddly self-contained character. Rather than showing any continuity with the lifeworld of an artist-engineer, they seem like fantastic interludes, more colorful and yet more fictive.

Around 1505, referring to his study of the flight of birds, Leonardo recalled or invented an emblematic life moment with the "childhood recollection" later made notorious by Freud: "This writing distinctly about the kite seems to be my destiny, because among the first recollections of my infancy, it seemed to me that, as I was in my cradle, a kite came to me and opened my mouth with its tail, and struck me several times with its tail inside my lips."[56] While mined by Freud for sexual metaphors, there is a strong possibility here that Leonardo is playing subversively with a hagiographic theme. He would have been familiar in Milan with the legends of Ambrose, the city's patron saint. Among them is an episode from the saint's infancy: "Ambrose . . . lay asleep in his cradle . . . when all of a sudden a swarm of bees flew in and covered his face and mouth so completely that the bees seemed to be moving in and out of their hive. Then they soared upward to such a height that the human eye could barely follow them. Witnessing this, the infant's father was astonished, and said 'If this child lives, something great will come of him.'"[57] The account in *The Golden Legend*—the most widely read collection of saints' lives—connected the saint's name with *ambrosium*, the honeyed food of the gods. The marvel was a sign of the saint's future "honey-tongued" eloquence.

The story of St. Ambrose can be connected with older stories about the Greek and Latin poets. For instance, the account of the infancy of the poet Pindar, where bees build a honeycomb in his mouth as he sleeps. Notably, the *Life of Pindar* that circulated with his verse suggested that the event might have been a dream vision, as Leonardo implies about the kite story. In the *Greek Anthology*, a collection of verse frequently translated and imitated by Leonardo's contemporaries, an epigram relates how the poet Stesichorus, shortly after his birth, had a singing nightingale settle on his lips. It is probable that Leonardo, who proudly styled himself as "a man without eloquence," was knowingly performing a parody of the theme of childhood oral inspiration. Instead of the benign bees with their sweetness or the sweet-voiced nightingale, the raucous kite crudely assaults the infant's mouth with the rear part of its body: Leonardo thus implies that he was destined to write without eloquence of the flight of birds. And as it turned out, in these observations he would correctly discern the importance of the bird's tail in the mechanics of flight. In other words, cultural and historical context can debunk myth-generating intuition.[58]

Another emblematic episode, from 1493 to 1494: a sheet in the Codex Arundel (155r) contains a long and vivid description of catastrophic meteorological and geomorphological events, with references to Scylla and

Charybdis, to Stromboli and "the flaming caves of Etna," which transitions suddenly to a first-person account of hesitation at the entrance to a cave: "drawn on by my eager desire, anxious to see a great multitude of varied and strange shapes made by formative nature, having wandered for some distance among overhanging rocks, I came to the entrance of a great cavern before which for a time I remained stupefied having been unaware of its existence. . . . And after remaining there for a time, suddenly there arose within me two emotions, fear and desire—fear of the threatening dark cavern, desire to see whether there might be any marvelous thing therein."

Editors of Leonardo's notebooks usually include the writings on the subsequent sheet 156r, as a sequel to the preceding, despite a long intervening block of text. Such characteristic editorializing allows the hesitation at the cave mouth to have a sequel—a startling apostrophe to a great fish or whale, as if its (fossilized?) remains were the "marvelous thing" that he sought within the cavern. In fact, there is probably no connection between the passages, but the encounter described similarly presents the character of an epiphany:

> O powerful and once-living instrument of formative nature, your great strength of no avail, you must abandon your tranquil life to obey the law which God and time gave to creative nature. Of no avail are your branching, sturdy dorsal fins with which you pursue your prey, plowing your way, tempestuously tearing open the briny waves with your breast.
> Oh, how many a time the terrified shoals of dolphins and big tuna fish were seen to flee before your insensate fury, as you lashed with swift, branching fins and forked tail, creating in the sea mist and sudden tempest that buffeted and submerged ships.

The account gives way to a meditation on time—disclosing, in fact, Leonardo's understanding of "deep" geological time—personified and addressed along with the petrified creature: "O Time, swift despoiler of created things, how many kings, how many peoples have you undone? How many changes of state and circumstances have followed since the wondrous form of this fish died here in this winding and cavernous recess?

Now unmade by time you lie patiently in this closed place with bones stripped and bare, serving as an armature for the mountain placed over you."[59]

The claim to have witnessed the petrified fish becomes a paraphrase of one of Leonardo's favorite classical sources, the speech of Pythagoras in Book XV of Ovid's *Metamorphoses*.[60] The archetypal philosopher's meditations on the instability of humans, the elements, and the earth itself—all as invented by Ovid—would permeate Leonardo's later writings on geomorphology. Scientific curiosity and the language of poetry and even prophecy are interdependent here.

This is not to say that the episode is necessarily invented: recently researchers in the history of paleontology have made the case that Leonardo could have seen cetacean remains on a hillside in Tuscany, and probably not far from Vinci, where whale fossils were reported since the late 1400s.[61] Yet if that is what Leonardo found, it is striking that he does not report it simply as a finding. He is framing it as a life event, but in a borrowed and Latinate rhetoric which he saw as appropriate to philosophical communication. His reading of poetry framed how he saw and how he described. Eyewitnessing and experience becomes an epiphany, with rhetorical "voicing" effects including Leonardo's favorite device of the apostrophe.

Whether it happened or not, the encounter is a moment of revelation envisioned as a turning point in a life, a life which is thereby given narrative form through an illuminating fragment. Years later, in the Codex Leicester, he reported finding fossil shells on mountaintops, claiming them as evidence of the elevation of the seabed. Although he has left the language of poetry far behind, he is still thinking with and echoing *Metamorphoses* XV, where Pythagoras says: "I have seen what once was solid earth now changed into sea, and lands created out of what once was ocean. Seashells lie far away from ocean's waves."

Leonardo, a man "without letters," appealed to experience as the ground of truth, but this was experience often mediated by "letters." The Achilles' heel of truth claims based on "experience" is that recorded experiences have nothing to do with the quotidian world: they are singular, extraordinary, and pertain to an individual. Recording them requires an act of representation, of verbal picturing with an array of rhetorical effects—what rhetoricians would have called *evidentia*—an artifice of words to produce the effect of seeing. The speaker of the passage on the cavern and the whale passes seamlessly from apostrophizing the great fish in its primordial habitat to the description of the remains lying patiently "in this closed place with bones despoiled."

"Experience," for Frank Ankersmit, "merely has the privilege of authenticity—and authenticity is desperately hard to recognize for others than the person having had an authentic experience of the world."[62] Such epiphanic experiences are to be distinguished from Leonardo's documentation of *repeatable* experiences, the observations of flowing liquids, of lights and spheres and measured distances and angles—what a later era will call "experiments," a derivative of the same Latin word, *experior*—to attempt, to find out, to prove, to experience, to put to the test.[63]

A few other notes in the first person recall curious events. On an anatomical study of the spine and nerves from ca. 1508, he wrote, "I once saw how a lamb was licked by a lion in the city of Florence." The lion licked the fleece from the lamb, "and having made it bare, ate it."[64] Leonardo occasionally describes meteorological phenomena like "a cloud shaped like a huge mountain made up of banks of fire," or the "blue color of the atmosphere . . . may be seen, as I myself saw it, by anyone who ascends Mon Boso [Monte Rosa], a peak of the chain of Alps that divides France from Italy." This kind of attentiveness to the effect of light and air on vast landscapes sometimes escalates to fantastical visionary evocations, where the recordkeeper imagines himself witnessing catastrophes in remote parts of the globe. One of the longest first-person narratives, bound with the Codex Atlanticus, purports to be a letter to the ruler of Syria from the Taurus mountains in the Caucasus, recounting travels as far as the Caspian Sea, the illumination of the peaks, and a great natural disaster: "The recent unforeseen event which has occurred in these our northern parts which I am certain will strike terror not only into you but into the whole world shall be revealed to you in its due order, showing first the effect and then the cause."[65]

Perhaps it was easier to write about imaginary and exotic catastrophes than ones that were occurring on a daily basis close at hand. As has often been noticed, Leonardo almost never refers to the invasions, the sieges, the plagues, the massacres, even, that he witnessed firsthand in the service of the Sforza, of the Florentine Republic, and of the notorious Cesare Borgia. One record—perhaps a list of points to include in a letter—stands out, since it records the downfall of the Sforza in 1499 as the French captured Milan, but it holds back from moralizing or evaluative comment of any kind.

> The Governor of the castle made a prisoner,
> Visconti carried away and his son killed,
> Giovanni della Rosa deprived of his money. . . .
> The Duke lost the state, his property, and his liberty and none of his
>   works have been completed.[66]

Another record of violence personally witnessed is severed from any historic contextualization, since it occurs on a sheet with several drawings and notes about the anatomy of the heart and the action of the blood vessels: "And I saw one whose heart burst as he fled before his enemies. And he poured out sweat mixed with blood through all the pores of his skin."[67]

That Leonardo's life is less articulate; that he adopted the experiential form of life-writing, with its explanatory turning points, to record a bizarre memory of a childhood assault by a bird; that contemporaries like Giovio offered little more than a non-narrative of successes and failures; and—finally and more damagingly—that Giorgio Vasari would supplement the lack of narrative in Giovio with a cautionary history of failed potential and wasted time—all of this points to an absence, but an absence with a distinctive form that I believe can be described and that is historically significant in itself.

LIFE IN THE SHATTERZONE

The elusiveness, the fragmentary character of Leonardo's life in written sources, is not just the result of the artist's own hesitancy or the prejudices of his first biographers. It is a symptom of the shattering of Italy itself during the final three decades of his career, the period to which most of his writing and artistic activity can be dated. Lombardy, with its violent changes of regime from 1499 to 1530, the resulting economic and social upheaval, the collapse of institutions of law and forms of government, has been described as a "shatterzone" by one recent historian. Conceived as the opposite of a "contact zone"—an area of the interaction between different geopolitical entities—*shatterzone* "evokes rupture, crumbling, fragmentation, and most obviously, percussive impact. . . . The fissures of a cracking political or social geography spread much quicker and farther than contact itself does, because disruption—contingent in duration and space—occurs in a wide and irregular starburst around the most contested territories."[68]

The shattering effects of the struggle for Milan between France, Spain, and the Sforza dynasty backed by the emperor had an impact throughout the peninsula, resulting in the violent and bloody unmaking of more than one community in which Leonardo attempted to live and work, and he was forced by circumstances to channel his talents and energies as a military engineer into the process of this unmaking. His records of his participation in the murderous campaigns of Cesare Borgia in Romagna and the Marches—beyond a celebrated map of Imola and a notebook of sketches and plans of fortifications—are copious but laconic. In addition to comments on fortifications, windows, and vaults, he notes the technologies of local farmers for carrying grapes and building carts, and how shepherds amplified the sound of horns using cave acoustics. There is one very rare moment of exasperation: the Romagna, he writes, is "capo d'ogni grossezza d'ingegno" (the chief realm of all thickened wits).[69]

Even more scarce are traces of Leonardo's participation in the military operations aimed at securing Milan for the French king; Leonardo toured the frontiers, making maps and inspecting fortifications. A substantive picture is lacking, because among these infrastructural casualties would have been the administrative archives of the Milanese state itself, partly destroyed before and during the French exit from Milan in 1512, and with further massive losses during the Allied bombings of 1943. On the other hand, as with Cesare Borgia, the actions of some of Leonardo's powerful associates leave a disturbing record.

The so-called Ligny Memorandum is probably from 1499: the tone, despite references to turnips, lily seed, and "garlic of Piacenza," and the self-exhortation to learn pastel technique from the French artist Jean Perréal, has a notable urgency: "Find [Count Louis de] Ligny and tell him that you will wait for him at Rome and will go with him to Naples. Have the donations paid and take the book by Witelo and the measurements of the public building. . . . Get from Giovanni Lombardo the [dimensions of the?] theatre of Verona. . . . Buy handkerchiefs and towels, hats and shoes, four pair of hose, a jerkin of chamois and skin to make new ones. Sell what you cannot take with you."[70]

The French royal chamberlain Louis de Ligny, with whom Leonardo here plans a rendezvous in Rome and Naples, was enfeuded by the French king with the territories of Bobbio and Voghera, confiscated from the Dal Verme family. In 1500, as punishment for ongoing loyalty to these Sforza partisans, Ligny's troops demolished the walls and castle of Bobbio and murdered two hundred Dal Verme supporters. Voghera was subjected to a crippling fine that necessitated the selling-off of municipal property to private buyers and debilitated its economy.[71] Ligny then created a sumptuous private residence in the castle of Voghera, professing his devotion to the liberal arts with serene frescoes of the nine Muses commissioned from the major Milanese artist Bramantino.

One of the reasons that Leonardo's career—and I would say, his very persona—appears so incoherent is because of the successive collapse of a series of regimes in which he had assumed an array of official roles: the state of the Sforza in Milan, that of the Borgias in Rome and central Italy, that of the Florentine Republic that replaced the Medici oligarchy between 1494 and 1512, that of the French crown in Lombardy, and that of his prematurely deceased Medici protector Giuliano, brother of Pope Leo X, who was trying to form a state of his own within the states of the church. Leonardo had little stability of habitation or employment; the apparatus of clientage was haphazard and unreliable. His projects came to nothing, in large part because they were broken off during political crises, or there was barely time for them to evolve beyond the drafting stage.

Think by contrast of Raphael. His career and private life are no better documented than Leonardo, but there is an illusion of greater familiarity and intelligibility because he is so intensively identified with the court society of papal Rome, whose image-maker he became with the spectacular history paintings, abounding in portraits of contemporaries, with which he adorned the Vatican apartments of Julius II and Leo X. Among scores of likenesses, the artist included his own, more than once, testimony to his standing as "insider" and enabler. The agonistic personality of Michelangelo also adapted itself to political and institutional tension—that between Florence and the papacy in the 1500s, and then from the 1530s between the post-Medici papacy and the new dynastic rule of the Medici in Florence. This was the *agon* of Michelangelo and it shaped rather than shattered his career.[72]

And yet in Leonardo's case, there is more. What does it mean that Leonardo—an artist so attentive to the body as a "marvelous machine of nature"—tells us nothing about his own, and probably never even drew his own portrait? It is from later sources that we learn about his fastidious attention to his appearance, his strength and physical prowess, his good looks and charisma, and his ill health late in life. Leonardo's restraint here is an absence that tells us something—his disembodied voice, his seeming paucity of personal memory, is in fact fundamental to Leonardo as a historical phenomenon.

We will return to the reticent and disembodied character of Leonardo in a later chapter. First, we need to understand how biographers compensate for such absences. I will turn to some characteristic themes repeated in modern accounts of Leonardo's life: key elements of the imaginary psychology through which modern biographers have tried to suture gaps in the notebooks, the works, and the tumult of historical events. In the main, these are inferences based on fragmentary information that repetition has turned into fact, especially when they enable the artist to be cast as an anticipation of modern traits and dispositions.

SEXUAL "SECRETS"

Of the few known facts about Leonardo's early life is the April 1476 denunciation of the twenty-three-year-old artist, along with three other individuals, for the crime of sodomy with a seventeen-year-old goldsmith named Jacopo Saltarelli. The documents were published in 1896, and arguably no other publication—even the engraved and much reproduced compendium of Leonardo drawings by Carlo Giuseppe Gerli first published in 1784, or the edition of his writings by Charles Ravaisson-Mollien from a century later—has had as significant an impact on popular and learned perceptions of the artist over the following century and beyond.[73] Since Sigmund Freud made this evidence into the foundation of his psychoanalytic study of Leonardo's "life and art" in 1910, the prosecution (from which all four accused were acquitted) has become the psychological master-key to Leonardo. It supposedly explains his lifelong bachelorhood, despite the fact that this was something Leonardo shared with some of the leading Florentine artists of the 1400s, including Masaccio, Brunelleschi, Donatello, Leon Battista Alberti, Verrocchio, Piero Pollaiuolo, Mino da Fiesole, Lorenzo di Credi, Piero di Cosimo, and Botticelli. It is believed to account for his apparent gravitation toward handsome young males, two in particular of whom were singled out insinuatingly by Vasari, who comments on their physical appeal.

One was the Milanese Gian Giacomo Caprotti, the infamous Salaì (or Salaino), nicknamed after the Ayyubid sultan Saladin, or perhaps after a devil who appears in Book XXI of Luigi Pulci's comic epic *Morgante* (Leonardo had the book in his library).[74] Salaì joined Leonardo's Milanese household in 1490 at the age of ten—probably as an apprentice. Leonardo's followers Marco d'Oggiono and Giovan Antonio Boltraffio may or may not have been apprentices, but we know of their presence in Leonardo's workshop in 1491 precisely because the artist recorded Salaì's theft of Marco's pen and Giovanni's silverpoint in the detailed list of the child's many misdemeanors already referred to. In an untypically personal outburst, Leonardo wrote in the margins the words "thief," "liar," "stubborn," "glutton."

The unruly Salaì stayed with Leonardo for nearly thirty years and learned to be a painter of some ability; he inherited part of Leonardo's estate, married in 1523, and was killed in a duel the following year. Salaì's relations with Leonardo provoked prurient comment, although many years after Leonardo's death. Vasari says that Salaì was taken on as a protégé (*creato*), and that Leonardo delighted in his beautiful hair. A later set of fictional dialogues by the painter/author Gian Paolo Lomazzo has the ghost of Leonardo admitting to engaging in the "game of the backside,

that Florentines like so much," with Salaì "because he was a very comely
young man around the age of fifteen." The same text, known as the *Sogni*
(dreams), also has Leonardo giving an elaborate eulogy of *amore masculine* (homosexuality) as a pastime worthy of philosophical minds and as
resembling the liberal arts because of its gratuitous character, its superflu-
ity to the necessities of existence.[75] In another of the *Sogni*, Leonardo's
heterosexual infatuation with a Milanese woman named Drusilla leads
to a lovelorn flight, a sea voyage, a shipwreck in the Levant, and his fam-
ished consumption of local fruit that transitions him temporarily into
a woman.[76] Biographers citing Lomazzo refer only to Leonardo owning
up to pederastic relations with his apprentice, since it fits the biographical agenda, and make no mention of Lomazzo's fantastical and patently
defamatory fictionalizations.

Throughout his life Leonardo drew numerous youthful and androgynous figures with curly hair, and although these are mostly quite generic,
they have inevitably been identified as portraits of Salaì (plate 22). A notorious verso in the Codex Atlanticus (132v and 133v), concealed until the
sheet was unglued during conservation in 1961, bears a crude drawing,
probably by a teenage apprentice, of two phalluses and a hole inscribed
"Salaì." Such marginalia have served Carlo Pedretti with the rationale for
identifying the ithyphallic, at least partly forged "Angel Incarnate" as a portrait of Salaì by Leonardo, a possibility that has convinced few Leonardo
specialists, although the claim is routinely repeated in recent Leonardo
biographies.[77]

The other was Francesco Melzi, who inherited Leonardo's vast archive
of notes and drawings, and would labor for years to prepare Leonardo's
draft treatise on painting for publication. It is often asserted, in the absence
of any corroborating information whatsoever, that Melzi, who joined
Leonardo's household as a teenager around 1506–8, was the elderly artist's lover.[78] The allegation appears to depend on an overzealous reading of
Vasari, who asserted in 1568 that the aristocratic Melzi "was a very beautiful youth and much loved by [Leonardo], just as now he is a beautiful and
courteous old man." Melzi wrote in heartfelt terms to inform Leonardo's
relatives of his teacher's death in 1519, but using expressions of devotion
conventional for intergenerational friendships: "He was like the best of

fathers to me. As long as I have breath in my body I shall feel the sadness, for all time. He gave me every day the proofs of his most passionate and ardent affection."[79]

It is entirely *probable* that Leonardo, just like other unmarried Florentine artists—Donatello, Botticelli, Michelangelo—engaged in sexual relations with younger males; Botticelli was denounced in 1502 for "keeping a boy." The leading artist of Venice, Giovanni Bellini (who was married), was complimented by a humanist poet for the beauty of his adolescent lover around the same time.[80] Working alongside Raphael and Leonardo in Rome was the painter Giovanni Antonio Bazzi from Vercelli, better known by his nickname "Il Sodoma." And the goldsmith and sculptor Benvenuto Cellini, a few generations younger than Leonardo, was sexually omnivorous, as well as predatory and violent. Cellini writes more than once in his life history about beautiful young assistants and models, one of whom—Paolino—he "loved to distraction." While Cellini shrugs off two accusations of sodomy as mere slander, he does not mention his two convictions for the same crime. Still in Florence, the painter-poet Agnolo Bronzino, and a generation later Giovanni di San Giovanni, specialized in a subaltern literary mode characterized by colorful sodomitical double entendres. For the artistic community especially in Florence by the 1500s, homosexual behavior or posturing was a recognized trait of a liminal social identity. If not exactly outsiders, artists were in a placeless "in-between," with regard to mechanical craft cultures, non-noble elites (although Giovanni secured a patent of nobility), and the intelligentsia.

Given the politically embattled circumstances of sexual minorities even in modern democracies, it is important to recognize the past visibility of same-sex sexual behaviors. Renaissance art history has historically been a prudish field, one in which a famous scholar—whose homosexuality was widely known if never openly avowed—could write, in 1990, that homoerotic interpretations of Donatello's sensuous nude bronze David "left a trail of slime on a great work of art."[81] Historians increasingly recognize that premodern urban cultures need to be understood in terms of male social and sexual exchanges, usually intergenerational and not exclusive of heterosexual relations and marriage by the participants. There is little evidence that anyone moving in and out of these sexual subcultures embraced anything that might correspond to a modern sexual identity.

One historian writes that in premodern Europe, "Christianity clearly condemned the practice of sodomy, but this did not change the nature of male desire. It was still presumed that both women and adolescent males were sexually passive and that men desired both."[82] Michael Rocke's research on the policing of sex between males in Florence, based on records of the magistracy known as the Officers of the Night and its operations during the period 1459–1502, indicates that "by the time that they reached the age of thirty, at least one out of every two youths in the city of Florence had been formally implicated in sodomy to this court alone; by age of forty, at least two of every three men had been incriminated."[83] (Evidence from other centers—Venice, Bologna, Lucca—indicates lower levels of prosecution: there is some controversy as to whether that indicates lower levels of activity or whether the data indicates something distinctive about the structure of male relations in Florence.)[84]

In Florence, penalties—mainly in the form of a fine—were relatively light, in order to encourage denunciations, and denouncers were usually granted immunity. Thus, Florence attempted to deal with circumstances endemic to its male culture, the so-called "Florentine vice" (another name for Lomazzo's Florentine "game") that brought the city notoriety throughout Europe. The well-preserved and detailed records of prosecutions for sodomy, and more anecdotal information from sources like the letters of Machiavelli, reveal that homosexual behavior involving adolescents and older men was widespread, an accepted fact of life if not exactly approved of.[85] Leonardo in this respect seems like a typical Florentine rather than a sexual outlier. It is a distortion when evidence is picked over to establish the anachronistic profile of either a discreet or closeted pre-Stonewall homosexual, who compulsively depicted the face and body of his lover(s); or the stereotype of a flamboyant one, fussing over his appearance and favoring rose-colored garments.

A single passing reference to Leonardo's *pitocco rosato* in the *Anonimo Gaddiano*—a form of dress that the author saw as noteworthy because it was "short to the knee, although long garments were then in fashion"—has served as the basis for speculative accounts of the artist's public persona, his extravagantly stylish self-fashioning. For one recent biographer, it shows that Leonardo "was tailor made for a Florence that had rebelled against Savonarola's bonfire of the vanities, and was again willing to embrace flamboyant, eccentric, and artistic free spirits."[86] We have no evidence, however, that Florence ca. 1500 was the moment to which the *Anonimo* is referring.

In the 1860s Jules Michelet was so carried away by Leonardo's pink tunic that he imagined the artist revolutionizing the couture of the French court.[87] Yet, if there was anything transgressive about Leonardo's rose-colored outfit it was its defiance of social categories. Cloth dyed in hues of red or crimson, referred to as *rubeo, rosso, rosato, grana, cremisino, vermiglio,* or *cardinalizio,* was a rarefied luxury, restricted by sumptuary laws to the upper classes during the 1400s. As the preacher Fra Bernardino da Siena thundered, "There is no one, of however little worth, who doesn't crave the scarlet, the purple or the pink."[88] In his *Florentine Histories* Machiavelli reported a complaint of Cosimo de' Medici: "two lengths of pink cloth can make a man of means [*due canne di panno rosato facevano uno uomo da bene*]."[89] We have seen that Leonardo spent lavishly to dress Salaì in stockings and surcoats of rose and purple, colors that occur in portraits of sumptuously clad members of the North Italian elite.[90]

Another example of such archival cherry-picking, which seeks to gratify a desire for a flesh-and-blood *biographical* Leonardo, is the cluster of pseudo-facts (and female nudes identified as portraits) that have clustered around the word *chermonese* in a list of names including those of Salaì, possibly Melzi, and the *garzone* Lorenzo on a sheet in Windsor. In 2004 a biographer connected this *chermonese* (to be read as *cremonese,* that is, a "person from Cremona") with an allegation based on an undisclosed source in an unpublished essay by Giuseppe Bossi, whom we encountered in chapter 1 as the maker of an influential copy of *The Last Supper* in the 1800s: "That Leonardo . . . loved the pleasures of life is proved by a note of his concerning a courtesan called Cremona, a note which was communicated to me by an authoritative source."[91] No such source has ever come to light, but needless to say the conjectures it has given rise to have sustained a more media-friendly production of Leonardo in a television drama series released in 2021. It is singularly difficult to identify any significant female presence in the Leonardo network or in his archive.

There is one reference to homosexual activity in all of Leonardo's writings—and it concerns the omnivorous sexual habits of bats.[92] Denialists have pointed to the lack of evidence of the artist's sexual life in his writings as an indication of a lifetime of celibacy, or even—following Freud—as signaling his aversion to sex: "The act of coitus and the parts employed therein are so repulsive that if it were not for the beauty of the faces and the adornments of the actions and the frantic state of mind, nature would lose the human species."[93] Yet this absence or aversion points to a more general lack of reference to physical and affective experience in his writings—no records of illness, of aging, of grieving, of anger, of pleasure. Such omission presents a contrast with the relative frankness of contemporaries about sexual and other bodily matters, notably Michelangelo, who openly engaged with homoerotic themes in his poetry and who wrote graphically about his melancholy, kidney stones, constipation, and physical disfigurement by age and by labor.

The point is not at all to deny or preclude a preference for sexual relations with other males: it is that disputing this on the basis of so little information distracts from a more important issue—that the aesthetic force of Leonardo's art lies in the powerful erotic relationalities it generates in the responses of other artists and with its implied beholders (we will discuss this further in chapter 5). If we find a work like the Louvre *St. John* (see plate 5) to have a queer or homoerotic dimension—which commentators did well before Freud—that is not because it is a personal manifesto or a symptom betraying itself. Such a work tells us as much, if not more, about Leonardo's audience or "public" as it does about Leonardo. Young male bodies, nude or adorned with physically expressive fashions, were sites of visual pleasure that appealed to premodern viewers. While such sensuous male nudes are rare in Leonardo's oeuvre (by comparison with Michelangelo's), they are prevalent in the paintings and drawings of Raphael, whose early biographies abound with the trope of the artist's ardent and possibly self-destructive love of women. That this most heterosexual of artists could confidently render the beauty and allure of ephebic male bodies is an indication that eroticism in premodern art primarily concerns the engagement of the viewer: it may or may not reflect the sexual life of its makers.

LEONARDO AND GOD

The same goes for matters of faith. How much biographical weight can be placed on what is *not* said? It is noteworthy that for an artist whose work mainly consisted of images of Christ and the Virgin Mary, Leonardo in his writings shows little concern with the meaning or function of religious images. His account of the Last Supper is a mechanical list of bodily motions and expressions: "One who was drinking has left his glass in its place and turned his head towards the speaker. Another wrings the fingers of his hands turns with a frown to his companion. Another with hands spread open to show the palms shrugs his shoulders up to his ears, and mouths astonishment."[94] And yet we have seen that in the case of the *Cenacolo* in Milan, Leonardo has intensely meditated on the theology of the Eucharist and the Passion, and sought the most effective means of conveying it through the mechanics of force—a relationship between what he would call *moto spirituale* and *moto materiale*: the motion and power of a primary force—a perturbing utterance (Christ's words, their impact on his hearers), and a derivative force (the expressions and gestures of the Apostles).

In his writings on the brain, on the mind or animating spirit, Leonardo kept his distance from theology—whether from skepticism, or from caution, it is hard to say. While in his skull studies of 1489 he sought to locate the place of the soul in the geometric center of the brain, by the time of his later anatomy studies around 1513 he tersely distinguished his use of the word "soul" as a strictly neurobiological and not a metaphysical entity: "the soul of the fetus at first remains asleep under the guardianship of the soul of the mother who nourishes and vitalizes it through the umbilical vein with all its spiritual members." And written below: "This discourse does not belong here, but is necessary for the composition of animal bodies—and the rest of the definition of the soul I leave to the minds of friars [*fratj*], fathers of peoples [*padri de popoli*]." Given the context of human generation, it is possible to see a vein of scathing anticlerical satire here—that priests are not so much spiritual "fathers of the people" as literal, fornicating "fathers" of people.[95]

Scripture is never invoked, except when—as in his writings on geomorphology—he contrasts his account of the Earth's history with the biblical account of the Flood: such arguments, he writes, require "miracles" in order to work, and are thus to be discounted.[96]

Sometimes, Leonardo writes vehemently and fancifully of other religions, like Islam and Hinduism, and in ways that have confounded scholars of premodern cultural transmission. For instance, following a tirade against cannibalism (to be discussed later in this chapter), on a sheet with drawings of a sectioned human heart from around 1511, he writes:

> And if any [person] be found virtuous and good drive them not away from you but do them honor lest they flee from you and take refuge in your deceits. If any such be found pay him reverence, for as these are as gods upon earth they deserve statues, images and honors. But I would impress upon you that their images are not to be eaten by you, as happens in a certain district of India: for there, when in the judgment of the priests these images have worked some miracle, they cut them in pieces being of wood and distribute them to all the people of the locality—not without payment. And each of them then grates his portion very fine and spreads it over the first food he eats; and so they consider that symbolically by faith they have eaten their holy one, and they believe that he will then guard them from all dangers. What think you Man! Of your species? Are you as wise as you set yourself up to be?[97]

A man of virtue, who deserves to be celebrated and memorialized, becomes the object of a Eucharistic cult whose images, deemed miraculous, are eaten by the faithful. It can't be ruled out that Leonardo had heard apocryphal stories about Hindu religious practice, or even reports about iconophagy (eating pieces of holy icon) among the devout in the Byzantine world, but it seems equally probable that he is adopting an oblique and satirical perspective on the Christian rites of the Eucharist, as he would do (also obliquely) in his pseudo-prophecies: "Then almost all the tabernacles where dwells the Corpus Domini will be plainly seen walking about by themselves on the various roads of the world. [Of priests who bear the Host in their bodies]."[98]

"In no accepted sense can Leonardo be called a Christian," wrote Kenneth Clark, sustaining a secularist vision of Leonardo that had emerged with Goethe, Michelet, and Taine a century before (a view that persists). "He was not even a religious minded man."[99] Yet the pre-Reformation world could sustain a wide spectrum of understandings, among individuals and communities, as to what it meant to be a Christian or to be religious. It is not at all clear that the majority of premodern Europeans (including the clergy) would have been attentive to contradictions between inner convictions and beliefs and conventional outward observances—a circumstance that would change radically in the decades after Leonardo's death.

Clark took some of Leonardo's pseudo-prophecies and riddles as a sign that he was "among the precursors of the Reformation": "Of the worshipping of pictures of the saints: Men will speak to men who hear not . . . they will implore favors from those who have ears and hear not; they will make a light for the blind." Some recent writers maintain the same view.[100] Gombrich, more judiciously, held back from ascribing agnosticism or an explicitly reformist mentality to Leonardo. The "prophecies," he writes, demonstrate "the power of words and the need for rational man to rid himself of the mental habits due to ordinary language." Gombrich finds a similar "detachment" in Leonardo's unconventional designs for church interiors with their "notorious" captions *logo dove si predica* (place for preaching) and *teatri per udire messa* (theaters for hearing Mass).[101]

In such passages Leonardo assumes a skeptical distance from popular religious observances of ordinary people, a point of view he shared with some of the critical minds of his time—among them Alberti, Giovanni Pontano, and Erasmus, who ridiculed popular cults of miracle images and relics while being observant themselves (Alberti was in minor religious orders, Erasmus deeply committed to the institutional reform of the church).[102] The reverence and awe that religious images could inspire served Leonardo well when he wanted to demonstrate the power of painting over language: "Do we not see pictures representing the divine beings constantly kept under coverlets of the greatest price? And whenever they are unveiled there is first great ecclesiastical solemnity with much hymn singing, and then at the moment of the unveiling the great multitude of peoples who have gathered there immediately throw themselves to the ground, worshipping and praying to the deity, who is represented in the picture, for the repairing of their lost health and for their eternal salvation, as if this goddess were there as a living presence."[103]

His attitude here resembles that of the first-century poet-philosopher Lucretius, whose poem *On the Nature of Things* was drawing controversy and avid attention in the late 1400s.[104] Lucretius taught that nature operated through the movement of atoms, without purposes of its own or in fulfillment of a divine plan; gods might exist but in an atom-like fashion, beyond care for mortal affairs; there was thus no afterlife, and the soul died along with the body. Lucretius also regarded the worship of gods in the form of images through a psychology of ritual. In book II (589–661) Lucretius writes of the frenzied devotees of the Magna Mater, the mother goddess Cybele, as the image is carried in procession: "And they have surrounded the top of Cybele's head with a mural crown, because embattled in excellent positions she sustains cities; which emblem now endows the divine Mother's image as she is carried over the great earth in awful state. . . . The tight drums thunder under the open palm, the hollow cymbals sound around, with hoarse echoing blare affright, hollow pipes prick up the spirits with their Phrygian cadences, martial arms show a front of violent fury, that they may amaze the ungrateful minds and impious hearts of the vulgar with fear through the goddess's majesty."[105]

Lucretius intended his sublime philosophical verse to deliver his readers from irrational fears propagated by religious superstition. Lucretian vocabulary and ideas, even a couple of quotations, surface occasionally in Leonardo's writing. He refers, for instance, to the Earth as the *macchina della terra*, which corresponds to Lucretius's *machina mundi* (V, 96).[106] Leonardo shared with Lucretius a vision of the ultimate decay of fertile nature and of human extinction, which seems soberingly resonant with our present: "the rivers will be deprived of their waters, the fruitful earth will put forth no more her light verdure . . . all the animals, finding no fresh grass for pasture, will die and food will then be lacking to the lions and wolves and other beasts of prey, and to men who after many efforts will be compelled to abandon their life, and the human race will die out. In this way the fertile and fruitful earth will remain deserted, arid and sterile from the water being shut up in its interior."[107] Here, Leonardo's conception of earth as an aging and infertile mother echoes the imagery in book II of *De rerum natura* where Lucretius writes of "the exhausted earth [who] scarce produces tiny creatures, she who once produced all kinds and gave birth to the huge bodies of wild beasts" (1150–52), or a similar passage in book V, "[earth] ceased to give birth, like a woman worn out by old age" (826). He may have known of these Lucretian themes only at secondhand, and he is not in any way consistently an Epicurean: he had little time for the doctrine of atomism, for instance. However, as a materialist in his view of nature, he adopted a nonsectarian "philosophical" attitude or demeanor, which distinguished itself from the received doctrines of Christianity or any form of metaphysical explanation. Mathematics and the mechanics of force and motion were his core principles (and here he certainly differs from Lucretius).

Leonardo's concern with the hidden causes of nature's perceivable operations requires a "creator," evoked many times in his writings, or a "First Mover." When in his writings Leonardo evokes a higher animating principle underlying the cosmos, this often suggests an allegorical personified Nature, but just as frequently there are references to "God" and "Heaven." In his writings on perspective, we find: "If the Lord—who is the light of all things—vouchsafe to enlighten me, I will treat of Light; wherefore I will divide the present work into three Parts: Linear Perspective, The Perspective of Colour, The Perspective of Disappearance." It is impossible to distinguish here between a profession of faith and a rhetorical means of connecting with an audience—in this case identified as "young painters." Yet there is something more than commonplace evocations of "the Creator" at work in another passage addressed to young painters, asserting the right of the painter to work on feast days: "For painting is the way to learn to know the maker of all marvelous things—and this is the way to love so great an inventor. For in truth great love springs from the full knowledge of the thing that one loves; and if you do not know it you can love it but little or not at all. And if you love Him for the sake of the good benefits that you expect to obtain from Him, you are like the dog wagging its tail, welcoming and jumping up at the man who may give him a bone. But if the dog knew and would be capable of understanding the virtue of this man how much greater would be his love!"[108] There is much to comment on here: Leonardo's habit of analogical thinking, resulting in a startling shift of perspective (and probably intentional satire), a tendency to call into question the boundaries between human and nonhuman animals, and most importantly a conception of popular as opposed to learned religious belief.

There are a few further clues that, whatever his attitude to divinity, Leonardo distanced himself from the beliefs and practices of ordinary people, which, like learned contemporaries, he regarded as superstitious and naive. Yet in the era before the Catholic Reformation, when orthodoxy in belief and behavior was rigorously prescribed and enforced, there was a wide latitude in what religious observance could entail.[109]

Biographies of Leonardo tend to conclude with the artist's will as a final profession of orthodoxy—he "commends his soul to our Lord, Almighty God, and to the glorious Virgin Mary, and to our Lord Saint Michael, to all blessed angels and Saints male and female in Paradise," and makes provision for his burial in the church of St. Florentin at Amboise, a funeral procession with sixty taper-bearing paupers, and an endowment "for the saying of three high masses and thirty low masses in his memory; for the distribution of 40 pounds of wax in thick candles to be placed in the churches where the masses were celebrated."[110] So, too, Leonardo's brief involvement with the Florentine confraternity of the Pietà in Rome in 1514 has been taken as a manifestation of spiritual needs late in life, because the organization provided medical care as well as care of the soul, in addition to funerary offices and a place of burial.[111]

However, when Melzi reported to Leonardo's brothers that his teacher had passed from his earthly life "with all the sacraments of holy Mother Church, and [was] well-disposed to receive them," it is hard to resist the sense that the disciple is trying to counter a different impression: that Leonardo was not regarded as someone who would be well-disposed to the sacraments of the church.

By 1550, when Vasari wrote his first life of Leonardo and the self-reforming, increasingly paranoid, and authoritarian church was concerned to set limits to orthodox belief and observance, "philosopher" was increasingly suspect as a social identity, now identified with risky pagan beliefs and free-thinking outside the teachings of the Church. The doctrines of Lucretius on the mortality of the soul had been condemned at a papal synod in 1513. It was Vasari who bequeathed the image of the atheist Leonardo to the nineteenth-century Romantic cult of the Faustian seeker of truth, and thence to Kenneth Clark and more recent commentators. Early in Vasari's first version of the life of Leonardo we find: "And so many were his caprices, that, philosophizing of natural things [*de le cose naturali*], he set himself to seek out the properties of herbs, going on even to observe the motions of the heavens, the path of the moon, and the courses of the sun. Leonardo formed in his mind a conception so heretical as not to approach any religion whatsoever: perhaps he esteemed being a philosopher much more than being a Christian."[112] It may not be a coincidence that *de le cose naturali* corresponds to the Latin *de rerum natura*, the title of Lucretius's poem.[113]

Vasari went on to report that in the last few months of his life Leonardo returned to the study of the Catholic faith, but with his second edition of the lives in 1568, at a moment when the Medici rulers of Florence reversed their protection of some religious nonconformists, he omitted the passage about Leonardo's heresy. It is possible that Melzi, the curator of Leonardo's legacy in the ultra-orthodox Milan of Archbishop Carlo Borromeo, the loyal disciple Vasari met in 1566, persuaded him to delete the controversial lines.

HUMANISM, HUMANS, AND NONHUMANITY

The same goes for the received idea of Leonardo the vegetarian (which has recently given rise to the internet cult of a "vegan Leonardo"). It is *possible* that Leonardo followed a vegetarian diet, as some contemporary Christian ascetics did, and many religious orders did during Advent and Lent ("Franciscan friars," Leonardo notes in one of his comic tales, "are wont, at certain times, to keep fasts, when they do not eat meat in their convents. But on journeys, as they live on charity, they have license to eat whatever is set before them").[114] But the evidence is slender: a 1516 letter by a contemporary Florentine Andrea Corsali, reporting to Giuliano de'Medici on a voyage to India: "The territory of Cambay is inhabited by certain infidels called Guzzarati [Gujarati, i.e., Hindus]. They are great merchants. . . . They are so gentle that they do not feed on anything which has blood, nor will they allow anyone to hurt any living thing, like our Leonardo da Vinci."[115] There is no categorical attestation of Leonardo's vegetarianism here: at best Corsali is attesting to hearsay about the artist's aversion to hurting living things. Vasari, writing decades later, seems to offer confirmation with his famous story of Leonardo buying caged birds in order to free them—but he makes no mention of vegetarianism. Leonardo and Corsali shared a common patron in Giuliano, but it is not certain that they knew each other (or, indeed, if Corsali knew of Leonardo's recent employment by the violently homicidal warlord Cesare Borgia, his scheme to drown the population of the Maremma during the war with Pisa, or his designs for cannons, exploding shells, and war chariots with scythes for severing the limbs of enemy combatants). What Corsali and Vasari have in common is the image of the Indian philosopher generated by a convergence of European eyewitnesses and classical sources that connected Pythagoras—the archetypal ancient philosopher and most famous exemplar of vegetarianism—with the "Indian sages" known as Gymnosophists, or "naked philosophers." Reports of Brahmans buying captive animals in order to free them began to circulate from around 1516, when the practice was recorded by the Portuguese Duarte Barbosa. His countryman Diego de Orta, in his *Colóquios dos simples e drogas he cousas medicinais da Índia*, published in Goa in 1563, states that the Brahman "Pythagoreans" purchased and released caged birds at the markets.[116] Vasari was conflating accounts like these with notions of the would-be Pythagorean philosopher he associated with Leonardo.

It has been noted that in the relatively detailed household accounts from between 1498 and 1504, the largest expenditures are for meat and wine.[117] If Leonardo observed a vegetarian diet for humanitarian reasons, he did not expect his household to follow suit.

In his "prophecies," Leonardo inveighs against the brutality of human beings as a species and writes of animal slaughter as atrocity: "Endless multitudes of these [cattle] will have their little children taken from them ripped open and flayed and most barbarously quartered." (Leonardo here and elsewhere drew on Ovid's account of the philosopher Pythagoras and his prohibitions of animal slaughter. However, there is additionally an evocation of Lucretius II.352–65, where a slaughtered calf is mourned by its mother.) And in another, captioned "Of human cruelty," "There will be no bounds to their malice; by their strong limbs a great portion of the trees in the vast forests of the world shall be laid low; and when they are filled with food the gratification of their desire shall be to deal out death, affliction, labor, terror, and banishment to every living thing; and from their boundless pride they will desire to rise towards heaven, but the excessive weight of their limbs will hold them down. Nothing shall remain on the earth, or under the earth, or in the waters that shall not be pursued, disturbed, or spoiled, and that which is in one country removed into another. And their bodies shall be made the tomb and the means of transit of all the living bodies which they have slain." (Again, an echo of Lucretius, who in V.991–93 portrays creatures becoming tombs for other creatures.) The reference to the desire for flight here is probably an ironic self-implication. And sometimes his scientific curiosity could overtake such humane scruples: "The frog dies instantly when its spinal medulla is perforated. And previously it lived without head, without heart or any interior organs, or intestines or skin. Here therefore it appears lies the foundation of movement and life."[118]

Leonardo, who investigated the comparative anatomy of humans and nonhuman animals, cast this *paragone* in more somber and moralizing terms, as in the following declamation on the bestial nature of man, written on the same sheet of drawings of a sectioned human heart referred to above: "King of the animals, as you have described him—I should say rather king of the beasts, you being the greatest—because you only help [animals], in order that they may give you their children for the benefit of your gullet, which you have attempted to make a sepulcher of all animals." He continues with a disturbing invective against the practice of cannibalism by human beings. Certain animals like "leopards, panthers, lynxes, cats, and the like" sometimes eat their children, "but you, besides the children, devour father, mother, brothers, and friends; nor is this enough for you, but you go hunting on the islands of others, taking other men and mutilating their members and their testicles, you make them fat and chase them down your own throat."[119] What could Leonardo possibly be referring to here?

The passage has been taken as a precociously anticolonialist protest by Leonardo in the wake of Columbus's voyages, when in fact it is a paraphrase of the Florentine explorer Amerigo Vespucci's lurid account of the dietary habits of the inhabitants of the Canary Islands, in his *Mundus Novus* of 1503.[120] Vespucci, whom Leonardo may have personally known, described having witnessed the indigenous people eating their own children and feasting on the flesh of enemies, and "in a certain city, where I stayed twenty seven days," he saw human flesh being smoked and salted "just as we hang up boar meat and especially sausages to dry out in the sun or the smoke."[121]

The passage, if it indicates anything, is about the shock of cultural encounter and—as with the dog/man = man/God analogy discussed above—a move seemingly calculated to dislocate the reader from complacent notions of the human. It is another of Leonardo's deliberately jolting shifts in perspective, an instance of his experimentation with the resources of language to create shifts in awareness. To complicate things further, Leonardo continues: "now does not nature produce enough simples for you to satisfy yourself? And if you are not content with simples, can't you create infinite compounds by mixing them, as Platina wrote, and other authors on feeding?" Who is Leonardo now addressing? Is it his Italian readers, or his Italian readers "as if" they were humankind in a primitive state, amply provided by nature with the means of its survival? Bartolomeo Platina's *De honesta voluptate et valetudine*, published in 1487, was in Leonardo's library. Far from being a manual of "natural diet" or vegetarianism, it is a philosophical defense of the pleasures of eating with moderation. While it includes recipes for vegetable dishes, it also has chapters on raising, slaughtering, and cooking beef, goat, and other animals.[122]

Several elements of the passage quoted suggest that Leonardo is drawing on Juvenal's 15th Satire, which following a lurid depiction of cannibalism among peoples of North Africa, with once again a nod to Pythagoras: "But in these days there is more amity among serpents than among men; wild beasts are merciful to beasts spotted like themselves." Lions, boars, tigers, and bears are merciful to weaker members of their own species, but "we now behold a people whose wrath is not assuaged by slaying someone, but who deem that a man's breast, arms, and face afford a kind of food. What would Pythagoras say, or to what place would he not flee, if he beheld these horrors of today,—he who refrained from every living creature as if it were human, and would not indulge his belly with every kind of vegetable?"

With "other authors on feeding," Leonardo might be referring to one of his favorite sources, the *Natural History* of Pliny the Elder, a standard source of information on "simples"—that is, plants beneficial to health. Pliny's reputation had tarnished somewhat by 1500, as humanists who read the Greek medical corpus—some actively involved in medicine— pointed to the unreliable and outrightly fanciful nature of many passages. Book XXVIII has spine-chilling passages criticizing medical remedies that employ human blood, brain tissue, or other body parts: "Epileptic patients are in the habit of drinking the blood even of gladiators, draughts teeming with life, as it were; a thing that, when we see it done by the wild beasts even, upon the same arena, inspires us with horror at the spectacle! And yet these persons, forsooth, consider it a most effectual cure for their disease, to quaff the warm, breathing, blood from man himself, and, as they apply their mouth to the wound, to draw forth his very life." Others seek cures in the marrow of the leg bones or the brains of infants. Certain Greek writers "have enlarged upon the distinctive flavors of each one of the viscera and members of the human body, pursuing their researches to the very parings of the nails! [It is as though] it could possibly be accounted the pursuit of health for man to make himself a wild beast, and so deserve to contract disease from the very remedies he adopts for avoiding it."

No one took this seriously in the Renaissance—or did they? Leonardo's older contemporary, the philosopher and philologist Marsilio Ficino, wrote a lifestyle manual called *On Life Lived in Harmony with the Stars*, in which he recommended that people "consumed by old age" might be regenerated through the ingestion of the blood of a youth. "A youth, I say, who is willing, healthy, happy and temperate, whose blood is of the best but perhaps too abundant. They will suck, therefore, like leeches, an ounce or two from a scarcely-opened vein of the left arm; they will immediately take an equal amount of sugar and wine. They will do this when hungry and thirsty and when the moon is waxing."[123]

The passage on cannibalism is an instance of Leonardo voicing a persona, employing rhetorical and other literary effects to produce a reaction in the reader (or listener, if the text was written, as some think, for oral performance). It is not a declaration of the ethics or health benefits of a vegetarian diet, which Leonardo never made, least of all regarding himself. The passage is a performance, on the order of the following lines in verse, mocking the poets who imitate Petrarch and his love lyrics to Laura: "If Petrarch loved the laurel so much, it was because it is good between sausage and thrush / I can't make a treasure from their stupid gush." Leonardo was not the original author of this terzina. It hardly matters—almost every passage from Leonardo quoted in this chapter is a borrowing or a citation from elsewhere: the terzina is the assumption of another persona, the channeling of yet another voice.[124] On the same sheet, aptly, appears seven grotesque profiles and a list of books—the grammar of Donatus, a lapidary, Pliny, a text called *Abacus*, and Luigi Pulci's mock epic *Il Morgante*.

The history of Leonardo as writer is the history of Leonardo as reader—of Leonardo in dialogue with multiple past voices, sometimes performing these voices, or adopting personae to address an imaginary antagonist in a debate. His modern biographers often accept such fictions at face value, leading them to fictionalize in turn. Each of the anachronistic identities assigned to Leonardo (gay, vegetarian, pro–animal rights, a religious agnostic) is supported only by excising Leonardo's works and pictures from their historical context, from refusing to see them as part of the dialogues in which he was enmeshed. Leonardo's own records of his many social encounters provides evidence that he conversed enthusiastically and widely, with social exchanges often involving the exchange of books.

So too, the little landscape drawing with which we began the chapter can also be seen as a pictorial conversation in a workshop, where Leonardo labors alongside other artists, or across Europe in its echoing of Netherlandish art. Da Vinci Worlds are made possible precisely by refusing to hear Leonardo's many interlocutors, both contemporaries and classical authorities, in order to reinforce the myth of solitary genius. We would be better-off ignoring the image of the silent, alienated loner and instead listening for the din of the workshop, the chatter of the marketplace, and the philosophical disputations resounding across the centuries.

Chapter 3

LEONARDO
AND THE
BIOGRAPHERS

In 1818, the young Jean-Auguste-Dominique Ingres painted *Francis I Receives the Last Breaths of Leonardo da Vinci*, based on Vasari's account of the unheard-of honors paid by a king to the dying artist (fig. 11): "his spirit, which was divine, knowing that it could not have any greater honor, expired in the arms of the King, in the seventy-fifth year of his age."[1] It was not the first time that the subject had been painted, but in 1818 it had a particular resonance with the resurgent Catholicism and monarchism of post-Revolutionary France: the work was made for Louis XVIII's ambassador to the Holy See.

Ingres sought to portray not just the Renaissance genius honored by France's great Renaissance king. Equally important to him and his client is Vasari's report that the painter "feeling himself near to death, asked to have himself diligently informed of the teaching of the Catholic faith, and of the good way and holy Christian religion; and then, with many moans, he confessed and was penitent."[2] Leonardo, in other words, for all his unorthodox philosophical beliefs, finally returned to the arms of the Church. The composition is framed by the figures of a kneeling Dominican confessor and a haughty cardinal, to whom Francesco Melzi appeals with a sense of urgency,

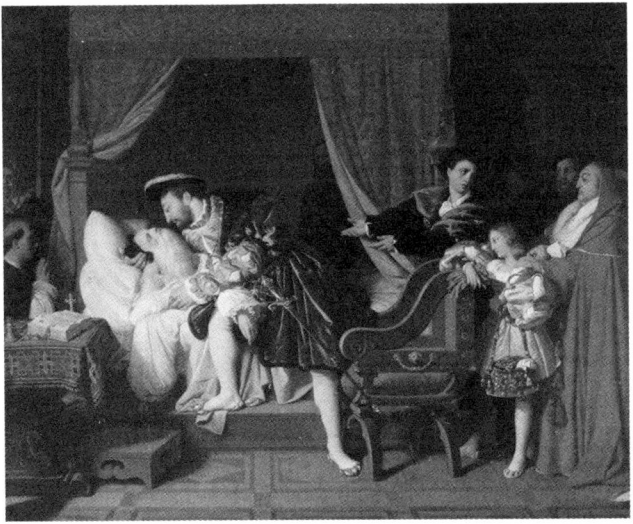

11. Jean-Auguste-Dominique Ingres, *Francis I Receives the Last Breaths of Leonardo da Vinci*. 1818. On canvas, 40 × 50.5 cm. Paris, Petit Palais.

as if appealing to the Church to take Leonardo back into its embrace. Of course, we can be amused in our more cynical age at the work's sentimental melodrama, and because we know better than Ingres (or his source, Vasari) that the king was absent from Amboise when Leonardo died there in 1519.[3]

Yet Ingres's public would already have known this—at least, some of them would have. As early as the 1790s, the historian of science Giovanni Battista Venturi published a short Leonardo biography in French showing that the episode reported by Vasari was apocryphal.[4] And the era of Romanticism, with its cult of the artist genius, was aware that its Leonardo was a fictive being, more lively as myth or symbol than as a historical person. "He died in the arms of a king," wrote the critic and novelist Théophile Gautier in 1867, "and if modern erudition doubts the truth of this legend, it is so fitting a crown to this happy and quiet life that everybody will certainly believe in it."[5]

"THESE ARE GODS, BUT SICK"

Leonardo, by then, was associated with other quasi-mythical characters through which Romanticism was inventing the Renaissance. For the historian Jules Michelet, to whom we owe the period term "Renaissance" itself, Leonardo was the prophet of a new order of defiant modernity, "the startling magician, the Italian brother of Faust, who astonishes and terrifies."[6] For the anti-Catholic historian Edgar Quinet, the *St. John* in the Louvre was a spiritual self-portrait of the artist as a Baptist-like harbinger of momentous change: he seemed to be pointing at "the vault of the heavens expanded by Galileo" or "the sail of Christopher Columbus's ship": "The religion of science, the Word of modern times, crying out in the new precursor."[7]

Mythical characters benefit from semi-visibility. Jacob Burckhardt, whose 1860 *The Civilization of the Renaissance in Italy* still casts a long shadow, wrote that "the colossal outlines of Leonardo's nature can never be more than dimly and distantly conceived."[8] Contemporaries of Burckhardt also found Leonardo personified in his art, with its veils of transparent shadow, its uncanny evocations of presence. For Gautier, writing in 1852, "His shadows are veils that he removes, or that he thickens in order to make you divine a secret thought; his tones are deadened like the colors of objects in the moonlight, his contours shroud and blend as though behind black gauze, and time, which is hateful to other painters, aids him by strengthening the harmonious shadows in which he loves to plunge himself."[9] Shadows and stains also indicate the process of decay, the degradation by which Leonardo is progressively lost—and the destructive work of time only enhances the posthumous afterimage.

Leonardo's style was seen as embodied or personified in mysterious smiling women and androgynous ephebes, or in grotesque scowling warriors and agitated old men. Michelet wrote that the knowing, seductive address of the *Mona Lisa* or the *St. John* to the beholder seemed to announce the dawning of a new epoch, but also seemed to threaten with the promise of annihilation: "Art, nature, genius of mystery and discovery, master of the profundities of the world, of the unknown abyss of the ages, speak! what do you want of me? The canvas attracts me, calls me, invades me, absorbs me: I go to it in spite of myself, as the bird goes to the serpent." For Michelet, the *Bacchus* and the *St. John* (plates 23 and 5) are really the same person in two different moments, with equal appetite for knowledge of good and for evil. He quotes Quinet, "A stunning gaze that brings the light, and laughs at the obscurity of time; the infinite avidity of the spirit of the new which searches for knowledge and proclaims 'I have found it!'" He concludes: "Only one thing needs to be said: these are gods, but sick. They are not a victory; Galileo is still a long way off. The Bacchus and St. John, those rude prophets of the new spirit, are consumed in suffering. You see yourself in their gaze."[10] For Michelet as for Quinet, the new spirit heralded by St. John and Bacchus, with their insinuating smiles and gestures, was a secularized modernity, a decay of the pure and naive Christianity of the Middle Ages, a new and sensuous openness to nature as it is—but also signaling a loss of innocence.

The image of the ancient gods lingering belatedly, awaiting recognition in the present, was pervasive in the mid-nineteenth century. Leonardo's interpreters would have known Heinrich Heine's 1845 story *Die Götter im Exil*, where the Olympians eke out a humiliated contemporaneous existence in disguise. Thus in 1869 Hippolyte Taine wrote,

> The mysterious smile [of Leonardo's figures] disturbs and vaguely
> unsettles. Skeptical, epicurean, licentious, deliciously tender, ardent
> or sad—what curiosities, aspirations, and discouragement are still
> to be discovered there! Sometimes, amidst young athletes as proud
> as Greek gods, we find a beautiful ambiguous adolescent, with a
> woman's body, slender and twisted with a voluptuous coquetry, like
> the androgynes of the imperial age—who seem, like those, to an-
> nounce a more advanced art, less healthy, almost sickly, so eager for
> perfection and insatiable for happiness that it is not content to put
> strength in man and delicacy in woman, but that, blending and multi-
> plying by a singular mixture of the beauty of the two sexes, it gets lost
> in the dreams and the quests of the ages of decadence and immorality.

Such figures stand for the artist himself, in all his portentous historical significance. They show with the characteristic intellectual and sensuous appetites of the age, who "after so many forays through all the sciences, in all the arts, in all the pleasures, manifest from their experience of so many things an indefinable quality of satiation, of resignation and melancholy. They stop in front of us with an ironic and benevolent half-smile, but under a veil."[11]

Catholic scholars, in the spirit of Ingres and his painting of the death of Leonardo, rallied to reclaim Leonardo for the heritage of Christian art. Arsène Houssaye, who claimed to have discovered the burial site and the skull of Leonardo at Amboise in 1865, published a monograph four years later that proclaimed the artist "a doctor of the faith and Father of the Church" and a "great patriarch of Christian painting." The spiritual and artistic heir of Fra Angelico, Leonardo "felt the paintbrush tremble in his hand" when he had to paint the face of Christ, so could not complete it for a long time.[12] "He had all the makings of a great thinker, but all the heart of a great believer. Nature did not conceal from him the final symbols of the greatness of God. By dint of moving away from God, we come back to Him. Leonardo's paintings are confessions. His testament was to God. It is said that he repented at his final hour. I would like to know what were the sins of Vinci."[13]

Walter Pater's review of Houssaye's monograph would become a chapter of his manifesto-like *The Renaissance* of 1873. Pater clearly regarded his Leonardo as an imaginary creation. There is not the remotest claim to be biographical—Pater self-consciously stages his imaginative generation of a persona from a corpus of works of art, one that speaks at least as strongly as the author's own thoughts and emotions as of the sensibility of a historical period. He is frank about his license with facts, which are the concern of "antiquarians." "A lover of strange souls may still analyze for himself the impression made on him by those works. . . . The *legend*, as corrected and enlarged by its critics, may now and then intervene to support the results of the analysis."[14]

Pater's Leonardo is less a character than an archetype, a creature of sensual transgression and curiosity for whom the satisfactions of Renaissance ideal form will never be sufficient. Hence the "fascination of corruption" in his art, born of a desire to know too much. He is haunted by "the smiling of women and the motion of great waters," which culminate in the *Mona Lisa*, "the presence that rose thus so strangely beside the waters . . . expressive of what in the ways of a thousand years men had come to desire." According to Pater's famously outlandish description, the wife of Francesco del Giocondo is "older than the rocks among which she sits; like the vampire, she has been dead many times, and learned the secrets of the grave, and has been a diver in deep seas, and keeps their fallen day all about her."

"The fancy of a perpetual life, sweeping together ten thousand experiences" had been evoked earlier in the essay with a mention of Gautier "thinking of Heine's notion of decayed gods," but also in the exquisite horror of *The Head of Medusa*, a seventeenth-century painting in the Uffizi, regarded since the late 1700s as a work by Leonardo mentioned by Vasari: "[Leonardo] alone realizes it as the head of a corpse, exercising its powers through all the circumstances of death. What may be called the fascination of corruption penetrates in every touch its exquisitely finished beauty."[15]

Pater's fascination is on one other occasion stirred by a work no longer given to Leonardo, and which appeared as the frontispiece for the second edition of *The Renaissance*: "a little drawing in red chalk which everyone will remember who has examined at all carefully the drawings by old masters at the Louvre. It is a face of doubtful sex, set in the shadow of its own hair, the cheek-line in high light against it, with something voluptuous and full in the eyelids and the lips" (figs. 12 and 13). The drawing is now given to Giovanni Agostino da Lodi, one of the so-called *leonardeschi*—the Italian term for Leonardo's closer followers—whom Pater characterizes as "men with just enough genius to be capable of initiation into his secret, for the sake of which they were ready to efface their own individuality."[16] I think Pater, however inadvertently, has had a moment of insight here, although it might be phrased differently: Leonardo's artistic "individuality" sought to be inclusive, or collective, from the outset. We'll return to this point in the concluding part of this book.

Ambitious writers following Pater filled in the blanks and invented their own Leonardo. In some cases, Leonardo served not as a character but as a model, or as a construction to think with. The poet and philosopher Paul Valéry sums up this approach in a retrospective comment on his early essay *On the Method of Leonardo da Vinci*, which he was commissioned to write in 1894: "Greatly bothered by my own totally hidden future, and living without any justification in the eyes of my family, I agreed to write an essay on Leonardo which Mme Juliette Adam had asked of me at the suggestion of Leon Daudet. Knowing very little about Leonardo, and

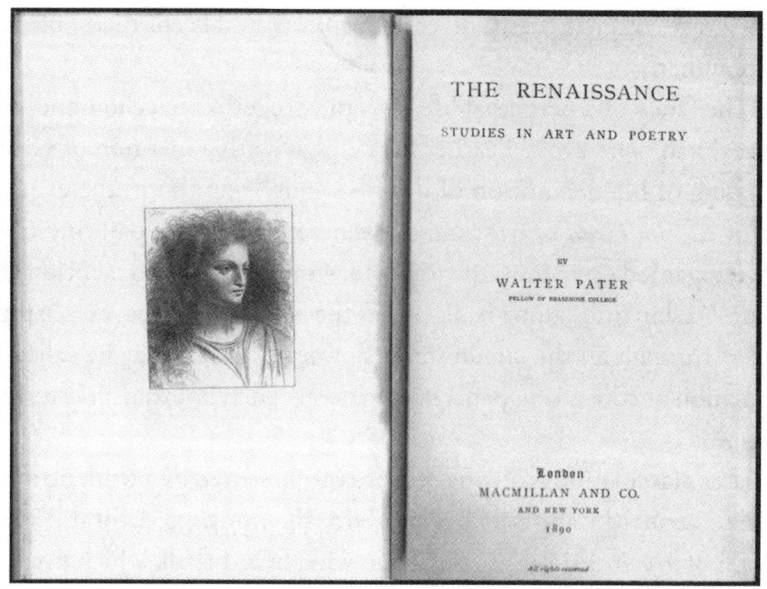

12. Walter Pater, *The Renaissance*, frontispiece to 1890 edition.

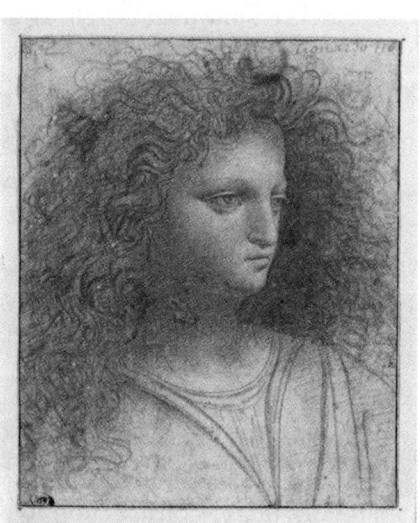

13. Giovanni Agostino da Lodi, *Head of a young man*. Ca. 1520. Red chalk, 10 × 8.5 cm. Paris, Louvre, Département des arts graphiques, INV 2252.

in short being surprised by her request, I accepted for the reasons stated above, and I imagined a Leonardo of my own."[17]

Valéry has little time for the aesthetic mystifications of Pater's generation. He was far more inspired by the recent publications of Leonardo's scientific writings in Paris and Milan, which had led to the painter's acclamation as a proto-Galileo.[18] The face of the *Mona Lisa*, he writes, "is buried beneath a mass of words and disappears among the many paragraphs that start by calling it *disturbing* and end with a generally vague description of a state of *soul*. It might deserve less intoxicating studies. Leonardo had no use for inexact observations or arbitrary symbols, or the *Mona Lisa* would never have been painted. He was guided by a perpetual sagacity."[19]

Valéry claimed that his objective was the philosophical investigation of a "universal mind." His "Leonardo" was a model of a superior attentiveness defined by an equilibrium of faculties and an absolute detachment, one that grasps the structure of the world through internalized images. Instead of distinct, fragmented phenomena, the universal mind is able to "construct" these visualized impressions as the continuum of nature in its totality, through analogy and through metaphor.[20]

Most notably, Valéry's anti-biographical meditation on a distinctive and superior consciousness seems to describe a kind of sentient machine: it does not require "character" or "personality."

> I am trying to give one view of the details of an intellectual life, one suggestion of the methods implied by every discovery, one, chosen among the multitude of imaginable things—a crude model, if you will, but preferable in every way to a collection of dubious anecdotes or a commentary upon museum catalogues, or a list of dates . . . I am not ignorant of such matters, but my task above all is to omit them, so that a conjecture based on very general terms may in no way be confused with the *visible fragments of a personality completely vanished, leaving us equally convinced both of his thinking existence and of the impossibility of ever knowing it better* [my emphasis].[21]

Valéry's notion of the "universal" Leonardo has inspired accounts both deeply historical and also celebratory to the point of hagiography. I find that it resonates with some of the most singular elements in Leonardo's thought, explored in chapter 5: on one hand, Leonardo's injunction to transform one's mind into the "mind of nature," which is also the "mirror of nature"; and on the other his idea of artistic pedagogy as an extended and deindividualized mirroring of the self.

The Leonardo we have inherited is shaped in both useful and misleading ways by the fictive constructions of Pater and Valéry. No less important was the "Leonardo" at the center of a novel by Dmitry Merezhkovsky, *Leonardo da Vinci: The Resurrection of the Gods* (1900), first translated into English as *The Romance of Leonardo da Vinci* (1903). The novel is both a lively historical epic with multiple characters influenced by Tolstoy and a vehicle for a philosophy of history inspired by Nietzsche (it is part of a trilogy titled *Christ and Antichrist*, preceded by a novel about Julian the Apostate and followed by one about Tsar Peter the Great). And there are elements of biographical nonfiction, drawing on the author's research in Italy, with citations of archival material.

Merezhkovsky's Leonardo, once again, is the lonely free-thinking harbinger of a new age signaled by the disinterment of the old gods and his confrontations with religious authority. He rescues an apprentice obsessed with Savonarola, argues with Machiavelli while wandering around the Roman forum, professes a pantheistic religion centered on the Sun, and practices vegetarianism. The mysterious and omniscient Lisa del Giocondo causes him to experience "a sense of awe, bordering on terror, as if she were a phantom," and he is haunted by the dream of his own mother's smile: "gentle, full of mystery, as though a little devious, unusual for such a down-to-earth, cheerless, stern, beautiful face." He encounters her likeness in the sculpture garden of the Medici: "a small bronze Cybele, the primeval Mother Earth goddess, with exactly the same enigmatic smile as on the features of his mother—the young village lass from Vinci."[22] Freud approvingly cited Merezhkovsky's conception of Leonardo's mother in his *Leonardo da Vinci and a Memory of His Childhood* a few years later.[23]

The connoisseur of Renaissance painting Bernard Berenson, by 1916, had had enough of the Leonardo "cult," as he called it. In his diatribe against artist and cult, he not only disavowed his youthful bewitchment by Pater's powerful writing but sought to lay bare Romanticism's overvaluation of Leonardo as an artist and a human being. Leonardo's flaw, he complains, lay in the corruption of his artistic character by the need to demonstrate theoretical principles, and this made him a "crank." But there was something else going on that provoked Berenson's extreme distaste. As a student he had been one of many budding aesthetes under the sway of Pater; on his first trip to the Louvre he had looked at the *Mona Lisa*, attempting to convince himself of the truth of Pater's text, which he had memorized. What follows reads like a palinode to Pater or Gautier: "What I really saw in the figure of *Mona Lisa* was the estranging image of a woman beyond the reach of my sympathies or the ken of my interests, distastefully unlike the women I had hitherto known or dreamt of, a foreigner with a look I could not fathom, watchful, sly, secure, with a smile of anticipated satisfaction and a pervading air of hostile superiority. And against this testimony of my instincts nothing could prevail."[24] The painting triggers powerfully xenophobic impulses along with misogynistic ones. He was intensely satisfied to learn of the painting's theft in 1911: "She had simply become an incubus, and I was glad to be rid of her." Berenson's art history famously had to do with the identification of artists, including previously unknown artistic "personalities" ("Amico di Sandro," etc.) but attempting to constitute and taxonomize Leonardo as a personality revealed a repulsive secret that had to be named, its bearer cut down to size, put in his place.[25]

The problem, as Berenson saw it, lay precisely in the kinds of illegibility or shadowy void that allowed spectators to fantasize about the nature of what was being disclosed or withheld: "We are, however, so centered, so socialized and so attuned that it is difficult if not impossible to avoid finding a meaning even where none was intended, and to cherish this meaning more perhaps than the object it sprang from. . . . We may call this inevitable parasite 'the over-meaning,' for it is probably over and beyond what the artist himself had in mind, and certainly beyond what he could hope to convey with precision."[26]

The effects of this pernicious authorial lack of control, amounting to a kind of irresponsible authorial absence, are seen in the *Mona Lisa*: "who would agree upon what is behind *Mona Lisa*'s look? Its over-meanings are not only as many as there are spectators, but more still, for it will appeal differently to the same spectator at different periods of his life and in different moods. If the artist has no control of the over-meanings except of the most elementary kind, it would surely be wise of him to avoid those intricate and uncertain expressions which lay themselves out to manifold contradictory interpretations, and to confine himself to the simplest looks and attitudes."[27]

The artist, as a fugitive nonpresence in his own work, had allowed a *parasitic* surplus of unintended meaning to take over. It seems clear, though, that the overmeaning—that which the artist "did not have in mind"— betrayed something about the artist, an involuntarily disclosed "truth."

> The *St. John* occupied the altar opposite [the *Mona Lisa*] in the
> imaginary shrine to Leonardo erected by my masters. I no longer
> recall what spiritual rewards I was to expect if I inclined my heart and
> understanding to worship here too. But though I was too innocent
> to suspect the reason, I felt far from comfortable in the presence of
> this apparition looming tenebrously out of the murky darkness. The
> face leered at me with an exaggeration of all that had repelled me in
> the *Mona Lisa* and in the *St. Anne*. And I could not conceive why
> this fleshy female should pretend to be the virile, sun-dried Baptist,
> half-starved in the wilderness. And why did it smirk and point up
> and touch its breasts? Inspired by my good angel, I concluded that
> I was too young to fathom such mysteries, and so I gave this picture
> no further attention until I became a Morellian and decided that it
> could not be by Leonardo. Then for a score of years and more, some-
> thing like a Freudian complex forbade my looking or thinking of the
> picture. At present I fear I must charge Leonardo with the crime.[28]

In his nauseated response to the *St. John*, Berenson lets the reader know that he is aware of Freud, whose *Leonardo da Vinci and a Memory of His Childhood*, with its clinical diagnosis of the artist's homosexuality, had appeared in 1910. We begin to suspect that there is another crime with which to charge Leonardo: the crime whose record as we saw had been published by Scognamiglio in 1896 and that motivated Freud's scrutiny of unintended meanings in Leonardo's paintings. Berenson was "too in- nocent" to understand why he found the androgyny of the St. John so disturbing—although he insinuates that his "masters," Pater and the aes- thetes, might have been rather less so.

This becomes clearer still when we read further in the essay about Mi- chelangelo, the practitioner of the "manly art" of fresco. Michelangelo, unlike Leonardo, had kept his dangerous impulses in check: sfumato and contrapposto are now the symptom of such impulses. Michelangelo in one instance conceived a marble figure with a sensuous posture like Leonardo's *St. John*, but "disgust got the better of him, and, after altering the posture somewhat, he let others complete the *Christ* of the Minerva. Besides, it never would have occurred to him to accumulate conflicting effects. In painting, he regarded fresco as the only manly art, and fresco admits no subtleties of sfumato. (It is significant, by the way, that Leonardo is not known to have painted in fresco)."[29]

And yet, Berenson registers the paradigm shift following the publication of Freud's book. Just as being a "Morellian" (that is, a follower of the methodical connoisseurship of Giovanni Morelli) meant scrutinizing a painting for inadvertent self-revelations of the artist's hand, so now the work was also haunted by psychopathologies of the artist. Kenneth Clark, a protégé of Berenson, began his study of Leonardo's "art, and the personality it reveals" with an acknowledgment that "our knowledge of psychology is fuller than it was. Whether or not we believe in the more elaborate doctrines of psychoanalysis, we are all aware that symbols come to the mind unsought, from some depths of unconscious memory and that even the greatest intellect draws part of its strength from a dark center of animal vitality."[30]

Clark proceeds to recount what was known of Leonardo's early life, including Leonardo's own recollection of the dream about a kite in his infancy, immediately acknowledging its centrality to Freud's psychological account of Leonardo. Freud's conclusions have been rejected "with horror" by Leonardo scholars, writes Clark, and his account "is perhaps as oversimplified as that of Vasari": "Yet it helps our conception of Leonardo's character by insisting that he was abnormal."[31] Some thirty pages later he gingerly takes up the subject of Leonardo's relationship with Salaì, which facts suggest "was of the kind honored in classical times, and partly tolerated in the Renaissance, in spite of the censure of the church." In an almost confessional mode, he declares that Leonardo's homosexuality "is implicit in a large section of his work, and accounts for his androgynous types and a kind of lassitude of form which any sensitive observer can see and interpret for himself." It accounts for "his foppishness in dress, combined with his remoteness and secrecy."[32] On the concluding page of his monograph, Clark reflects, ominously: "In all his writings—one of the most voluminous and complete records of a mind at work which has come down to us—there is hardly a trace of human emotion. Of his affections, his tastes, his health, of his opinions of current events, we know nothing."[33]

To Clark the spectacle of a reputedly sociable, popular, and even flamboyant Leonardo who tells us nothing of himself was deeply troubling. If in Leonardo's writings Clark could detect "hardly a trace of human emotion," there was some compensation in his drawings where Clark found "the subtle and tender understanding of human feelings which is not solely due to the efficiency of the optic nerve."[34] It is as if Clark were haunted by the possibility that Leonardo was something far more disturbing than a courtly dissimulator, and more insidious than a Machiavellian operator; something rather on the order of a barely human intelligence that was chiefly embodied in its optic nerve. Something, perhaps, resembling the Leonardo as supreme universal intelligence without personality that Valéry had envisioned.

Crucially, however, between these two visions of Leonardo—Valéry's and Clark's—was the cataclysmic watershed of 1914–18: not just a global war but the looming twentieth-century threat of annihilation by the machine, a dark fulfillment of the "universal man's" construction of the world. It was Fascist Italy that in the 1939 Milan exhibition *Mostra di Leonardo da Vinci e delle Invenzioni italiane*, with its reconstructions of the artist's inventions, anointed Leonardo the father of the machine age: "The purpose of the exhibition is to celebrate the universal and unequalled genius of Leonardo da Vinci, who is practically the symbol of all Latin and Christian, and therefore Roman, civilization, and to highlight the spiritual connections uniting this great creator and man of accomplishments with the achievements of Mussolinian and Imperial Italy. The combining of the Vinci celebrations with the exhibition of Italian inventions aims to demonstrate the continuity of the creative genius of the race and the great possibilities opening up to those within the climate of Fascist will."[35]

LEONARDO BIOGRAPHIES: THE INDUSTRY

The modern psychopathological Da Vinci had arrived: the artist/author chillingly absent as a humane agent from his own work, his paintings and drawings populated by a queer masquerade of freakish, androgynous, and seductive beings, all pointing and gesturing at . . . you name it. Even before *Black Swan*, *The Imitation Game*, or *The Queen's Gambit*, Western popular culture had long embraced the logic that superior talent and intelligence has its downside—especially if the hapless genius is female or queer. Film or television had little use for Leonardo in the twentieth century: he was simply too risky a subject. It was easier to do what the organizers of the 1939 Milan exhibition had done and to celebrate a modern Leonardo for an age of speed, mechanical force, and technological progress.

Leonardo specialists regrouped and kept their distance, focusing less on the life story than the body of work—the artist as practitioner, inventor, as a maker of knowledge, as a writer. The works would become highly visible case studies in the scientific examination and technical investigation of works of art. Defining events of this pre–Da Vinci World were the 1967 discovery of a group of Leonardo's engineering and machines studies—the Madrid Codices—in the Biblioteca Nacional de España; the acquisition from the princes of Lichtenstein of the portrait of Ginevra de'Benci by the National Gallery of Art in Washington in the same year; the publication of the Royal Collection drawings by Kenneth Clark in 1968; the facsimile with translations of the anatomical manuscripts by Kenneth Keele and Carlo Pedretti in 1979; and the acquisition and display of the Codex Leicester by Armand Hammer in 1980. All of these occurrences served to keep Leonardo prominent in the news media, but it was Leonardo the artist/scientist and not Leonardo the "character."

Less celebrated, but destined to be highly influential, was a monograph on Leonardo's scientific thought by Vassilii Pavlovich Zubov, published in Russian in 1961 and in English in 1968.[36] Zubov, an authority on late medieval science, departed from heroizing accounts of Leonardo as the spiritual ancestor of Galileo and Newton, and equally from emerging revisionist views of Leonardo as a "failed scientist" or "non-scientist."[37] He affirmed Leonardo's relation to scholastic (Aristotelian) traditions of natural philosophy—demonstrable from his notes and his lists of books—and concluded that Leonardo, as a craftsman and technician with acute powers of observation, was able to modify or challenge the Aristotelian orthodoxies that had dominated scientific thinking in the premodern era.

Past the turn of the mid-century, as polemicists like the chemist C. P. Snow decried the fragmentation of intellectual life into the increasingly irreconcilable "two cultures" of the sciences and the humanities (laying heavy blame on the latter), the art historian Ernst Gombrich immersed himself in Leonardo's optics and mechanics as the key to understanding his art, while applying a psychological perspective to Leonardo's grotesques and caricatures. This is emphatically a psychology without Freud: Leonardo's rapid "brainstorming" sketches and his constant return to the same visual motifs are a lifelong attempt to "break the mold" of stereotypes acquired in training through analysis and permutation.[38]

Gombrich's writings, as well as his lectures at the University of London on the relation between "seeing and knowing" in Leonardo, influenced a Courtauld student named Martin Kemp, who had switched to art history from a background in the natural sciences. In 1981 Kemp would publish what would prove to be the most influential study of Leonardo from the past fifty years: *Leonardo da Vinci: The Marvelous Works of Nature and Man*. Kemp sought to put the brakes on popularizing accounts that assessed Leonardo in terms of his anticipation of—or "breakthrough" into—modern science: "I have been concerned with the reasons why his anatomies took the form they did, rather than running him beside Vesalius and Harvey in a historical race towards 'observational accuracy.' I have been concerned to understand his theory of vision and its implications rather than trying to mould him into an ancestor of Kepler. I have been concerned to illustrate the personal flavour that he brought to a broadly Aristotelian range of physical sciences rather than to draw up a historical balance sheet of scientific credits and debits. And ultimately, I have been concerned to show how his art profoundly reciprocates his scientific vision but is not identical to it."[39]

Kemp followed his study of Leonardo with a short biography that abandoned a birth-to-death chronological narrative: an opening chapter is devoted to details of the career, the remainder deal with the leading themes of Leonardo's thought as revealed in his writings, his mechanical and scientific drawings, and his paintings.[40] Daniel Arasse's monumental *Leonardo da Vinci: The Rhythm of the World* (1997) is also emphatically nonbiographical in its organization, going even further than Kemp in its insistence that we see the artist and his thought in relation to his times: "How should [Leonardo's] exceptional qualities be interpreted *historically*?" Arasse asks.[41] In answering the question, Arasse refuses linear narratives of historical progress as well as of his subject's personal history. He regards Leonardo's precocious yet impact-free scientific findings—those "discovered" all over again as Newton's Third Law of motion, the principle of inertia, the functioning of the valves of the aorta—as manifestations of a paradigm shift, the breakdown of an Aristotelian view of nature as Leonardo tested traditional knowledge with close observation: "to be 'the first' to set out or discover an idea, an invention, or an observation, is only a criterion of excellence within a conventional anecdotal history of science." A chronological survey of the life and career thus "would appear artificial because of frequent repetition and the cyclical, 'spiral' nature of Leonardo's activities."[42] The book concludes with short sections on "Leonardo as a person" and "Leonardo and Freud." Both Kemp's and Arasse's books were published not by specialist university presses but by trade imprints, which provide larger print runs, much broader distribution, lower retail prices, and in-print longevity.

Earlier, in 1967, a group of historians, scientists, and artists led by Frank Malina had founded an organization named after Leonardo, with an eponymous journal that sought to further collaboration between technology and the sciences, the visual arts, and research in the humanities. While the journal *Leonardo*'s main activity consisted in documenting "ways in which artists have appropriated almost all fields of scientific research and new technologies," it has featured work by historians and art historians, including original research on Leonardo. More short-lived was a sumptuously produced annual journal from the Armand Hammer Center for Leonardo Studies at UCLA, *Achademia Leonardi Vinci: Journal of Leonardo Studies & Bibliography of Vinciana*, which appeared from 1988 to 1997. It included primarily short articles on topics that could mainly be regarded as Leonardo minutiae—individual drawings and many minor sketches, passages or single words in the notebooks, archival gleanings. One of the effects of this publication was its constitution of a network community or even guild of Leonardo studies, in that it linked the names of a series of major scholars with more marginal and perhaps eccentric contributors. Alessandro Parronchi, Paul Joannides, Martin Kemp, Carmen Bambach, Pietro C. Marani, Richard Schofield, Francesco Paolo Di Teodoro, Francesca Fiorani, Janis Bell, Alessandro Vezzosi, Carlo Vecce, Constance Moffat, and—above all—the editor Carlo Pedretti, who appeared as the author of as many as eight items per issue. Pedretti, who had mastered Leonardo's difficult handwriting and undertaken pioneering work on his manuscripts, had begun to attribute paintings and drawings to the artist, with overzealous criteria of attribution, and was becoming an outlier in the field.

Thus, by the end of the twentieth century, while Leonardo studies could be said to have been flourishing, it usually took the form of knowledge slowly and painstakingly obtained in conservation studios, libraries, and archives, and though sometimes extravagantly publicized, it was—and remains to this day—seldom of the sensational kind that captures newspaper headlines or lights up the online artworld media.

What distinguishes the present-day industrial complex of journalists, documentary producers, bloggers, curators, "scientific experts," and professional biographers is the promise to gratify the need for a "real" Leonardo. We've already looked at the ways Leonardo's pictorial oeuvre has been scrutinized for personal disclosure, to find his self-portrait, or his fingerprints, or for evidence of personal pathologies, his DNA, and his descendants (or at least his collateral descendants, since as far as we know the artist was childless). Specialist publishing in the humanities and the fine arts has declined since the 1990s: so too has the style of museum catalog that seeks to serve both a general and a specialist public. The last Leonardo catalog that a professional researcher might still consult was for the Louvre exhibition of 2012 on *The Virgin and Child with St. Anne*: most museums now produce picture books with thematic essays, mostly nontechnical summaries. There has been a parallel increase in commercial books about "genius artists"—chief among whom has been Leonardo. And the preferred mode is the biography, in the sense of "personal story"—what the artist was "really like." There have been more biographies of Leonardo than of any other artist in history, and they have been appearing in ever-greater quantities over the past twenty years.

The "Leonardo biography" in many ways has come to be a genre of its own, distinct from life histories of other artists or other figures of the premodern world. In part this is due to the seemingly disturbing incompleteness of an unusually large body of writings by the artist, and a lack of other kinds of documentation (again we might cite the contrasting case of Michelangelo, whose long career left a rich deposit of personal correspondence, business records, poetry in a highly personal vein, and long mutually contentious narratives of his life by acquaintances). The lack is supplemented by a constant rehashing of the same story. A life history structured by gaps and absences seems to call out for de-encryption, to uncover its hidden motives. As suggested above, one characteristic of a burgeoning nonspecialist literature on Leonardo from the past twenty-five years is an obsession with Leonardo as a mystery to be solved—whether as a clinical case requiring diagnosis or as a case study in human "creativity," right-brain thinking, and entrepreneurial success, or because the mystifying business of art needs to be cut down to size and rendered intelligible.

According to the Leonardo scholar Matthew Landrus, around two hundred and fifty books on Leonardo were published or republished on the occasion of his quincentennial in 2019. Of these, more than fifty titles were concerned specifically with the life of Leonardo, almost all aimed at a nonspecialist audience (this is not counting numerous short books aimed at young readers).[43] That more than doubles the quantity of trade books on Leonardo's life produced since the 1990s. While some of these popular titles are written by academics, the majority of the authors—strikingly almost all male—are journalists or freelance professional writers.[44] Among the others: a retired surgeon interested in Leonardo's anatomical research; a self-described former surgeon, inventor, and "bestselling author"; an art conservator and biographer of Michelangelo and Bernini; a former pop musician, science journalist, and author of nine biographies including lives of Tolkien, Newton, and Stephen Hawking; a former rock drummer; a journalist, former editor of *Time* magazine, and CEO of CNN, also the author of lives of Henry Kissinger, Einstein, Benjamin Franklin, Steve Jobs, and Elon Musk.[45] Such books receive glowing reviews from other nonspecialists that read more like press releases. A colleague of mine was asked to review one of them for a national newspaper: because her review pointed out the book's lack of depth or engagement with specialist literature, it was canceled.

Some of these books are useful and enjoyable: they tell a colorful story, their authors can sometimes read and interpret Italian sources, they recast specialist research in more reader-friendly form. The readable and well-informed biographies by Charles Nicholl and Serge Bramly are much-cited (and much-cannibalized) examples of this type.[46] And then there are those books that actually make claims for originality, invariably of a *groundbreaking* kind. In publishing, as in the world of conservation and the art market, Leonardo tends to attract would-be sleuths and codebreakers. Many claim to get closer to their subject than their predecessors, especially by refusing to be distracted by historical minutiae or *academic discussions*, above all by being *anti-elitist* and *relatable*. One author is described by his publisher as a "passionate Da Vinci fan": "much is known about Leonardo, but modern scholars and biographers have routinely avoided making assumptions based on that evidence, either out of academic caution or the impulse to be p.c." Instead, he promises to provide "a thrilling and fascinating journey into the life of a ferociously dedicated loner, whose artwork in one way or another represents his noble rebellion, providing inspiration that is, quite apparently, timeless."[47] The result, delivered with much "stump the experts" irreverence, is often entertaining. He warns, "I recommend you keep a legitimate biography alongside this bastard of my brain so as to remain constantly in tune with the truth as it is generally understood." Much effort is on display in the process of making Leonardo into a character that a contemporary male reader, perhaps one who doesn't see himself as normally interested in art or as a habitual museum goer, perhaps a player of *Assassin's Creed*, might identify with. Such books will lead off with Leonardo the proto-scientist, *ahead of his time* as usual, rather than Leonardo the painter and sculptor.

Another demystifying voice from outside the Leonardo guild promises to explain how "Leonardo was, through the scope of his investigations and his desire to push back the boundaries of knowledge, nothing less than 'The First Scientist.' Exploring the legacy of research he left behind . . . [he]

finds evidence not just of a true polymath but of a true man of science," making the case "for a re-evaluation of this most remarkable man and a study of the definitive amalgamation of art and science."[48] The book, however, does not say much about Leonardo and science, let alone anything new: it is a retelling of the life of the author's "childhood hero," with the usual mixture of facts, pseudo-facts, and psychological speculations, most of the latter second- or thirdhand.

The dual authors of *The Young Leonardo* (2017)—most of which, despite the title, deals with Leonardo's mature years in Milan—are identified as a correspondent to *National Geographic* on biblical archaeology and "the historical Jesus," and as an entrepreneur, "art connoisseur," and surgical specialist in facial reconstruction.[49] Thus equipped, they offer a "provocative" solution to the mystery of why Leonardo failed to complete so many of his works: Leonardo, supposedly, was misunderstood and thwarted by his uncomprehending Italian contemporaries in Florence and Milan, who preferred now-obscure artists working in an outmoded "late Gothic style." The French, on the other hand, far surpassed the Italians in their appreciation and support of Leonardo's unique and forward-looking gifts. Thus, the young Leonardo reacted against "Verrocchio's cloying stereotypes," and surpassed Filippino Lippi, whose *Vision of St. Bernard* (by any account an extraordinary painting) is deemed "a very static and conventional composition."[50]

Leonardo's *Adoration of the Magi* is compared to a Savonarola sermon because of its "social criticism." It presents no difficulty that the work dates from more than a decade before Savonarola preached in Florence. Social criticism is manifest, however, because "the good and the bad, the faithful and the wicked of fifteenth century Florence" are on full display. Maurizio Seracini is cited as the authority for the groundless claim that the monks rejected the altarpiece and that Benci had the controversial elements painted over.[51]

Matters are only worse in Milan. It is alleged as a sign of a still "medieval" artistic culture that Milanese painters worked in anonymous collectives (but collective production was the hallmark of the Verrocchio workshop, as we have seen, and Florentine artists regularly organized themselves into partnerships to share studio facilities and commissions).

Milanese art and architecture were supposedly retarded by the contaminating influence of French and German and Netherlandish "late Gothic" art, as a result of which "the region of Lombardy had yet to produce any artist of real note."[52] Scholars of Michelino da Besozzo, Donato de'Bardi, Pisanello, Giovanni Antonio Amadeo, Vincenzo Foppa, the Mantegazza brothers, or the astonishing Bramantino might disagree: the latter in particular constituted an artistic vanguard, lasting well into the 1500s, that was largely indifferent to Leonardo. It is true that many elite commissions in Milan went to non-Milanese artists; that is because princely patrons managed appearances on the world stage through a cultural cosmopolitanism. It is an error to identify such pluralism, which operated in places like papal Rome, Naples, Genoa, and Messina, as provincialism.

The historian and biographer William St. Clair has commented on the tendency in recent publishing to throw out the key principle of scholarly biography—that of Ockham's razor, "which demands that . . . the simplest explanation which connects the recorded facts should be preferred." "The abandonment of Ockham's razor has encouraged a kind of restless biographical consumerism, a constant repackaging of the same materials in ways which give the appearance of novelty."[53] "While purporting to be an investigative discipline," he writes, "proceeding from detailed empirical observation of individuals to more general conclusions, or testing the validity of provisional theories by adducing investigated cases against which they can be compared, is biography not in practice reversing this process, fitting the choice of facts to match ideologies of essential human nature already firmly settled in the biographer's mind?"[54]

For one historian of life-writing, "the 'biographical' information that millions of readers want is the stuff of the first-person interview and the psychologist's couch. Second-hand dish suffices, but the subject's own story is better. Even biographers get in on the autobiographical act. . . . They confess how immersing themselves in someone else's life helped them understand their own, as if self-diagnosis were a benefit of writing biography, not just of reading it."[55]

Janet Malcolm is more damning: the biographer's demonstration of their tireless industry and "personal journey" seeks to make the reader believe "that he is having an elevating literary experience, rather than simply listening to backstairs gossip and reading other people's mail. The transgressive nature of biography is rarely acknowledged, but it is the only explanation for biography's status as a popular genre." The reader's tolerance of such an enterprise "makes sense only when seen as a kind of collusion between him and the biographer in an excitingly forbidden undertaking: tiptoeing down the corridor together, to stand in front of the bedroom door and try to peep through the keyhole."[56]

Leonardo biographers tend to refer to themselves a good deal. Or, the writer's first-person experience and assertive selfhood become the grounds for filling in the blanks. On the failure of Leonardo's writings to disclose "an idea of his personality," one biographer writes, "I look around at other talented outsiders, misunderstood and perhaps angry about it, and I think he wanted to temper his rashness, his tendency to talk too much perhaps—or his tendency to offer the critical remark." The world of the biographical subject is the biographer's, thinly disguised. Leonardo's inclination to be critical was because he was surrounded by people who "were semi-literate at best." Leonardo's world was one "of subjective chaos riddled with misperception and ignorance. . . . And his abhorrence of that stupidity drove him like a dog on fire. I believe he fashioned a new persona and dressed the part and started over in Milan as a reinvented man, like Ben Franklin, or Mark Twain, or Isaac Newton, or as so many others have done since."[57] A biographical portrait makes its subject not only universal—with comparisons to "talented outsiders" everywhere— but strangely familiar. For the world without words in which rumor and "subjective chaos" flourish is nothing other than the image-ridden world we live in, the dystopic media-landscape that fashions history as a mirror of itself.

Walter Isaacson is to be singled out for his openness about his debt to specialist scholarship. His book presents itself as a "gateway" biography, providing access to more specialized sources, "that little-tapped trove of academic articles and doctoral dissertations on Leonardo."[58] While Isaacson affirms the virtues of "knowledge for its own sake," he is up-front that this biography is about the relevance of his subject for our world: "The fifteenth century of Leonardo and Columbus and Gutenberg was a time of invention, exploration, and the spread of knowledge by new technologies. In short, it was a time like our own. That is why we have much to learn from Leonardo. His ability to combine art, science, technology, the humanities, and imagination remains an enduring recipe for creativity. So, too, was his ease at being a bit of a misfit: illegitimate, gay, vegetarian, left-handed, easily distracted, and at times heretical."[59]

It would be less interesting to dwell once again on the confident anachronisms here—chiefly the way that fields of human activity are treated as more distinct than they may once have been, so Leonardo can be singled out for "combining" them—than to note the resonance with the rhetoric of *creativity* and *interdisciplinarity* as it manifests itself in the corporate boardroom and in the administrative sectors of the contemporary university. In those contexts, specialization or disciplinary expertise—or the investigation of matters that do not map onto present concerns—tends to be regarded as an obstacle to progress.[60]

Leonardo here represents the *skill sets* necessary for survival in a world order where originality is increasingly synonymous with entrepreneurism: this is what the word "creative," now used as a noun as often as an adjective, has come to mean. The word seems to have acquired its modern ubiquity following psychobiological experiments in the 1980s, notably in the "split brain" theory that assigns logical and more intuitive forms of thinking to, respectively, the brain's left and right hemispheres. Models of "creative" brain activity—the ability of some individuals to move rapidly between left and right brain functions—translated rapidly into the corporate management sector, particularly through the influence of Ned Hermann's 1988 book *The Creative Brain*. The well-regarded neuroscientist and literary scholar Nancy Andreasen, who undertook research into the relationship between artistic ability and mental illness, with subjects drawn from the Iowa Writers' Workshop, went on to produce a popularizing account of "creativity and genius" adorned on the cover with portraits of Shakespeare, Leonardo, Mozart, and Neil Simon.[61]

Creativity is distinguished from intelligence and defined in terms of *originality*, *utility*, and the generation of "a product of some kind" (we should already begin to worry about the applicability to Leonardo). Much of Andreasen's book concerns the pathologies of the "genius brain," alleging that 43 percent of creative people showed indications of bipolar disorder, as opposed to only 10 percent of subjects in a control group. Such conclusions are sustained by extrapolating "data" from the biographies of famously dysfunctional (and mostly long-deceased) artists and writers, including Samuel Taylor Coleridge, Emily Dickinson, and Vincent Van Gogh. A Netflix documentary series also named *The Creative Brain* delivers the insight that our brains "remix preexisting inputs" with "stimulating new knowledge" to come up with something "truly creative." And that being a "creative" somehow means not being a "critic." (Critics analyze, while creatives deliver; this is presumably why such books presuppose that academics are not creatives.) And that the proof of creativity means the delivery of "innovations" (products) that "transform your career": it is measured by material success. The celebrity subjects, musicians, and actors (Nick Cave, Michael Chabon, Tim Robbins) are primarily white men; the STEM end of the spectrum is the domain of women and people of color.

The words "creative" and "creativity" resound through the opening pages of Isaacson's book, where he lays out his theory of Leonardo's importance. The words are nonetheless absent from the index and there are no citations to the literature on creativity: the concepts are treated as if they were utterly transparent in meaning: "I embarked on this book because Leonardo da Vinci is the ultimate example of the main theme of my previous biographies: how the ability to make connections across disciplines—arts and sciences, humanities and technology—is a key to innovation, imagination and genius. . . . Steve Jobs climaxed his product launches with an image of street signs showing the intersection of the liberal arts and technology. Leonardo was his hero. 'He saw beauty in both art and engineering,' Jobs said, 'and his ability to combine them was what made him a genius.'"

Isaacson goes on to elaborate on the different types of "genius": "[Leonardo's] genius was of the type we can understand, even take lessons from. It was based on skills we can aspire to improve in ourselves, such as curiosity and intense observation. He had an imagination so excitable that it flirted with the edges of fantasy, which is also something we can try to preserve in ourselves and indulge in our children."[62]

Nothing could seem more reasonable. Succinctly, the educational value of the past lies in learning that history is made by innovators. Leonardo is more than the "hero" of Steve Jobs; he is his historical pre-incarnation, a formula for the reproduction of a certain personality type that connects a future of technological progress and wealth creation with the past. Leonardo makes the past usable. Once again, anyone involved in higher education will note the resonance with the professional rhetoric of education management. This is the way in which education has been reconceived as a set of *learning outcomes*, based on a synergy of humanities and STEM fields (themselves dichotomized through the same "two cultures" managerial policies), where the value of studying history, or poetry, or mathematics is measured through *skill sets*.

Of course, it would be no bad thing for humanists to have a better literacy in the forms of scientific writing, or if more STEM authors would think and write with more ethical and historical perspective—but our biographer is not calling for this. His holding up of Leonardo as a role model points to a corporate reengineering of a "Renaissance man," an ideal product who designs ideal products. The book ends with a set of maxims, "Learning from Leonardo." *Be curious, relentlessly curious. Seek knowledge for its own sake. Retain a childlike sense of wonder. Go down rabbit holes. Procrastinate. Let the perfect be the enemy of the good* . . . and so on. The last of these is glossed with a cautionary note that "sometimes you ought to deliver a product even while there are still improvements that could be made. That is a good rule for daily life. But there are times when it's nice to be like Leonardo and not let go of something until it's perfect."[63] Leonardo's failure to complete commissions is neatly encompassed with a diagnostic from the self-help manual, "perfectionism."

Isaacson claims that his starting point is "not Leonardo's art masterpieces, but his notebooks."[64] He makes "pilgrimages to see the originals in Milan, Florence, Paris, Seattle, Madrid, London, and Windsor Castle." Quite what he learned from direct consultation of the sources, as distinct from facsimiles and translations, is never disclosed. Nor are we told how Isaacson mastered the acquaintance with Renaissance paleography, codicology, connoisseurship, and other skill sets necessary for navigating the quite extraordinary difficulties in understanding the huge and disorderly Leonardo corpus of seven thousand pages and more.

The claim in any case is contradicted by erroneous descriptions of the manuscripts; for instance, the Windsor sheet (RCIN 919005r), dated

1510–11, showing the head of an old man, along with the musculature of the right arm and studies of the veins in the left and right arms, is asserted to be "the centenarian and his muscles."[65] But the centenarian is the subject of an entirely different sheet of notes and drawings based on an earlier dissection of ca. 1508 (RCIN 919027), where a study of the veins of the arm appears with Leonardo's famous record of an old man, who "a few hours before his death, told me that he was over a hundred years old, and that he felt nothing wrong with his body other than weakness. And thus, while sitting on a bed in the hospital of Santa Maria Nuova in Florence, without any movement or other sign of any mishap, he passed from this life. And I dissected him to see the cause of so sweet a death."

The casualty here is expertise, and the currency of such well-intended misrepresentations points to a clear failure of the means by which professional scholarship is supposed to reach a larger public. We are quite remote here from any notion of a historian's ethical responsibility to past lives and past societies. It increasingly seems as if scholars like Martin Kemp, who have written for nonspecialist readers, pursuing public outreach through museum programming as well as television, might be doing so in vain. Increasingly, trade publishing both exploits and undermines hard-won scholarship in the service of a *Da Vinci* that is increasingly the construct of commercial interests, whether mass entertainment, the media, or the art market. What once might have been a thought experiment in imagining the lifeworld of a figure from the past and visualizing history through their experience has now become the publishing equivalent of mass tourism. By analogy, we might think of the mega cruise ship mangling fragile historical environments. Scholarship is also a fragile environment. The fiscally precarious habitus of research and training, of conservation and display, is treated as virgin real estate awaiting speculation and development. Given the lacunose state of the evidence, the narration of a life history spirals rapidly into speculation, psychological projection, fictive conversations, and the making of characters with *human interest*.

Since the writing of history is always perspectival and represents the worldview of the historian, the ethical principle is that of how one speaks for an Other and a self-awareness that has acquired a new degree of urgency with the postcolonial critique of Eurocentric bias and blindness. At stake is the pursuit of an entrepreneurial mastery of the past, solving the problem of the unknowables of history in order to instrumentalize them. With the claim to make the past visible and uncomplicated, its messy complexity and ambiguity are obliterated.

There are abundant fragmentary stories visible in the copious archive of Leonardo's career. The greatest illusion of the Leonardo legacy—paintings, drawings, eyewitness reportage by contemporaries, thousands of pages of notebooks—is that there is a complete life hidden within the material legacy that can be reassembled and made to produce the historical character of our imaginations. What is there, however, is singularly interesting, and no less so are the absences. It is to both of these that we now turn. What is it that the records of Leonardo's life do not tell us? Rather than trying to fill in the blanks, we need to address instead why those blanks exist.

Chapter 4

THE SHAPE OF PREMODERN LIVES

To produce a life history or to consider life as a history, that is, as a coherent narrative of a significant and directed sequence of events, is perhaps to conform to a rhetorical illusion, to the common representation of existence that a whole literary tradition has always and still continues to reinforce.

—PIERRE BOURDIEU, "THE BIOGRAPHICAL ILLUSION"

Many readers will know that for the influential Swiss historian Jacob Burckhardt, writing in 1860, the "discovery of the world and of man" and "the birth of the modern form of the self" were foundational to the very notion of a Renaissance. The idea of Renaissance as the emergence of a distinctively *modern* kind of individualism shows no signs of going away, despite challenges from generations of historians who pointed out the indifference of Burckhardt's individualism to differentials of geography, of gender, and of class, its privileging of elite and literary voices, and its exaltation of timeless genius.[1] More recently, and especially since the critical postmodernisms of the 1970s and 1980s, there has been a tendency to rethink Renaissance individualism in terms of performance, of "fashioned" selves, of selfhood as masquerade. This, however, made the Renaissance seem no less modern than it had been in Burckhardt's conception. The radical questioning of the unity of the self by Bourdieu (see above) or Michel Foucault, or post-Freudian psychoanalysis and feminism, has even, in the meantime, been mainstreamed. The idea of a nonessential and fashioned self now seems to do little more than hold up an affirmative mirror to our own age of celebrity, social media profiles, and networked personae.

Leonardo's was undoubtedly a fashioned self, manifest in situational shifts of voice and appearance between the court, the workshop, the military encampment. In crucial ways, however, premodern subjects were not at all like contemporary celebrities who "reinvent themselves," whose audience is always assured of a core of personhood and "personal journey." That core is elusive in the case of a well-documented individual like Leonardo, and his various stagings of a voice or a persona seem fragmented and unresolved. Is the artist an outlier, in an age of increasingly robust and articulate identities? Was his assertive "*I*" and "*you*," his idiomatic play of voices and personae, actually part of a deliberate strategy of withdrawal on his part? We might like to think that Leonardo's apartness, his alienation from ties of family and class in Florence, might have reinforced a sense of distinctness, an "identity" if a rather solitary one. Yet the evidence from the notebooks considered in chapter 2, where we see Leonardo inscribing himself in multiple social and professional relations with craftsmen, humanists, courtiers, and merchants, suggests a significant effort of integration. Or might the "I" and "you" of Leonardo's writings finally be symptomatic of larger transformations happening in his lifetime, which had a bearing on how individuals of his class and profession thought of and presented themselves? Especially since historians have drawn attention to a singular phenomenon of Leonardo's century, against which his case might be assessed: the manifestation of individual lives in new forms of writing and the construction of personal legacy through written records. While these might include the recording of experiences and life episodes, they are not limited to what we would now recognize as biography or autobiography, and do not correspond to Burckhardtian ideas of modern individuality.

We briefly considered an early example of a written life without a narrative of life events—the third-person epigraph on Giovanni Pisano's marble pulpit in Pisa. Although conventionally regarded as uneducated and plebian "mechanicals," craftsmen were among the very first non-elite persons to assume the role of author throughout the 1400s, and even earlier. In the 1280s, the goldsmith, painter, and miniaturist Restoro of Arezzo wrote an influential vernacular treatise *On the Composition of the World*, with chapters on meteorology and geology that would be consulted by Leonardo. Importantly, Restoro extolled the figure of the craftsman, with his hands-on, bodily experience of nature, as wielding forms of knowledge second only in prestige to astronomy.[2] The "exalted ancient masters," according to Restoro, possessed "an almost godlike subtlety in carving and sculpting the things of nature, such as animals and plants and rivers and mountains and rocks and every other thing that can be sculpted and drawn. And this very great subtlety and great knowledge does not impede the intellect, rather it enabled the writing of this book; and without this knowledge this book could not have been written, because it has to deal with images and figures and other things which require knowledge of the greatest subtlety."[3]

Lorenzo Ghiberti is often seen as a role model for Leonardo, in that he combined craft wisdom and a sophisticated grasp of medieval sciences like optics. Yet the key difference is that Ghiberti set down a detailed record of his own accomplishments in the art of bronze sculpture. Ghiberti wrote himself into the first modern history of art, modeled on the Roman writer Pliny the Elder whose records of the careers of artists of Greece and Rome had been read throughout the Middle Ages. Ghiberti's formidable rival, the sculptor-architect Filippo Brunelleschi, was the subject of a *vita* with a colorful focus on that rivalry written by the mathematician and Dante scholar Antonio Manetti, probably as a means of preventing Ghiberti from having the last word. Around 1480 Manetti wrote out a manuscript copy of Restoro's *Composition of the World*, which is probably how Leonardo came to know it.[4]

Leon Battista Alberti, who was primarily a writer and scholar, but whose practice of architecture earned him a *vita* in Vasari's *Lives of the Artists*, wrote of his own complicated life in Latin and in an objectifying third person, focusing on illness, professional disappointment, and family conflict, and on the therapeutic role of art and intellectual pastimes in managing spiritual and physical afflictions.

Such life-writing is just one instance, however, of a dramatic rise of the artisan as author in the 1400s. Most of those who wrote wanted to be remembered for systematizing the principles of their craft, sometimes recalling key achievements of their career. In the wake of Ghiberti, his grandson Buonaccorso, his pupil Antonio Filarete, the polymath Francesco di Giorgio, and the painter and teacher of arithmetic Piero della Francesca all wrote texts glorifying their profession or reformulating its central precepts based on their own learning or experience. And much authorial activity by artists and craftsmen takes the form of more fragmentary and occasional writing, including (as we will see) verse invective and satire.

Such authorial activity outside the church, the court, or university points to broader social transformations. There are clear signs of a reshaping of professional identity among artisans that challenged hierarchies of class and knowledge and in ways that brought reactions from elites.[5] Artists were mechanicals who *knew things*, who commanded intellectual and political capital in addition to lucrative public commissions. The mathematician and astronomer Biagio Pellacani (ca. 1350–ca. 1416) talked to craftsmen and recorded metalworkers' use of burning mirrors in his widely read 1415 treatise on optics, *Questiones super perspectiva communi*, which may have been read by Leonardo in a vernacular reduction.[6] The Venetian Giovanni Fontana (ca. 1395–ca. 1455), a mathematician and physician who dedicated a treatise on optics to the painter Jacopo Bellini, was in close communication with makers of mirrors, builders of clocks and musical instruments, locksmiths, boat builders, and foundry workers, both as sources of knowledge for his treatises on engineering and automata and in order to realize some of his spectacular theatrical machines. The Florentine mathematician and astronomer Paolo Toscanelli (1397–1482) sought to improve the mathematical basis of mapmaking, an endeavor that throws light on his friendship with Brunelleschi as well as with Alberti. Leonardo, who took notes from his works and owned manuscripts in Toscanelli's hand, probably knew him personally.[7]

There is a sense with this literature of the writers being embroiled, of their pushing against a status quo. Elite custodians of knowledge—the Aristotelian professors of natural philosophy and the literary professionals—often looked askance at the prominence of artisans in scientific application and discovery. The spectacle of mechanicals who seemed no longer to know their place incurred amusement and suspicion as well as admiration.

Such a conflicted perception is already manifest in the appearance of artists as comic or trickster characters in vernacular storytelling. In the mid-1300s, Boccaccio included humorous stories about Giotto's repartee, and the painter Buffalmacco's ability to outwit his superiors, in his *Decamerone*. From the 1400s there are several stories about Donatello, some of them disturbing. In a collection of *facezie* thought to have been compiled by the humanist Angelo Poliziano, Donatello appears as an irascible, uncouth foreman who smears the faces of his handsome apprentices with dirt so other bosses won't steal them away, or chases a runaway apprentice to Ferrara vowing to kill him.[8] In the novella of the "fat woodcarver," adapted from earlier sources by Antonio Manetti, Donatello and Brunelleschi both appear as accomplices in an elaborate joke played against the unfortunate woodcarver of the title. Brunelleschi brings about the annihilation of the craftsman Manetto's identity by convincing him that he is no longer Manetto but another individual called Matteo, for whose misdemeanors he is subsequently arrested and imprisoned. When the joke is discovered, Manetto, the butt of general ridicule, is so mortified that he goes into exile in Hungary, where he effectively rebuilds a personhood from tabula rasa. The tale of Manetto's "loss of face" points to the contingent nature of selfhood and the alienability of social identity. Such properties can be lost, in the logic of the tale, because they depend on one's place in a social network, the strength of one's connections with the rich and powerful, and the recognition of one's neighbors and coworkers.

However, the story also points to the emergence of new forms of community that traverse social and professional hierarchies: a social circle of "men from the governing class," according to Manetti, along with members of what he calls "the more intellectual and imaginative of the crafts [*maestri d'alcune arti miste e d'ingegno*], such as painters, goldsmiths, sculptors, woodcarvers, and the like" who are all in on the joke. Their solidarity as a unified group is affirmed through the victimization of a hapless craftsman, "since they were almost all of a higher rank and station than he."[9]

Artists in Florence came to excel at performing these out-of-place, boundary-crossing social identities, mechanicals who could talk back to the intelligentsia—although the voice and persona they would adopt would be deliberately strange, pointedly anomalous. Two sonnets by Filippo Brunelleschi are preserved in a fifteenth-century manuscript, where they are referred to as "counterfeits of Orcagna"—that is, as written in the persona of the fourteenth-century painter Andrea di Cione, known as Orcagna, who had supposedly invented the colloquial, invective-laden anti-Petrarchan form.

Around 1430 Brunelleschi had been attacked in verse by the poet, jurist, and Dante scholar Giovanni di Gherardo, unconvinced of the viability of Brunelleschi's project for a mechanical boat, the *badalone*.

> *O, you depthless fountain and pit of all ignorance,*
> *You pauper beast and imbecile,*
> *Who thinks uncertain things can be made visible:*
> *But as regards your alchemy, there is no substance to it.*
> *The simple fickle mob, its hope all lost, is still credulous*
> *But never will you, man without substance,*
> *Make that come true which is impossible.*
> *So, if the Badalon, your water bird,*
> *Were ever finished—which can never be—*
> *I would no longer teach Dante in the school*
> *But vow to terminate my existence at my own hands.*
> *Because I am certain that you are mad, as you hardly know*
> *How to warp, let alone how to weave.*[10]

The weaving metaphor assigns the artisan to his place among the mechanical crafts. Donatello would similarly be criticized by the poet Gentile de'Becchi, who devised the epigrams for the statues of *David* and *Judith*. Donatello is inventive, says de'Becchi, but he's the kind of artist who excelled more at inventing and sketching rather than finishing, who could "warp without doing the patient weaving."[11] Brunelleschi, portrayed as a mere artisan seeking to rise above his station through spurious science or "alchemy," is something worse, a bestial entity, a man without substance, possessing depth only in his ignorance.

Brunelleschi responds, unmasking in verse the pretensions of his attacker:

> When hope is given to us from above,
> O you, the very effigy of a laughing beast,
> We become men who rise above corruptible matter
> And gain the highest power in judging.
> False judgement loses its power,
> because it is put to flight by experience
> To [such] a wise man nothing remains unseen,
> except that which is not, for it has no existence.
> As to the fantasies of a would-be scholar
> Wrong thinking won't let you see what is there
> for art reveals that which nature hides.
> So, unravel the tangles of your verses
> Since they strike discordant notes
> For my "impossible" will come into being.

The craftsman becomes a philosopher: through judgment gained by experience, the wise artisan rises above the mechanical manipulation of matter to the apprehension of general principles. Practitioners of book learning are the ones grasping after mere figments. Nearly all of these themes will appear again sixty years later in Leonardo's famous polemics against men of letters, doctors, alchemists, and astrologers. For example, "there are books full, declaring that enchantments and spirits can work and speak without tongues . . . and can carry the heaviest weights and raise storms and rain; and that men can be turned into cats and wolves and other beasts, although indeed it is those who affirm these things who first become beasts."[12]

Alberti himself wrote his own verses in this idiom, exchanging witty and insulting sonnets with the popular barber-poet Burchiello, whose verses are often a verbal chaos of body parts, foodstuffs, and sexual and scatological double entendres.

Alberti begins the poetical duel by insulting Burchiello's poetic pretensions:

> *Burchiello ["little boat"] rickety, and without oars,*
> *Made together with bottomless baskets,*
> *The Muses can no longer hide*
> *Because of so many moans at the prow . . .*

He continues with a series of obscure jibes at "feeble and diverse rhymes" and "an animal who does not esteem himself."

Burchiello accepts the challenge and responds using the same rhymes (a form known as *tenzone*): Alberti's writings are worthy only to be used as a table napkin:

> *Battista, so that it would seem like I do not fear*
> *Your herbed fritters, as I do not do,*
> *I often dry my sweaty lips with dignity*
> *On your great proems . . .*

The sonnet proceeds to mark the professional and social hierarchy between the contending rhymers:

> *But revering your grand rhyme,*
> *Your haughty speech, that I avoid,*
> *Craft [mestiere] was never my escort or guide*
> *Because the sky from the highest summit*
> *Breathed virtue into me as soon as I was born,*
> *Under whose shield my genius trusts . . .*

And the tenzone continues until Burchiello concludes it by demanding a carnival dinner of roasted capons turned on a spit (probably an innuendo).[13]

This exchange between Alberti and Burchiello was probably known to Leonardo, who listed a volume by Burchiello among his books, and it may leave a trace in some of his facetious "prophecies" and riddles. A manuscript produced in Verrocchio's workshop contains sonnets by Burchiello,

Brunelleschi, and Alberti, as well as another comic tale of identity confusion concerning the twins Geta and Birria, sometimes attributed to Brunelleschi.[14]

And the idiom was taken up in prose in 1479 by the sculptor Bertoldo, the pupil of Donatello, in a bizarre letter of protest to Lorenzo de'Medici replete with imagery of kitchens, poisons, and latrines. Florence was then at war with the papacy and Naples. Bertoldo protests his annoyance that one Luca Calvanese has been promoted for his "cooking skills" (a possible reference to military pyrotechnics, or possibly poisoning) while the sculptor bemoans his choice of profession: "Magnifico Lorenzo, etc. I have this moment thrown away chisels, scalpels, compasses, T square, wax, straw, [theory of] architecture and perspective and have given four kicks to this terracotta and returned the clay to the potter to make chamberpots, since I understand that the spicy stews of our Commandant of Prato, Messer Luca Calvanese, are more highly regarded than all other abilities, sciences or arts, by Count Girolamo [Riario, the pope's nephew], seeing that he managed to become a knight by means of them; . . . and would to God I had [studied] under that fool rather than under Donatello." Once reunited with his "cookery book," Bertoldo looks forward to seeing "the Pope, the Count and Messer Luca stifled in a vat of pepper [gunpowder?], and that [God] may protect you from their treachery."[15]

Finally, Leonardo's friend Bramante again sounded the theme of disgruntled dependency in a sonnet to his patron, the noble Milanese poet Gaspare Visconti, bemoaning the wretched state of his stockings "all stained like the towels in the taverns."[16]

Leonardo, too, can be aligned with this tradition of artists who write, and whose selfhood is mediated by writerly personae, sometimes facetious and transgressive, and to be understood to be a kind of role-playing. Yet Leonardo's relation to these artist predecessors is complex.

He was mindful of the precedence of Alberti (fig. 14): like Alberti, he engaged with the artists' vernacular tradition without fully positioning himself within it. At the same time, he could not fully embrace Alberti's humanist milieu. Alberti's humanistic training and command of Latin and Greek meant that he was out of Leonardo's league as a professional role model, although the younger artist could draw profitably on Alberti's treatises on painting and on architecture.

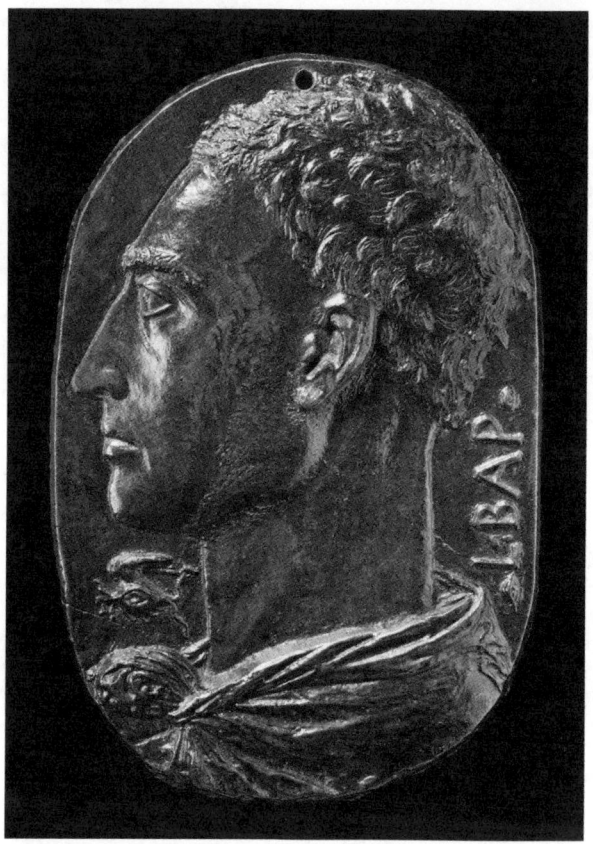

14. Leon Battista Alberti, *Self-Portrait*. Ca. 1435. Bronze plaquette, 20.1 × 13.55 cm. Washington, DC, National Gallery of Art, Kress Collection.

There are striking similarities between the two. Alberti, like Leonardo, was illegitimate: his short autobiography does not mention this but refers at length to the callous neglect and obstruction of his relatives. Leonardo experienced comparable treatment from his own siblings especially after 1500 when they contested his right to a bequest on the grounds of his illegitimate birth. Although he did receive a university education and a low-level position in the Vatican bureaucracy, illegitimacy would have limited Alberti's possibilities for inheritance and professional advancement. For both, the social barriers to illegitimates led to the development of compensatory skills and forms of expertise that they might not have acquired had they settled into professional roles normally available to families of their status.

And yet, Alberti *does* write the story of his own life—in the third person, as if by an anonymous author. The so-called *Vita anonima* is emphatically a narrative of embodied experience, where physical accomplishments are as important as intellectual ones, and bodily sufferings as significant and self-defining as mental afflictions. This circumstance can provide a point of departure for thinking about why we have nothing comparable in the writing of Leonardo.

Alberti writes of his devotion to "knowledge of the most strange and difficult things," of his striving "to obtain a name in modelling and painting," his ability to construct "wonders" in the form of small peep-show models of the cosmos and the oceans, and of his absorption in the artisanal world: "We would inquire of artisans, architects, shipbuilders, and even from shoemakers and tailors, whether perhaps there was some technique in their craft which was unusual and little known and which they carefully preserved as something peculiar to their art; and he eagerly explained these same things to his eager fellow citizens."[17] For recreation, he would leave his house to see craftsmen working in their shops, and this would lead him to hurry home "as though he had been warned by some rigorous censor, saying to himself 'And we too must exert ourselves in the task we have undertaken.'"[18]

Indeed, Alberti regarded intellectual work as akin to physical labor. In a striking passage he emphasized the heavy toll reading and writing had taken on his own body during his youth: "the force and vigor of almost his whole body broke down in a state of exhaustion. This terrible ill health brought him to the point where, as he read, his eyesight at once seemed to fail amid a sudden dizziness and bowel pains, while bangs and long hissing noises resounded loudly in his ears." Alberti ignored his doctors, who advised him to labor less. He did not obey, "grinding himself down with studying because of his love of learning." When the reading of books causes him pain, so that "the letters themselves seemed to coil up before his eyes like scorpions," he turns to music, painting, and physical exercise.[19]

Alberti, by his own account, was an athletic prodigy, who could leap over men standing by, who had no equal in throwing the javelin, who could pierce iron breastplates when he fired an arrow. Some of these accomplishments are peculiar, as if to guarantee their authentic and nongeneric character. In a church, he could throw a coin in the air so as to strike the vault. And on horseback, "he would hold an elongated rod, one end of which was placed on the top of his foot and the other he held in his hand, and with this he would guide his horse in every direction, with the stick constantly moving for hours on end."[20]

Although Alberti writes of his contact with "various princes," you would learn nothing in the *Vita anonima* of his elite connections at courts and chancelleries, which included some of the most famous intellects of his time. He barely mentions a classical author, and cites none (as he does unfailingly in his other writings). There is a dimension of the sensory and the concrete that on one hand aligns with the milieu of the workshops, the habitus of Manetti's woodcarver, and on the other anticipates the piquant detail of the sculptor Benvenuto Cellini's coarsely physical true-life confessions from a century later.

Why such a corporeal dimension to the self-portrait of a man of letters? Alberti's aspiration to achievements in the world of *techne*, of making and doing, reflects an awareness that knowledge produced among the mechanicals was not mere empirical wisdom and mindless labor but, through the ingenuity of Brunelleschi, Ghiberti, and others, was transforming the physical and intellectual environment in startling ways. During Alberti's lifetime, the sculptures at Orsanmichele, the dome of the cathedral, and the doors of the Baptistery all brought fame to the city and to their makers. Alberti, like Restoro long before him, considered that artisans, who sounded out the secrets of matter and its fashioning through training and expertise that were not based on textual authority, whose knowledge was grounded in hands-on experience, had a special purchase on the natural world that the university-educated "natural philosophers"—the science experts of the day—did not.

De pictura is the work where Alberti seeks to systematize knowledge gained among the artists of Florence—especially perspective, the principles of which were worked out by Brunelleschi and Ghiberti based on medieval optics—packaging them in elegant Latin and sprinkling them with exempla from Pliny the Elder, Lucian, and Cicero. Particularly important is the claim he makes in *De pictura* for an embodied, empirical expertise that enables a learned capacity of discernment: "Mathematicians measure the shape and form of things in the mind alone and divorced entirely from matter. We, on the other hand, who wish to talk of things that are visible, will use a more fleshy Minerva in writing."[21] The phrase *pinguiore Minerva*, adapted from Cicero *De amicitia* v.19, means "coarser form of wisdom"—that is, a sensory as opposed to purely cerebral way of knowing. (He himself began a treatise on metal casting, only recently discovered.)[22] Regarding the autobiography, it is as if Alberti's attention to, even momentary identification with, the artisanal world allows his own body to appear, even in glimpses.

Alberti wrote elsewhere of the embodied artisan, the follower of "fleshy Minerva" who thinks in the act of making, who proclaims wisdom in sensate form through a coarse antiliterary poetics. He included an example of such a "painter's fiction" in his Latin novel *Momus* around 1450. *Momus* is a dystopian fable of catastrophic encounters between the Olympian gods and the newly created human race. Toward the climax, Charon the boatman of Hades relates a philosophical tale to the ghost of a philosopher named Gelastus. Charon says he learned the tale not from a philosopher, "for all your reasoning revolves only around subtleties and verbal quibbles," but from a painter. "By himself this man saw more while looking at lines [*lineamentis contemplandis*] than all you philosophers do when you're measuring and investigating the heavens."[23]

For Alberti, the attribution of this fable to a "painter," whose artisanal wisdom is held up at the expense of the bickering sects of philosophers, needs to be taken seriously. Alberti's term *lineamenta*—which can be translated as "outlines" in the sense of "fundamental principles" as well as "drawings"—had been employed a few years previously by the Ghiberti in *Commentaries* and is used by Alberti himself in his *De re aedificatoria*.[24]

Charon continues: "This painter used to say that the artificer of a great work had been selecting and purifying the material from which he was to create man. Some said the material was clay mixed with honey, others said warm wax." Yet some of the creatures fashioned by this artificer were unhappy with the bodies they have been given and were allowed to refashion their own appearances. In the course of various misadventures, they took on various bestial and monstrous forms: "rejected by their fellow humans, and realizing that they were all made from the same clay, they put on masks fashioned to look like other people's faces. This artificial method of looking like human beings became so commonly employed that you could scarcely distinguish the fake faces from the real ones, unless you happened to look closely at the eye holes of the masks that covered them. Only then would observers encounter the varied faces of the monsters. These masks, called *fictiones*, lasted until they reached the waters of the River Acheron and no further, for when they entered the river they were dissolved in its steaming vapor."[25]

It looks like an allegory, but of what? Above all, the painter's fable suggests a disturbing ontology of the human as something other than human, of the face as an inscrutable dissembling surface, rendering human and animal natures indistinguishable. Nowhere is it made so blatant that identity is a matter of artifice, or artificial matter that can be cast off. The Christian duality of hylomorphism—that is, of body inhabited by spirit—is displaced by bodies of clay bearing additional layers of clay, masks made of earth, that betray their nonhuman alterity only at the eyes.

Alberti's fable is particularly suggestive given that fashioners of images were increasingly recognized and in demand as fashioners of portraits, whether of wax and clay, or paint and marble. Around 1490 Giovanni Pico della Mirandola would celebrate the chameleon-like nature of man in general, *plastes et fictor sui ipsius*—"his own sculptor and fashioner."[26] Alberti, who rendered his own portrait in a bronze plaquette, was already, a generation before, *plastes et fictor* of his own features, as was Ghiberti, who included his self-portrait in both sets of doors for the Florence Baptistery, and Filarete, in his doors for St. Peter's, and in a bronze medal (fig. 14). Brunelleschi is not known to have portrayed himself, but his likeness was preserved with a molded cast of his face made on his deathbed in 1446 (Florence, Opera del duomo).

There is no particular reason to think that Leonardo read Alberti's *Momus*. Yet we have already seen in chapter 2 that there is much in his own writing that is consonant with Alberti's pessimistic anthropology, especially as manifest in his disturbing and violent fables and prophecies:

And many will be robbed of their stores and their food, and will be cruelly submerged and drowned by folks devoid of reason. O justice of God! Why dost thou not awake to behold thy creatures thus abused? (Of bees).

He drew on the same tradition of classical antihumanism as Alberti, who in another text, *Profugiorum ab aerumna*, cites a maxim from Plautus, "man is wolf to man" (*homo homini lupus*). On one hand, Alberti's characterization of artisanal wisdom as an eccentric perspective, as an outlier voice, is one that Leonardo's writing often affirms, with its earthy, oral character, its salty wit and invective. In his later writings, however—in the last decade or so of his life—he styles himself as an *author* (still a far from conventional one), with language as a frame for geometrical demonstration, with sideways moves from descriptions of the motion of water to melancholy reflections on the future of the earth and of humanity. It is as if he was seeking legitimation as a *vernacular* philosopher, in the mold of Paolo Toscanelli or Luca Pacioli; both geometry and melancholy were essential attributes of the philosopher.[27]

In Alberti's masquerade of multiple personae, which earned him the epithet "chameleon" from Landino, he could reconcile a multiplicity of voices, forms of writing, and professional roles. He was the humanist sage, the practitioner of knowledge grounded in labor and craft know-how, and, most strikingly, the narrator and subject of a life where his embodied being bears witness as the ground of experience, sensation, and knowledge.

By contrast, what appears as a reconciled multiplicity in Alberti manifests itself in Leonardo as tension and fragmentation. If Leonardo can be said to manifest a persona, it is shaped by contradictory imperatives: on one hand, the claim that his authorship and authority lie in a philosophical valorization of "experience" through *scienza*. On the other, and increasingly over time, a progressive sense of alienation from the world of the workshop, craft secrets, making as knowing, labor and the body, where experience is conceived in terms of the eye's engagement with the world and not the hand's. His very intellectual distinctiveness is the outcome of these contradictions. Recall in addition the violent political disarray and its impact on the places where Leonardo worked, and on his patrons and publics.

LEONARDO'S ABSENT BODY

Alberti could put his body on display in his own text because he himself would never be regarded as a "mechanical." There was far more at risk for Leonardo. There is only one very early passage in Leonardo's notes, from around 1480, where his vocation as seeker into nature's mysteries is described in terms of bodily experience. That is the text on a leaf of the Codex Arundel (155r), discussed above in chapter 2, where he recorded his hesitation before exploring a cave, both physical sensations and inner emotions. "Bending my back into an arch I rested my tired hand on my knee and held my right hand over my downcast and contracted eyebrows, often bending first one way and then the other, to see whether I could discover anything inside, and this being forbidden by the deep darkness within, and after having remained there some time, two emotions arose in me, fear and desire: fear of the threatening dark cave, desire to see whether there were any wondrous thing within it."[28]

We don't even have a verifiable self-portrait. What does the faceless, nonconfessional, nonphysicality of Leonardo signify? Especially since his writings and drawings are full of observations about the bodies, the facial expressions, the emotional behaviors of others, and copiously refer to the physical habits, often stated to be repulsive, of human beings in general? In fact, as a self-styled seeker of truth, concerned with the nature of physical reality and the relation of matter and motion in living things, his writings betray a profound ambivalence about the materiality of the human and animal bodily life that he saw, touched, smelled, and drew—in the latter case with more attentiveness than anyone before him. More than one passage reduces a common human and animal nature to the digestive tract: "Man and animals are really the passage and conduit of food, the sepulcher of animals and resting-place of the dead, making life out of the death of the other (taking pleasure in the misery of others), making themselves the covering for corruption."[29]

Or even more graphically: "The flesh of the animals is made anew by the blood which is continually produced by that which nourishes them, and that this flesh is destroyed and returns by the mesaraic arteries and passes into the intestines, where it putrefies in a foul and fetid death, as they show us in their eliminations and the steaming like the smoke and fire."[30]

In a note from ca. 1495 on the planning of a new city with canals for transportation and waste disposal, Leonardo advises Ludovico Sforza that "[the prince] may also draw revenue from ten cities of five thousand houses with thirty thousand habitations; and you will disperse so great a concourse of people who, herding together like goats one upon the back of another filling every part with their stench, sow the seeds of pestilence and death. And the city will be of a beauty equal to its name, and useful to you for its revenues and the perpetual fame of its growth."[31]

It is as if Leonardo recognized that to tell of his life would be not only a history of his body, of physical pleasures and sufferings, but a revelation of the labor and strife of the workshop, especially as it becomes a dissecting room or what we'd now call a laboratory. In his manuscript notes on the preparation of artists' materials, there are recipes for the washing of panels with urine, the making of caustic salts for the casting of the Sforza horse by burning human excrement, the treatment of oils with vinegar to remove their foul odors.[32] Yet none of this prosaic material found its way into the drafts for a *Libro di pittura*, dominated by precepts from applied optics and Aristotelian psychology.

Such constant contact with human matter probably underlies the peculiar misanthropy of Leonardo's caricatures (plate 24) and the sense of philosophical despondency that appears as a constant vein throughout his writings. And note that in such moments it is as if we see Leonardo in dialogue with himself through second-person address, a dimension to be discussed shortly.

[Nature] has ordained that many animals shall be food for others. Nay, this not satisfying her desire, to the same end she sends forth certain poisonous and pestilential vapors and frequent plagues upon the vast increase and congregation of animals, and most of all upon men, who increase vastly because other animals do not feed upon them. . . . This earth therefore seeks to lose its life, desiring only continual reproduction, as **you** continually demonstrate in **your** arguments; like effects always follow like causes, animals are a type of the life of the world [my emphasis].[33]

While some of the prophecies and fables, like the caricature drawings, target the pompous delusions of the rich, it often appears that the laboring poor "herded together like goats" are far more exposed to the catastrophic rhythms of generation and corruption, the cruel *motus* and *impetus* of nature. In a proto-mechanistic organization of society like the one Leonardo offered his lord at Milan, bodies become not just objects of knowledge in themselves but are put to use as massed assemblages for the performance of labor. While nature is a great machine, a machine-like operation of society can protect against nature's malignancy, its scattering of dirt and disorder. In futuristic visions like the cannon foundry, these massed struggling bodies have come to look like extensions of the great instruments of annihilation that they have worked to bring into being (plate 25). As one who sees, draws, and writes about the mechanical principles underlying labor, Leonardo maintains a cold perspectival distance. Thus, about his own bodily engagement he will remain silent.

Leonardo wrote, in his projected *Libro di pittura*, that the sculptor's art is "an extremely mechanical operation, generally accompanied by a great sweat and much perspiration which mingled with dust becomes converted into mud. His face becomes plastered and powdered all over with marble dust, which makes him look like a baker, and he is covered in minute chips of marble, which makes him look like he is covered in snow. His house is in a mess and covered in chops and dust from the stone." A painter, by comparison, is like a humanist in his study: "he may dress himself in whatever clothes he pleases. His residence is clean and filled with delightful pictures, and he often enjoys the accompaniment of music or the company of the authors of various fine works that can be heard with great pleasure without the crashing of hammers and other confused noises."[34]

Leonardo is not alone in this respect. One of his contemporaries, Pomponius Gauricus, published a book in humanist Latin about the art of sculpture in 1503. His chapter on the process of casting in metal, for which he employs the Greek word *chemiken*, "that ignoble art that has been widely practiced over the centuries, which deals with the transformation of metals," begins with an apology: "Since it is a dirty and smoky work, it might seem more appropriate if we left it out. For it concerns the handling not of wax and boxwood tablets, but of clay, dung, coal and the bellows."[35] He nonetheless proceeds to give a detailed description, clearly informed by observing the foundries of Padua and Venice, of lost wax and other casting processes. As Pamela S. Smith writes in *The Body of the Artisan*, "Many observers were baffled by about how to clearly describe techniques that were learned by observation and imitation, much less how to transmit the nonverbal components of artisanal practices." They tended to attribute their own bafflement "to the messiness and nontheoretical character of manual work, rather than to their own lack of ability to articulate artisanal practices."[36]

It is as if Leonardo and Gauricus saw the enterprise of knowing the physical world as potentially contaminated by the very visceral conditions of obtaining this knowledge: the artisan's domain of matter and clutter, the dirty, sweaty, malodorous world of physical labor, that marks the lives and writings of artists like Pontormo, Cellini, Bertoldo, Michelangelo, and Bronzino.[37] In their world, the artisan's body—and its collision with the courtly world of refined bodily constraint—seems almost the basis for a professional solidarity. Not so for Leonardo, whose aspirations to write philosophy and *scientia* grounded in experience were undermined by his mechanical, autodidact, and outlier status—or rather by prejudice against it.

This is the prejudice that he famously confronted throughout his writing: in his styling of an authorial self, the very energy and heft of his prose are sustained by rivalry with the literary professionals.

LEONARDO AND THE ANTIPICTORIAL TRADITION

In Leonardo's time, a relatively new class of Latin literary scholars constituted an intellectual establishment of which he was very conscious. They were sometimes known as humanists because of their expertise in *humanae litterae*—that is, the liberal arts in the traditional academic curriculum, which were defined as the intellectual disciplines worthy of "freeborn minds." The scholarship of figures like Guarino of Verona, Angelo Poliziano, and Erasmus combined the study of Latin (sometimes Greek and Hebrew) texts with a historical perspective, a scientific approach to language that enabled them to distinguish authentic ancient texts from medieval forgeries and interpolations. That sometimes put them at log-gerheads with the ecclesiastical establishment, and so too did their defense of reading and imitation of literature seen as "pagan" or profane.

Prejudice against the mechanical arts often served the ends of humanist self-definition. Although Alberti defended "fleshy Minerva," arts contami-nated by base matter could not be "liberal," worthy of free minds. Petrarch had even sought to undercut the prestige and self-importance of physicians by insisting on their contamination by the malodorous corruption of the human body.[38] In turn, professors of medicine themselves maintained a hierarchical distinction between their own book-based knowledge and the low-level "empirics" who prepared remedies and the barber surgeons who opened bodies for anatomical demonstrations carried out at the medical schools at the end of winter each year: the professor, his hands unsullied, read from canonical texts by Galen and Aristotle (fig. 15).

Detractors of painting were particularly derisive of its ability to convey more than mere appearance, its reliance on surface and sensual charms, its precarious materiality. Teachers of the *humanae litterae* drew on the long-standing idea that the appeal of painting was only sensual, even de-ceptively meretricious—akin to sophistry in rhetoric. In 1452 the great humanist Guarino of Verona complimented his son Battista on a "prose portrait" of the Byzantine scholar Manuel Chrysoloras: "You warn us well and prudently of the greater power and dignity of the use of writing than painting, for the latter lies silent while the former is always alert and speak-ing; the former also inspires us to an imitation of the good and towards the imbibing of honesty, but to the latter only remains the power of feeding

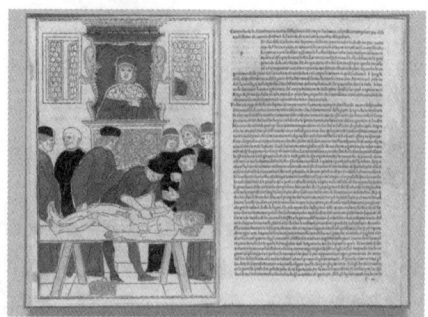

15. Johannes de Ketham? *Fasciculo di medicina* (Venice: Johannes and Gregorius de Gregoriis, 1493). Printed book with hand-colored woodcuts, 31.6 × 21.5 × 1.5 cm. New York, Metro-politan Museum of Art.

the eyes. Therefore, Cicero referred to painting as a pastime for boys, and Virgil wrote 'painting is fodder for empty minds.'"[39]

In the tradition of Restoro, some artists were aware of and responded to such prejudices. The painter Cennino Cennini, a contemporary of Guarino, wrote a handbook where he disputed the humanist distinction between poetry and painting—both were equally dependent on the mind's power of visualization: "[painting] calls for imagination, and skill of hand [*fantasia, con operazione di mano*], in order to discover things not seen, hiding themselves under the shadow of natural objects, and to fix them with the hand, presenting to plain sight what does not actually exist [*dando a dimostrare quello che non è, sia*]. And it justly deserves to be enthroned next to science [*scienza*, i.e., theoretical knowledge], and to be crowned with poetry." Just as the poet can compose by putting things together, so too "the painter is given freedom to compose a figure, standing, seated, half-man, half-horse, as he pleases, according to his imagination."[40]

The arguments of the literati against painting and sculpture were repeated ad nauseam well into the sixteenth century, but by the late 1400s artists in the wake of Cennini were answering back. In 1490, while Leonardo was working on the great equestrian monument for Ludovico Sforza, the court poet Francesco Puteolano composed a preface to the vernacular edition of Giovanni Simonetta's *Sforziada*. The short text collates some shopworn humanist commonplaces on the superiority of literature to paintings, sculptures, and public works, in securing the fame of the deceased: "Many painted and many sculpted the likeness of Trajan, but far more expressive and everlasting was the image that Pliny the Younger left in his letters, which the ravages of time cannot extinguish, and of the work of the ancient painters and sculptors hardly anything remains intact," and so on.[41] It has been suggested that Leonardo began to compose his polemics in defense of the superiority of painting at that point, and in 1498 he would have an intellectually powerful ally in the person of the mathematician Fra Luca Pacioli, who engaged in a "laudibile e scientifico duello" with various physicians and astrologers of the Sforza court.[42] Pacioli's account was included in the preface to his treatise *De divina proportione*, which appeared in print in 1509 with illustrations designed by Leonardo.

Luca recalls Leonardo's presence at the disputation and praises his Sforza monument and his *Last Supper*. He goes on to proclaim the superiority of mathematics to a whole array of arts and sciences that are dependent on its principles, including astrology, warfare, theology, philosophy, and law. In the traditional two-part scheme of the Seven Liberal Arts, the basis of the arts curriculum in the medieval university, the so-called quadrivium had included the sciences of Arithmetic, Geometry, Astronomy, and Music. Luca now insisted that there should be a fifth, Perspective. Just as Music is concerned with harmonic ratios intelligible to the sense of hearing, Perspective—which includes the science of painting—concerned the geometric laws governing human vision. This bold reassignment of painting to a place within the Liberal Arts, grounded in its theoretical or scientific basis in mathematics, had been recognized earlier in the century by Alberti and by his humanist contemporary in Padua, the physician Michele Savonarola. Recalling Giotto's activity in Padua, Savonarola had written: "[Painting] provides a particular embellishment for our city as it is to be associated with the study of letters and the cultivated arts more than the other arts are, as it is a part of perspective, which deals with the projections of rays. And this is a part of philosophy."[43] Anticipating Pacioli, the Florentine goldsmith Antonio Pollaiuolo included Perspective in his own allegorical scheme of Eight Liberal Arts on the tomb of Pope Sixtus IV in St. Peter's in Rome, completed just a few years before (fig. 16).

That a fellow Florentine artisan, whom Leonardo undoubtedly knew, could take this bold step of challenging the traditional organization of knowledge indicates that Leonardo could have acquired the idea independently of Pacioli. There is no need to determine who influenced whom on this point; we might consider both authorial enterprises as conjoined, or co-inherent. Around the time of the "scientifico duello," Leonardo wrote that painting was "a subtle invention which brings philosophy and subtle speculation to bear on the nature of all forms . . . which are enveloped in shade and light." Painting was not only "a science, the true-born child of nature, for painting is born of nature"—or rather since painting is born of and also represents nature, it might be thought of "as the granddaughter of nature and as the kin of God."[44]

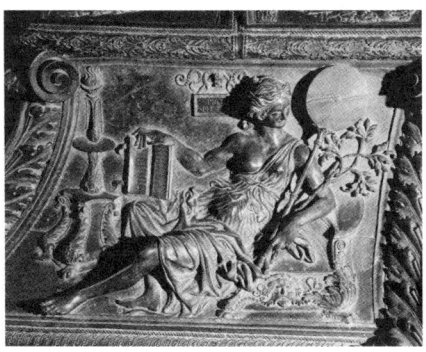

16. Antonio Pollaiuolo, *Allegory of Perspective*, from the monument to Sixtus IV. 1484–93. Bronze. Rome, Vatican, Grotte Vaticane.

Also significant is Pacioli's mockery of poetry, "vague fables and other ridiculous and false trifles, unbelievable poetic fictions, vague notions that please the ear," which he contrasts with the certainty of geometry. The attack is very similar to Leonardo's energetic polemic against poetry, in the lengthy *proemio* intended for his treatise, where painting is proclaimed to be superior by virtue of its association with true science, and its effect of simultaneity or immediacy.[45]

"The eye, which is said to be the window of the soul, is the primary means by which the *sensus communis* [i.e., receptor of sensory impressions] of the brain may most fully and magnificently contemplate the infinite works of nature; and the ear is the second, acquiring nobility through the recounting of things which the eye has seen. If you, historians or poets or mathematicians, had not seen things through your eyes, you would only be able to report them feebly in your writings. And you, poet, should wish to depict a story as if painting with your pen, the painter with his brush will more likely succeed and will be understood less laboriously. If you assert that painting is dumb poetry, the painter may call poetry blind painting."[46]

Two strikes here: first, against poetry (or literature in general), which is "tedious" because it can only represent phenomena word by word and detail by detail. Second, against the "blindness" of literature, because the immediacy of vision is mediated, even obscured, by the opacity of written signs. Painting works through the simulation of space and form, unlike poetry, and delivers more "satisfaction"; though poetry attempts to describe forms, actions, and places in words, the painter employs the actual similitude of the forms, in order to reproduce them. Consider, then, which

is nearer to the actual man, the name of the man, or his image? The name
of the man changes with change of country; but his form is not changed
except by death.

A portrait is "truer" than a name. Humanists had a ready answer to
this one, as we saw: that artists could only portray extrinsic characteristics,
not the qualities of mind or soul—in fact, they were resisting the prevailing
attitude implied by Leonardo here, that the body is the grounds for, if
not identical to, what we now call a "self." Leonardo knows well not to
go down this philosophical path, because his framing is polemical and
rhetorical, not metaphysical or psychological. He practically concedes this
point in a further passage, which accepts the duality of mind and body: "If
poetry embraces moral philosophy, painting is natural philosophy. If poetry describes the operation of the mind, painting considers the action of
the mind in bodily motions."[47] (The mind or soul, however, as we shall see
in chapter 5, is ghost-like and even depersonalized in Leonardo's writings.)

Leonardo proceeds undaunted by his apparent admission of painting's
superficiality, its concern with externals. A painter's depiction of a furious
battle will draw far more attention than a poet's description of one, if you
put them together in public: "Inscribe the name of God in any place and set
up His image opposite and you will see which will be most revered. Painting
embraces within itself all the forms of nature, while you have nothing but
their names, which are not universal as form is; and if you have the effects
of demonstrations, we have demonstrations of the effects. Take a poet who
describes the beauty of a lady to her lover and a painter who portrays her
and you will see where nature guides the enamored judge. Certainly, the
proof should be allowed to rest on the verdict of experience."[48]

There is undoubted boldness here, and not a little risk. The simulations of painting include the simulation of divinity itself, thus raising the
specter, or abomination even, of pagan idolatry. This is even more the case
when Leonardo makes painting into a (female) divinity who simulates the
operations of God: "we should conclude that [painting] is not only a science but a goddess which should be duly accorded that title. This deity re-
peats all the visible works of almighty God."[49] The "goddess of the science
of painting extends over works human as well as divine." Not only does
she guide architects, potters, goldsmiths, weavers, and embroiderers, "she

has invented the characters in which the different languages are written, she has given the numbers to the mathematician, and has described the figures of geometry, she teaches perspectivists, astronomers, mechanics, and engineers."[50]

More radically, Leonardo affirms many of the negative characterizations of painting leveled by its literary enemies: it is not only literal but traffics in illusion, working on the senses just as effectively as the objects or bodies it represents: painting can arouse love "which is the main motive of the species in the whole animal world." Artists "have represented acts of wantonness and lust which kindled these passions in the beholders. Poetry could not do as much. And if you write a description of gods, such writing will never be worshipped in the same way as paintings of divinity." Finally, in an echo of Cennini, he holds that painting's powers of simulation are such that it conjures into being what does not exist, and is not limited by what exists in nature: "It was wrong, O writers, to leave painting out from the number of the Liberal Arts, because she deals not only with the works of nature but over an infinite multitude of things which nature never created."[51]

The defense of painting—or image-making in general, from the logocentrism or linguistic bias of the humanists—tactfully avoids an affirmation of the materiality and handmade nature of the plastic arts, and the importance of craft knowledge. In one of Leonardo's few references to contemporary artists, the glazed ceramics of the della Robbia are praised for their permanence, less even as sculpture than as a more permanent form of painting: "Painting can be made . . . worthy of esteem by the use of glazed pigments on metal or terracotta, which are melted in a furnace and then polished with different tools to produce a smooth and shining surface, as can be seen . . . with the family della Robbia, who have discovered a process of producing large works of all kinds by painting on terracotta and covering it with glaze. . . . As regards permanence they compare with sculpture, but they are incomparably superior in beauty because they combine both kinds of perspective, while in sculpture in the round there is no perspective except what is supplied by nature."[52]

Leonardo's rejoinder to the humanists, poets, and literati (often incorrectly referred to as the *paragone* or "comparison," a term not applied to these writings until 1817)[53]—is taken to be among the most radical manifestations of his thought and a proto-modern theorization of what painting is.[54] Its apparent grounding in medium specificity—how painting prevails against sculpture, poetry, or music through qualities particular to itself—has, for some commentators, seemed to prefigure the mid-twentieth-century manifestos of pictorial formalism and abstract art, which called for painting to stress the flatness of its support, to reject simulation of space and relief, and to shun literary reference.

Poetry, in Leonardo's invective, seemingly has no autonomy as an art. Poets, he writes, claim that they are superior to painters because they can rouse people to argue, to take up arms, or describe the sky and the stars and nature. "To which we reply that none of the things which he enumerates pertain to his own profession and that in the making of speeches and orations he will be beaten by the orator; that in speaking of the stars he is stealing his subject from the astronomer, in speaking of philosophy from the philosopher, and that as matter of fact poetry has no domain of its own and does not have one any more than a shopkeeper [*merchaio*] who collects all sorts of merchandise from various artisans."[55]

He was captivated by the idea of the poet as a petty trader or thief, a turning of the tables on poetry's claim to be a liberal art, and made two drafts of this passage (Melzi included both in his compilation of the *Libro di pittura* from Leonardo's notes). Thus at the conclusion of the first part of the *Libro*, the poet is described as not only a merchant who stocks goods made by different artisans but a broker (*sensale*) "who gathers various persons together to conclude a deal. If you wish to discover the true office of the poet, you will find that he is nothing other than an accumulation of things stolen from various sciences, with which he fabricates a deceitful composition—or we more fairly say a fictional composition."[56]

The polemics resurface in his anatomical drawings of 1508–13. On one Windsor sheet (RCIN 919071), a tour de force drawing of the heart, the lungs, and the bronchial blood vessels of an ox, Leonardo inveighed against the arrogance of authors: "Oh writer, with what words will you write about the perfection and complete portrayal which this drawing here presents . . . with what words will you describe this heart here so as not to fill a book? And the longer you write about details the more you will confuse the mind of the audience and you will always feel the need to have interpreters, or return to the example of experience" (plate 26).[57]

The polemics transcribed in the first part of Melzi's compilation of Leonardo's notes on painting (the Vatican Codex Urbinas 1270), and revived in the anatomical drawings, are a series of ideological or political claims staked against literature, drawing on widespread and long-standing antiliterary prejudice and on the more assailable claims made on literature's behalf. Leonardo knew that poetry was itself under attack, along with all the cultural capital that humanists had claimed for it since Dante had proclaimed his *Commedia* to be divinely inspired. In the wake of Dante, and most influentially with Giovanni Boccaccio, Coluccio Salutati, and Leonardo's contemporary Cristoforo Landino, poetry was asserted to be a kind of universal knowledge, even spiritual insight, veiled in the artifice of language. The pre-Christian poet Virgil was believed to have prophesized the coming of Christ in his 4th Eclogue, and Dante, who cast the ghost of Virgil as guide through the afterlife in the *Commedia*, was regarded as a theological visionary and encyclopedic source of wisdom.

Yet some learned members of the clergy acquainted with the world-view of humanism challenged these claims. In 1455 Ermolao Barbaro the Elder, Bishop of Verona, had deployed his own classical erudition to ridicule the notion that poetry was a form of theology—it was pagan lies, it bore the taint of the evil license and hedonism of the ancients, and its inventor, Orpheus, was a pederast.[58] During the 1490s Leonardo would have known that the Dominican friar Girolamo Savonarola, whose preaching had brought about the downfall of the Medici regime and the creation of a new Florentine Republic, had been railing against secular literature and other vanities, including painting.

He mostly avoids the central and most controversial target of the *contra poetas* backlash—the insistence by Boccaccio and Salutati that the self-hood of poets is permeable by powerful supernatural forces beyond themselves, that poetry could thus be a form of theology or prophecy. That idea is central to the great pictorial ensemble created by his colleague Raphael in the apartment of Julius II in the Vatican. The pictorial scheme reveals the harmony of Philosophy, Poetry, Theology, and Law. Poetry is represented in the great lunette of Apollo and the Muses with the great poets

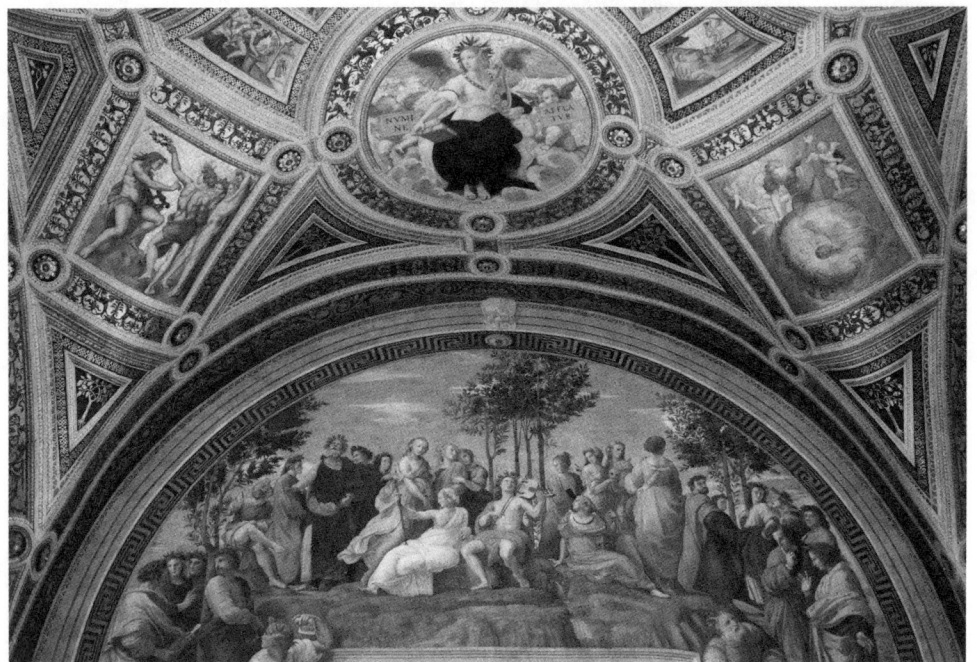

17. Raphael, *Parnassus* and the *Allegory of Poetry*. 1511. Fresco. Vatican, Stanza della Segnatura.

of antiquity and more recent times: Apollo looks heavenward, toward the personification of Poesia in the vault, an angelic figure with the inscription NUMINE AFFLATUR—"filled with the breath of the divine" (fig. 17). Dante appears among the poets, and a second time among the theologians.

Leonardo's invective is a manifestation of a phenomenon recurring in the Greco-Latin tradition since the time of Socrates: the challenge to the presumed authority of literature, a rhetorical act of war that seeks not only to limit but to occupy the territory of the literary. In fact, there may be no more inclusive conception of what literature actually is other than that provided by the detractors of literature and their constant return to the same cluster of arguments. For William Marx, "Literature is what remains when the other discourses have completely taken over the field. It claims the smallest share. Literature is what is attacked. Even the smallest share can still be reduced, can't it? (read: scribblers, be happy with what you've been left—it's already more than you deserve)."[59]

In *The Hatred of Literature*, Marx argues that literature is challenged because of its perceived authority. Thus, Plato attacks the authority of poetry in order to advance the claims of philosophy; proponents of AI have lately declared the venerable college essay to be a dead letter. Literature is challenged for its untruthfulness (think of Barbaro's repudiation of "poetic theology"); on moral grounds (the perspective that the "fables of the poets" are corrupting, irreligious, pagan, or that certain novels propagate un-American values in public schools); and on social grounds (as in the idea, sometimes encountered in education op-eds, that teaching premodern literature is elitist and irrelevant). Leonardo can be aligned with the antiliterary arguments from authority—he targets literature's unwarranted prestige, its reliance on theological and philosophical content—and truth: it fails to convey nature "as it is." Marx notes regarding Leonardo that he employs the antiliterary trope of virtue-signaling, in his claim to be a "man without letters" (*omo sanza lettere*): "Good letters are born of a good disposition; and since the cause is more to be praised than the effect, I will rather praise a good disposition without letters, than good letters without the disposition."[60]

This is as close as Leonardo gets to laying claim to a selfhood—where "good disposition" is manifest through a lack. To be sure, the claim to be "without letters"—that is, to lack a formal education in Latin—reflects a real social disadvantage, an intractable restriction on who could be considered producers of knowledge or science. Yet the claim is also a challenge to that state of affairs, a bid to undermine the citadel of official forms of learning. Leonardo obtained access to learning of all kinds—he read Latin works in vernacular versions and summaries, increasingly available through commercial printing; he sought to teach himself Latin (apparently with some success); he owned a wide array of books in Italian, both literary and technical (including manuals on composing letters); and he was surrounded by people who could relay the contents of books by Galen, Euclid, Archimedes, Aristotle, and many others.

In his longer writings and drafts for books, moreover, such as the text on water and geology preserved as the Codex Leicester, he was also concerned with sounding lettered, cultivating a sonorous and declamatory written style. Even as he protested "with what language and with what vocabulary

will I be able to express or tell of the vile ruination, the incredible desola-
tion, the inexorable rapacity of rapacious rivers in flood, against which no
human resource can avail?" he collected lists of vocabulary with which to
register the "impetus and acceleration" of water: "rebound, circulation,
revolution, rotation, turning, repercussing, submerging, surging, declina-
tion, elevation, depression, consummation, percussion, destruction, collapse, impetuosity, turnings about, beatings upon, collisions, floodings,
ripplings, boilings, saggings, slowings, scattering."[61] As Gombrich noted,
"If anything is striking in these studies and notes about water, it is the
predominance of the word and the role assigned to language. Whether
he knew it or not, in the paragone between word and image the word was
here very often in the lead."[62] Yet it was not just the denotative function of
language that was in the lead; syntactically and rhythmically, Leonardo's
writing manifests effects of cacophony and turbulence that evoke what he
seeks to describe.[63]

Marx observes that the opponents of literature seek to occupy not just
the ground occupied by the poets but their technical means: "The exile of
the poets does not necessarily entail the end of poetry. . . . One discourse
drives out another, truth drives out falsehood, philosophy drives out the
epic. Poetry as such may disappear, but its performative and truth-telling
function remains, taken up by a variety of people other than poets." He
concludes, aphoristically, "Convict the Muse of lying and then hang her:
the first thing to do is to eliminate her in order to take her place."[64]

It was an old maneuver, for an outlier seeking to challenge a professional status quo that excluded them. Leonardo and his interlocut-
ers probably associated the rejection of eloquence with the vocation of
the professional philosopher—which had been the thrust of Petrarch's
complaint about the university Aristotelians ("scholastics"): "They assert that I do not have a trace of knowledge. As for eloquence, if I have
any at all, they despise it as our modern philosophers do, and reject it as
unworthy of learned men. At present, the only thing which they honor
in a philosopher are babyish and puzzled babbling." They ignore the
eloquence of Aristotle himself: "They deviate and depart so far from
their leader that they think eloquence an impediment and a disgrace to
philosophy."[65]

Artisanal writing was also typically characterized by claims to be communicating without eloquence, a "rhetoric of non-rhetoric," as if plain writing sought to be more transparent to real experience: "I saw this with my own eyes."[66] The claim of writing plainly, without learning or art, was one typical of members of a class who were not *literatus*— learned in Latin. Leonardo's self-image as a philosopher is imagined in terms of "natural" wisdom, without degrees or academic curricula, where being non-*literatus* is a guarantee of authentic witnessing, of unfalsified experience, *autopsia*: "[presumptuous persons] will say that I, having no literary skill, cannot properly express that which I desire to treat of; but they do not know that my subjects are to be dealt with by experience rather than by words; and [experience] has been the mistress of those who wrote well."[67]

Leonardo's self-definition against eloquence and literariness may have been an impetus to one of his more idiosyncratic scientific speculations. In his drafts for his treatise on painting, he sought to give his elevation of painting over poetry a neurobiological basis: a description of perception and cognition that played fast and loose with Aristotelian teaching on the faculties of the brain, the relation between sensation and knowledge. He claimed that the images of the poet's imagination (*immaginatione*) are conceived without any intake of sensory impressions from outside the mind, and thus are bloodless figments with little impact or duration in the brain of the poet—or of his readers: "The imagination does not see as excellently as the eye sees, because the eye receives the species or similitudes of objects and gives them to the *impressiva* [receptor of sense impressions in the brain], and the *impressiva* gives it to the *senso commune* [common sense, the area of the brain concerned with cognition] and there it is judged." But imagination is disconnected from the eye; it has access only to the less vivid sense impressions in the memory, where imagination "stops and dies if the thing imagined is not of great excellence. And indeed, the work of the poet is [only] in the mind or imaginative faculty of the poet who feigns the same things as the painter . . . therefore, with regard to these [poetic] fictions it would be true to claim that there is the same proportion between the science of painting and poetry as there is between the body and its derivative shadow."[68]

By contrast, the painter draws on an image-forming faculty that is pneumatically responsive to sensory impressions received through the eye. Leonardo invents an entirely new faculty in the front ventricle of the brain (displacing the "common sense" from its traditional location)—the *impressiva* (or *imprensiva*), which registers the impetus of visual impressions almost like tactile imprints in wax.[69] This contravened Aristotelian and scholastic teaching on the relation between the senses and the higher cognitive functions of the brain, which assigned the imagination a primary role in the transmission of sense impressions to the intellect and thence to the ventricle of memory. Well-informed readers or listeners would not have taken Leonardo's alternative formulation seriously—one wonders if he expected them to.

LEONARDO AS LITERATURE

Leonardo's attack on poetry does not claim to be a manifesto or a theory of painting. If that were the case, it would be disingenuous; it is clear from his writings that he does not regard painting as more autonomous than poetry, and that painting can only be made to seem so by reducing it to the immateriality of geometry and optics. His body of work testifies to an understanding that painting works through visual conventions as much as through simulation and illusion, and that it achieves its end through taking on the "picturing" qualities of language—the specialty of the poet and the rhetorician.

Leonardo knew that his own over-rigorous territorial boundary between word and image risked limiting the scope of the art of painting itself. In the more technical chapters of his treatise, which mostly eschew the language of polemic, he walks back some of the more extreme rhetorical claims of his comparison of painting and the arts of language. The following appears under the heading "Rule to be given to boys learning to paint."

> We know clearly that vision is one of the swiftest actions that there is,
> and in one instant we see infinite forms; nevertheless, we understand
> only one thing at a time. Suppose that you, reader, were to glance rapidly
> at all this written page, and you will quickly perceive that it is full of
> various letters, but in this time you could not recognize what letters

they are nor what they were meant to tell. Hence you need to proceed word by word, line by line, to be able to understand these letters. Again, if you wish to mount to the top of an edifice you must go up step by step; otherwise it will be impossible to reach the top. So I say to you, whom nature turns to this art, if you wish to have knowledge of the forms of things, you will begin with their details, and not go on to the second until you have the first well fixed in memory and in practice.[70]

Knowledge of phenomena through the sense of sight turns out not to be so "simultaneous" after all. The artist needs to grasp nature in its particulars before a synoptic re-creation of nature can be achieved.

And there is the manifest fact that Leonardo's painted works refuse to be considered solely according to the phenomenological or "scientific" terms in which he appears to defend painting against poetry, as simulacra of optical experience. More radically and powerfully than the works of other painters of his time, Leonardo's paintings are fundamentally ordered not by the laws of optics but by the fulfillment of the visualizing functions of language—deictic (signaling an addresser and an addressee), expressive, informative, metaphoric, and above all *persuasive*.

An obvious example: a viewer who does not know or recall the text of Matthew 26:21 will not be properly equipped to understand *The Last Supper* in Milan. The subject traditionally represented the institution of the Eucharist, but Leonardo went to the evangelical text in order to add an additional dramatic layer—the Apostles' reaction to Christ's alarming utterances and his impending betrayal by Judas. Without a grasp of the scriptural density of the pictorial invention, the viewer will be in the same predicament as the ultra-formalist Bernard Berenson, whose indifference to the painting's narrative and exegetical dimensions led him to have distasteful reminiscences of a Southern Italian market: "to us Northerners the sounds and sights of a Neapolitan crowd are deafening and fatiguing, if not positively repellant." He was, he wrote, "too repelled by the illustrative side of Leonardo's *Last Supper* to be able to do full justice to the design as decoration."[71]

The late and enigmatic *St. John the Baptist* in the Louvre (see plate 5)—which confounded and intrigued Berenson, Michelet, Pater, and numerous others—becomes electrifying and vital when seen in the light (as it were) of the opening of his namesake's Gospel: "In the beginning was the Word, and the Word was with God, and the Word was God. . . . In him was life; and the life was the light of men. And the light shineth in the darkness; and the darkness apprehended it not. There came a man, sent from God, whose name was John. The same came for witness, that he might bear witness of the light, that all might believe through him. He was not the light, but came that he might bear witness of the light."

Leonardo's figure bears witness not just with his gesture and his address to the viewer but through illumination by a mysterious source. In other words, Leonardo's close observation of shadows and reflected light on complex surfaces is invested in making John's mystical text tangible and meaningful, if no less portentous. Painting operates through the simulation of sensory phenomena, but those simulations have a signifying function. As Paul Barolsky notes, "The *Saint John* is not mere 'illustration' in Berenson's disparaging sense of illustration without 'form,' for it is precisely Leonardo's chiaroscuro or form that generates the mystery in his painting, that so subtly endows it with significance. In the root sense of the word illustration (*illustrare*: to embellish; to enlighten; to give glory; to illuminate, to light up; to clarify; to elucidate) Leonardo's painting is an illumination, not an equivalence, of the enigmatic words of the Gospel on the mystery of the Word who was God who was the true Light."[72]

According to the same principle, *The Adoration of the Magi* in Florence would not be an illustration but an "illumination" of Jewish Bible texts in the Book of Isaiah on the Tree of Jesse, the birth of the Messiah, the coming of the kings, and—it would seem—the restoration of the Temple in Jerusalem (plate 12). The prominent tree by the Virgin and Child visualizes the metaphor of the Tree of Jesse in Isaiah 11, which may also have inspired the tumult of men and horses around the central group: "A shoot will come up from the stump of Jesse; from his roots a Branch will bear fruit. . . . In that day the Root of Jesse will stand as a banner for the peoples; the nations will rally to him, and his place of rest will be glorious." Most importantly of all, the dramatic chiaroscuro of the foreground, where figures emerge from dark into light, visualizes one of the most famous passages in the book, Isaiah 60: "Arise, shine; for your light has come, and

the glory of the Lord has risen upon you. For behold, darkness shall cover
the earth, and thick darkness the peoples; but the Lord will arise upon
you, and his glory will be seen upon you. And nations shall come to your
light, and kings to the brightness of your rising."[73]

None of this is to say that Leonardo's paintings only mean what the
scriptural texts are understood to mean. Referring to the Book of Isaiah is
in no sense adequate as an account of what the *Adoration* "means." Yet the
naturalism of the *Adoration* and Leonardo's other religious paintings are
deeply motivated by the multilayered significance of the scriptural texts in
Christian tradition, and they open up scriptural subject matter to dimensions of exegetical meaning that go beyond any scriptural commentary.
Only Leonardo represented the *Adoration* as a tumultuous and even terrible
event, a convulsion in historical time where past catastrophe, prophecy,
and eschatology all collide. Painters had previously normally only rendered
Christ's death on Golgotha in such cataclysmic terms, never his infancy.
Even as some of his figures might be borrowed from a near-contemporary
Adoration by Botticelli, Leonardo resisted the habitual formulas for particular subjects and sought out the historical basis for the *historia* he had to
paint—a procedure of which Alberti would have approved.[74]

Leonardo's interest in allegory and rebuses parallels his interest in
geometry: they were, after all, two parallel systems, a structural logic of
nature and a symbolic logic of culture, although unlike contemporary alchemists, astrologers, and Neoplatonists, he resisted seeing analogy and
proportional correspondence in symbolic and magical terms.[75] His allegories are exercises in invention in the interstices between picturing and
verbalization, in the fruitful mutual contaminations of word and image.
But allegory is also a habit of thought that enables the description of ho-
mologous structures: the body as microcosm of the Earth, for example—a
metaphor he borrowed from Restoro of Arezzo. Guided by analogy, where
"animals are a type of the life of the world," Leonardo's descriptions seem
to affirm a deep level of identity: "The body of the earth is of the nature
of a fish, a grampus, or a sperm whale, because it draws water as breath
instead of air."[76]

Leonardo owned a copy, in Italian translation, of Aristotle's *Meteorology*.[77] In *Meteorology* II.3, the philosopher cautioned against the use of

metaphor in the writing of natural history: "It is equally absurd to suppose that anything has been explained by calling the sea 'the sweat of the earth,' like Empedocles. Metaphors are poetical and so that expression of his may satisfy the requirements of a poem, but as a scientific theory it is unsatisfactory." Aristotle explains that the saltiness of the sea is caused by similar processes to the saltiness of urine and of sweat as liquids acquire an admixture of other substances in the course of digestion. For premodern readers like Leonardo, however, such passages may have reinforced the possibility that the analogy of microcosm to macrocosm was more than just a similitude. Leonardo resisted the reading of singular natural phenomena, like comets or monstrous births, as portents from which present or future catastrophes could be read. But these may still have been available to understanding in terms of macrocosmic analogy. When reports circulated in 1506 of a monstrous winged newborn, hermaphroditic, with one claw in place of its legs and its body marked with strange signs, one of Leonardo's assistants drew it, giving it some features of a human infant, and hence a touch of pathos (plate 27). Quite how he understood it, we don't know—but it probably reinforced an increasingly catastrophic view of nature, unsettling his habitual analogy of the harmony between microcosm and macrocosm. If man is an image of the cosmos, then what did this unfortunate child signal about the cosmos?[78] It lies hidden in his graphic output like a disturbing Other to the *Vitruvian Man* (plate 8), signaling a grasp of nature as erratic and willful.

A few years later, in 1513, Leonardo drew a rapid but convincing likeness of a boy with a conjoined parasitic twin who was being exhibited for a fee in Florence and throughout Italy (Codex Atlanticus 48r; plate 28); the drawing occurs within a period when Leonardo's art—as we will see in chapter 5—repeatedly imagined (as was the case with Cennino's centaur) the permeability and even fusion of bodies.[79] Nature, art, and language resemble and throw light on each other in their flux, their instability, their *poetic character*. The word "poetry," *poesia* in Italian, is rooted in the Greek *poiein*, "to make," as well as *poiesis*—the coming into being of that which had not existed (recall again Cennini's poetic definition of painting, above).

Working for various powerful masters in the 1490s and 1500s, Leonardo designed a number of allegorical inventions involving a monstrous fusion of bodies—for instance, Pleasure and Pain, joined at the hip (plates 29 and 29b). It is said all too frequently that Leonardo's interest in allegory is out of character, somehow anachronistic or inconsistent for an artist on the cusp of "modernity." Gombrich lamented the regressive, incipiently medievalizing character of Leonardo's allegories, as if he only produced them to gratify the "feudal" mentality of his courtly employers. Leonardo, still for some writers, is "modern" because he liberated art from "literary" meaning, turning instead to a proto-scientific view of nature.

According to this logic, Leonardo must have portrayed the young mistress of the Duke of Bari in 1489 (or probably earlier) as the fond owner of a monstrously outsize white-pelted pet stoat (plate 7).[80] Stoats, or ermines, resist being handled by humans and cannot be domesticated: that is the whole point of Leonardo's portrait—Cecilia, by her grace and virtue, has made gentle a fierce and untamable creature. While some have complained that Leonardo made the animal too large, it seems clear that we are supposed to notice the anomaly, which itself signals that the ermine is a literary conceit. The painting deliberately, even monstrously, deforms the conventions of mimesis to signal that there are meanings at stake beyond the literal subject—that appearances have been turned into signs, that poetic devices like allegory and metaphor are at work. The ermine's very aesthetic appeal lies not just in its febrile vitality, the way that Leonardo has invested it with a sense of animal intelligence, but in a poetic multiplicity of meanings: it refers to Cecilia because of its fabled purity, noted by Leonardo in one of his notebooks—it would rather die than stain its fur; moreover, the Greek word for ermine, *galée*, is a play on the name Gallerani. And Ludovico Sforza's membership of the chivalric Order of the Ermine means that the creature also stands for him, rendered gentle by his mistress's surprisingly powerful hands, more particularized than her face and looking older than Gallerani's tender years. We're a long way from the "bella mano" of the poet's beloved in the Petrarchan tradition: the hand even seems creaturely, its form echoing the animal's head. The ermine is a poetic ornament, a kind of prosthesis to the factual portrait—but little else could have so effectively conveyed the amorous mergence or co-inherence of the lovers Cecilia and Ludovico.

Leonardo's derision at the limitations of language strategically and ironically omits challenging the qualities of language that increasingly intrigued him: not just its picturing qualities but the capacity of words to make denotative meaning unstable and even chaotic.[81] Gombrich, more insightfully, saw them as demonstrations of the pitfalls of "ordinary language."[82] His collections of riddles and pseudo-prophecies draw on the possibility that a verbal account of prosaic everyday reality can be rendered fantastic and even terrifying by small lexical adjustments or circumlocutions, by irony and double entendre. Leonardo called these "propositions contrary to nature—as to speak of a substance which the more is taken from it the more it grows." The opacity of words permits unsettling shifts of tone, and above all of perspective: the ruling principle is shifting point of view.[83]

Such shifts of perspective are manifest in the panoramic geographical excursions, conveying infinite vistas and the sense of airborne motion through space, such as the conclusion of the Leicester Codex, where "Hercules breaks open the sea to the West," and the Mediterranean begins to pour forth into the Atlantic: "and, because of this great lowering, the Red Sea remained higher, and therefore the waters, having left the course through here, have always poured ever since through the Straits of Spain."[84] Elsewhere, Leonardo's speaker-persona claims instead an extraordinary, frequently preposterous breadth of Olympian vision, with vivid evocations of places—Ethiopia, the English Channel, Gibraltar, the Danube, the Black Sea—sometimes evoking an epic catastrophe of flood or of earthquake: "The trees of the great forests of Taurus, and of Sinai and of the Apennines and of Atlas shall be seen speeding by means of the air from east to west and from north to south; and transporting by means of the air great multitudes of men. Oh, how many vows! Oh, how many deaths! Oh, how many partings between friends and relations! How many will there be who shall nevermore see their own country or their own native lands! and who shall die unburied and their bones scattered in divers parts of the world."[85] Unless the reader/listener knows the caption (or "punch line"), "of sailing ships," they might experience an escalating sense of alarm, and then relief. But on reflection, how long are we supposed to be relieved by the bathos of the punch line? Has something else, some alarming present or future possibility, not been called to mind in the doleful prognostication?

Some prophecies simply do not let us off the hook so easily: "Men will have such cruel maladies that they will tear their flesh with their own nails." The answer that lets us down gently is "an itch," but itches of a ghastlier order of magnitude haunted the generations around 1500 that first felt the ravages of syphilis, that left its literary deposit in Poliziano's exquisitely revolting *Sylva in Scabiem*.

Writing—and, correspondingly, painting—is finally not just a question of seeing things as they are: Leonardo knows that seeing means seeing something *as* something, under particular conditions internal and external to the eye. The shift of perspective becomes particularly devastating when turned on the mass delusions of religion: "Many will there be who will give up work and labor and poverty of life and of goods, and will go to live among wealth in splendid buildings, declaring that this is the way to make themselves acceptable to God." (Of churches and the habitations of friars.) Or, "A vast multitude will sell, publicly and unhindered, things of the very highest price, without leave from the Master of those things, which never were theirs nor within their power; and human justice will not prevent it." ("Of the sale of paradise"—that is, of indulgences: we are probably no more than a decade before Luther's condemnation of the practice.)

On one hand, Leonardo disenchants the worldview of occult and divinatory agency that sustains belief in prophecy, but revitalizes it with catastrophic physics: "All the Elements shall be seen mixed together surging in huge tolling mass, now borne towards the center of the world, now towards the sky, at one time coursing in fury from the southern regions towards the icy north, at another time from the east to the west, and then again from this hemisphere to the other."[86] The caption/punch line is "Of the water which flows in a turbid stream mingled with Earth and Mist; and of mist mingling with Air, and of the Fire which is mingled by its heat with each." This apocalyptic vision from the "prophecies" is a massively concentrated encapsulation of Leonardo's writings on water and geomorphology in the manuscript known as the Codex Leicester.

Verbal games merge with the technical drawings of dynamics of flux to give rise to the late images of ecological collapse, which Leonardo renders through the codependency of words and of images: words evoke the sense of cataclysmic events unfolding in time, while images produce the terrifying sense of scale and proportion, as diminutive buildings and human and animal bodies are engulfed by flood and tempest.[87]

THE PAGE AS BODY

For a thinker seeking to reject professional hierarchies and the stigma of being an artisan or a mechanical, command of the resources of language was as necessary as command of Euclidian geometry. The world of making, of knowledge acquired through bodily engagement, did not "demonstrate" itself, as Leonardo sometimes claimed, nor could it be reduced to a series of theorems. Language was necessary for the communication of *lineamenta*, for the description of what was seen and what was deduced, in an abstract sense. He will not be just an eye, or a pair of hands. And Leonardo knew that language is not only indispensable to his laying claim to knowledge: it is generative of thought and invention, a medium of experiment in itself.

The poets—and their rhetorical annihilation—provided a convenient staging ground for an appeal to experience as "hands-on" expertise, as immediacy. On the other hand, that experience, by being given philosophical moment as investigation, research, and the formulation of principles, has to leave behind the artisanal world of making, of messy engagement with the matter of the world. The *experience* of what it was like to be in the body of Leonardo can never enter the picture.

This is also why Leonardo's "self" is an artifact of language, a screen or veil of words. The effect of a self that is fabricated or called into being is maintained by Leonardo's declamatory mode of writing, the effect of a series of disembodied authorial personae that materialize themselves on the page, called into being with the sometimes relentless "*You . . .*" or "*O reader . . . ,*" exhorted to have patience as they cope with the constant repetitions and jumping back and forth, and with promises of a more systematic organization in the later fulfillment of the project.

> When you are painting you ought to have by you a flat mirror in
> which you should often look at your work. The work . . . will seem to

be by the hand of another master and thereby you will better judge its faults.

But, as we asked above, who is this reader? On an obvious level it is *you* when *you* read (or try to read) Leonardo's challenging pages—you will need more than a mirror to do so. Yet preeminently the reader being addressed must be Leonardo himself. The texts perform a splitting and division of personae, calling into being not just Leonardo as brainstorming speculator and inventor, Leonardo as the self-celebrating maker of new knowledge, Leonardo as the prudent quantifier of visible and tactile reality—but Leonardo as writer and as reader. The "you" function is analogous to the pointing gesture or pointed gaze of Dürer, in his self-portrait drawings, or Pontormo, who points at his own image in the mirror—a deictic motif that implicates the addresser before it implicates any notional addressee (fig. 18). And here we might pause to think of pointing hands in Leonardo's painting, self-implicating gestures that displace self-embodiment to a non-place constituted in void; we might think of the active agency of the left hand of Christ in *The Adoration of the Magi* (plate 12), of the Virgin in the early *Annunciation* (plate 31) and *Madonna of the Carnation* (plate 17). Or foreshortened *left hands* that seem to project forth from the painting, as if mirroring the left-handed artist's own in the course of making (plate 10).[88]

And we might think of the urgent, importuning address of the notes on the later anatomical studies, where the almost hectoring *"you . . . you"* is inscribed within an extraordinary collocation of dense text and autopsied bodily organs: as if the body of the speaker were only manifesting him through detached and dismembered organs (see plate 26). On RCIN 919070 (plate 30) we find: "Though *you* may have a love for such things, *you* will perhaps be impeded by your stomach; and if this does not impede *you*, *you* will perhaps be impeded by the fear of living through the night hours in the company of quartered and flayed corpses, fearful to behold. And if this does not impede *you*, perhaps *you* will lack the good draughtsmanship which such a depiction requires; and even if *you* have skill in drawing, it may not be accompanied by a knowledge of perspective; and if it were so accompanied, *you* may lack the methods of geometrical demon-

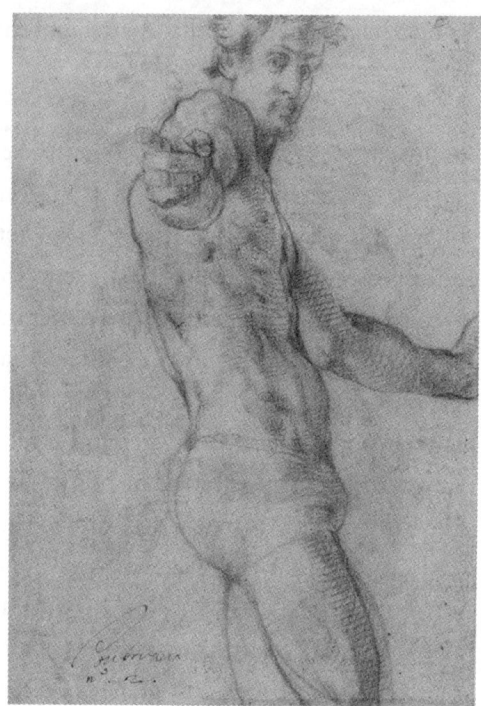

18. Jacopo Pontormo, *Self
Portrait*. Ca. 1525. Red chalk,
28.1 × 19.5 cm. London, British
Museum, inv. 19.361,010.10.

stration and of calculating the forces and strengths of muscles; or perhaps
you will lack patience so that *you* will not be diligent. Whether all these
things were found in me or not, the 120 books composed by me will give
the verdict, yes or no. In these I have been impeded neither by avarice nor
negligence, but only by time. Farewell [my emphasis]."⁸⁹

Reflect, also, that such sheets are densely inscribed in mirror-writing—
which asks us to regard them into a simulation of the surface of a mirror.
But what is reflected in the bodily imprint, the hand, is not the face of
the author but his *voice*. In other words, the self here will not be pictured
but dispersed and displaced by a trace or residue that marks that self's
absence, its disembodiment, but in a staged orality that also calls on that
self as residue or aftermath—the writer who reads the injunction to go on
writing—from the surface of the page.⁹⁰

Leonardo's own writing constituted a mirror for a selfhood that was
gathered together and embodied only on the page. This written Leonardo
provides us too with a mirror of sorts, a cloudy one in which we will never

be able to see the man himself in other than fragmentary terms, no matter what present-day biographers might claim. I thus make no claim to have unearthed a truer, more entire form of his personality, and I consider it unlikely that we will ever be able to close the many gaps in his own archive. The very absence of his body from his writing helps us see only a small, but important, part of his struggle to join with contemporary artisans in undercutting the bias against those who labored *ingeniously* with their hands. Part of this shared defiance meant laying claim to literary authority while disputing the very authority of literature, and knowing full well how vulnerable that authority was. The result was a tension manifest across the whole corpus of his writings, just as his aspiration to the sublimity of philosophical knowledge was in tension with the experiential basis of his professional identity. Tensions in Leonardo are both structural and productive, as we will see in the following chapter.

Chapter 5

LEONARDO, EXTENDED

The authenticity of painting as a form of second nature, grounded in a *scientia* based in experience, is at risk from the very body—the artist's—that is the site of that experience. Leonardo's precepts on the training of painters sought not only the erasure of any lingering influence of earlier masters. It was also a defect in a painting, he wrote, if it betrayed the "air" or "figure" of the artist who made it. What his contemporaries called *maniera*, and what we now would call "personal style," or "self-expression," was the sign of a weak painter. A painter's faculty of judgment had to be on guard against betraying inner temperament or disposition—or as Leonardo called them, "motions of the soul." He wrote that "it is a fault in the extreme of painters" to repeat the same movements and styles of drapery in the same picture "and to make most of the faces resemble their master . . . for I have known some who, in all their figures seem to have portrayed themselves from the life, and in them one may recognize the attitudes and manners of their maker."

Such an auto-mimetic compulsion determines far more than a propensity for self-portraiture. An artist who is lively in his speech and movements will make figures who also appear so. Painters with "bad proportions" portray figures with similar proportions, and painters who are devout make figures with heads piously bent. Painters who are "mad" will reveal themselves in the irrational and distracted figures of their paintings. "And thus each peculiarity in a painting follows from the painter's own peculiarity. I have often pondered the cause of this defect and it seems to me that we may conclude that the very soul which rules and controls each body directs our judgment before it is our own."[1]

The artist is locked in a struggle with an invisible double of his own body that threatens to become visible in his portrayal of human figures. Note the possessive "our own" above, with regard to the painter's judgment—it is stated to belong to the painter's soul before it belongs to the painter. Our judgment "is powerful enough to move the arm of the painter and makes him copy himself, since it seems to this soul that this is the true way of representing a man, and those who do not do as it does commit an error." This daunting image of the soul's despotic domination of the body and the will shows Leonardo's idiosyncratic interpretation of Aristotelian theories of the mind and its faculties: no academic interpreter of Aristotle's *De anima* would have held such a view. Leonardo's concept of auto-mimesis or compulsive self-imitation drew as much on common wisdom, like an older Tuscan proverb "Every painter paints himself," or "A leopard cannot change its spots" (itself based on Jeremiah 13:23, "Can an Ethiopian change his skin or a leopard its spots? Neither can you do good who are accustomed to doing evil").[2]

Leonardo's views could explain the nonexistence of an undisputed self-portrait. The paradox, of course, is that certain facial types *do* recur through Leonardo's corpus of drawings, notably images of the delicate profile of a young man and of a rugged, heavy-jowled elderly male (plate 22). For Ernst Gombrich, Leonardo's grotesque heads—hugely popular with later Renaissance artists and among the best-known of his productions—are an attempt to *rid* himself, through deformation and exaggeration, of the facial types that came to him through force of habit (plates 19 and 24).[3] Again we have to wonder whether Leonardo is not, in these passages from the projected treatise on painting, in some way writing to himself.[4]

There might be more to this artistic auto-cancellation in the name of fidelity to nature: the logistics of artistic production through a division of labor demanded a disciplined and compliant team. The master's control of the process required a subordination of individual expression, a self-extension through the accommodating labor of apprentices and assistants. The consequences of Leonardo's operation as an "extended" author or producer, to be examined shortly, are very much still with us, manifest in a distinctive phenomenon of one twenty-first-century Da Vinci World: the fact that replicas of Leonardo's paintings emerge on the market with an uncanny frequency.

Very rarely are these new discoveries. Mostly, the replica has been known about for years, and the "reappearance" is due to a new claim: that the replica might be more than just a copy. That even if it is not quite an autograph or partly autograph alternative version, Leonardo's presence somehow adheres to it. In chapter 1 we considered the cases made on behalf of some alternative versions of the *Mona Lisa*. A debunked alternative version of *La Belle Ferronnière*—the occasion of a notorious lawsuit in 1920 when the dealer and connoisseur Joseph Duveen was successfully sued for declaring the painting to be a copy—resurfaced in 2010 and was sold for $1.5 million, three times its estimated sale value: the co-chairman of Sotheby's Old Master Paintings department observed that Leonardo is "such a potent name that there are people who want to touch anything that has to do with him."[5]

The cartoon of a half-length nude female with strong similarities to the *Mona Lisa* was acquired as a Leonardo by the Duc d'Aumale in 1861 (fig. 19). A few years later Walter Pater referred to the "latest gossip [about] an undraped Monna Lisa, found in some out-of-the-way corner of the late Orleans collection,"[6] but mostly demoted in the twentieth century to the status of "Leonardo Imitator." Yet an exhibition at the Museé Condé in 2019 made a tentative case for Leonardo's partial involvement—close technical examination revealed delicate high-quality under drawing and some traces of left-handed hatching in the face. And the drawing, pricked for transfer, was intended to serve as a prototype, not a single-use cartoon: the punched holes were for the production of a second cartoon, to preserve the original from the pouncing process. There are several other painted versions of this so-called *Monna Vanna* by artists with ties to Leonardo and his followers. While the findings are interesting in themselves, it is not clear what should be the conclusion—other than that we can see in the Chantilly cartoon a set of techniques for reproducing or even

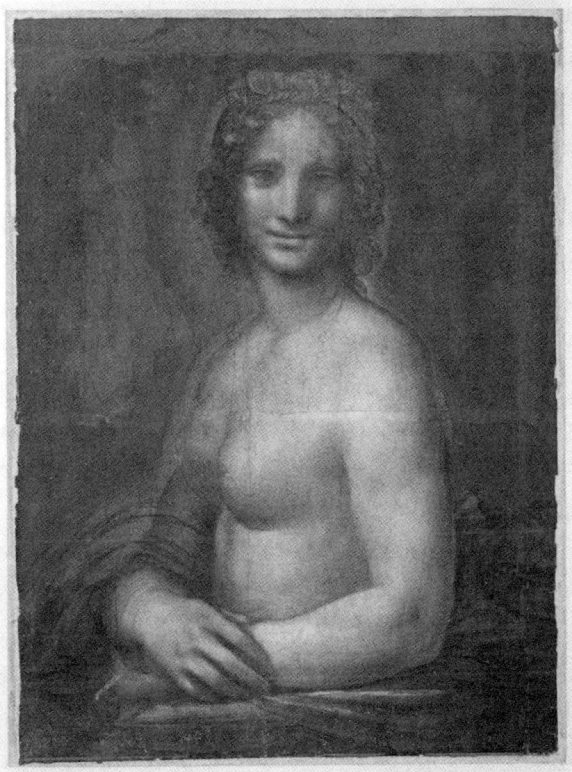

19. Followers of Leonardo da Vinci, *Female nude half-length, known as "Monna Vanna."* 1520s. Black chalk and white heightening on brown paper, 72.4 × 54 cm. Chantilly, Museé Condé.

counterfeiting a "Leonardo," possibly authorized by the master, among them the left-handed hatching, which followers like Melzi sometimes imitated in their drawings. And yet authors of technical studies are often under pressure to deliver more newsworthy results than this, to lean on the possibility that an object is more significant than previously thought.

Little is known about the industry of Leonardo replicas and variants in the 1500s, and of the extent to which the derivations were made inside or outside the workshop. It is apparent, as we saw in chapter 1, that full-scale replicas of his most famous work from his lifetime—*The Last Supper*—were being commissioned within a few years of the mural's completion in 1499. A version attributed to Andrea Solario had found its way to

Tongerlo Abbey in Flanders by 1545. Recently the Tongerlo painting has been promoted—with no convincing evidence—as a partly autograph work by Leonardo, who is alleged to have painted the faces of Christ and St. John.[7]

And so it goes for most of Leonardo's works—an industrial level of production of replicas and variants. The Louvre *Virgin and Child with St. Anne*, which Leonardo began (or recommenced) around 1508, generated numerous variants at different stages of the process of completion. The London cartoon gave rise to no less than fourteen adaptations by Lombard and Flemish artists of the full composition, with more of the figure of the Christ and the Lamb, a first intermediate version (sixteen derivations), a second intermediate version (seven known derivations), and the final version (about six derivations).[8]

Many of the most popular Leonardo compositions have no surviving original; sometimes it is probable that workshop collaborations like the *Madonna of the Yarn Winder* are the originals—the prototypes in a series of replicas and variations (plates 32 and 33). The same goes for the Louvre full-length *St. John/Bacchus* (plate 23) and for the infamous *Salvator Mundi*, where the "originals" may already not be fully autograph. The former has recently been attributed by the Louvre to Francesco Melzi, the latter, following its controversial sale for $450 million, to Giovanni Antonio Boltraffio under Leonardo's direction (although there is much disagreement about this). With few other artists does replication seem to conjure the promise of an original—Caravaggio and Artemisia Gentileschi, buzzworthy artists with violent life histories, would both fit the bill. There is far less excitement over the regular appearance of replicas and versions of the Brueghel family, or Titian, or Rubens.

Such replicas and variants may have been produced by Leonardo's workshop, about which we know little, or by independent artists who had access to his designs. The result, according to Luke Syson, was that "an individual style was transformed into a collective one, and the artist himself became a kind of multiple."[9] The production of Leonardo multiples was visible to contemporaries, and clients seemingly knew what they were getting—an authentic "Leonardo" manufactured by hands not entirely his, if at all. That is the substance of Fra Pietro da Novellara's report to

Isabella d'Este from Florence on April 4, 1501, when the *marchesa* asked him to look into progress on a portrait promised by Leonardo while passing through Mantua: "Since he has been in Florence he has only done one drawing, in a cartoon [i.e., of *Virgin and Child with St. Anne*]. He has not done anything else, though two of his assistants make copies [*dui suoi garzoni fano retrati*], and he from time to time adds some touches to them. He devotes much of his time to geometry, and has no fondness at all for the paintbrush."[10]

The process of delegation to assistants is probably why so many early modern collectors could claim to own "Leonardos" and why, two centuries later, Carlo Amoretti and Luigi Lanzi could provide lengthy lists of "Leonardos" in Milanese collections.[11]

What if we were to rethink our conception of the Renaissance artist as an autonomous, sovereign individual? What if our standards for determining the limits of an oeuvre were actually anachronistic, inappropriate under the conditions of premodernity? The notebooks cast light on the degree to which Leonardo's pedagogical methods, and the distinctive painterly effects associated with him were conceived as a means to overcome disparities of individual artistic hands or styles. Such methods not only would enlarge the productivity of a workshop—that mode of organization existed already; more profoundly, his precepts conceived the very personhood of the artist as transcending his own physical limits, as operating through the bodies of others.

Contemporaries like Perugino, Botticelli, and Ghirlandaio already organized their workshops to meet a demand for replicas and alternative versions. Sometimes, the demand for replicas was triggered by a prestigious original: a miraculous image attracting votaries and pilgrims, or the glamor and allure of a work produced for clients like the Medici by artists like Pesellino or Fra Filippo Lippi. Entire enterprises specialized in the production, from tracings, of low-cost adaptations (some could be called decorative simplifications) of such works.[12] In some cases an original appears to have been created as a prototype, geared toward the generation of replicas. A considerable portion of Ghirlandaio's workshop output consisted of replication (with small variations) of popular prototypes. For instance, the Ghirlandaio tondo of *The Virgin and Child with St. John* in the Louvre generated at

least twenty-two replicas that we know of, and it is likely that there were
more. Many Botticelli compositions survive as multiples: and some again
seem to have been designed specifically for serial production within the
workshop, but independent artists also appropriated and reproduced Botticelli compositions—notably Jacopo del Sellaio, Bartolomeo di Giovanni,
and the so-called Masters of Marradi, of the Campana Panels, and of the
Gothic Buildings (recently identified as Jacopo Foschi).[13] Leonardo would
have been aware of the successful operation of his fellow Verrocchio alumnus
Lorenzo di Credi, who inherited the teacher's business. Lorenzo did a brisk
trade in replicas and variants of his works, some of which themselves were
pastiches of Leonardo's early Florentine Madonnas. Credi's designs had an
extraordinary persistence, well into the mid-1500s, and in some cases were
taken up by artists in northern Europe. Again, some of Credi's imitators—
the so-called Tommaso di Credi, the Master of the Johnson Magdalen—
seem to have operated independently of Lorenzo's shop.

Such methods of workshop organization led to the prolific output of
Raphael's studio in the Rome of Julius II and Leo X, as young aspiring artists flocked to the city from all over Italy and beyond.[14] Among Raphael's
followers, the practice arose of assembling not a team of apprentices and
assistants but a massed force of day laborers. The consequences, according
to the painter and writer Giovanni Battista Armenini, who experienced
similar working conditions in Rome in 1550, was the degradation of the
art of painting itself. Raphael's follower Perino del Vaga, when he received
commissions, "would have them carried out by those who would serve him
more willingly and for lower wages; this madness, once introduced, led
to the cursed custom of paying assistants by the day, as if they were abject
peasant laborers, something which, until then, had always been avoided;
yet in our own time this shabby and disgraceful practice has flourished,
so that in many places we see the most beautiful and famous buildings
painted, or rather, defaced, by this mode of working. There are even those
who pay by the hand's breadth."[15] Armenini's account of the degradation
of painting is in sharp contrast with Giorgio Vasari's celebration of the
efficiency of the mid-century generation of painters, the triumph of *bella
maniera* marked by facility and speedy production.

Leonardo's operation participates in this larger development, but his output was smaller, his mode of clientage irregular. Paintings long in gestation and regularly revised seem to have outgrown the circumstances of their original commission (a marriage portrait, an altarpiece in a Florentine or French church) and given rise to works produced on speculation. Modes of association by junior partners may have been looser. While the *Madonna of the Yarn Winder* appears to have been generated in multiple versions as a commercial function of the workshop, it is not clear who benefited financially from the proliferation of replicas of the *St. Anne*, the *St. John*, the *Leda*, the *Mona Lisa*, and the *Salvator Mundi*. It is possible that Leonardo allowed his associates to produce and market Leonardesque pictures based on his reservoir of originals, and it is certain that this continued well beyond his death in 1519.

However, while economic and marketing explanations have a concreteness and familiarity from a twenty-first-century perspective, I believe we need to see Leonardo's collective production in a register other than a purely economic one. There is something distinctly strange and nonmodern also at work. On one hand, there is the normalizing of style to void traces of the artist's own persona; on the other, there's the extraordinary receptivity to Leonardo's style in the 1500s that goes beyond what art historians normally mean by their use of the word "influence." We are confronting a trans-personal or supra-personal production of art, that at times resembles a *depersonalization* but could be better referred to as an *aesthetics of extension*, a powerful affective dimension that operates across the boundaries between individual makers, and between makers and beholders. That is, the effect of Leonardo's works lies both in their powerful capacity to engage their viewers and in an analogous impulse—their capacity to generate a mimetic response on the part of other artists. The works engage a community of response, what we might call an intersubjective aesthetics, involving artists and beholders, one that would be resisted in the orthodoxies of later sixteenth-century academic theory. In the academic theory of Vasari, Lomazzo, and Federico Zuccari, a dogmatic protocol of imitation replaced what amounted, in the case of the *leonardeschi*, to impersonation.

The *Libro di pittura* or *Treatise on Painting*, left in more than one incomplete draft when Leonardo died (the most comprehensive transcription, that by Melzi, had very limited circulation before the 1600s), would
have laid out much of this rationale. Leonardo's theories of artistic production and his ideas of pedagogy suggest an ensemble operation that
transcends individual identity or "personal style." Individual mannerism or
idiosyncrasy was something to be worked against, since it interfered with
the goal of rendering truthful appearances that revealed their inner causes.
There is the well-known note on the history of art on a sheet in the Codex
Atlanticus, adapted from Ghiberti and probably intended for inclusion in
the *Treatise*: "How from age to age the art of painting continually declines
and deteriorates when painters have no other standard than work already
done. The painter will produce pictures of little merit if he takes the works
of others as his standard: but if he will apply himself to learn from the objects of nature he will produce good results. This we see was the case with
the painters who came after the time of the Romans, for they continually
imitated each other, and from age to age their art steadily declined." Giotto
then discovered his vocation as a painter "reared in mountain solitudes,
inhabited only by goats and suchlike beasts, turning straight from nature
to his art, began to draw on the rocks the movements of the goats which he
was tending." Predictably after Giotto art declines again "because all were
imitating paintings already done," until "Tommaso the Florentine, nicknamed Masaccio, showed by the perfection of his work how those who
took as their standard anything other than nature, the supreme guide of
all the masters, were wearying themselves in vain."[16]

It is telling that this unconventional advice was omitted in Melzi's compilation of a treatise on painting from Leonardo's chaotic archive of drafts.
Melzi's text, seemingly intended for a publication that never occurred,
is preserved in the Vatican Library manuscript known as Codex Urbinas
latinus 1270. Melzi may have regarded such passages as too unorthodox for
readers in the decades after Leonardo's death. The first chapter in Melzi's
Parte Seconda (Urb.lat.1270, 31r), devoted to the training of artists, ex-
trapolates far more conventional advice from his teacher's notes: "First a
youth needs to learn perspective and understand the measure of all things,
then, little by little learn from a good master to get used to the well-formed

parts, and [only] then from nature to reinforce the reason for the things learned. Eventually youths should look at works from the hands of many masters in order to form the habit of putting into practice and implementing everything learned."[17] The precept is reiterated a few folios later (34r): "First, the painter should train the hand by copying the drawings of good masters and, having acquired that training with the judgement of a tutor, should then train to copy things well in relief."

Melzi's manipulation of Leonardo's text was guided by the concerns of more conventional artistic pedagogy. In chapter 4 we saw that Cennino's handbook for painters (early 1400s) had exhorted the copying of proven masters before the "triumphal gateway" of drawing from nature. The ultimate goal of such internalization was the achievement of personal *maniera*—a style of one's own. Melzi was also mindful of the concerns of mid-sixteenth-century artistic training, which embraced the principles of systematic *imitation* of older artists. Artistic achievement was measured by comparison to authoritative models, and the work itself pointedly alluded to those models by borrowing and quotation. By the time Giorgio Vasari and his colleagues formed the Academia del Disegno in 1563, the principles were formalized in training.

In a note in the Codex Atlanticus (199va/534v)—another passage not incorporated by Melzi, or by the editors of the first printed edition of the treatise in 1651—such a point of view is ascribed by Leonardo to an "adversary."

> The adversary says that to gain practice and to produce a quantity of work it is better to devote the initial study period to drawing on various compositions that have been done either on paper or on walls by various masters, and that, in doing this, practice is speedily acquired together with good habits. To this I reply that the habits would be good if based upon the well composed works of studious masters. But since such masters as these are so rare as to be seldom found, it is safer to go to the objects in nature than to those imitated to much worse effect from nature and accordingly thus to acquire bad habits. He who can go to the fountain does not go to the vessel.[18]

Once again it has to be borne in mind that the "adversary" here is none other than the writer himself. There is little evidence of independent study from nature and from live models among Leonardo's followers—Boltraffio, Marco d'Oggiono, Francesco Napoletano, Cesare da Sesto, Melzi—who tended to adhere to a repertoire of compositional formulas and figure types from Leonardo's designs.[19]

Leonardo's primary concern is the training of the hand and the memory, the formation of habit through repetition. Diligence, in his prescriptions on training artists, is inseparable from *scienza* or *teorica* (theory).[20] He has nothing to say about personal style, except negatively: "A painter must never imitate the style [*maniera*] of another because he will be called the grandson and not the son of nature. Since natural things are available in such great abundance, turn to nature itself rather than to masters who have learned from it."[21] Later commentators found the point objectionable: in 1649, the French academician Abraham Bosse, who had access to Leonardo's treatise prior to its 1651 publication, rejoindered, "I don't think it would be disadvantageous for [the painter] to take [the style of] Raphael, Mr. Poussin, Domenichino, Correggio, the Carracci, Pietro da Cortona, and similar others."[22]

Leonardo's repudiation of imitation—the principle that when a young artist copies an established artist he is absorbing not just the forms but the *maniera* of his model, in the long process of developing a *maniera* of his own—is a rejection of the very basis through which workshop and local traditions constituted and sustained themselves. His negation, in his remarks on Giotto and Masaccio, of the principle that art is generated through the exemplarity of previous art is pointedly ideological. It is grounded in an appeal to "Nature"—tradition kills, and requires moments of "restart" in Nature. The circumvention of style is positioned against the practice of his most successful contemporaries, their methods of training and marketing, and their investment in a recognizable (and reproducible) *maniera*. The "universality" enjoined by Leonardo is a versatility that can appeal to the "judgments" of different beholders, based on the normativity of vision; it is also supposed to transcend the traditions, the stylistic branding, of the traditional workshop. For Leonardo's trainee artist, the quantitative adjustment of qualities of light and relief must become *second nature*: "make sure there are things of great *oscurità* (obscurity, darkness), and shadows of great *dolcezza* (softness, or sweetness) in the same composition, making the causes of such shadow and sweetness known." At the same time, such qualities of *dolcezza* and *oscurità*, which are the goal of technical simulation of visual experience, also possess affective and poetic qualities. They resonate in the language of Italian vernacular poetry, from the *dolce stil nuovo* and the *selva oscura* of the age of Dante (one of Leonardo's favorite poets) onward.[23]

These prescriptions, often grounded in Leonardo's research on optics, are often held up, understandably, as an instance of Leonardo the "modern scientist," but again there is something more complex and nonmodern at work. In the *Libro di pittura*, the strictures against auto-mimesis can seem very strange indeed. In the Codex Urbinas (43v) and in chapter 42 of the 1651 published *Trattato*, there is a section titled "How we become deceived in judging bodies." Leonardo writes: "If the painter has ungainly hands, he will make similar ones in his work. The same will happen with any part of the body unless prevented by prolonged study. Therefore, every painter ought to observe his ugliest part, and fix that in each study."[24] Following two chapters on the study of the internal structure (*intrinseca forma*) of the body and warning against the tendency to repeat drapery folds, movements, and heads in the same painting, there is a chapter in the form of a "Precept": "So that a painter is not deceived in selecting a figure made out of habit . . . he should have himself measured and see where the body varies a lot or a little from what is generally considered praiseworthy. Having acquired this knowledge, he should make every effort through study not to fall into the same errors in the figures he makes as he finds in his own body. You must defend against this vice to the utmost, since it is an error that was born together with your judgement. Because the soul is master of your body, and that of your own judgement, it readily delights in works similar to those that it made to compose your body."[25]

The struggle for self-mastery seems deeply fraught: habits, intrinsic dispositions, are compensated by other habits inculcated by art, by precept. So, too, the "nature" that the young artist should strive to produce is to be realized through highly abstracted and artificial conditions: he prescribes "a dwelling . . . open to the air, with flesh-colored walls [*pareti di colore incarnato*]," for the portrayal of faces and nudes from life. "Alternatively, you could make the walls on the south side high enough that the rays of the sun do not strike the walls on the north side so that its reflected rays will not spoil the shadows."[26] Against this anguished strife of the body and soul, Leonardo comes to envision a relational continuum of skilled bodies working in synchrony, their sensory powers enhanced by training, their quirks and idiosyncrasies tamed and contained.[27]

Leonardo, of course, did not come out of nowhere. While he never directly mentions his training under Verrocchio, his approach to making art bears the stamp of some of the more radical experiments in drawing within that studio environment. As Christina Neilson points out, Verrocchio's startling "Head of a Woman" (1470s, Oxford, Christ Church), rendered in black chalk with touches of brown ink and gray wash, is the earliest known example of sfumato technique, where the artist smudges the chalk to create a rich tonal range and to suggest the softness of living flesh.[28] Leonardo would take this further, blurring the outlines of heads and faces to suggest the optical atmospheres in which they are seen. Drawings by Botticelli, who probably interacted with Leonardo in Verrocchio's shop, manifest the same interest in soft modeling and subtle effects of relief. Yet while Leonardo developed a technique of painting that could maintain this effect, Botticelli's finished pictures assert the priority of flowing line and crisp silhouettes. The works of Botticelli and his pupil Filippino Lippi, as well as many other painters of that generation like Domenico Ghirlandaio, reflect a tradition of firm and assertive drawing rooted in goldsmithing and metalwork. Their crisp and flowing linear *ductus*, manifest in windblown draperies and hair, create a distinctive sense of graceful motion and decorative rhythm.

The well-turned line had a currency beyond Florence as well: it signaled manual skill and poetical effect in many centers of late fifteenth-century Italy.[29] Mantegna's masterly line and its capacity to render sculptural volumes lent itself to circulation in the form of the reproductive engraving, of which he was a pioneer.[30] Line was the means by which the manual skill and ingenuity of Martin Schoengauer and later Albrecht Dürer was transmitted from beyond the Alps. Leonardo would have come to see line as the sign of painting's affiliation with pattern-making and a craft aesthetic, and as an expression of the artisanal hand. By the time he came to make notes for the *Libro di pittura*, and already in his practice as a painter since the late 1470s, he was pitting himself against it: "Do not give a finished or a sharply bounded effect to those shadows which you make out with difficulty and those boundaries you cannot discern . . . lest your work look wooden as a result."[31] Later, around 1510 or as late as 1515, he wrote more emphatically, "The outlines of bodies are the least of all things. The proposition is proved to be true, because the boundary of a thing is a surface, which is not part of the body contained within that surface; nor is it part of the air surrounding that body, but is the medium [*mezzo*] interposed between the air and the body." Such a line is of "invisible thickness [*grossezza invisibile*]." "O painter! Do not surround your bodies with lines."[32] It was a principle that Leonardo only very questionably adhered to in practice.[33]

Such emphatic contours and edges were to be regarded as an intrusive artisanal fiction, the assertion of medium and mechanical operation at the expense of optical truth. His own elimination of the conspicuous contour, his arrival on the Milanese scene with a new way of painting based on the rendering of softly modeled bodies and faces in crepuscular light, would have been seen as a radical challenge to the crisp contours and decorative silhouettes manifest in the work of the Da Preda brothers, in Vincenzo Foppa, and in the early work of Bramante and of his protégé Bramantino.

Sandro Botticelli is one of the very few contemporary artists to be named in Leonardo's writings.[34] In the note included in the Melzi transcription he wrote of artists who failed to be "universal," who do not

love equally all the elements in painting, as when one who does not like landscapes[35] holds them to be a subject for cursory and straight-forward investigation—just as our Botticelli said that such study was of no use because by merely throwing a sponge soaked in a variety of colors at a wall there would be left on the wall a stain in which could be seen a beautiful landscape. He was indeed right that in such a stain various inventions are to be seen. I say that a man may seek out in such a stain heads of men, various animals, battles, rocks, seas, clouds, woods, and other similar things. It is like the sound of bells which can mean whatever you want it to. But although these stains may supply inventions, they do not teach you how to finish any detail. And the painter in question makes very sorry landscapes.[36]

The remark seems to have very little to do with Botticelli's approach to the painting of landscape, or of anything else. There is nothing in Botticelli's surviving work that suggests he generated compositions through blotting or staining. That, of course, would be more typical of Leonardo, who elsewhere advised painters to "look at stained walls or mottled stones [where] you may be able to see inventions and likenesses of different landscapes, different battles, the dynamic actions of figures, because the *ingegno* is aroused to new inventions by indeterminate things."[37] The notion of "potential images" in nature comes from Pliny; it was taken up by Petrarch in his *Rime Sparse*, and by the 1470s was a signature motif of Andrea Mantegna, the most celebrated artist in Italy.[38] Contrary to what Leonardo implies, Botticelli excelled in the detailed depiction of flora and foliage, where the effect is often consciously artificial, redolent of tapestry or embroidered textile. We see here one of several signs of self-transference or projection by Leonardo onto the figure of Botticelli, notwithstanding other passages of implied criticism.

Back in Florence around 1502 he carps at a painter called "Sandro" for neglecting the proportional diminution of figures in the middle ground and background; Leonardo's criticism of an *Annunciation* where the angel's movements were so vehement that he appeared to be assaulting the Virgin, who "seemed as if she was going to throw herself in despair out of the window," has been regarded as referring to Botticelli's Guardi *Annunciation* in the Uffizi (fig. 20).

And yet in the 1470s, as Leonardo sought to establish himself without much success in the Florentine artistic profession, Botticelli was a rising star, and some of his most signature qualities had an impact on Leonardo. He was especially attentive to Botticelli's depiction of luxuriant and fantastical hairstyles, with their elaborate braids and jeweled ornaments. The *Madonna of the Carnation* (plate 17) of ca. 1474–78 responds to female head studies by Verrocchio. It would also have solicited comparison with recent works by Botticelli, especially in the elaborate hairstyle, while signaling its distance from Botticelli in its attention to luster and reflection and shifts of tonal value in indoor lighting conditions (fig. 21).[39] Leonardo's *Adoration of the Magi* borrows figures from Botticelli's painting of the same subject now in Washington.[40] And in 1481, shortly after leaving

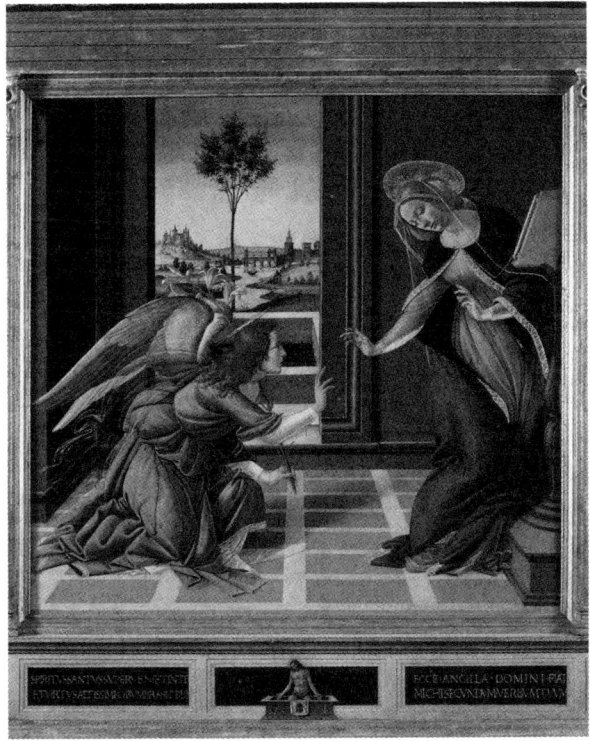

20. Sandro Botticelli, *Annunciation* (Cestello or Guardi
Annunciation). 1489. On panel, 150 × 156 cm. Florence,
Uffizi.

Florence, Leonardo made a vigorous sketch of an allegorical figure and a
flying angel of the Annunciation, the latter in a turbulent, hurtling motion
(precisely contradicting his strictures on decorous movement in his notes
on painting, quoted above) (plate 34).[41] The typology of both figures—
slender, with flowing hair and drapery—is thoroughly Botticellian; the
handling, with the smears of ink and rough pen strokes, is decidedly not.
In its insistent chiaroscuro and coarse spontaneity, the drawing might also
be a conscious and perhaps conflicted repudiation of Botticelli's linear
refinement, his signature stylistic feature. Around 1515, several years after
Botticelli's death and not long before his own, Leonardo revisited the typology of the Florentine *ninfa* in a more meticulous study of three dancing

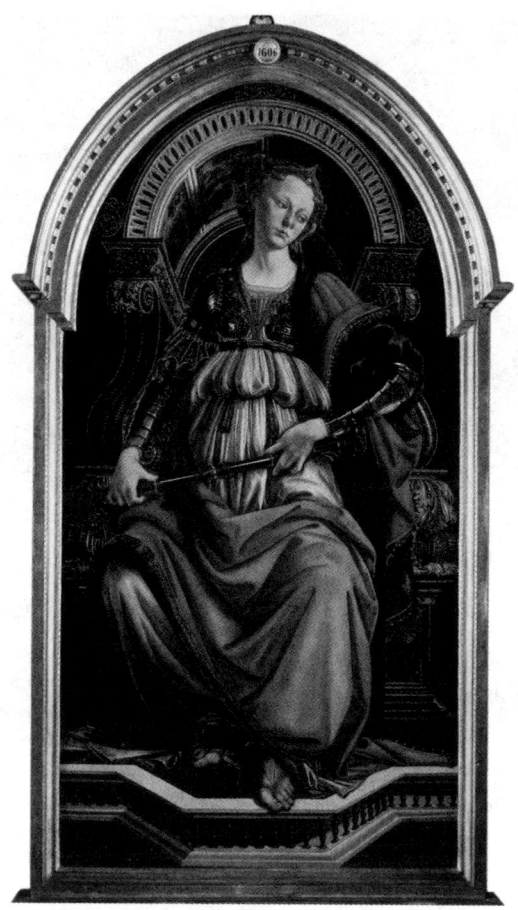

21. Sandro Botticelli, *Allegory of Fortitude*. 1470.
On panel, 167 × 87 cm. Florence, Uffizi.

figures with flowing hair and billowing drapery, far more reminiscent of
the graphic qualities of Botticelli's Sistine *Daughters of Jethro* or the atten-
dant divinities in the *Birth of Venus* or *Primavera* (plate 35). In another late
study of around 1517 (RCIN 912581), Leonardo drew a mysterious pointing female in fluttering drapery, strongly reminiscent of Dante's Matelda
(*Purgatorio*, cantos 28–29) in Botticelli's *Commedia* illustrations, although
the Botticellian effect is tellingly mitigated through the adaptation of a
figure from Mantegna's *Triumphs of Caesar* in Mantua, which Leonardo
would have known through prints or drawings.[42]

Such instances suggest a lifelong preoccupation with, if not incorporation of, the figure of Botticelli—a drive to both assimilate and resist a close contemporary, the Medici insider, the famous muralist of the Sistine Chapel, who was under consideration by the Sforza in 1493 when they sought out illustrious Florentine artists to make altarpieces for the Certosa in Pavia; it seems that Leonardo was not invited.[43]

In the case of Leonardo responding to Botticelli, however, we might recognize a kind of "blocking" directed by the artist against a habit acquired in his own training, a skill so ingrained as to become involuntary. Above all, it is the decorative and edge-like quality of Botticelli's outline—a line characteristic of one trained in chasing on metal, the kind of line taken up by print engravers—that is the object of Leonardo's relentless focus. Instead, he pursues a line that will erase its own traces as pictorial form and manifest itself instead as optical species.

In his own words, which anticipated later Renaissance strictures against *maniera*, this would be a turning from "art" to "nature"; or in Gombrich's relativistic view, from pattern or "schema" based in training to "correction" based on observation. Yet nature is not a given, a picture of reality already existing "out there" to be reproduced through close looking. We might rather say that in Leonardo's painting "nature" is a set of optical effects achieved by experimenting with theories and techniques—optics and the anatomy of the eye, aerial perspective, rapid "brainstorm" sketching (plate 34), oil painting, chalk, mirrors, lamps, and geometric solids—that enable the blocking of habits and second-nature skills, which for Leonardo are personified by Botticelli.

We might take this further: when Leonardo writes that the painter has to turn himself into "the mind of Nature," he is gesturing in an unprecedented sense away from the artist as sovereign creator toward the artist as a self-less, trans-personal, biophysical energy that connects the human with the nonhuman, the body with the larger world of phenomena. Hence the appeal of that line quoted above from Dante's *Convivio* that Leonardo copied into one of his notes for the *Libro di pittura*: "It is impossible to paint a figure, if the painter is not able to be that figure (Chi pingie figura se non pò esser lei non la pò purre)."

Leonardo's resistance to calligraphic and edge-like qualities in drawing corresponds to some distinctive features of his writing. When Leonardo writes conventionally, from left to right, his hand will usually feature the calligraphic flourishing of mercantile script. In general, the right-to-left "mirror" script hand is purged of this decorative aspect: it is an almost independent graphic system with the writer's own idiosyncratic forms of abbreviation, streamlined into a limited array of strokes in which descenders predominate (see plate 30). His script is more of a notation than an autograph "hand," as if he wanted it to be as transparent to the instantaneity of the voice as possible.[44] Writing is his body rendered mechanical, like an acoustic recording device. Once, in a very late mathematical note dated 1518, it records a suspension of its own operations, where the writer indicates that he is stopping "and so on, because the soup is getting cold" (eccetera: perchè la minesstra si fredda)—when other claims of the body (almost never acknowledged in Leonardo's writing) begin to assert themselves.[45]

Such a preoccupation with line as notation as opposed to line as ornamental flourishing, arising from a conflicted absorption of Botticelli, will manifest itself in two ways, each in tension with the other. Leonardo responded to the cultural prestige of the artfully turned line by, on one hand, making it more abstract and geometric, as mathematical calculation and pattern, in decorative knot-patterns, meanders, and labyrinths—as in those that appear in the symmetric entwined boughs in the forest landscape of the "Room of the Boards" in the Sforza castle, the geometric pattern on the robe of the *Salvator Mundi*, and in the "puzzle" engravings inscribed *Academia Leonardi Vici* (plate 36).[46] With an irony probably intentional, these prints constitute the one single opus of Leonardo that bears the name of its author, and they are the one instance where the vagaries and idiosyncrasies of the hand—or hands, for there are likely to be several who brought them into being—are brought under control through depersonalizing rigors of geometry. In theory, both the mathematically calculated labyrinth pattern and the helix form possess an objective or impersonal quality that shows off but regulates the artist's skill as a pattern-maker; geometry reins in craft, the arbitrariness of the virtuosic line.

On the other hand, Leonardo naturalized the calligraphic flourishing line, making it into the kernel of his renderings of the dynamic forces of nature—flowing hair and flowing water are both representable in terms of the spiral and the double helix (plate 37). For Leonardo, geometry made visible the hidden order of nature, a truth that cannot be rendered according solely through the perspectival logic of light, shadow, and sfumato.[47] The painter, as seeker of truth who has to think like and "transform himself into Nature," is under an obligation to disclose the operations of geometry within the dynamics of water, wind, smoke, the growth of plants, and so forth. Stylistic flourishes and artisanal caprice are retranslated into operations of nature. The sense of Leonardo absorbed in Botticelli is the result of—to paraphrase Cézanne on his relation to Poussin—a commitment to redoing Botticelli over again from nature, or to derive/reinscribe the operations of style within the operations of the cosmos.

Here, I'd like to return to a well-known but neglected drawing in Leonardo's oeuvre, which briefly surfaced in chapter 2 (plate 19). None of the commercial biographies discuss it at all; Carmen Bambach's recent monumental survey, which mentions it only briefly, reproduces the drawing with the caption, "Leonardo, nearly grotesque, bearded old man with braided hair in bust-length profile view (recto), a drawing of the Roman period, ca. 1513–16."

Martin Clayton provides a bit more: "The neck is vigorously muscular, the beard luxuriant, and the long hair is twisted into plaits reminiscent of Leonardo's *Leda* of the previous decade or of his master Verrocchio's drawings of many years before. The hair suggests that Leonardo intended a certain exoticism, as if the man were a magus, and the conspicuously hooked nose would be in keeping with such a conception." Clayton adds that the drawing can be dated to the last years of Leonardo's life, when Leonardo was known to have had a full beard. He reflects cautiously on the possibility of an intended resemblance to the aging artist himself, "an old bearded man drawing an old bearded man cannot have been oblivious to an element of self-portraiture."[48]

The drawing looks like a variation of Francesco Melzi's portrait of Leonardo (plate 21). Perhaps it is an *almost-portrait* as much as it is *almost grotesque*, not drawn from his own features but from his pupil's rendering of his own features, emphasizing the deforming and estranging quality of the line that embellishes and betrays.

I see the almost-portrait as a reflection on the dichotomy in Leonardo between the line that forms patterns, the trace of handiwork or craft,

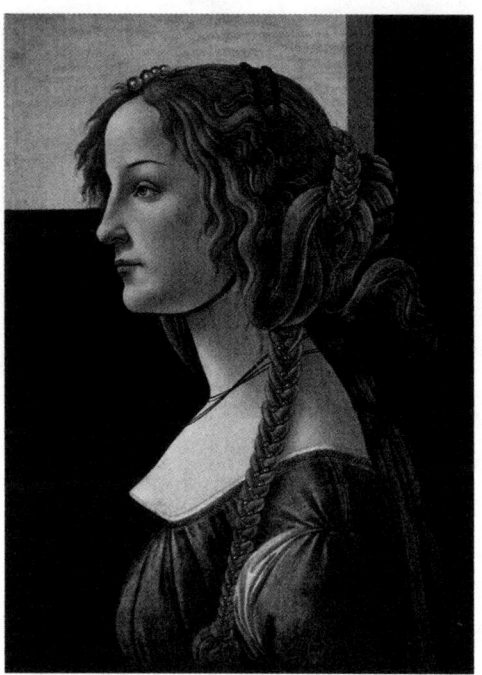

22. Sandro Botticelli, *Portrait of a woman* ("Simonetta Vespucci"). 1475–80. Tempera on poplar panel. Berlin, Gemäldegalerie.

and the mode of describing the figure—sometimes called sfumato—that makes the line disappear. As a study that manifests the principles of sfumato, it also provocatively recapitulates elements of the idealized female heads of Botticelli, manifest in particular in the artfully arranged braids (compare fig. 22). And this suggests that the old man with braids might be a final impersonation, in the form of a travesty, of the same Florentine rival. (The extremely rough and sketchy version on the reverse is its negation.) Leonardo's strange attachment to Botticelli is a paradoxical outcome of his preoccupation with auto-mimesis, the painter's self-manifestation within his own work. Whatever "self" Leonardo is striving against, it appears to be a set of effects best personified by Botticelli.

Those effects also include ornamentation in the broadest sense, not just pictorial, but bodily adornment and its social cachet. As a portraitist, Leonardo was regularly called upon to produce depictions of the adorned and ornamented body: for the most part, in the earlier portraits and in the *Mona Lisa*, he minimizes the more ostentatious effects of fashion. When he can't avoid doing so, he becomes absorbed in the logic of fashionable bodily adornment as a fashioning of the body, as framing, constriction, *outlining*. North Italian court costume was designed to make its chief impact in profile, and portraiture—especially of female subjects—was tasked with turning the body into a kind of blazon of power and status. Portraits assigned sitters a taut silhouette, registering the way costume articulates the rigid syntax of braided hair and flesh demarcated by jewelry, the junctions of sleeves and bodices, of borders lit up with pearls. Leonardo's portraits signal and disrupt that mapping of the body, making the logic of costume more elusive through the sitter's pose, to the extent, for instance, that the hairstyles of Cecilia Gallerani or Lucrezia Crivelli, with the heavy *corrazzone* or braid designed to make maximum impact in profile, only minimally disrupt the delicate contour of the head (plates 6 and 7).[49]

Clayton's association of the late profile drawing with the lost painting of *Leda and the Swan* (1505–10) is also suggestive. The designs for the *Leda* explore an erotics of the incongruous—in this case a cross-species coupling (plate 38). Leda's famous triple twist renders motion and energy, a flowing volume in three-dimensional space, resisting containment by the plane. Yet as if to offset this visualization of fluid bodily motion, Leonardo in one of his drawings for the head of Leda (RCIN 912515) writes of her artfully braided hair as a prosthesis—"this kind [of wig] can be taken off and put on without being damaged"—a luxury accessory rather than a natural complement to bodily beauty. Artifice is objectified in order to be portrayed, demarcating the labor of the craftsman, the wigmaker, from that of the artist who makes Ovidian fable plausible as "nature." By way of contrast, Leonardo produced a study of a female head in sfumato at some point during his work on the Leda. It is unlike the Leda in a key respect, which gives the work the title by which it came to be known, *La Scapigliata*: "the woman with disheveled hair" (plate 39).

The one moment that Leonardo comments at length on fashion, in a chapter of his projected *Treatise on Painting*, is marked by an element of the monstrous as well as the satirical: In his childhood, he writes, men had

all the edges of their garments scalloped at every place . . . and it even appeared such a beautiful invention to that generation that

they further scalloped the scallops, and they wore hoods and shoes
in the same style, and scalloped cockscombs which extruded from
the seams of garments. . . . In another era sleeves began to grow
and were of such size that each one by itself was larger than the
gown. Then garments began to rise round the neck, so that in the
end they covered the whole head. . . . Then the garments began
to lengthen, so that men continually had their arms laden with
clothes in order not to tread on them with their feet. Then they
reached such an extreme that they wore clothing only as far as their
hips and elbows, and they were so tight that they suffered great
torment and many of them split underneath, and the feet were so
constricted that their toes were pushed over one another and were
full of corns.[50]

Through fashion, the body, the *marvelous work of nature* as Leonardo
called it elsewhere, is made freakish by art. His remarks suggest the impos-
sibility of a self-sufficient natural body free of a compulsive attachment
to precious and prosthetic enhancements. The natural in Leonardo, not
for the first time, appears as something fleeting, estranged, and obscured
by habits and mundane preoccupations. Leonardo wants us to see the
tension between the purposeful body and the vexations of costume, but
also the ways in which the costumed body traversed by borders, as an
assemblage of the human and the nonhuman, makes that borderline uncertain. Ornament is more than superficial or superadded, it becomes
supplemental, even potentially constitutive of bodies. While working up
studies for *The Battle of Anghiari*, Leonardo began with his famous head
studies, rendering the *pazzia bestiale* of the warriors' aggression (plates 13
and 14). When weaving the individual studies into a whole, the warrior
anatomies are transfigured by a fantastical imagining of mercenary battle
gear, analogized to the shells of snails, fish scales, and the horns of rams.
Clothing externalizes bestial fury into bodily alteration, so it demands to
be seen as grafting and prosthesis (plate 15). Leonardo knew the passage in
Lucretius where the ancient writer contrasted the naked defenselessness of
human beings with animals, not born naked and unarmed but equipped
with fur, teeth, and claws.[51]

LEONARDESCHI

The London version of *The Virgin of the Rocks* (plate 11) is usually described as an autograph painting, yet it involved the participation of unnamed workshop partners or young trainee painters. These assistants closely followed methods of rendering effects of illumination and reflection corresponding with Leonardo's contemporaneous notes—in the notebooks known as Paris MS C and A—on optics and on shadow projection (some of the material was incorporated into the Melzi *Libro*). By comparison with the version now in the Louvre (see plate 10), with its elegances of soft flowing hair and drapery characteristic of early Leonardo, with its layers of transparent shadow, the exquisite distinction between different kinds of rock and species of flowering plants, the pictorial construction of the later version is more streamlined and schematic. Leonardo and his assistants economized on detail and on delicate layered effects, first establishing the dark tones in a monochrome underpainting, then working on top of this with lead white and a limited range of color; the metallic, even leaden, quality contrasts with the warm luminosity of the Louvre version, and the approach to the botanical specimens and rock formations is more generalized and abstracted. However, the behavior of light on complex forms, proportioned according to the disposition of the bodies in relation to the fixed frontal light source, is meticulously observed. Light falls at fullest intensity on surfaces notionally closest to the viewer: look at the golden highlight on the Baptist's left cheek, and the painstaking gradations of light and dark to articulate the fleshy surface anatomy of the infant Christ (plate 40).[52]

At a certain point, however, the relentless insistence on truth to optical effects becomes deeply estranging: the body of the Christ child begins to look less like a vigorous fleshy human infant than an inchoate mass of flesh covered in crater-like dimples, or a spongy growth with human head, hands, and feet. The continuity of the huge thigh with a torso of equal thickness means that the logic of anatomy has been deprioritized in favor of a method-bound rendering of appearance that has become detached from actual structure or substance. The topography of irregular surfaces lit at different aspects and intensities takes precedence over the grasp of the inner forms of the body.

The work, installed in a Milanese church without being fully finished in 1508, but probably begun well before Leonardo's initial return to Florence in 1499 or 1500, has been a point of departure for piecing together what can be known of the *leonardeschi*—a term used to categorize Leonardo's disciples and commemorated in one of the master's rebuses (Windsor RL 12692v: a lion -*lione*, in flames—*arde*: he burns, and two tables—*deschi*). The pictogram is a less formal statement of group identity—or extended authorship—than the geometric labyrinth woodcuts that call into existence an *Achademia Leonardo Vinci*. The *leonardeschi* are a heterogeneous and elusive group of a dozen or more artists, only a handful of whom can be connected even conjecturally to Leonardo's workshop. There are references in Leonardo's notebooks to a "Giovanni" (Giovanni Antonio Boltraffio), Salaì (Gian Giacomo Caprotti, who went by the nickname until his death in 1522), "Marco" (Marco d'Oggiono), Francesco Melzi, and possibly Giampietrino (Giovanni Pietro Rizzoli). Other artists, notably Cesare da Sesto, are named as Leonardo pupils by later sixteenth-century sources. Still others, like Bernardino Luini or Andrea Solario, are part of a broader "circle" of Leonardo that developed largely during his long absences from Milan after 1500 and final departure in 1513.[53]

Some of these artists continued to traffic in the "Leonardo effect" after setting up independently—Francesco Napoletano (who died young in 1501), Marco d'Oggiono, and Giampietrino; although their works are not hard to recognize and distinguish, they were frequently confused with Leonardo's in the 1500s and sometimes have been since, especially when their works are on the market.[54] Preeminent here is the *Madonna Litta* now in the Hermitage, a high-quality example of a "Leonardo" not painted by Leonardo, but by at least one pupil, Boltraffio, with access to his drawings. Ironic, perhaps, given Leonardo's contempt for "influence" or imitation in art, but I maintain that these artists need to be seen in other terms: as manifestations of Leonardo's trans-personalized artistic program, even as extensions of an artistic subjectivity beyond an individual authorial subject. There were practical reasons why Leonardo sought to extend his sphere of operation as an artist but also social, psychological, and aesthetic ones.

Cesare, Boltraffio, and Luini went on to cultivate assertive artistic identities of their own, responding to new currents in Venice, Rome, Bologna,

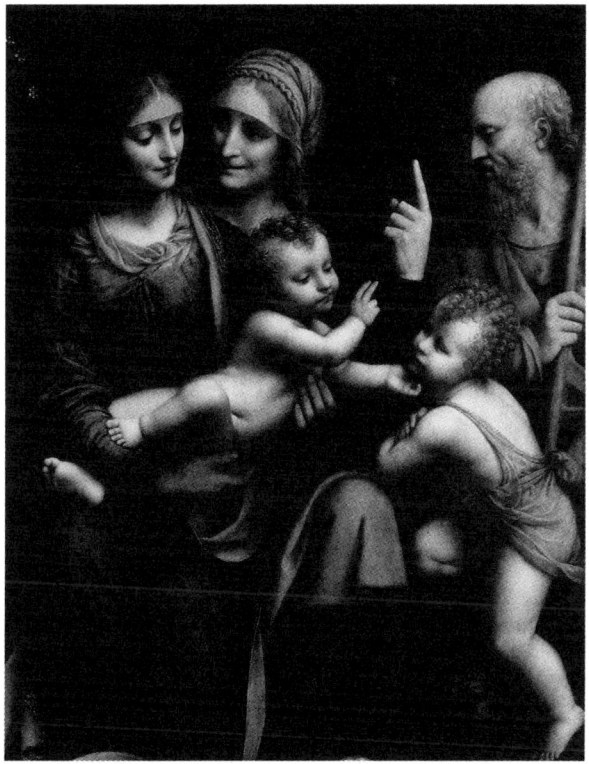

23. Bernardino Luini, *The Holy Family with St. Anne and St. John*. Ca. 1520–30. On panel, 118 × 92 cm. Milan, Ambrosiana.

and Southern Italy.[55] They advertised a connection to Leonardo through carrying over signature effects like sfumato modeling, the blithe smiles of figures, and the soft flowing coils of hair. In general—like many Leonardo followers—they broke away from the monochrome tonal unity of the Leonardo prototypes and adopted a palette of bold and rich color with oranges, greens, and violets. Luini was a versatile and independent artist who may never have known Leonardo in person, but he came to own a vital piece of the *leonardesco* legacy: the cartoon of the *Virgin and Child with St. Anne* now in London, and he produced a painted version, adding a St. Joseph, in the 1520s (fig. 23).[56] The darkness, the haunting and ambiguous qualities of the original are all carefully edited out, especially through a cropping or close-up effect that minimalizes the uncanny anatomical fusion of the original and gives greater prominence to the young St. John. Luini uses color decoratively, ignoring Leonardo's precepts on the color of shadows and reflected color. Color serves to demarcate bodies and render them coherent, while the inclusion of St. Joseph makes the sculptural cluster into a group composition extended in the plane.

With Leonardo and his followers, we need to broaden our normative idea of artistic discipleship, collaboration, or "influence" and attend to other possible modes of association and affiliation. We know very little of the normal daily life of any Renaissance artist's workshop: the weight of documentary evidence indicates a commercial, hierarchical, and masculine space of work. There is sparse additional evidence of the workshop as household, a space of sociability and intimacy. Leonardo's notebooks record numerous comings and goings of male part-time residents in his house, occasionally identifying a particular skill (often metalwork) or indicating that they paid rent. There are other graphic traces in Leonardo's paper legacy, in the constant inscription of proper names, in the interventions of other hands that draw and write on the same surfaces. A sheet in Windsor bears canceled notes on the flow of water by Leonardo along with notes by Melzi, studies of a leg and of valves of the heart, and drawings of mountains and a naked embracing couple by Melzi and others (RCIN 912641; plates 41a and 41b).[57] The couple are invariably identified as a man with a woman, but the identification of the figure with defined pectorals as female is doubtful: flip the sheet and anatomically similar male bodies are depicted wielding mallets and blowing a horn, along with drawings of syphons, notes on canal systems, and calculations. The multiple hands on the sheet render energy, flow, and affinity, the intertwining of like with like.

If Lomazzo was correct, some products of the workshop might be seen to have thematized these modes of association as a form of queer incorporation. Lomazzo, who knew Melzi, wrote in his *Treatise on Painting* of 1583: "many monsters are worthy of being remembered, among them those which Leonardo da Vinci portrayed in Milan, one of them being a very beautiful youth with a penis attached to his forehead and without a nose, and with another face on the back of his head with a penis below its chin and ears attached to the testicles; and which [conjoined] two heads had faun's ears. The other monster had the male member just above the nose and the eyes beside the nose, and the rest was the body of a very beautiful boy. They are both owned by the sculptor Francesco Borella."[58]

Writing at mid-century, Giorgio Vasari seems to have seen Leonardo's mentorship of the Florentine sculptor Giovan Francesco Rustici in terms of a trans-personal affinity rather than the grind of workshop training: "Rustici, being pleased by the beautiful manner and ways of Leonardo, and considering that the expressions of his heads and the movements of his figures were more graceful and more spirited than those of any other works that he had ever seen, *attached himself to him*, after he had learned to cast in bronze, to draw in perspective, and to work in marble [my emphasis]." Rustici lives with Leonardo and serves him "with the most loving submission," while Leonardo conceives so an affection for the talent and diligent young artist "that he did nothing, either great or small, save what was pleasing to Giovan Francesco." Rustici, moreover, was from a noble family, "and therefore practiced art more for his own delight and from desire of glory than for gain." The invocation of Rustici's nobility, the image of a noncommercial "partnership," where art is pursued as a liberal form of knowledge and not "for gain," is reminiscent of the loving attachment of another Giovan Francesco—the noble and "beautiful" Milanese youth Giovan Francesco Melzi—to Leonardo's person and studio.

Vasari writes that when Rustici was working on the clay models for the Baptistery bronzes, "he would have no one about him but Leonardo da Vinci, who, during the making of the molds, the securing them with irons, and, in short, until the statues were cast, never left his side; wherefore some believe, but without knowing more than this, that Leonardo worked at them with his own hand, or at least assisted Giovan Francesco with his advice and good judgment."[59] It is almost as if Vasari wants to identify the Rustici statue group on the Baptistery as coauthored, or even authored by Leonardo *through* Rustici's hands and body—thus beginning a mythical quest for sculptures by Leonardo that continues with constant new attributions to the present day.

PAINTING AS ATMOSPHERE

"Influence" is a notoriously lazy term in the history of art. It usually implies a simplification of the many possible relations, including but not only involving resemblance that a work of art might bear to another work of art, or that one artist might bear to predecessors or contemporaries. Concepts of influence have been deployed with more circumspection and analytical force in literary studies, and more recently in post-human studies, political theory, philosophy, and quantum physics—modes of inquiry attentive to the myriad forms of human and nonhuman interaction, the biological and the inorganic.[60] On one hand Leonardo embraces a notion of influence as an openness to the world beyond the boundaries of the self, through his figure of the artist as a mirror, or via the already-quoted words of Dante: "It is impossible to paint a figure, if the painter is not able to be that figure."[61]

Or, in rhapsodic passages on painting as a form of climate, like the following: "Endeavor, painter, to make sure your works draw spectators to stop in admiration and delight, and do not attract them only to drive them away again, as the air does to someone who during the night leaps naked from bed to ascertain whether the nature of such air is cloudy or clear. Immediately repelled by the chill, he returns to the bed whence he rose. Rather make your work resemble the air which in hot weather draws men from their beds and detains them pleasurably as they partake of the coolness of a summer's night."[62]

Vasari, always ambivalent about Leonardo, insinuates that the influence of a Leonardo painting, manifest in its impact on the beholder, is like intoxication or contamination. He twice associates Leonardo's work with the baleful head of Medusa: once in reference to a now lost painting of the Gorgon's head, and also in a famous anecdote about the seemingly morbid naturalism of the young painter, who spends weeks among the decaying bodies of dissected reptiles and rodents to generate the image of a monster that broke the constraints of pictorial illusion and terrified Leonardo's father. In a darkened room reeking of rotting animal corpses, the *animalaccio* seemed to come alive, polluting the room with venom and fire and surging forth from a cleft rock: "belching venom from its open maw, fire from its eyes and smoke from its nose." A few pages later Vasari refers to Leonardo's tendency to engulf his pictures with deep shadow to provide the maximum effects of relief, so that the "pictures finally seemed to portray an effect of night rather than of clear daylight."[63] The tacit disapproval here becomes more pronounced, as we will see, in accounts of artists influenced by Leonardo's tenebrous atmospheres.

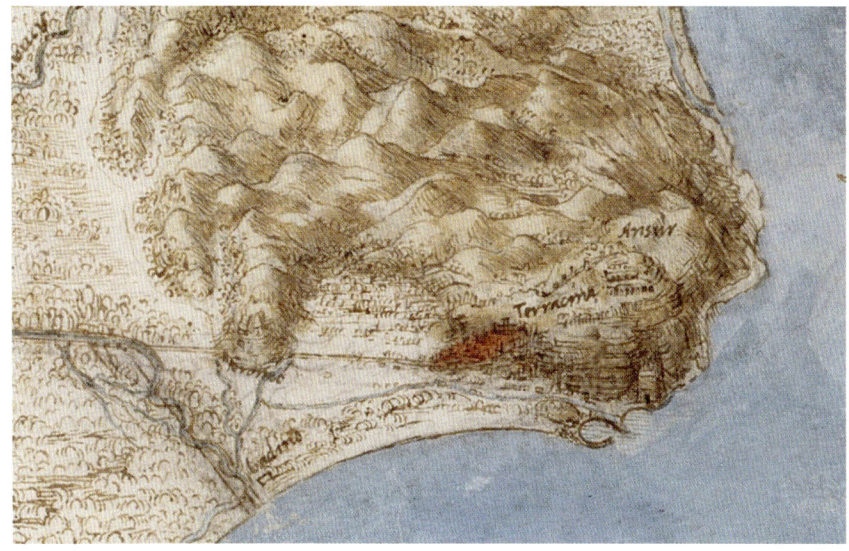

1. Leonardo da Vinci, a map of the Pontine marshes. Ca. 1514–15, detail. Stylus, black chalk, pen and ink, brown and red wash, blue bodycolor, 27.7 × 40 cm. (sheet of paper). Windsor, Royal Library, RCIN 912684.

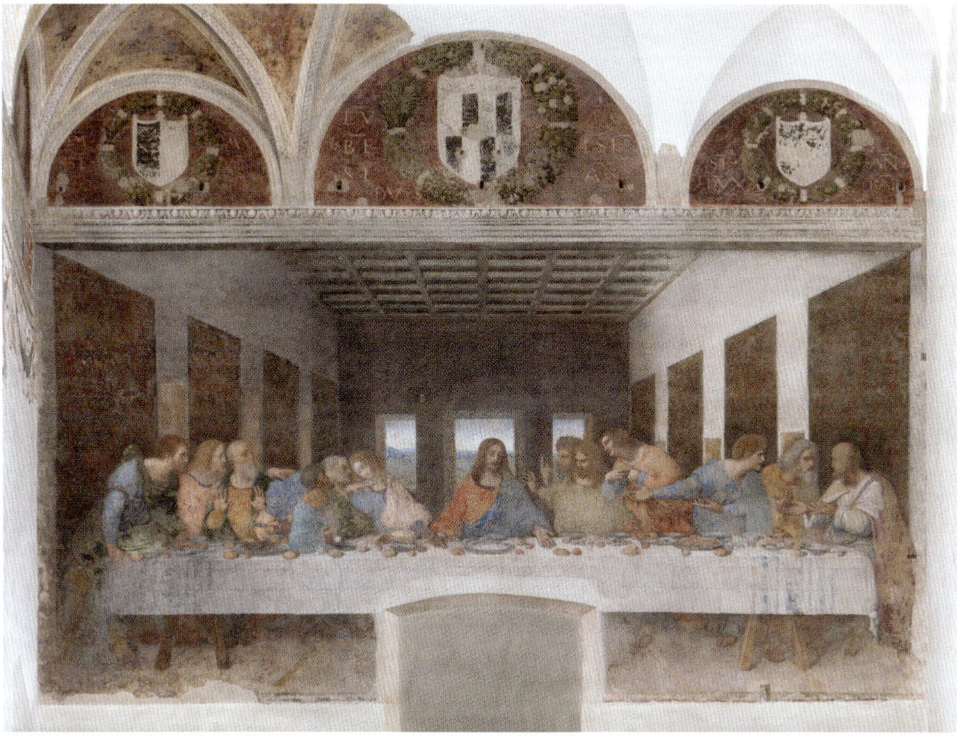

2. Leonardo da Vinci, *The Last Supper*. Ca. 1495–98. Milan, Santa Maria delle Grazie.

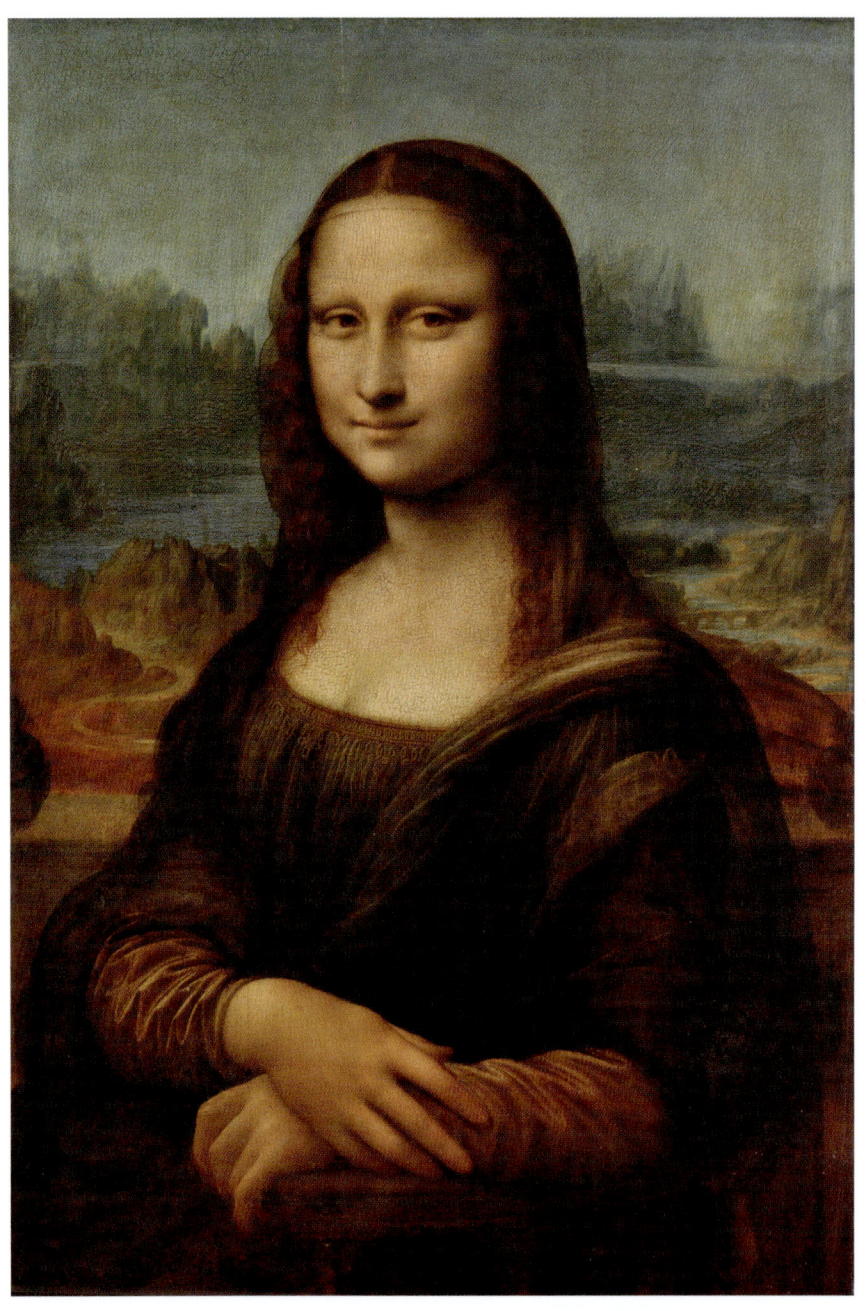

3. Leonardo da Vinci, *Portrait of Lisa Gherardini del Giocondo* (*Mona Lisa*).
Ca. 1500–1506, with additional work until ca. 1517. On panel, 77 × 53 cm. Paris, Louvre.

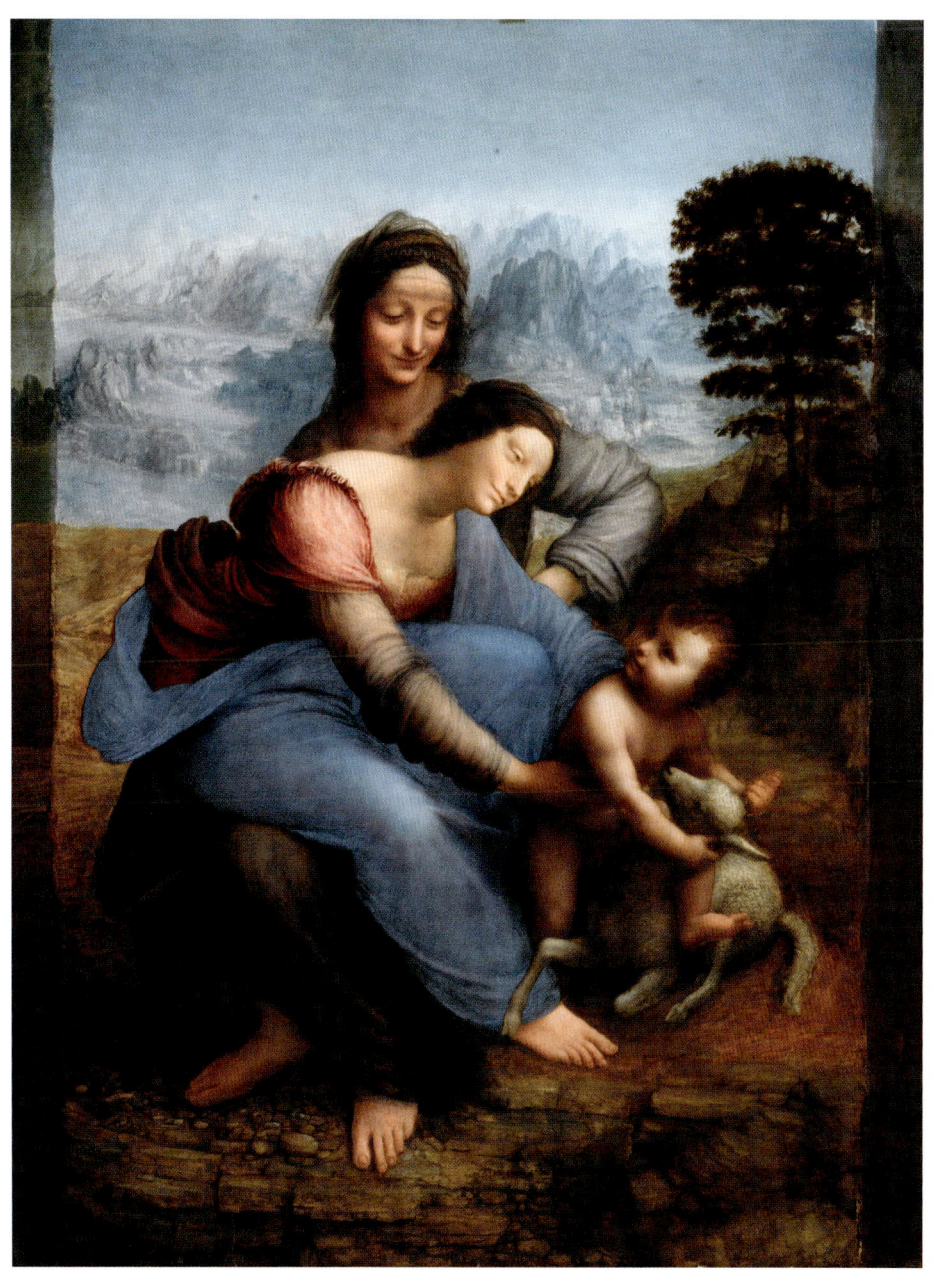

4. Leonardo da Vinci, *Virgin and Child with St. Anne*. 1510. On panel, 168 × 130 cm. Paris, Louvre.

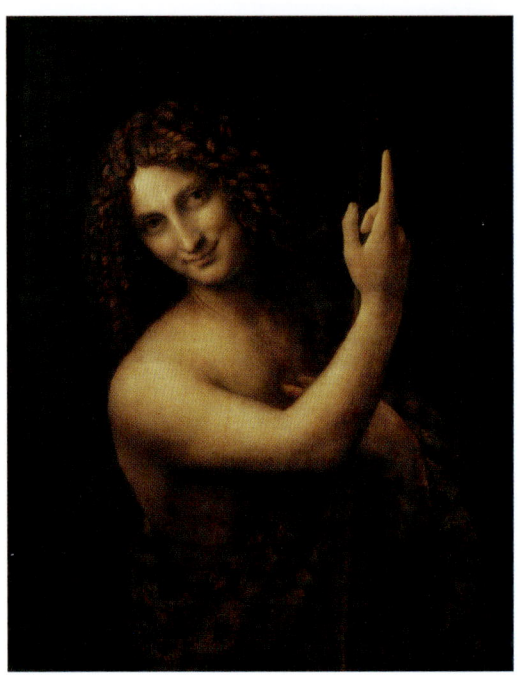

5. Leonardo da Vinci, *St. John the Baptist*.
Ca. 1513–16. On panel, 69 × 57 cm. Paris, Louvre.

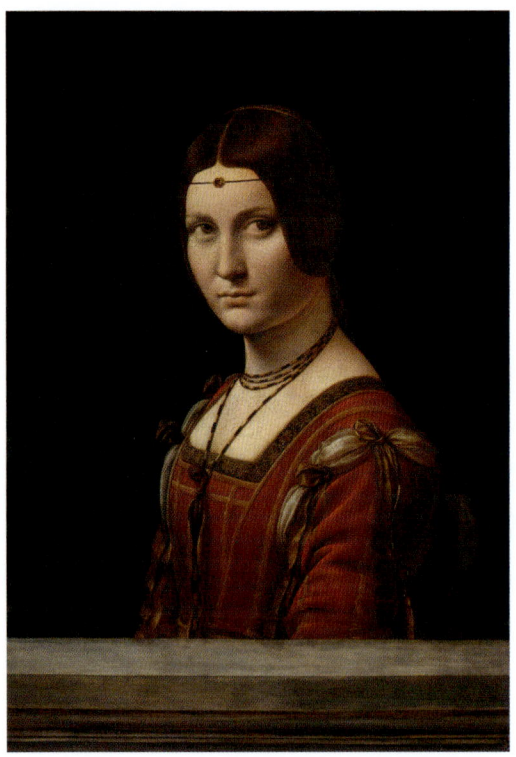

6. Leonardo da Vinci, *Portrait of a Lady, known
as "La Belle Ferronnière."* 1490–99. On panel,
62 × 44 cm. Paris, Louvre.

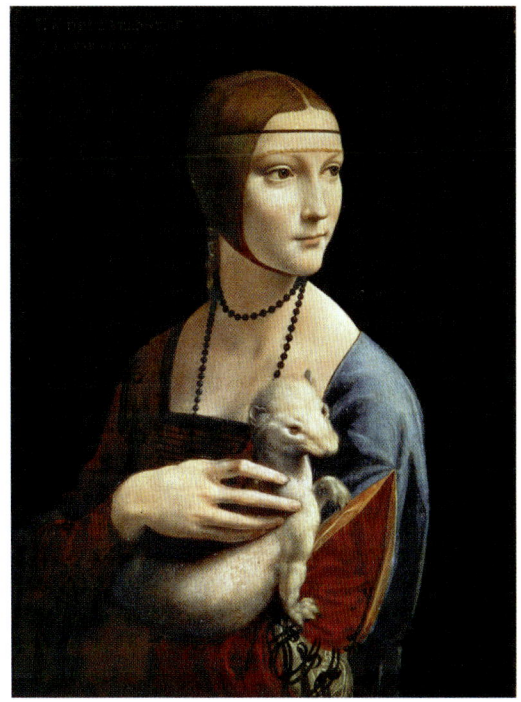

7. Leonardo da Vinci, *Lady with an Ermine* (*Cecilia Gallerani*).
Before 1490. On panel, 54 × 39 cm. Cracow, Czartoryski Museum.

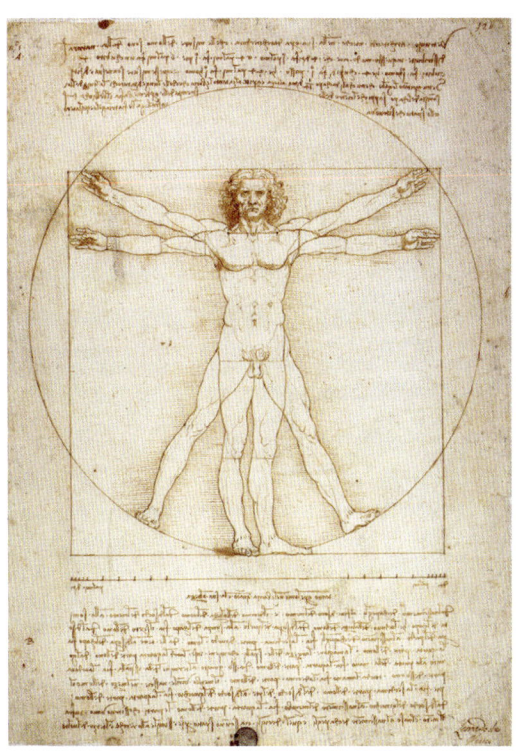

8. Leonardo da Vinci, *The Vitruvian Man*. Ca. 1490. Pen and ink with wash
over metalpoint on paper, 34.6 × 25.5 cm. Venice, Gallerie dell'Accademia.

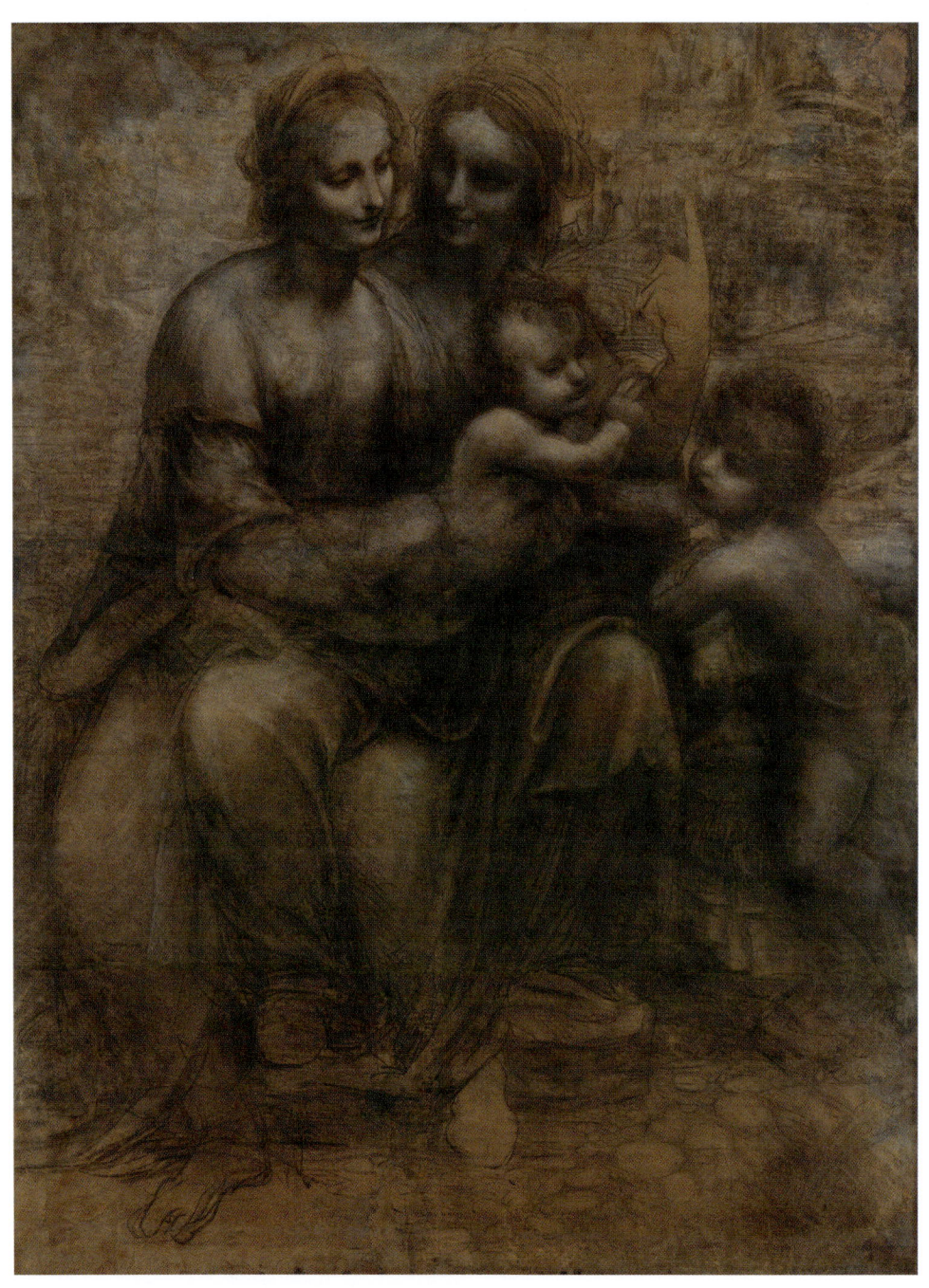

9. Leonardo da Vinci, *The Virgin and Child with St. Anne and St. John* (Burlington House Cartoon). 1506–8. Charcoal, black and white chalk on tinted paper mounted on canvas, 141.5 × 104.6 cm. London, National Gallery.

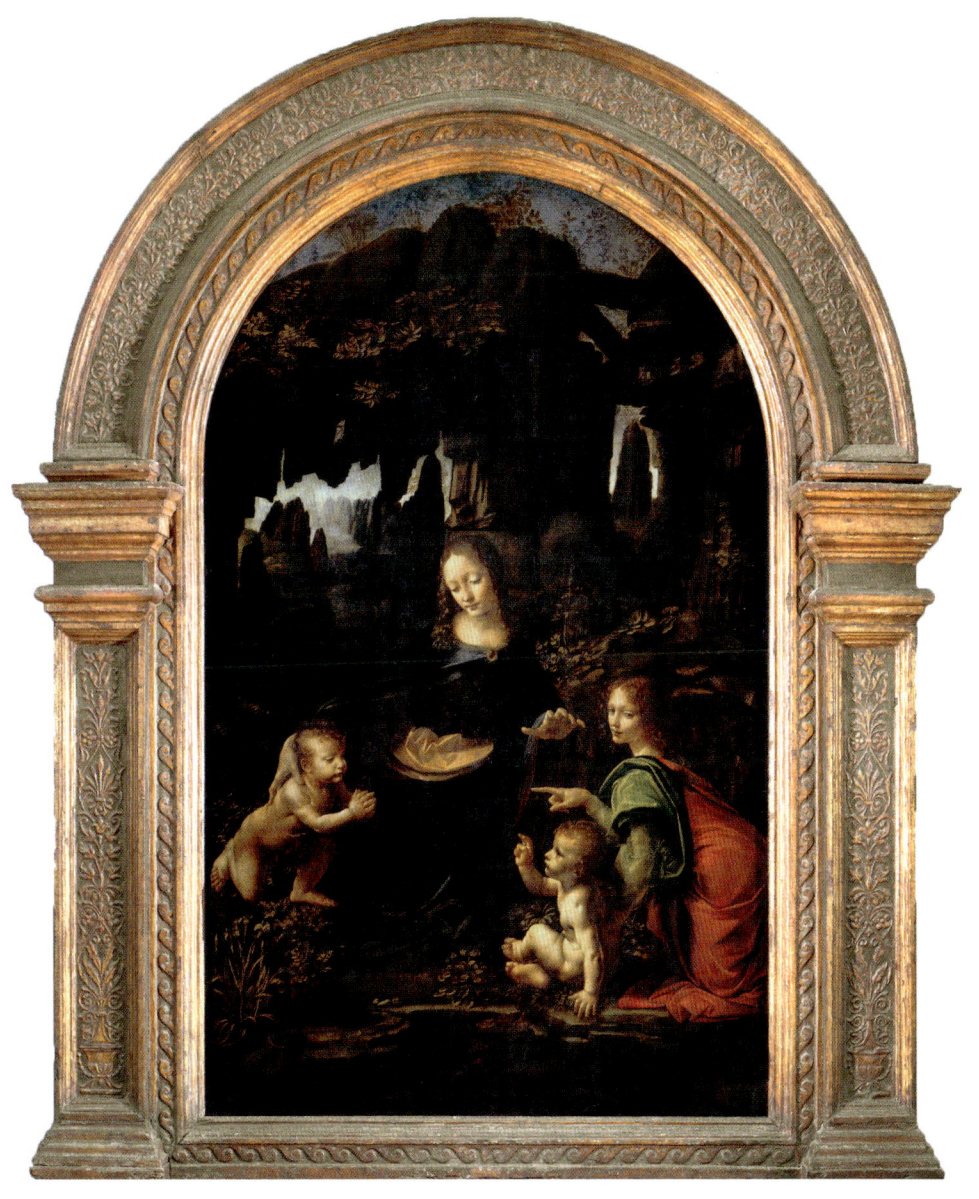

10. Leonardo da Vinci, *The Virgin of the Rocks*. 1483–86. On panel, 199 × 122 cm. Paris, Louvre.

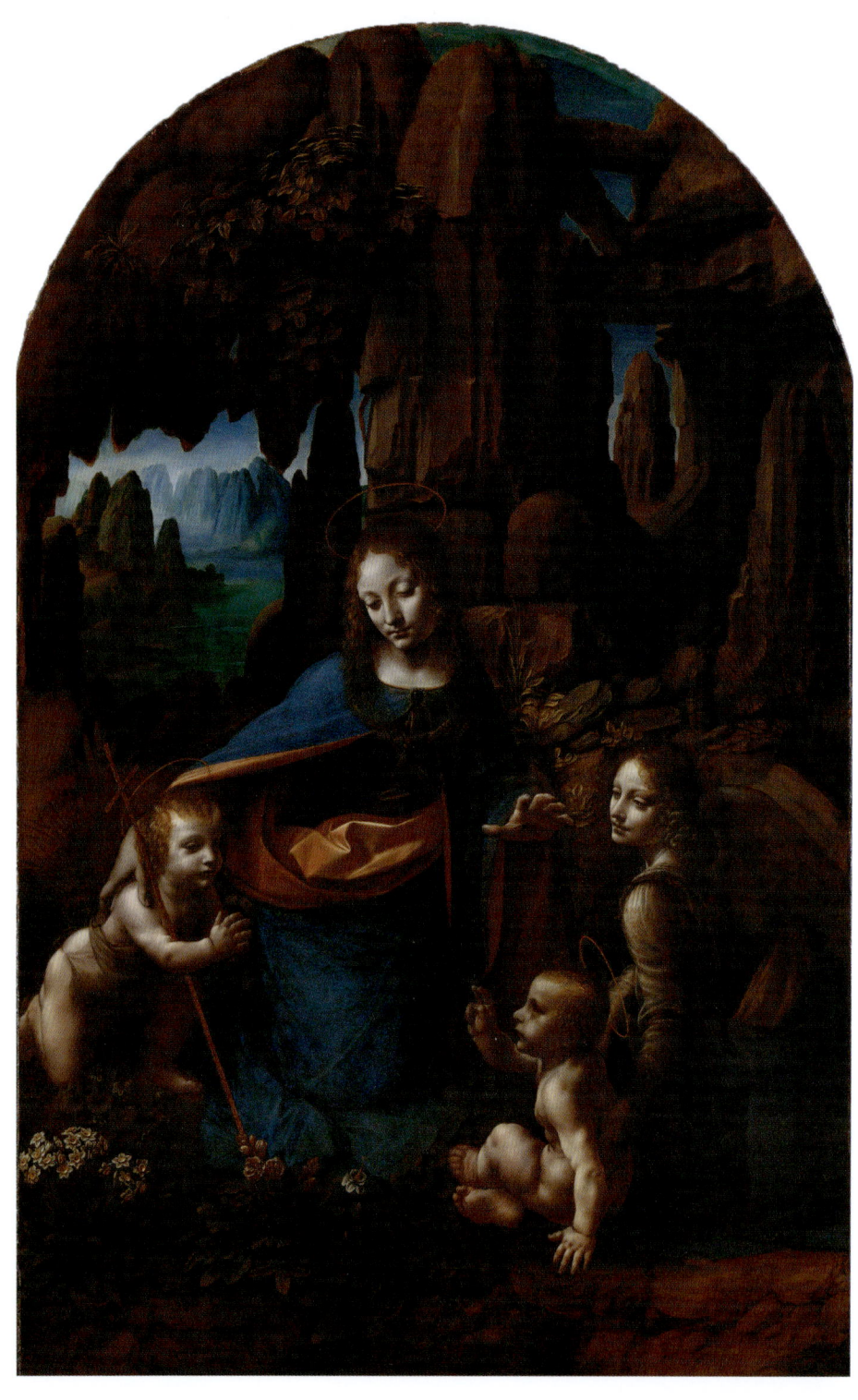

11. Leonardo da Vinci, *The Virgin of the Rocks*. Ca. 1495–1508. On panel, 189.5 × 120 cm. London, National Gallery.

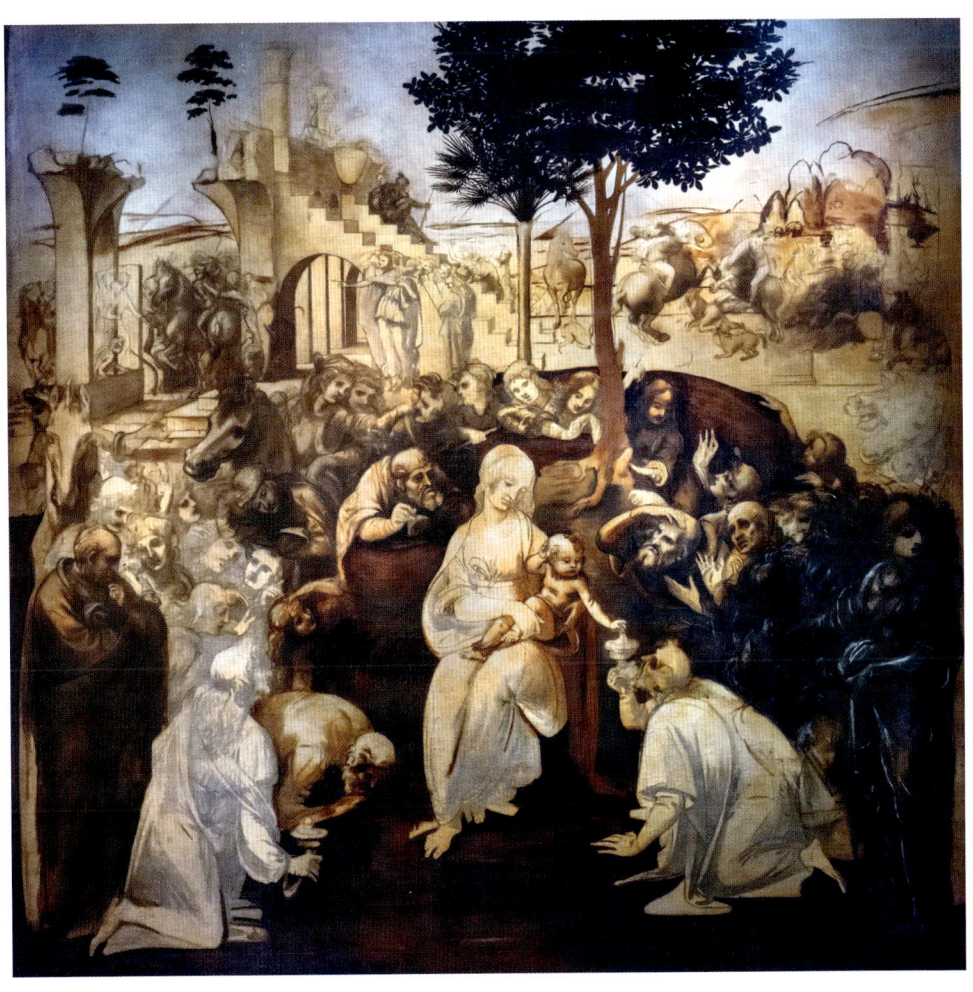

12. Leonardo da Vinci, *The Adoration of the Magi*. 1481. On panel, 246 × 243 cm. Florence, Uffizi.

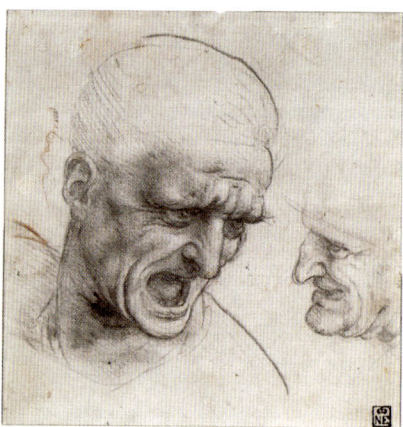

13. Leonardo da Vinci, study for *The Battle of Anghiari*. Ca. 1505. Black chalk or charcoal, some traces of red chalk on paper, 19.1 × 18.8 cm. Budapest, Museum of Fine Arts.

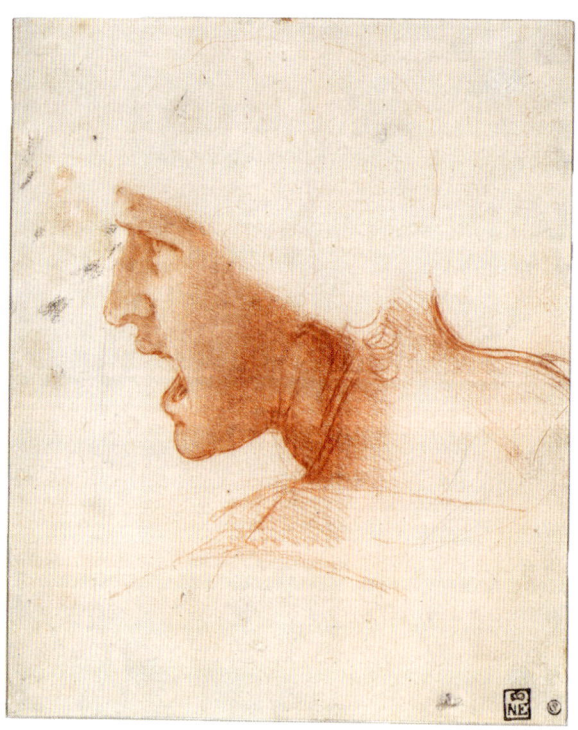

14. Leonardo da Vinci, study for *The Battle of Anghiari*. Ca. 1505. Red chalk on pink prepared paper, 22.6 × 18.6 cm. Budapest, Museum of Fine Arts.

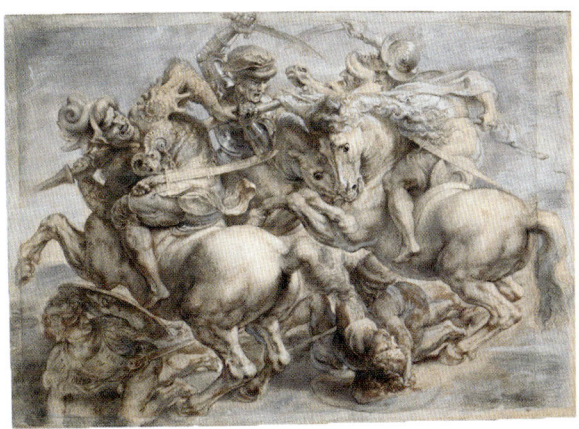

15. Unknown draftsman after a design by Leonardo, retouched by Peter Paul Rubens ca. 1603, *The Battle of Anghiari*. Black chalk, pen in brown ink, brush in brown and gray ink, gray wash, heightened in white and gray-blue, 45.3 × 63.6 cm. Paris, Louvre.

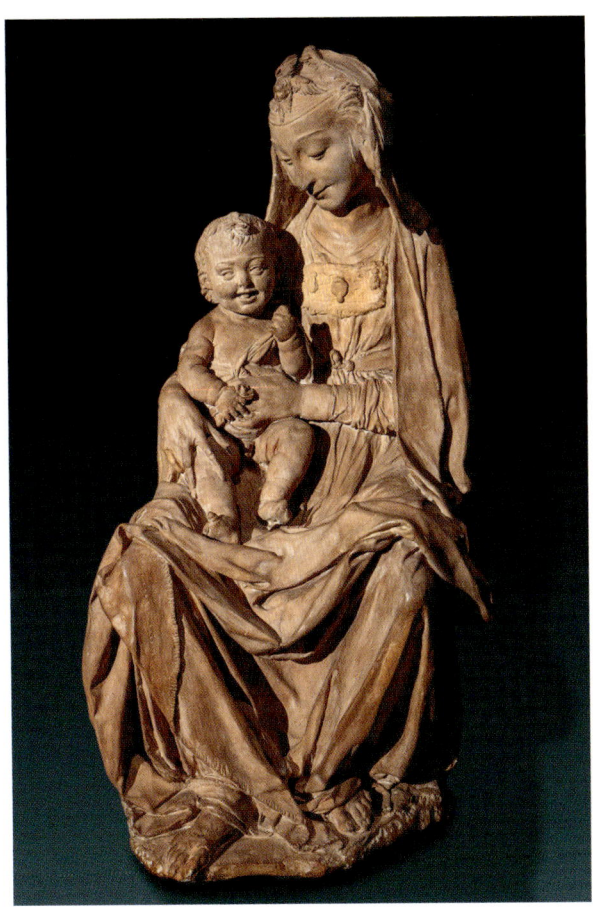

16. Attributed to Leonardo da Vinci, *The Virgin with the Laughing Child*. After 1470. Terracotta, 49 × 27 cm. London, Victoria and Albert Museum.

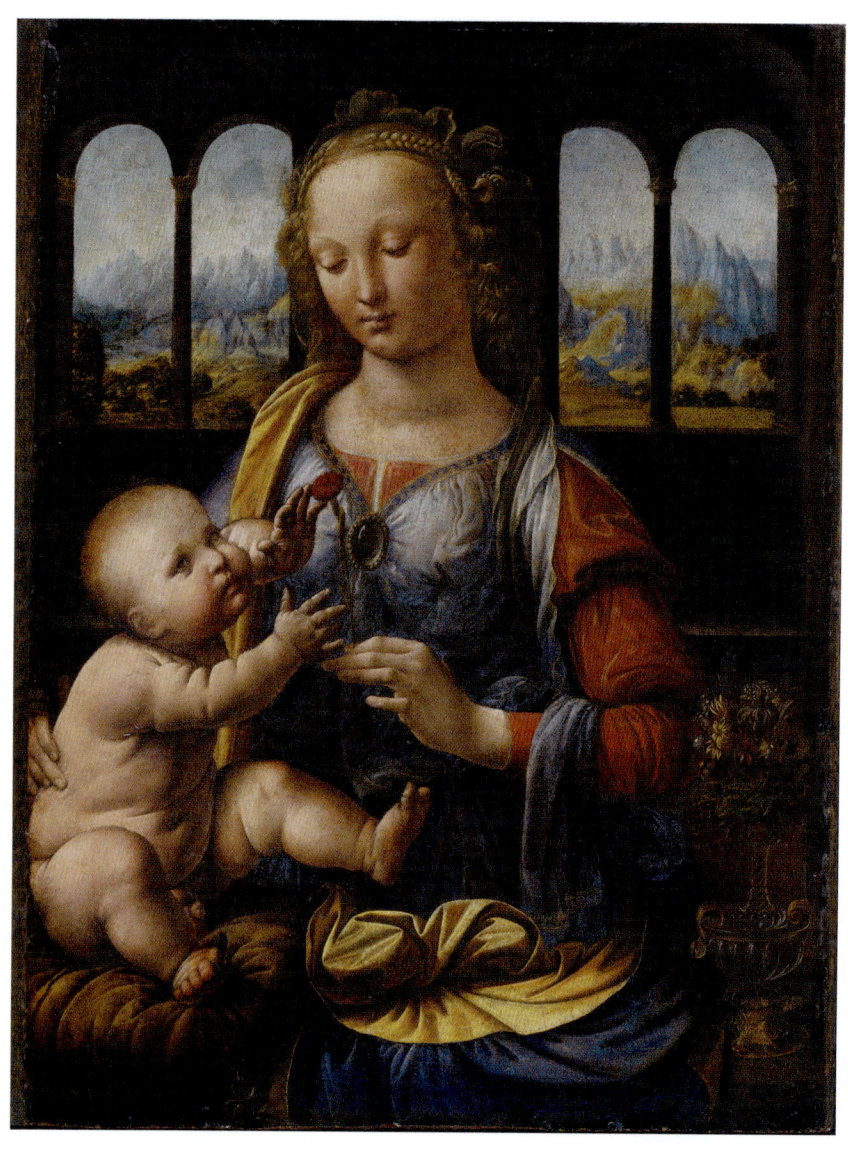

17. Leonardo da Vinci, *Madonna of the Carnation*. 1474–78. On panel, 62 × 47.5 cm. Munich, Alte Pinakothek.

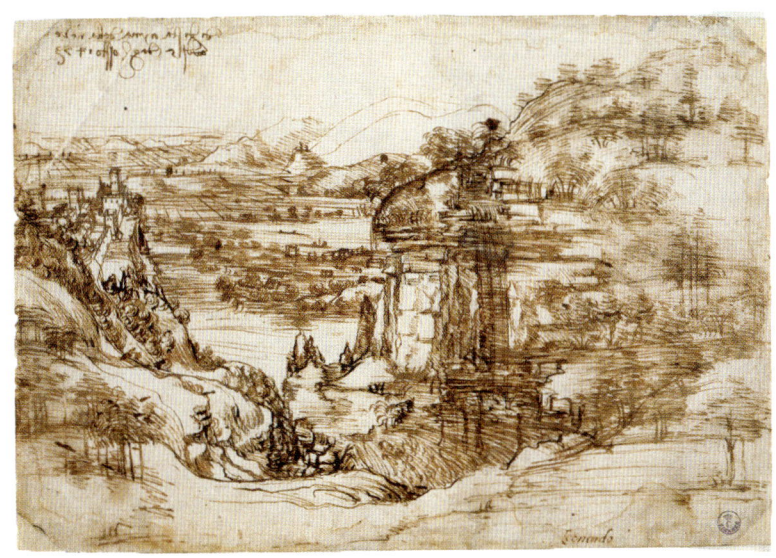

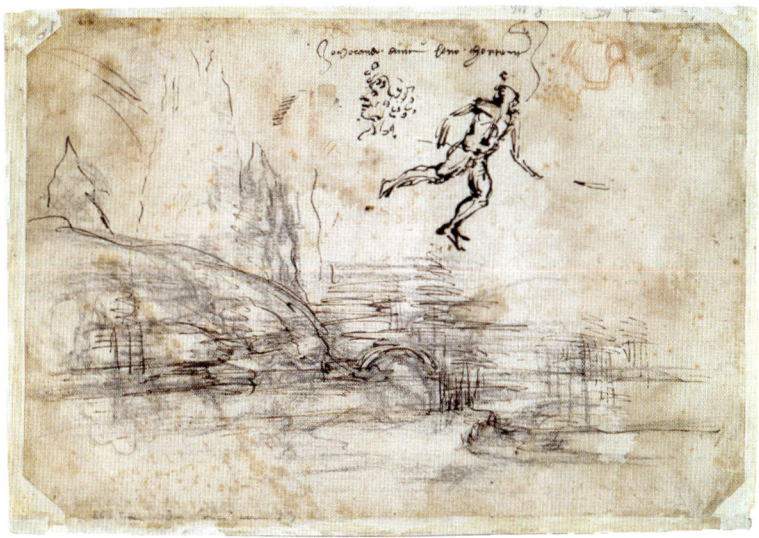

18a and 18b. Leonardo da Vinci, *Arno Valley landscape*. Dated August 5, 1473.
Ink over black chalk on paper, 19 × 28.5 cm. Verso: landscape, flower, male figure, and
geometrical motifs. Black and red chalk. Florence, Uffizi.

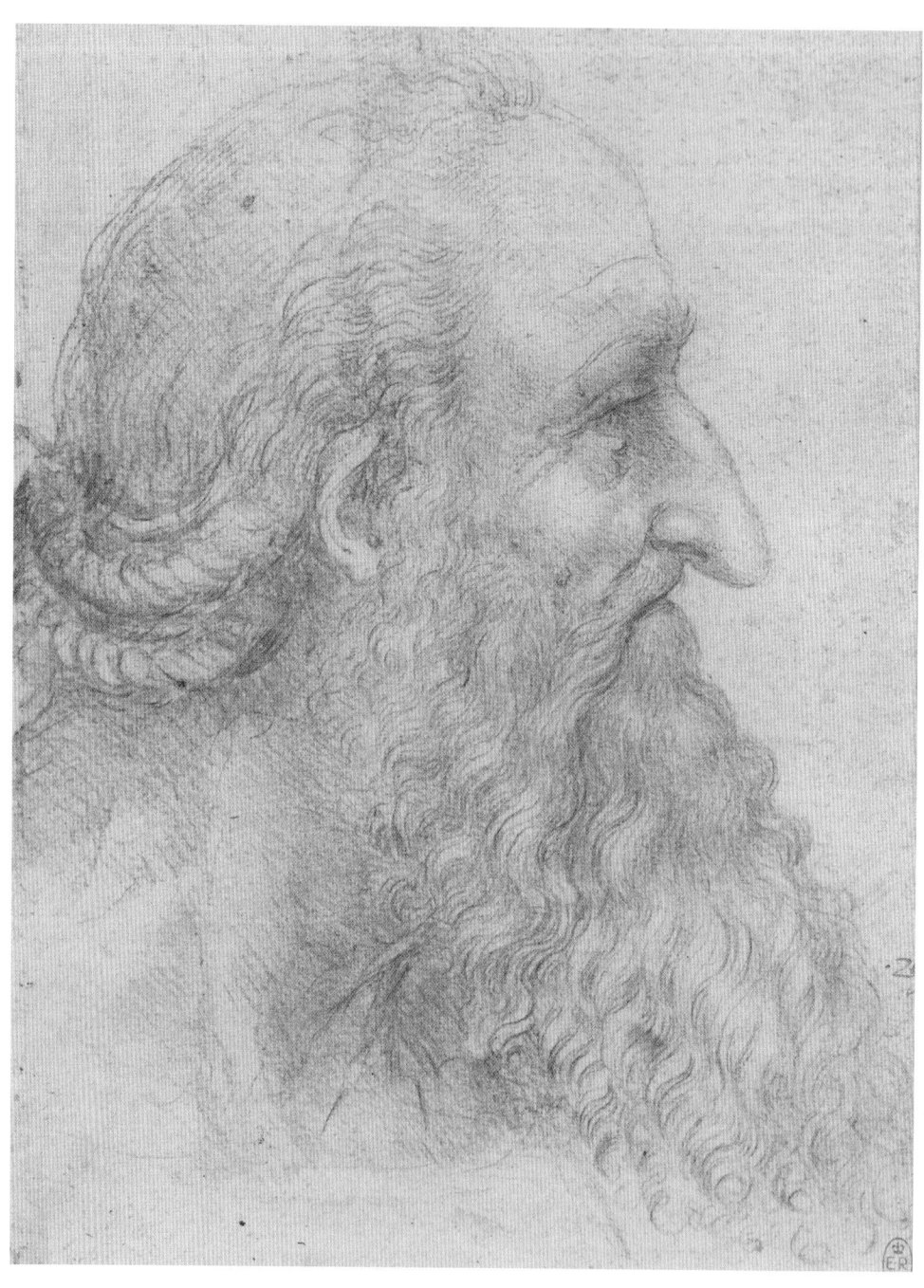

19. Leonardo da Vinci, *The head of an old bearded man*. Ca. 1515. Black chalk, 21.3 × 15.5 cm. Windsor, Royal Library, RCIN 912499.

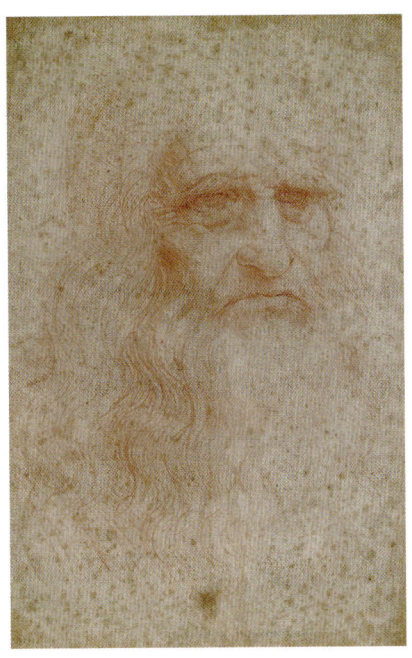

20. Leonardo da Vinci, *Portrait of an Elderly Man*. Ca. 1500–1505. Red chalk, 33.3 × 21.6 cm. Turin, Biblioteca Reale.

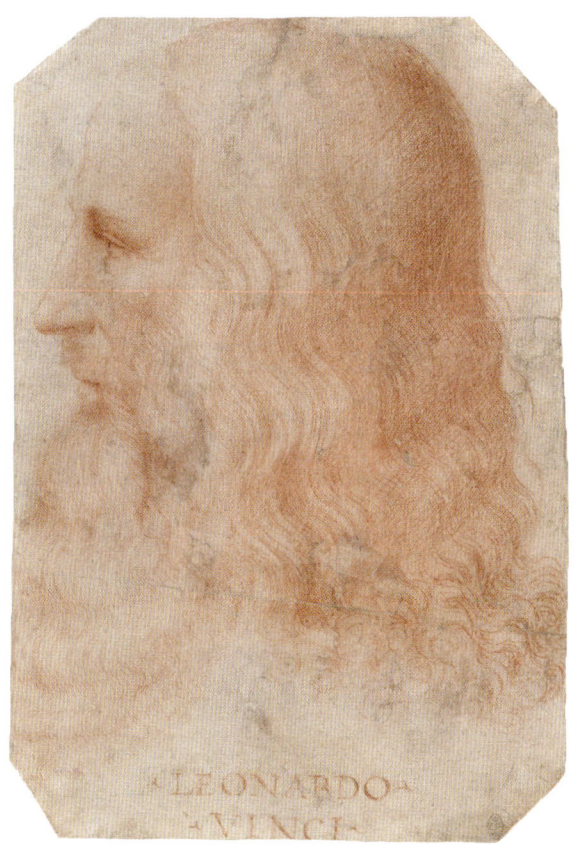

21. Francesco Melzi, *Portrait of Leonardo da Vinci*. Ca. 1515. Red chalk, 27.5 × 19 cm. Windsor, Royal Library, RCIN 912726.

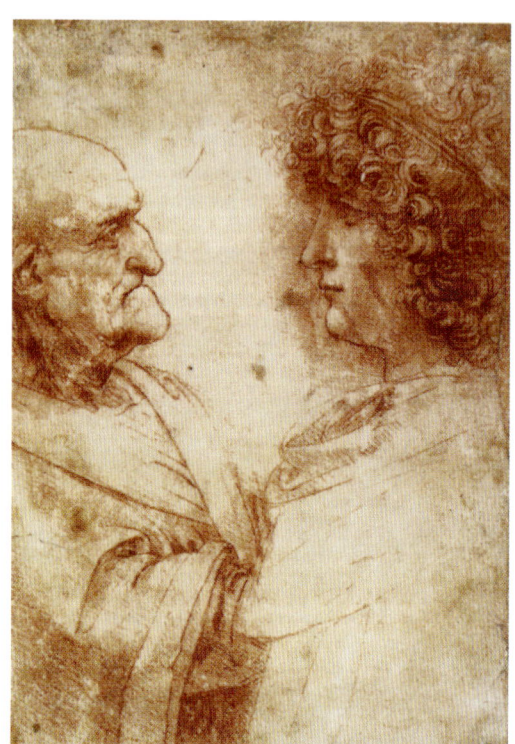

22. Leonardo da Vinci, *Heads of an old man and a youth*. 1495–1500. Red chalk on paper, 20.8 × 15 cm. Florence, Uffizi.

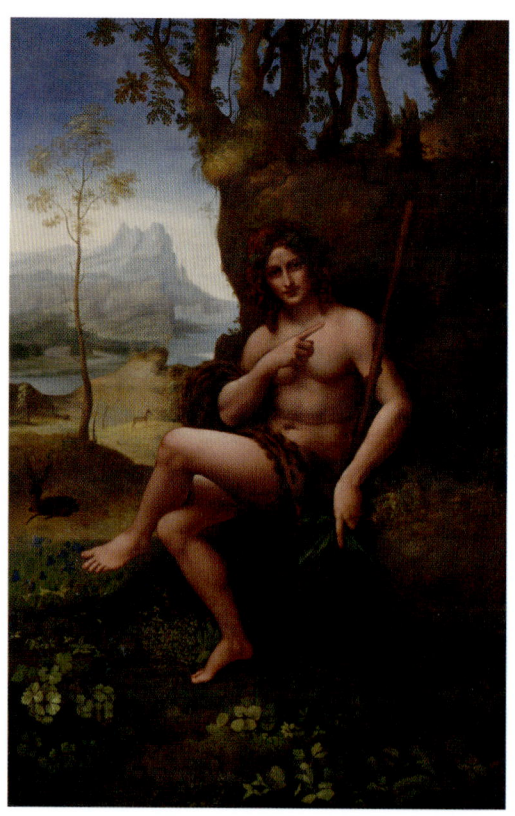

23. Leonardo da Vinci and assistants, *St. John the Baptist* ("*Bacchus*"). On panel, transferred to canvas, 177 × 115 cm. Paris, Louvre.

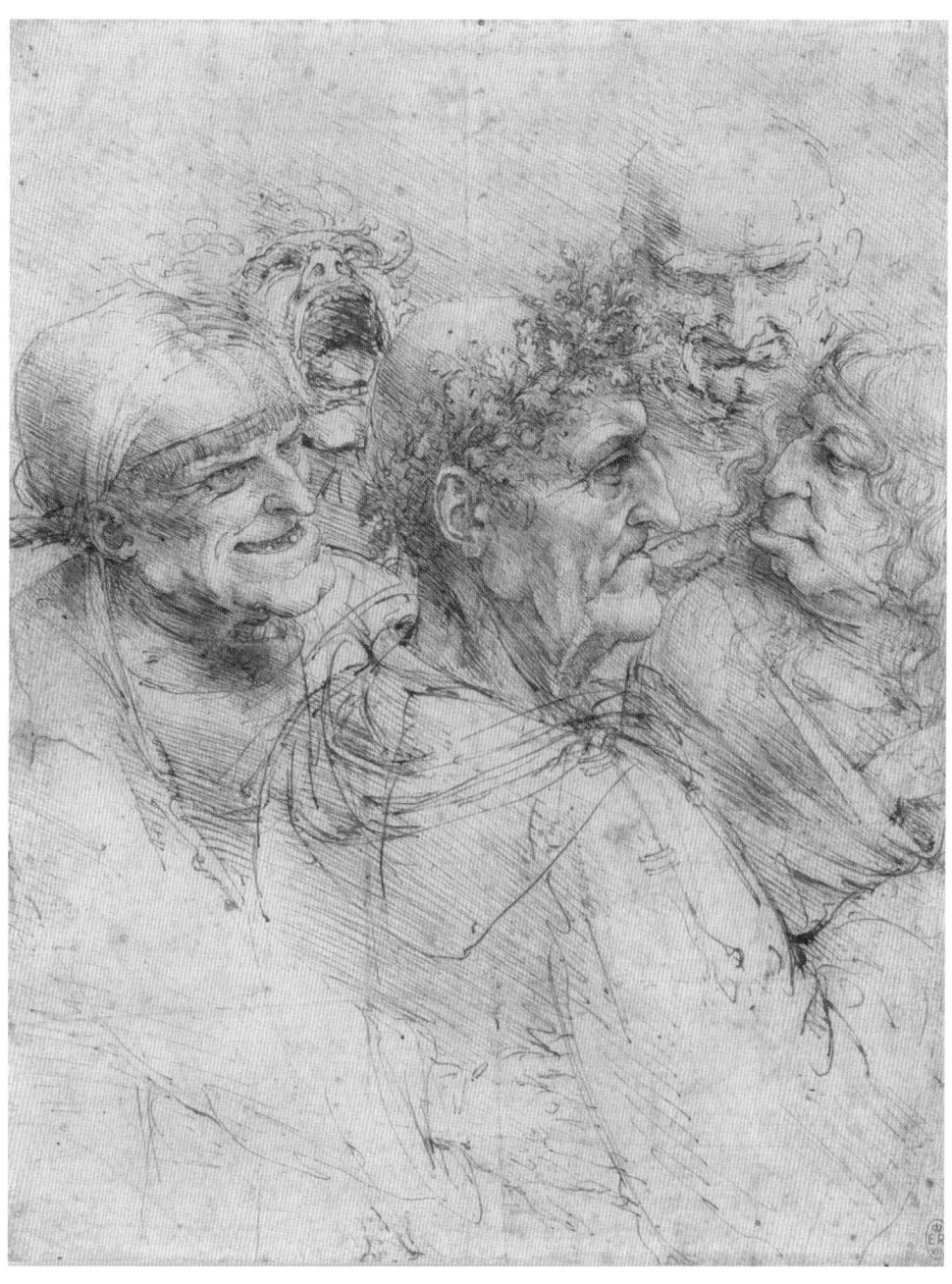

24. Leonardo da Vinci, *Five grotesque heads*. Ca. 1493. Brown ink on paper, 26 × 20.5 cm. Windsor, Royal Library, RCIN 912495.

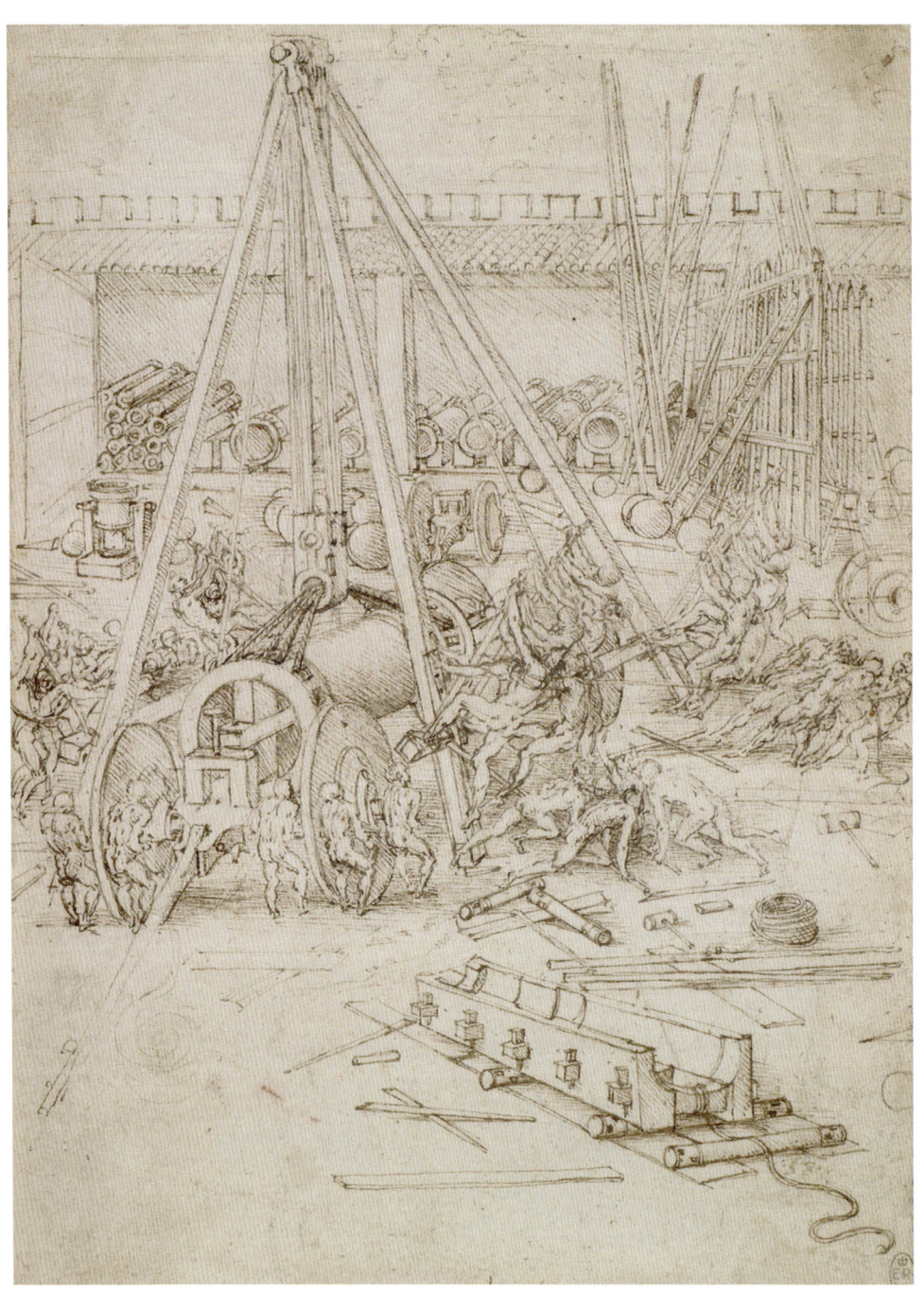

25. Leonardo da Vinci, *A scene in an arsenal*. Ca. 1485–90. Pen and ink, 25 × 18.3 cm. Windsor, Royal Library, RCIN 912647.

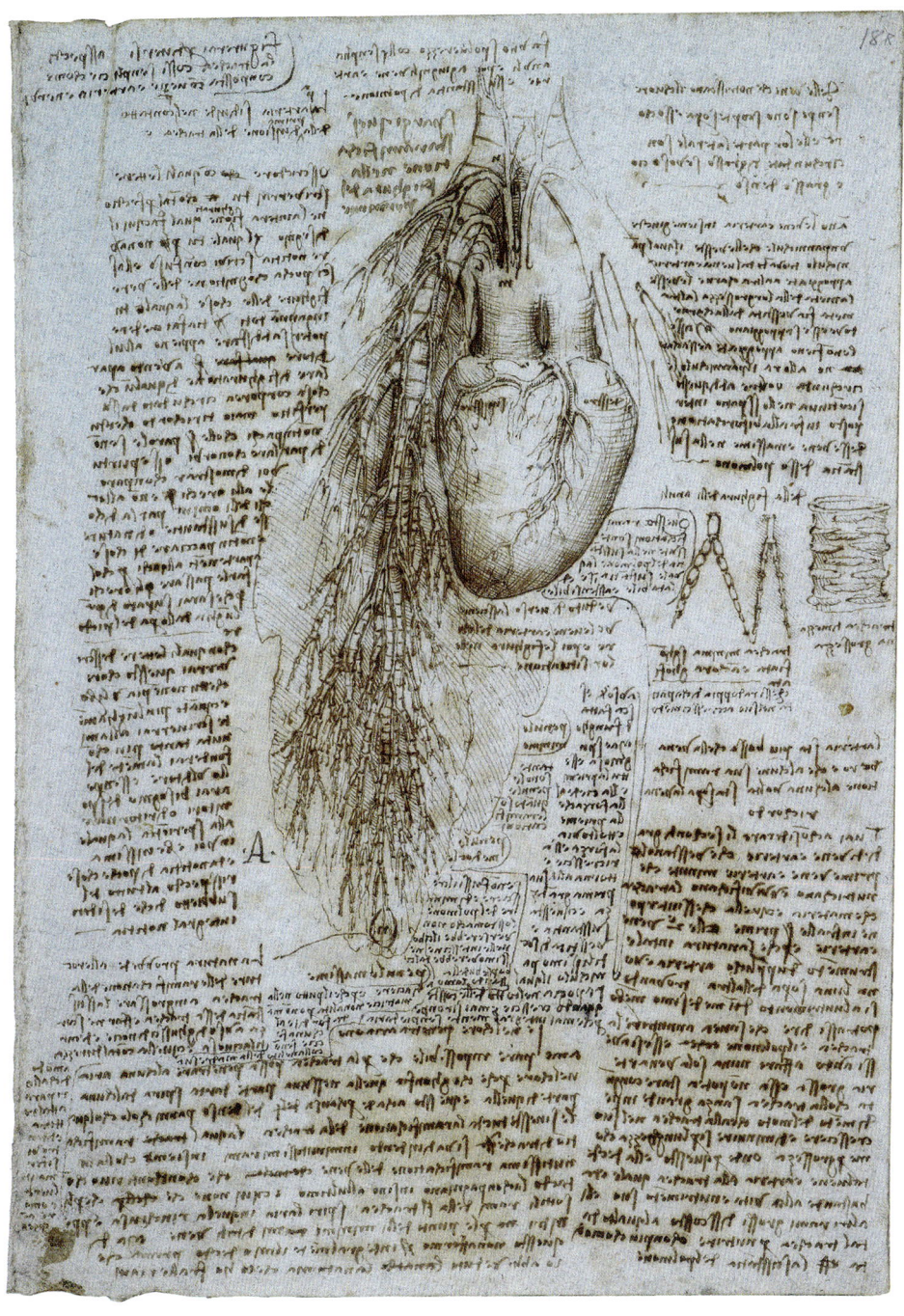

26. Leonardo da Vinci, *The heart, bronchi and bronchial vessels of an ox*. Ca. 1511–13.
Pen and ink on blue paper, 28.8 × 20.3 cm. Windsor, Royal Library, RCIN 919071.

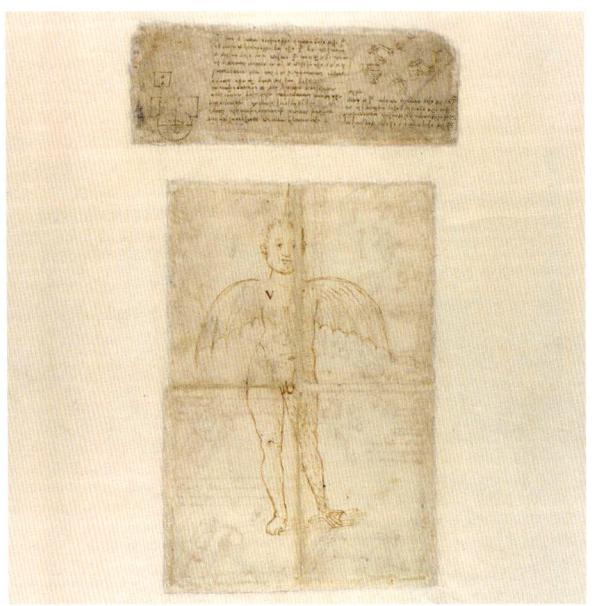

27. Leonardo da Vinci, sheet from Codex Atlanticus 58r. Milan, Ambrosiana.

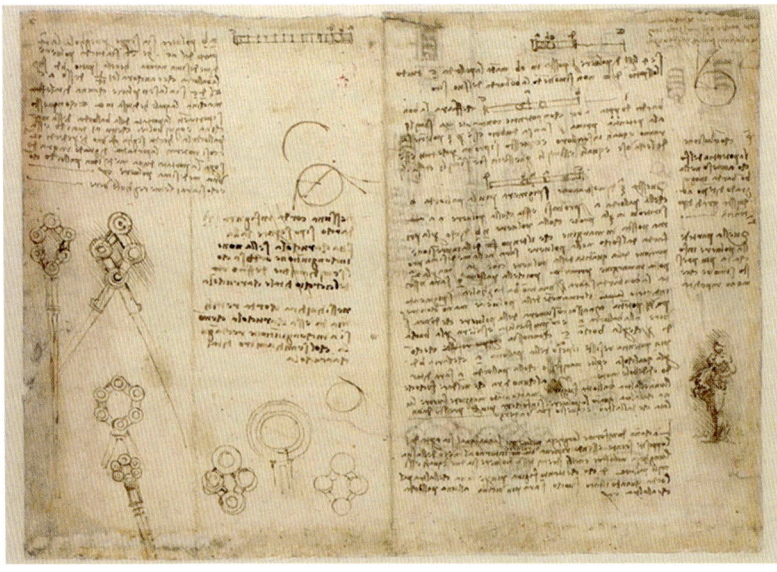

28. Leonardo da Vinci, sheet from Codex Atlanticus 48r. Milan, Ambrosiana.

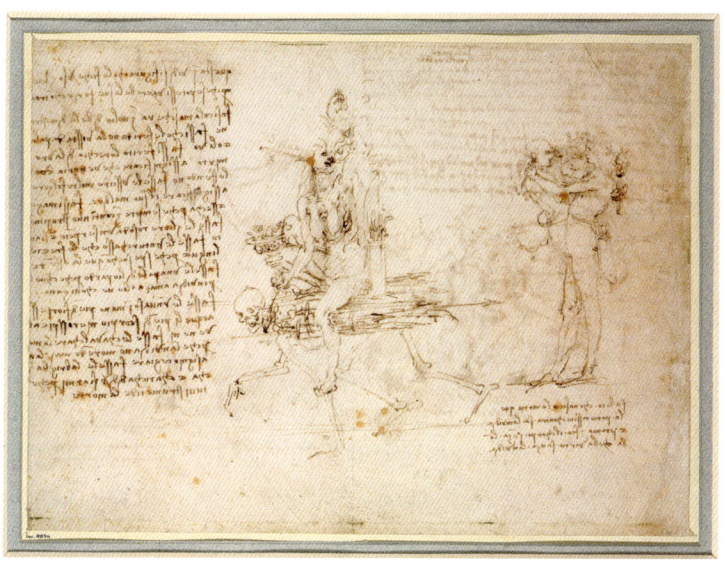

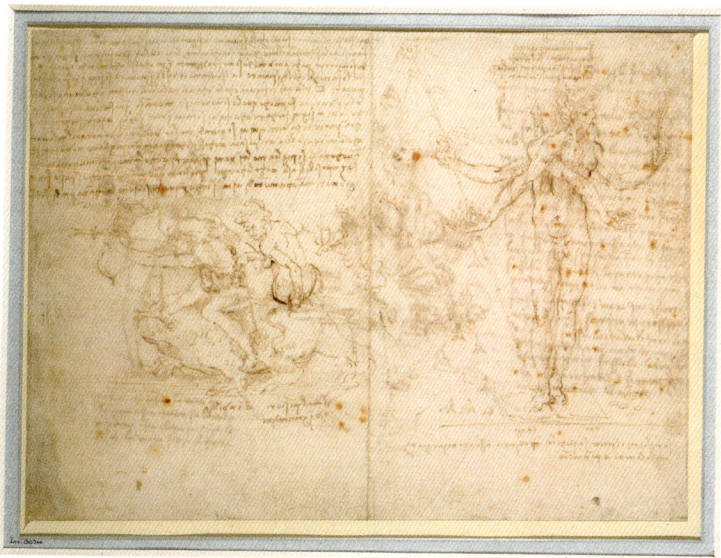

29a and 29b. Leonardo da Vinci, recto: *Two allegories of Envy*; verso: Two allegories:
(a) *Ingratitude, Envy and Death*; (b) *Pleasure and Pain*. Ca. 1490. Pen and brown ink,
21 × 28.9 cm. Oxford, Christ Church Gallery 0034r and v. (JBS 17).

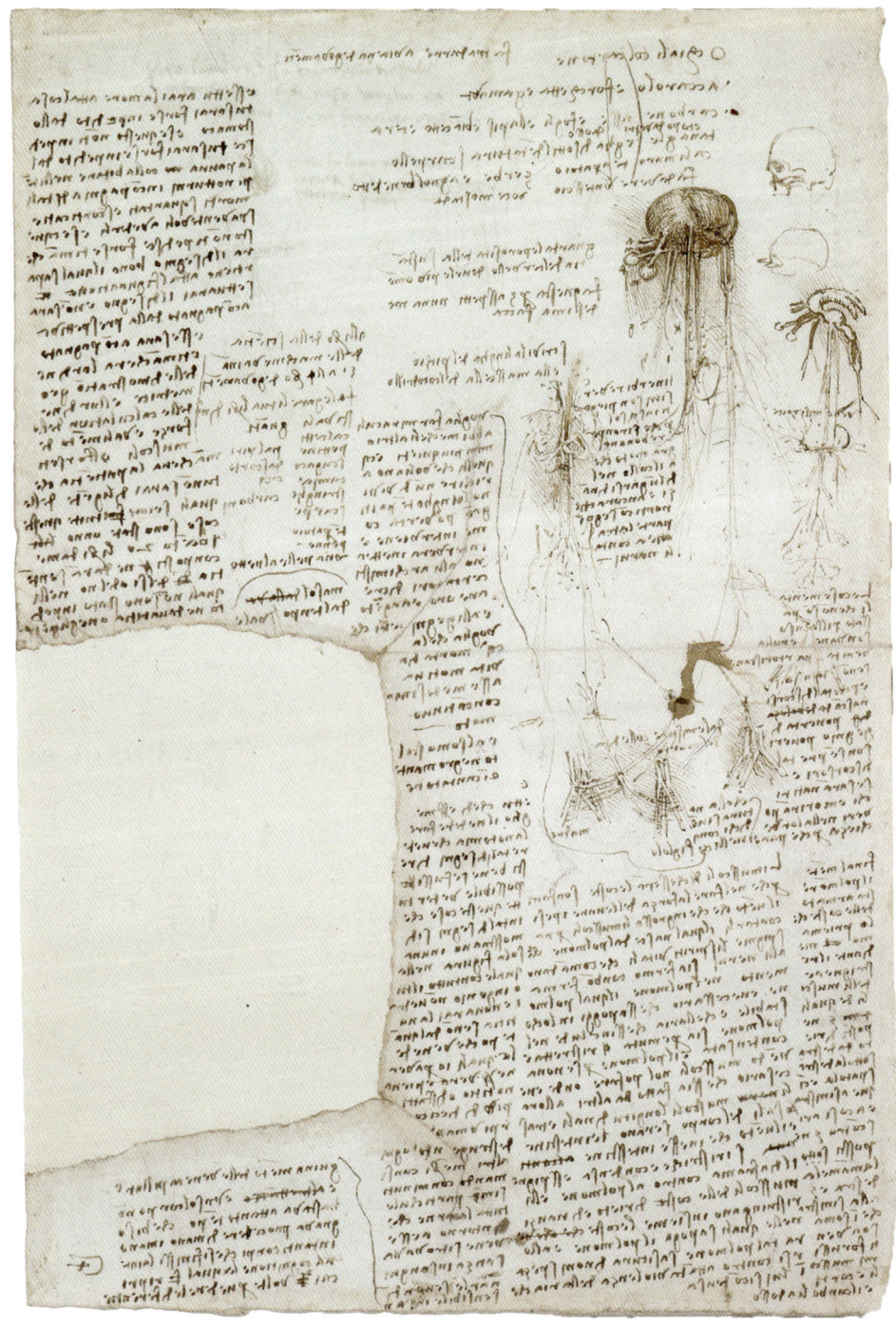

30. Leonardo da Vinci, *Miscellaneous notes and anatomical sketches.* Ca. 1508–10. Pen and ink, 32 × 22.1 cm. Windsor, Royal Library, RCIN 919070.

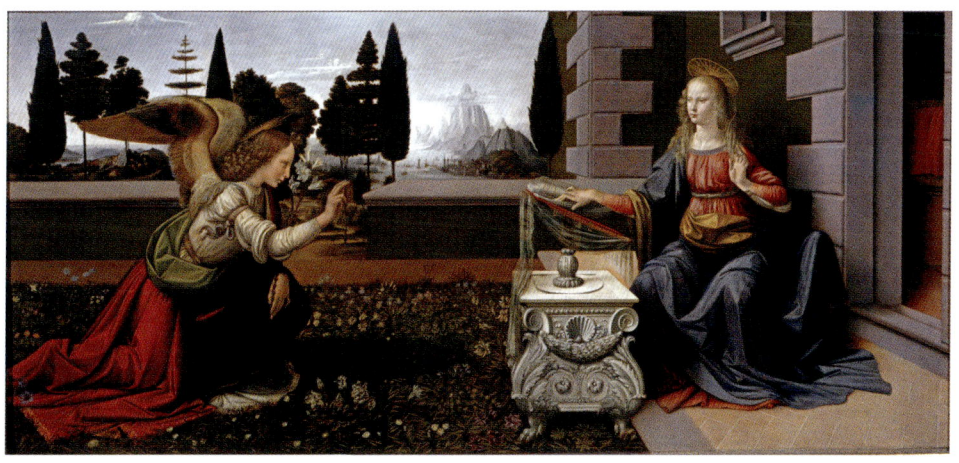

31. Leonardo da Vinci, *Annunciation*. Ca. 1472–75. On panel, 98 × 217 cm. Florence, Uffizi.

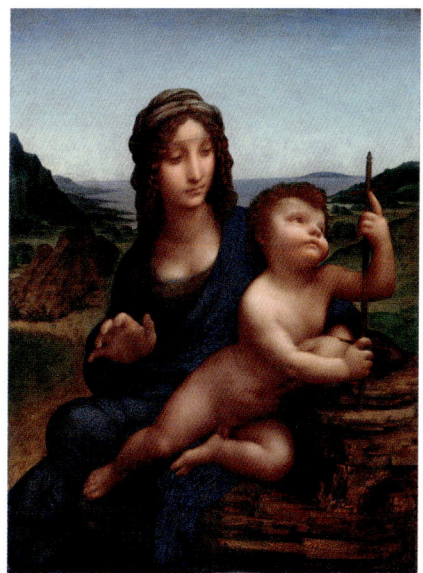

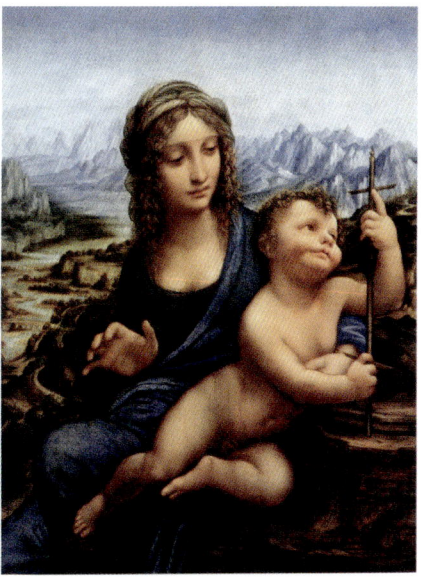

32. Leonardo da Vinci and assistant, *Madonna of the Yarn Winder* (*Buccleuch Madonna*). Ca. 1501. On panel, 48.3 × 36.9 cm. Edinburgh, Scottish National Gallery.

33. Leonardo da Vinci and assistant, *Madonna of the Yarn Winder* (*Lansdowne Madonna*). Ca. 1501. On panel, transferred to canvas and relaid on panel, 50.2 × 34.6 cm. Private collection.

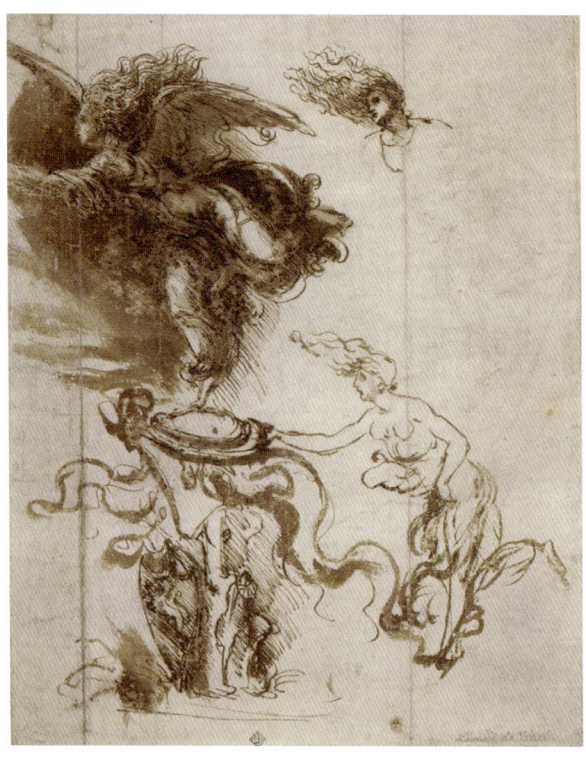

34. Leonardo da Vinci, *Study for a winged figure, an allegory with Fortune*. 1480–85. Pen and brown ink, with brown wash, 24.9 × 20.1 cm. London, British Museum.

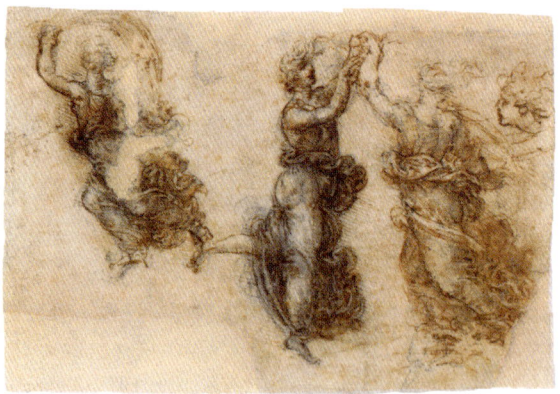

35. Leonardo da Vinci, *Dancing Figures*. Ca. 1515. Pen and brown ink and wash on paper, 10.9 × 16.7 cm. Venice, Gallerie dell'Accademia.

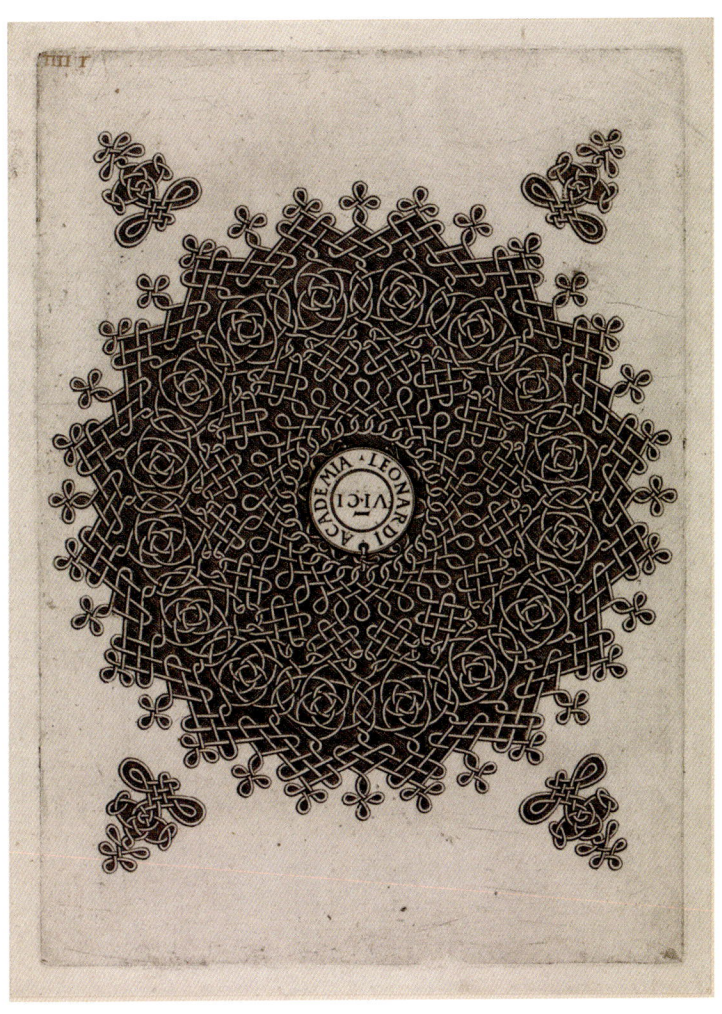

36. Knot design, with around the central circle the words "ACADEMIA
LEONARDI" and in the center "VICI." 1490–1500. Engraving,
29 × 21 cm. London, British Museum.

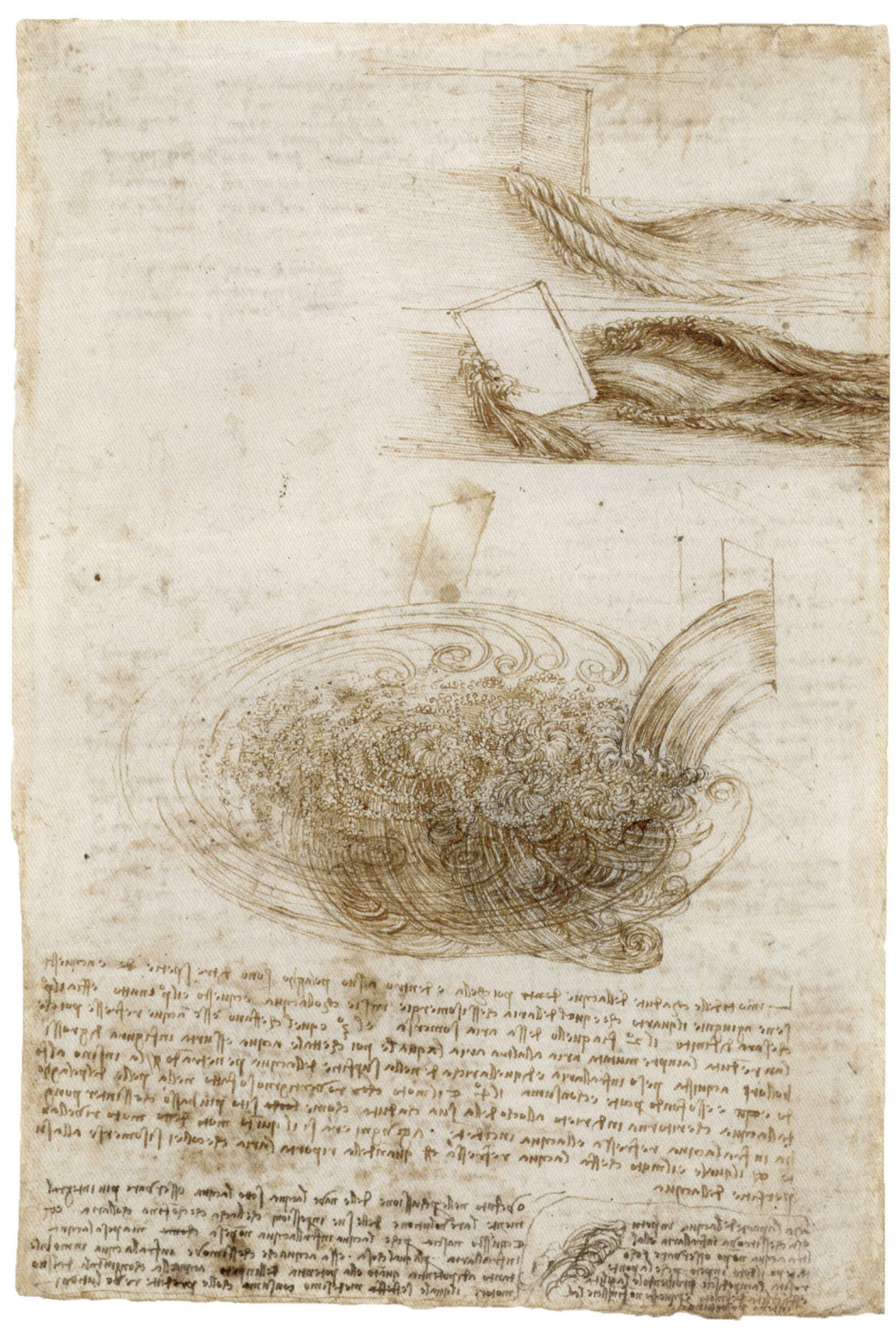

37. Leonardo da Vinci, *Studies of water*. Ca. 1510–12. Pen and ink, traces of black chalk, 29 × 20.2 cm. Windsor, Royal Library, RCIN 912660.

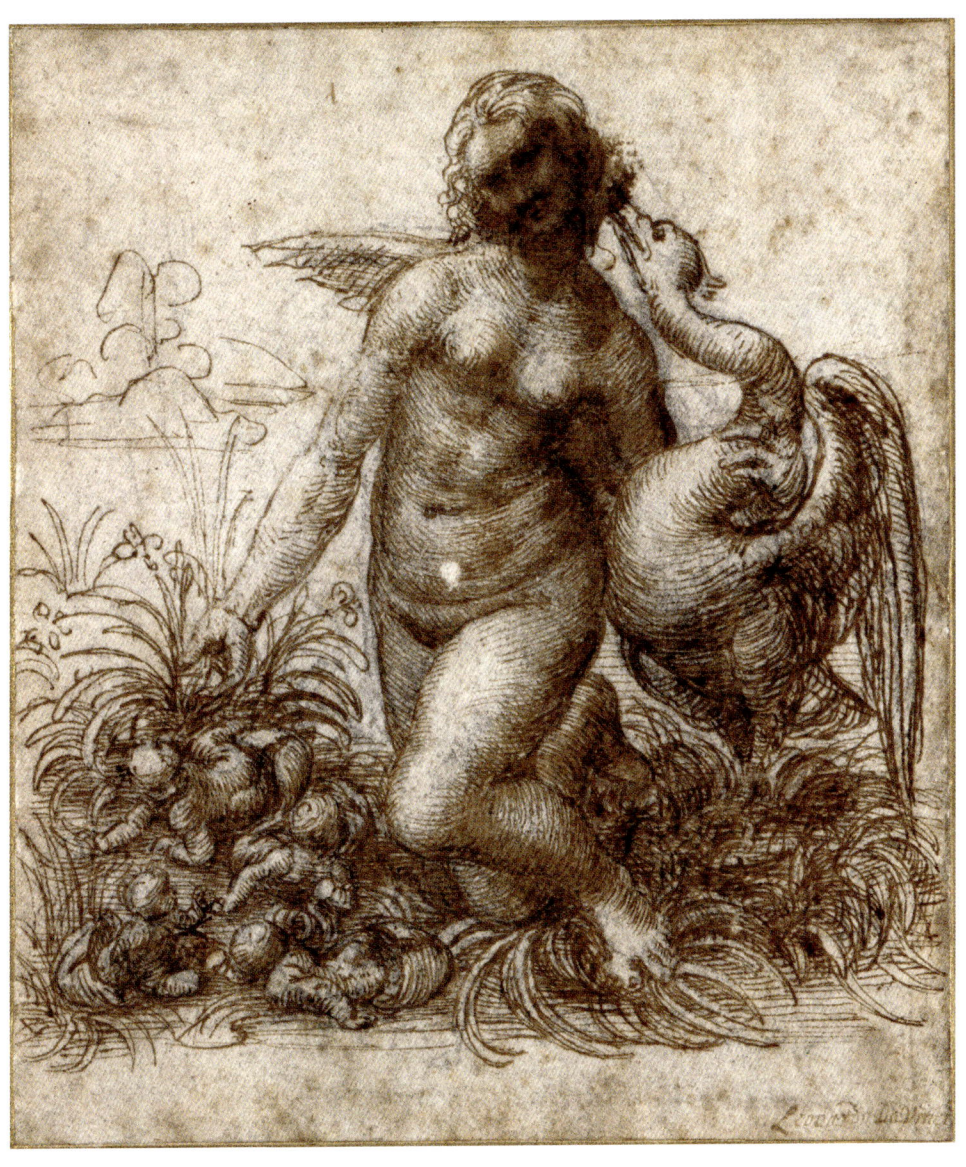

38. Leonardo da Vinci, *Leda and the Swan*. Ca. 1506–9. Pen and brown ink and wash over black chalk, 16 × 13.9 cm. Devonshire Collection, Chatsworth.

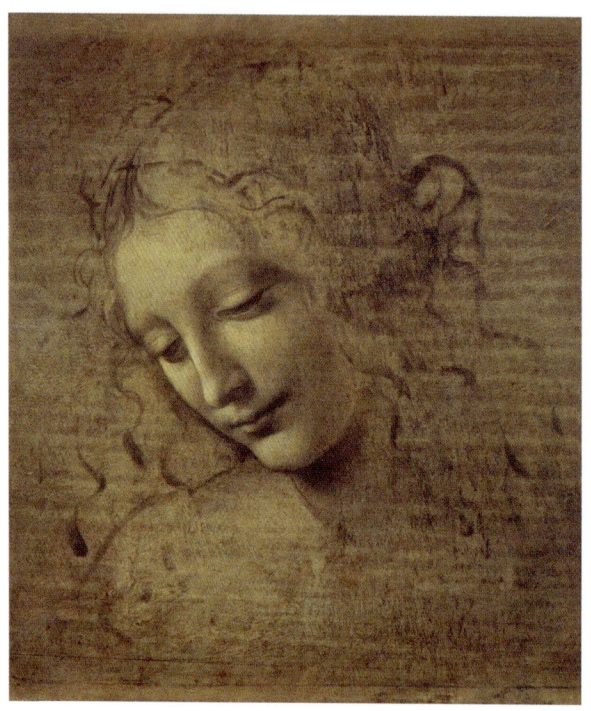

39. Leonardo da Vinci, *Head of a woman* (*La Scapigliata*). Ca. 1506. Oil, earth, and white lead pigments on poplar, 24.6 × 21 cm. Parma, Galleria Nazionale.

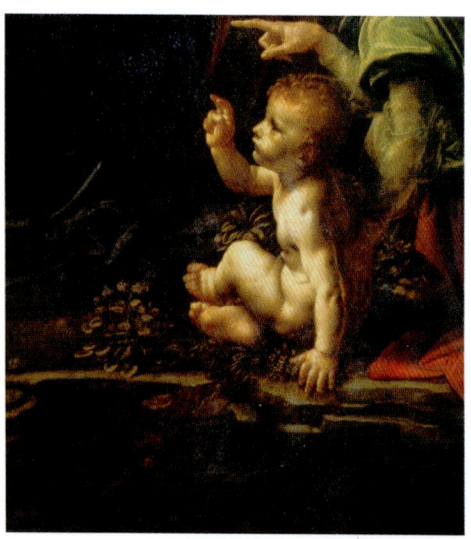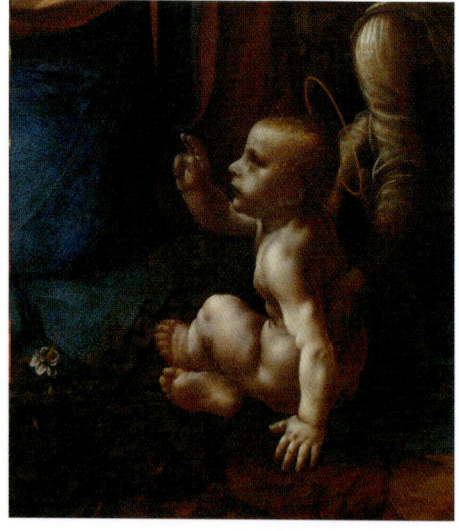

40. *Virgin of the Rocks*: details of the Paris and London versions (plates 10 and 11).

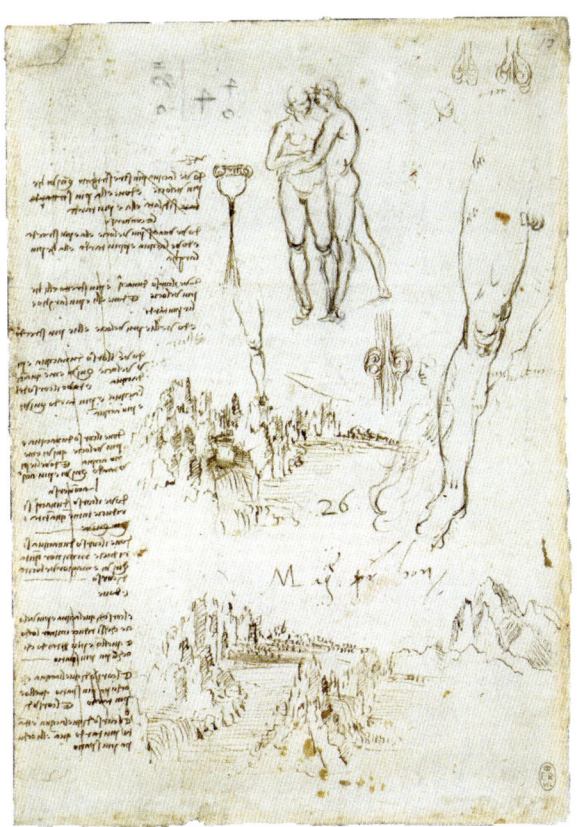

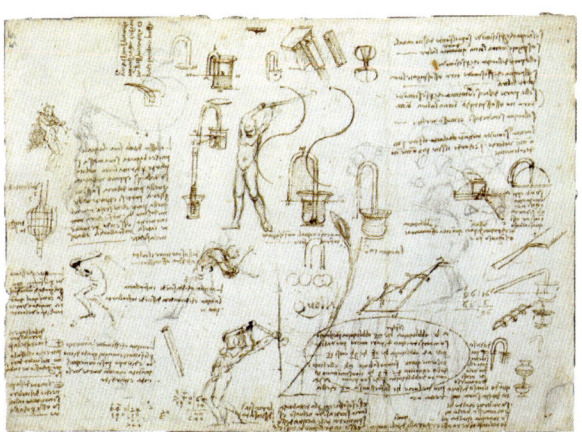

41a and 41b. Sheet with notes by Leonardo da Vinci and drawings by Leonardo da Vinci and Francesco Melzi. Ca. 1512–15. Recto: Notes on the flow of water; a vase/siphon; a couple embracing; the valves of the heart; an Alpine landscape; a man's leg. Verso: numerous drawings of siphons, studies of men delivering blows and blowing a horn; notes on canal systems; calculations. Windsor, Royal Library, RCIN 912641.

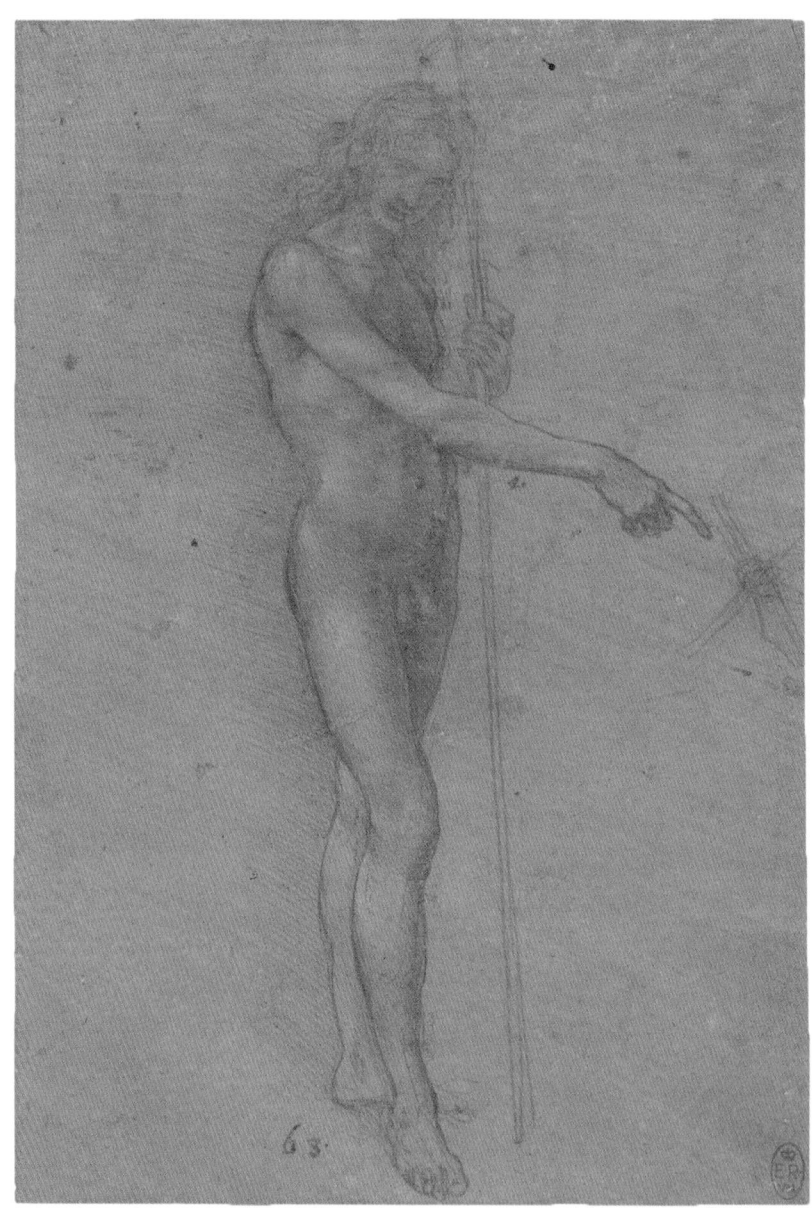

42. Leonardo da Vinci, *A nude youth as St. John the Baptist*. Ca. 1485. Metalpoint, white heightening, on blue-gray prepared paper, 17.8 × 12.2 cm. Windsor, Royal Library, RCIN 912572.

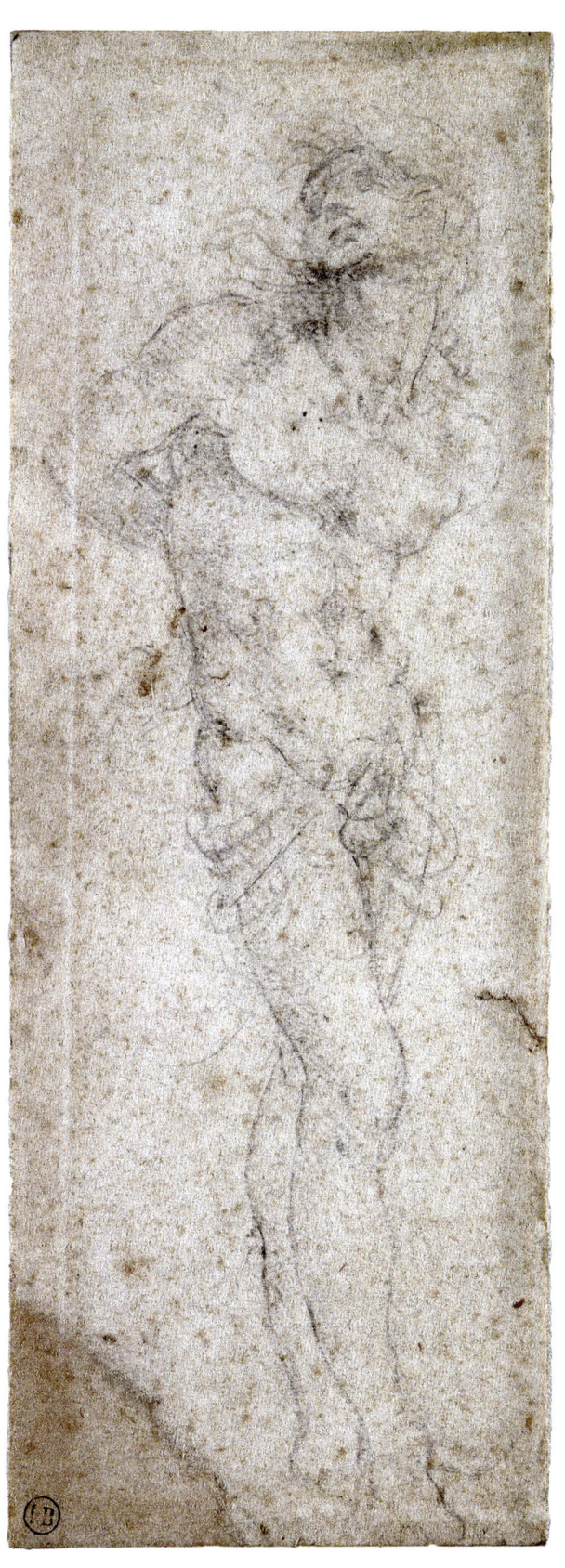

43. Leonardo da
Vinci, *St. Sebastian*.
Ca. 1480. Bayonne,
Musée Bonnat-Helleu.

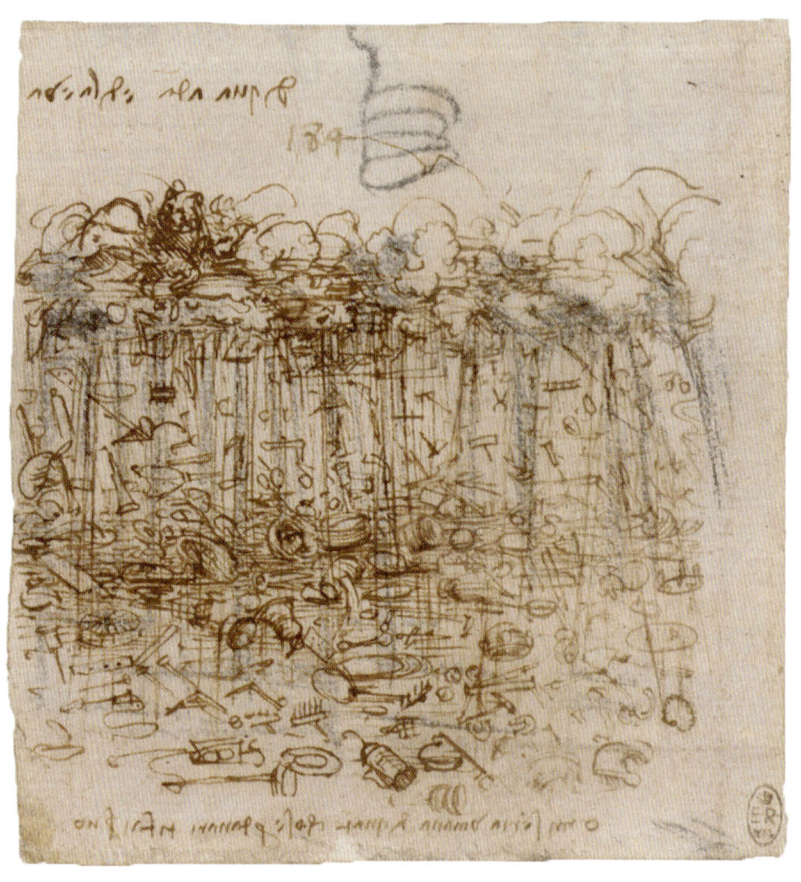

44. Leonardo da Vinci, *A cloudburst of material possessions*. Ca. 1512–14. Black chalk, pen and ink, 11.7 × 11.1 cm. Windsor, Royal Library, RCIN 912698.

I have suggested that Leonardo's departure from linear perspective after the completion of *The Last Supper*, toward a development of compositions of figures modeled in soft veils of shadow, suggests a changing relation to the beholder.[64] It is as if there is a shift from a purely optical conception of the observer—an "I" reduced to an eye, addressed in the convergence of rays in the retina—to a subjectivity that is more mobile, dispersed, or extended. The composition of forms softly modeled in sfumato displaces geometric perspective as the mode of address to the spectator. The experience (and here we can evoke the Greek root of the word "aesthetics," αἴσθησις—sensory perception or experience) is the effect of a soft, crepuscular, atmospheric closeness. Compositions like *The Virgin and Child with St. Anne*—both the London cartoon (almost certainly made in Milan 1506–8, plate 9) and the Paris painting (plate 4)—model strange new forms of embodiment.

It has been hard for some scholars to reconcile these compositions with the idea of Leonardo as the diligent student of anatomy or perspective, which—as with *The Virgin of the Rocks*—become oddly arbitrary in the works in question. In the London cartoon, Anne seems to lack a right shoulder and arm; the Virgin and Christ child twist at the waist in ways that hardly seem anatomically possible. It has often been commented that Leonardo's research into the creation of organic figure groups, what the formalists described as the "High Renaissance pyramidal composition," results in a sense of bodily recomposition and corporeal fusion. Freud saw in the fusion of bodies a resemblance to "badly condensed dream-figures"; his analysis of Leonardo turns on how an apparent "defect in composition" might yield up its secret meaning—that "the two mothers [i.e., his birth mother and his adoptive mother] of his childhood were melted into a single form."[65]

More recent commentary preserves the observation without the Freudian diagnosis: "one of the most brilliant features of the Leonardo 'invention' is the fact that, while being clearly articulated and dynamically distinctive, the figures tend to fuse into each other; the group now forms a living organic whole in a state of restrained separation, captured at the instant of the transformation."[66] Another commentator takes things further: "the parthenogenetic implications of the doubling of the maternal figure are of a piece with the undifferentiated way in which the central figures seem to emerge from one another: Saint Anne's splitting off from her daughter's body; the confusing, slightly monstrous multiplication of legs below; the Christ child's swimming emergence from the Virgin's body, as if he were the barely differentiated continuation of her arm."[67] In the cartoon, Anne's head seems to proceed from Mary's shoulder; Mary's left arm seems to dematerialize and be replaced by Anne's. In the panel, Mary's right arm seems visually to become that of St. Anne.

David Summers writes that naturalism as a tenet of Leonardo's art entails more than mere description of appearances. For Summers, Leonardo's naturalism in practice means faithfulness to a truth or logic *internal to painting*, an aesthetic logic determined by a "judgement of sense": "Beginning with what were presumed to be optical elements, the 'right' relation among these elements was found in the case of *this* painting, not by consulting the laws of optics or the study of light and shadow to which Leonardo was so devoted, but by doing what seemed best to the eye. In fact, these 'right' relations could be found in no other way."[68]

But we need to press further here, to think about what might be motivating that sense of "rightness," beyond post-Enlightenment theories of aesthetic judgment—the notion (typified by Immanuel Kant) that we have an innate capacity to appreciate system and order in art. Just *why* does this particular arrangement of bodies and body parts carry a formal and emotional conviction? Because, we might say, Leonardo is not only depicting an uncanny extension of physical being, of flow and continuum between one body and another. He is also portraying psychological connectedness—the drawing forth of inner responses from one figure by another, in ways that body, gesture, and expression make visible. There is a strong sense of emotional continuum between the Virgin and St. Anne, who addresses her and gestures upward, as there is between the Virgin and Christ child. The child's features and expression seem to "double" the Virgin's, and the upturned face of St. John completes the axis of their downward gazes.

The effect of flowing seems to permeate the beholder's space. In the lower foreground, Anne and the Virgin have placed their right feet into a rocky spring. These body parts—the closest to the beholder—seem to merge or dissolve with the watery edge of the image. In the landscape, three enormous bodies of water are connected by the waterfalls that flow between them, mirroring the three human generations in the foreground and the dynamics of flow that draws them together and to the beholder beyond the painting. For Fritjof Capra, the more radical underlying idea is that organic life depends on the mechanics of flow. As Leonardo knew, organisms manifest the principle evident in liquid motion of forms that remain stable despite constant transformation.[69]

As in *The Adoration of the Magi*, which seems to break upon the viewer like a wave, in this composition of intertwined bodies there is no figure that addresses the beholder, no gaze to arrest the viewer's own. Such figures— think by contrast of Botticelli's self-portrait and outward gaze in his Lamo *Adoration*—seem to bid the beholder to maintain distance, to contemplate the composition as a whole. The absence of such an effect in Leonardo facilitates a kind of empathic and intimate closeness with the monumental but delicate and seemingly porous bodies. Even today, the conditions of its display in London, in an isolated chapel-like enclosure, reinforce that sense of closeness.

We might even find a glimmering here of Leonardo's thinking about *coinherence* that he postulated in his notes on gestation and fetal development, composed during dissections at the end of the first decade of the 1500s. On the famous Windsor drawing of the fetus in the womb (RCIN 919102r), he writes that a single soul unites the bodies of mother and child, and the soul of the mother composes that of the fetus: "And one and the same soul governs these two bodies, and desires, fears and pains are common to this creature as to all other animated parts. From this it arises that a thing desired by the mother is often found imprinted on those parts of the infant that have the same qualities in the mother at the time of her desire; and a sudden terror kills both mother and child. Therefore, one concludes that the same soul governs and nourishes both bodies."

Leonardo's imagery is predictably understood in terms of his scientific interests. On the other hand, a Christian beholder in the 1500s might have thought, looking at the liquid imagery and confluence of bodies in the Louvre *St. Anne*, of the watery symbolism of mystical union in devotional writing and poetry in the tradition of St. Bernard of Clairvaux, St. Francis, and St. Catherine of Siena. In the latter's *Dialogue*, Catherine acclaims the "abyss, the Eternal Godhead, the profound sea" and "pacific sea." She addresses the Trinity as "a deep Sea, into which the deeper I enter the more I find, and the more I find the more I seek; the soul cannot be satiated in Your abyss, for she continually hungers after You." "As the hart desires the spring of living water, so my soul desires to leave the prison of this dark body and see You in truth. . . . Melt at once the cloud of my body."[70] Leonardo's writings provide little indication of any interest in devotional mysticism, but we have seen that several of his religious works do indicate a rigorous address to the religious investments of his audiences.[71] Michelangelo made a drawing in response to the lost Florentine version of the St. Anne composition, and his *Doni Tondo* of ca. 1506 responds to Leonardo's nestling and layering of figures, vigorously accentuating the orientation toward the surface of the composition and toward the beholder. With his tight contour and brilliant color, he resisted Leonardo's anatomical ambiguities and the veils of shadow that obscured the boundaries between figures.[72]

The London cartoon's impact can for the most part be identified only in artists working in Lombardy, a strong indication that it was made in Milan. Before Luini's adaptation of ca. 1530, the composition served as the basis for Melzi's mythological painting of *Vertumnus and Pomona* (fig. 24). Melzi's voluptuous and profane adaptation reduced the composition to its two central figures, extracted from the cartoon probably through tracing, with the Virgin recast as the bare-breasted goddess of gardens, Pomona. The seducer-god Vertumnus, who disguises himself as an old woman to get close to Pomona, is also a "disguised" version of Leonardo's St. Anne. A tree with a twisting vine now forms an axis to the composition. Melzi retained the arrangement of the feet, and the body of water at the threshold.

The compositional experiments for *The Virgin and Child with St. Anne* prove to be the most generative of all the works of Leonardo, entwining and enfolding the work of dozens of artists, beginning with those in his immediate circle. It is as if the works were designed with this effect of artistic self-extension in mind, and that this effect of extensiveness is enacted in the dynamic fusion of moving bodies in the compositions themselves. Its impact is comparable to that of a groundbreaking archaeological discovery made in Rome in January 1506, in the presence of Michelangelo and Giuliano da Sangallo: the *Laocoön*, a work famous in antiquity, changed the future

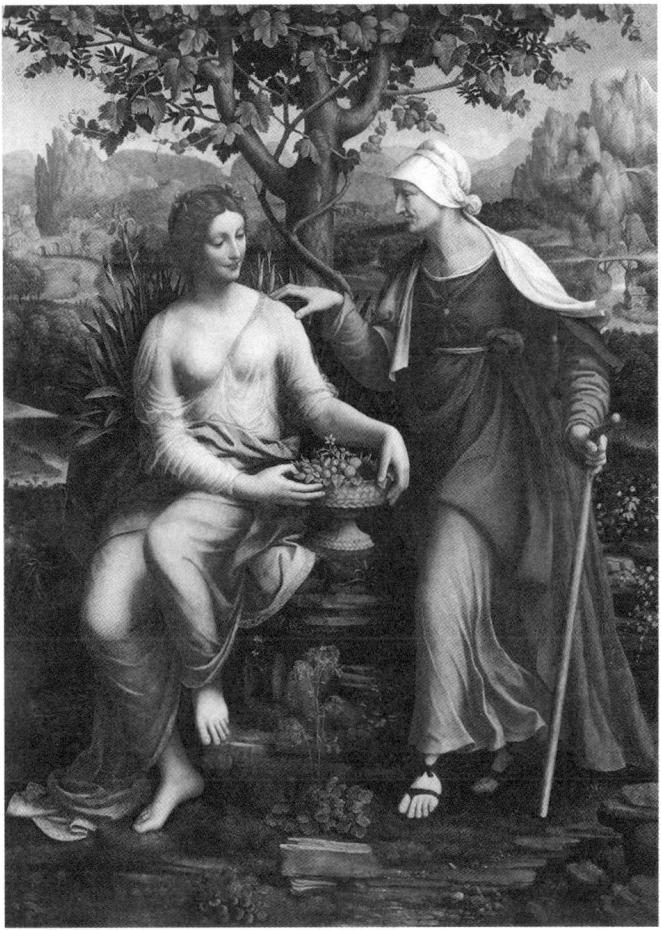

24. Francesco Melzi, *Vertumnus and Pomona*. Ca. 1518–22. On
panel transferred to canvas, 186 × 135.5 cm. Berlin, Gemäldegalerie.

course of painting and sculpture, setting new agonistic criteria for compositions with multiple moving figures (fig. 25). The marble group transformed
the art of Michelangelo, now Leonardo's chief artistic rival following the
dueling *Battle* designs for the Salone dei Cinquecento in Milan. Although
Leonardo had been experimenting with the imitation of antique sculpture
in these years, especially in *The Battle of Anghiari*, where struggling warriors
with open, screaming mouths anticipate the violence of the *Laocoön*, he
would demonstrate no interest in the sculpture.[73] Even on moving to Rome
in 1513, when he was working in the Belvedere a stone's throw away from

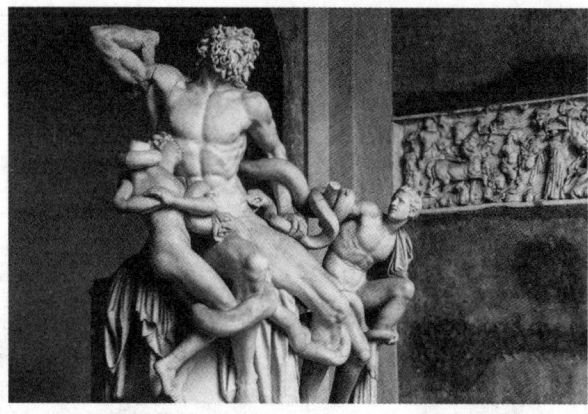

25. Greek or Roman sculptors, *Laocoön and His Sons*.
Ca. 27 BC and 68 AD. Marble, 208 × 163 × 112 cm. Rome,
Vatican Museums.

the famous sculpture group, it left no trace of any impact in his drawing
or painting. Could he really have been so impervious? The apparent lack
of engagement could indicate the degree to which the ancient sculpture
was regarded as a concentration of effects of superhuman bodily struggle
associated with Michelangelo, who by 1512 was modeling his two Captives
for the tomb of Julius II, now in the Louvre, on the sons of Laocoön.

The lost *Leda and the Swan* of 1506–9 could be seen as an alternative
formulation of the dynamic and idealized classical body, for which Leonardo produced two groups of compositional drawings. It is in his serial
inventions for the *Leda* that Leonardo popularized the dynamic contrapposto spiraling figure that would later be baptized the *figura serpentinata*
by Lomazzo. Leonardo started to sketch the figure of Leda on a sheet with
studies for *The Battle of Anghiari* in 1503–4—a figure resting on her right
knee, her hips turned accordingly, while her shoulders move toward the left
and her right arm is drawn across her body. It is clear that some time has
elapsed before we get to the more fully worked-up studies in black chalk
and black ink, which now include the swan (Jupiter) and their oviparous
offspring. By 1508, if not earlier, Leonardo had finalized a composition with
a standing and static Leda, the energy of curvilinear hatching now relayed
instead in vigorous botanical growth and in her elaborately braided hair.[74]
Perhaps there's just an echo here of the "serpentine" figure of the younger

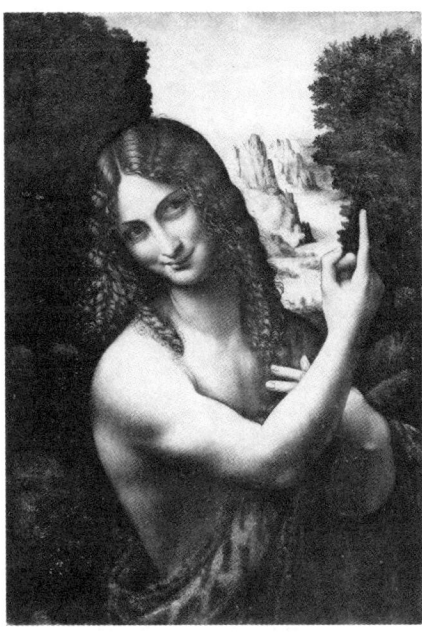

26. Follower of Leonardo (attributed
to Gian Giacomo Caprotti, known as
Salaì), *St. John the Baptist*. Ca. 1520. On
panel, 73 × 50.9 cm. Milan, Ambrosiana.

son from the *Laocoön* group, whose spiraling pose—twisting at the neck,
shoulders, and hip—is involuntary, as the boy is lifted from the ground
in the serpent's coils. The Leda is hardly a quotation, but a revision, transformed in gender and in the motivation for the pose: it is now the power
of Eros rather than divine nemesis that bends limbs and hips.

Raphael, who left Florence for Rome in 1508, made a sketch from
Leonardo's painting or its cartoon, and the standing *Leda* became the
more popular composition, generating versions attributed to Melzi, Cesare da Sesto, Giovanni Agostino da Lodi, and Fernando Yáñez, and adaptations as a *Venus and Cupid* by Giampietrino and the Sienese Domenico
Beccafumi. The crouching and twisting Leda of the Chatsworth and Rot-
terdam drawings had far less significant progeny: Giampietrino made an
ungainly painting in Milan around 1510, subsequently sold as a Leonardo
by the landgrave of Hesse-Kassel in 1756, and admired by Goethe as a
Leonardo masterpiece.

Eros is clearly also part of what motivates the extension of the *St. John*
composition in the work of several artists, as if the hailing gesture of the
alluring saint were calling other versions of himself into being (figs. 26 and

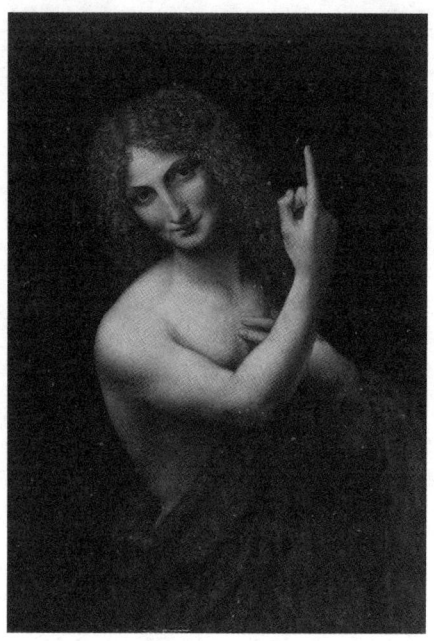

27. Follower of Leonardo da Vinci
(Giampietrino?), *St. John the Baptist*.
Ca. 1512–30. On panel, 74.1 × 52.7 cm.
Baltimore, Walters Art Museum.

27). This is not as odd as it may sound. If the multifigure composition draws
the viewer into a state of close, immersive contemplation, this half-length
single figure—which like the *Salvator Mundi* aligns with the long Christian
tradition of the devotional icon—makes painting's power of address more
explicit. It is noteworthy that in this late painting, Leonardo returns to possibilities of earlier experiments—an Angel of the Annunciation, now lost
and only known from a sketch, and an even earlier drawing on blue paper
of a slender, long-haired, studio model, with the attributes and pointing
gesture of the Baptist (plate 42). The drawing, dated around 1485–90, is
distinctive in being one of very few drawings by Leonardo made after a live
nude model. Among life studies, it is noteworthy in registering the model's
awareness of being looked at.[75] There is an effect of extraordinary intimacy,
of wordless communication, which is altogether absent in contemporary
studies from nude models by Botticelli, Filippino Lippi, or Luca Signorelli,
where the model never seems conscious of the draftsman.

The study itself drew the attention of artists in Northern Italy. In Milan
around 1490, Marco d'Oggiono drew on the figure for his *St. Sebastian*
now in the Museo Poldi Pezzoli. Fernando Yáñez de la Almedina, generally

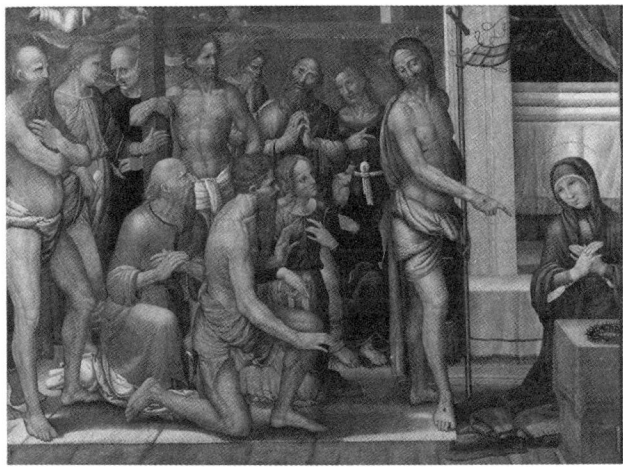

28. Fernando Yáñez de la Almedina, *Christ presents the Redeemed from Limbo to the Virgin*. 1510–18. On panel, 129.8 × 172.5 cm. Madrid, Museo del Prado.

identified as the Ferrante Spagnolo who assisted Leonardo on *The Battle of Anghiari*, had access to the drawing, as can be seen in his far more ascetic *Christ presents the Redeemed from Limbo to the Virgin* of 1510–18 (Prado; fig. 28).[76] By 1510, Correggio included a hirsute redaction of Leonardo's epicene figure in his *Mystic Marriage of St. Catherine* (now in the Detroit Institute of Arts), and another a few years later in his *Madonna of St. Francis* altarpiece (Dresden, Gemäldegalerie). It is a mark of the small drawing's singular power that it came to play a role in constituting a continuum of artists who attached themselves to Leonardo, and that it remanifested itself in his last painting.

TRANSREGIONAL LEONARDO

Writing at mid-century, Vasari singled out only Giovan Francesco Rustici as an instance of the positive impact of Leonardo in Florence, even presenting the sculptor as a kind of extended embodiment of an artist who had otherwise failed to deliver on his major Florentine commissions. The biographer is far more censorious of Leonardo's influence on other artists of Rustici's generation. These included artists born in the 1490s or slightly earlier—Andrea del Sarto, Baccio Bandinelli, Rosso, Pontormo—who witnessed Leonardo working on *The Battle of Anghiari*, and who could study its cartoon, as well as the unfinished *Adoration of the Magi* at the house of the Benci. From 1504 to 1506, they could have seen, as works in progress, the *Mona Lisa* and the earliest version of *The Virgin and Child with St. Anne*.

A characteristic instance of Florentine adaptation of Leonardo is manifest in a work by Andrea del Sarto, of uncertain date but probably 1512–15. When called upon to make a portrait of Christ for the shrine of the Santissima Annunziata, possibly as a votive offering to the most prestigious Marian cult image in Florence, Sarto would have been expected to evoke the tradition of holy icons of the face of Christ—such as the Sancta Sanctorum in the Lateran, a far more ancient and distinguished sacred site in Rome, or the Mandylion in Genoa (fig. 29). Instead, he turned to Leonardo's example. Not, however, to the *Salvator Mundi* (which was probably in Milan) but to a composition that by 1512 was equally "iconic"—the *Mona Lisa*: in both, the subject regards the viewer with a calm but somehow knowing expression charged with inner life, slightly turned away, the hands crossed at the wrist. The new Leonardesque approach to the portrait is being brought into line with the much older conventions for Man of Sorrows or Christ the Redeemer, but the iconography, rethought in terms of domestic portraiture, corresponds to neither. While its identification as a work by Sarto was never forgotten, it was regarded by the late sixteenth century as a work of the highest devotion and almost as a sacred relic: "Seeing it, one is inspired to a sense of majesty and reverence," wrote Francesco Bocchi in his 1591 guidebook to Florence, "contemplating it, the flame of devotion is lit." In 1617, by order of a brother of the Grand Duke Cosimo II, it was given an elaborate silver and *pietra dura* frame, with candelabra and two adoring angels—treatment indeed worthy of a holy relic.[77] Andrea del Sarto and Leonardo crossed paths in 1518–19 when both were employed by the French king at Amboise, and Sarto made an adaptation of Leonardo's *Leda* (Brussels) and *St. John* (Worcester).

Vasari's life of Andrea del Sarto, his own teacher, damns the older artist for his hesitancy and "lack of boldness." Although Vasari doesn't mention Leonardo in relation to Andrea, his generally negative assessment of Leonardo colors his account of other Florentine artists. Younger artists seem contaminated by a pernicious "Leonardo effect," incubating one or other of Leonardo's unpalatable or heterodox opinions, eccentricities,

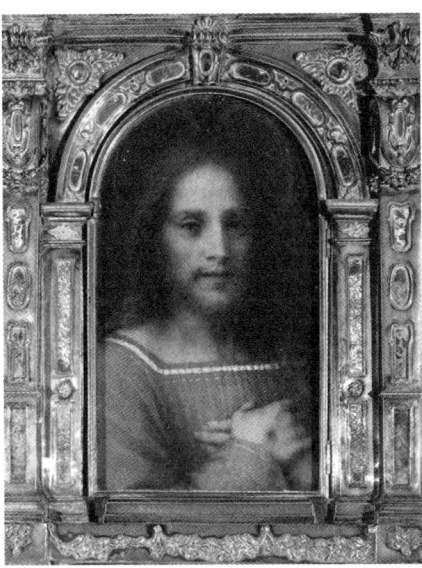

29. Andrea del Sarto, *Christ the Redeemer*. Ca. 1515–20. On panel, 47 × 27 cm. Florence, Santissima Annunziata.

or professional shortcomings. The painter Piero di Cosimo—"uncouth in his ways . . . held to be a madman"—is, in Vasari's terms, a pathological magnification of certain Leonardesque traits. In the 1550 version of the *Life*, Piero is condemned as a solitary and eccentric false philosopher misled by his own charlatanism, drawn into investigating the secrets of nature for their own sake, and not to any useful purpose: "[such men] fleeing the practice of men, seek only solitude. Becoming accustomed to solitude, they incur only greater obstacles in their life, and submitting to the fog of ignorance, they make plain to everyone that they do what they do for the love of philosophy, or more likely charlatanism [*filosofia, anzi più tosto furfanteria*], which is truly theirs." Men like Piero manifest "a spirit very contrary to that of others, along with a certain subtlety in investigating certain subtleties of nature that they would penetrate, without regard to time or effort, only for their pleasure."[78]

The passages are cut in the 1568 edition (we have seen a similar downplaying of Leonardo's heterodoxy between Vasari's two editions), but many Leonardesque traits remain: "[Piero] would sometimes stop to gaze at a wall against which sick people had been for a long time discharging their spittle, and from this he would picture to himself battles of horsemen, and the most fantastic cities and widest landscapes that were

ever seen; and he did the same with the clouds in the sky." Leonardo's Plin-
ian prescription for generating compositions is associated with filth and
disease. Vasari writes that Piero paid close attention to Leonardo's works
in oil "executed with that gradation of color, and finished with that extraordinary diligence, which Leonardo used to employ when he wished to
display his art [*quando e'voleva mostrar l'arte*]. And so Piero, being pleased
with his method, sought to imitate it, although he was afterwards very
distant from Leonardo, and worlds away from any other manner."[79] To be
noted here is the touch of condescension to Leonardo's revolutionary oil
technique as a means to "display his art." Like the young Leonardo, Piero is
noted for the painting of "monsters," as well as "plants, animals, and other
things as Nature at times creates out of caprice."

Painters like Baccio della Porta, known as Fra Bartolomeo, and his some-
time associate Mariotto Albertinelli were Leonardo's peers and colleagues.
They attended closely to his rapid and loose methods of sketching with
chalk and emulated his twilight pictorial world and his sfumato modeling.
Both were censured by Vasari for drenching their works in inky shadows.
"And in truth, in this manner of coloring, [Bartolomeo] imitated to a great
extent the works of Leonardo; particularly in the darks, for which he used
printer's smoke—black and the black of burnt ivory. The [*Mystic Marriage of
St. Catherine*] has now become much darker than it was when he painted it,
on account of those blacks, which have kept growing heavier and darker."[80]

Vasari's account of Albertinelli's methods in his *Annunciation* (fig. 30)
does not mention Leonardo, but a critique of Leonardo's exacting studio
procedures—with its modifications of walls and windows—is implied:
"He undertook to make, in the Company of S. Zanobi, near the Chapter-
house of S. Maria del Fiore, a panel picture of the *Annunciation*, which
he executed with great labor. For this he caused special windows to be
made, wishing to work on the spot, in order to be able to make the views
recede, where they were high and distant, by lowering the tones, or to bring
them forward, at his pleasure. Now he had conceived the idea that pictures
which have no relief and force, combined with delicacy, are of no account."

Albertinelli torments himself to achieve forceful relief in his painting,
reworking it several times: "he wished to find a white that should be more
brilliant than lead-white, and set himself, therefore, to clarify the latter,

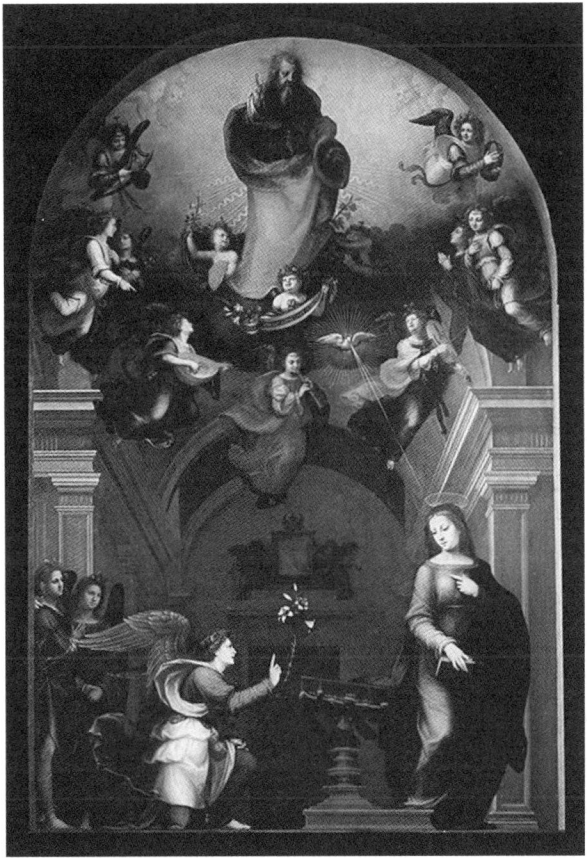

30. Mariotto Albertinelli, *Annunciation*. Ca. 1510.
On panel, 345 × 2467 cm. Florence, Accademia.

in order to be able to heighten the highest light to his own satisfaction.
However, having recognized that he was not able to express by means of
art all that the intelligence of the human brain grasps and comprehends,
he contented himself with what he had achieved, since he could not attain
to what it was not possible to reach."[81]

Vasari here understands the two artists to be painting "in the shadow"
of Leonardo, and with negative results: the passages recall his own criticism
of Leonardo's lengthy and allegedly unproductive technical procedures.
Similar criticisms are leveled at Jacopo Pontormo, whom Vasari believed
to have been a pupil of Leonardo, and whom he described in his later years

as a solitary misanthrope who betrayed his early promise. The life of Pontormo concludes: "At times, going out to work, he set himself to think so profoundly on what he was to do, that he went away without having done any other thing all day but stand thinking. And that this happened to him times without number in the work of S. Lorenzo may readily be believed, for the reason that when he was determined, like an able and well-practiced craftsman, he had no difficulty in doing what he desired and had resolved to put into execution." The parallel with Leonardo's ponderous inaction and excessive deliberation while painting *The Last Supper* seems intentional.

Why would Vasari have such strong misgivings about Leonardo, and about the Florentine artists of the generation just preceding his own, and why did he insinuate that the shortcomings of the latter were somehow the result of Leonardo's *influence*, almost as if he were jinxing their work at a distance? Part of the reason is political: all of these artists served under the Republican regime of 1494–1513 that had forced the Medici into exile, and Sarto and Pontormo—while successfully weathering the Medici restoration of 1513–27—were associated with the anti-Medicean Republic of 1527–30; Sarto had died of plague during the Siege of Florence by Medici and Imperial forces. Piero di Cosimo had served as a kind of pageant master to the earlier anti-Medicean Republic: his macabre and terrifying Triumph of Death for the carnival celebration of 1512 was seen as signaling the imminent return of the Medici.

Vasari's deep bias is grounded not just in his own pro-Medici affiliation—he was a court functionary of the Medici dukes Cosimo I and Francesco—but in the highly institutionalized and ideological organization of the artistic profession operating in the later sixteenth century. Art making, centered on the Academia del Disegno, was an apparatus of the centralized Medici state, dedicated to orthodoxy in religion and the affirmation of the regime. The generation that Vasari writes about with such ambivalence were vestiges of an older artisanal culture whose subaltern and outsider status with regard to political authority meant that it could weather changes of regime, but equally that its conformity and acquiescence could not be counted on. That older artists like Donatello, Castagno, and Piero di Cosimo were wayward and ungentlemanly was a recurring theme of Vasari's *Lives*.

Vasari's generation saw the transformation of artists into courtiers and intellectuals, with their own spheres of public discourse and publication. As the proto-modern state came into being, its administration tightly centralized around the Medici sovereign, sites of civic discourse and cultural production were equally spheres of surveyance and regulation. It was in this milieu that Leonardo's theoretical and pedagogical ideas began to circulate—but in a heavily edited form. Melzi's original compilation of the *Libro di pittura* languished mostly unread in the ducal library at Urbino, while abridgments (and abridgments of abridgments) circulated among Florentine artists and *literati*. Leonardo's polemical statements on painting as natural philosophy, on the superiority of painting to poetry, sculpture, and music, on the painter's powers of invention, on painting as a liberal art not practiced for financial gain, were all omitted, as were some of the sections on aerial perspective. Moreover, in some of the manuscripts, passages from other authors' writings on linear perspective were interpolated.[82]

The late sixteenth-century circulation of these manuscripts and their impact showed that Leonardo's writings were appreciated more for their scientific content than for his authorship of them. The authors who cite from them invariably omit any attribution to Leonardo. As Claire Farago has shown, lacking the name of an author they were considered all the more "scientific" or objective for that reason—the common property of men of knowledge. Vasari acknowledges Leonardo's historical importance but never mentions the treatise on painting. This omission, as Robert Williams has pointed out, "is part of an anxious insistence that Leonardo thought too much, and that thinking too much is dangerous for artists."[83] On one hand, Vasari's evident urgency about elevating Raphael's example at the expense of Leonardo's motivates the portrayal of an insidiously ubiquitous "extended" Leonardo that intertwined himself in the labors of his peer artists. In Vasari's view, this was a phenomenon that had to be relegated to a disorderly political past before the rise of the Medici monarchy. On the other, it is apparent that Vasari recognized a premodern collectivizing of creative labor, one that he sought to displace with a different form of collectivization modeled on courtly and academic decorum, on literary refinement and religious orthodoxy, on the emerging absolutist state centered on the prince: the Florentine Academia del Disegno, under the joint presidency of Michelangelo and Duke Cosimo de'Medici.

And yet that earlier workshop culture, a fellowship of wit and skill often openly transgressive of polite social and sexual norms, persisted among some of Vasari's contemporaries: for instance, the circle around the supposedly isolated Pontormo, whose reputation Vasari deliberately sought to undermine.[84] The painter-poet Bronzino indicated his authorship of at least two of his most ambitious works by including not only his own portrait but that of his mentor Pontormo and his protégé Alessandro Allori—a masculine lineage of artistic fathers and sons, each an extension and projection of the other.[85] And Vasari himself is ambivalently aware of such an affective mode of artistic association, one that he sometimes characterized in erotically loaded terms, distinguishing such fellowship from the normal sphere of hierarchical master-assistant obligations and productive efficiency.

As characterized by Vasari, Pontormo's own relation to Michelangelo similarly possesses a quality of homosocial co-inherence. With regard to two paintings—the *Noli me Tangere* and the highly carnal *Venus and Cupid* designed by Michelangelo and painted by Pontormo around 1531—Vasari writes that the younger painter "gave over his soul to Michelangelo, and resolved to imitate his style insofar as he was able."[86] In his life of Giovanni Antonio Lappoli, Vasari writes that the young artist might have joined the workshop of Andrea del Sarto but instead "attached himself to [*si mise col*] Pontormo, under whose discipline he was forever drawing, spurred to incredible exertions, out of emulation [*concorrenza*]." What drew Lappoli to Pontormo, it appears, was not just the mastery or prestige of the older painter but the emotionally invested forms of attachment manifested by other young artists in his workshop, above all Bronzino: "[that which] spurred him more strongly was the sight of Agnolo, who was called Bronzino, being much brought forward by Jacopo on account of his loving submissiveness [*una certa amorevole sommessione*] and goodness and the untiring diligence he showed in imitating his master's works."[87]

Thus Leonardo's "shadowy" manifestation in Florentine art around 1500 is more than just a projection by Vasari. There is no "school of Leonardo" corresponding with the *leonardeschi* of Lombardy, who worked in Leonardo's *maniera*. Leonardo's presence is more diffused, more phantasmic, a threatening *ombra*. I use the word "phantasmic" quite deliberately to indicate qualities of the uncanny, of strange or even queer embodiment that younger Florentine artists picked up on in the artist's work, and to which they sometimes exploited with pointedly oppositional results. Leonardo, that is, was understood in terms of an *oppositional* relation to the art of the past, to antiquity, and to Florentine tradition. A key point of reference for this subversive strain in Florentine art of the 1500s was *The Adoration of the Magi*, a work that still has the power to disturb in its radical departure from conventional iconographies or modes of pictorial organization, and that even recently has resulted in interpretations that sound more like conspiracy theories.

Consider the composition in the Uffizi (6499F) known as *The Skeletons* or *The Triumph of Death*, the attribution of which has pivoted between Baccio Bandinelli and Rosso Fiorentino; although there are compelling grounds for both (Vasari referred to a "*scheletri* di Baccio," but I tend to favor Rosso), such undecidability is telling in itself (fig. 31). A winged skeleton and a cadaverous male figure with pendulous breasts seem to dispute over the skeletal remains of a corpse. A host of old and emaciated men cluster around with what could be called morbid curiosity, several kneeling, bending and clutching their heads. Some are close quotations of Leonardo's wizened, fascinated, ancients in the monochrome *Adoration*. It is as if the recourse to Leonardo entailed a license to indulge in the grotesque, or to parody an image of the tumultuous advent of the Messiah with an epiphany of death and decay. Following Leonardo, for the young Rosso (or Bandinelli), entailed the unflinching study of cadavers for anatomical knowledge in order to determine the structure of the human body and to derive structural principles of pictorial composition; the *Skeletons* is a macabre and witty parody of—but also homage to—Leonardesque composition and Leonardesque science. Rosso would constantly reintroduce such macabre cadaverous figures in his religious works, in one case shocking and alienating his client who saw him as painting "devils," "for it was Rosso's custom in his oil sketches to give a sort of savage and desperate air to the faces, after which . . . he would sweeten the expressions and bring them to a proper form."[88]

Another artist, yet more extreme than Rosso, who made similar subversive use of Leonardesque models is the extravagantly nonconformist Jacopo di Giovanni di Francesco, known as Jacone, on whose uproarious

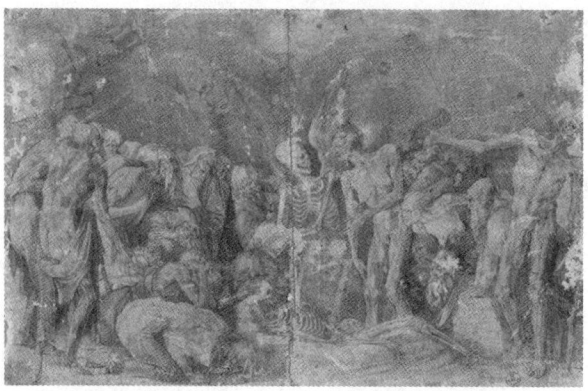

31. Rosso Fiorentino, or Baccio Bandinelli, *The Skeletons* or
The Triumph of Death. Ca. 1515–18. Uffizi (6499F).

and slovenly life—and more goadingly, indifference to making a living—
Vasari writes at length. Jacone too styled himself as a "philosopher,"
which meant that he and his friends "lived like swine and brute beasts."
Jacone "spent the best part of his life in jesting, in going off into cogita-
tions, and in speaking evil of all and sundry. For in those days the art of
design had fallen into the hands of a company of persons who paid more
attention to playing jokes and to enjoyment than to working, and whose
occupation was to assemble in shops and other places, and there to spend
their time in criticizing maliciously, in their own jargon, the works of
others who were persons of excellence and lived decently and like men
of honour." Jacone's unsettling and irreverent approach to design is
manifest in a drawing at Christ Church, Oxford, in which Leonardo's
Virgin and Child with St. Anne is reenvisioned as a tangle of ogre-like
and brutish figures, the Virgin partly nude and with her legs widely
splayed and prodded by a simian-looking St. John, while the ferocious
St. Anne seems to drag the left leg of the Christ child well beyond any
plausible extension (fig. 32). I would see Jacone's gravitation to Leonardo
here not just in terms of subversion and parody but as a recognition of
possibilities suggested by Leonardo's art—and which would receive far
wider dissemination with the circulation of Leonardo's caricatures and
grotesques.

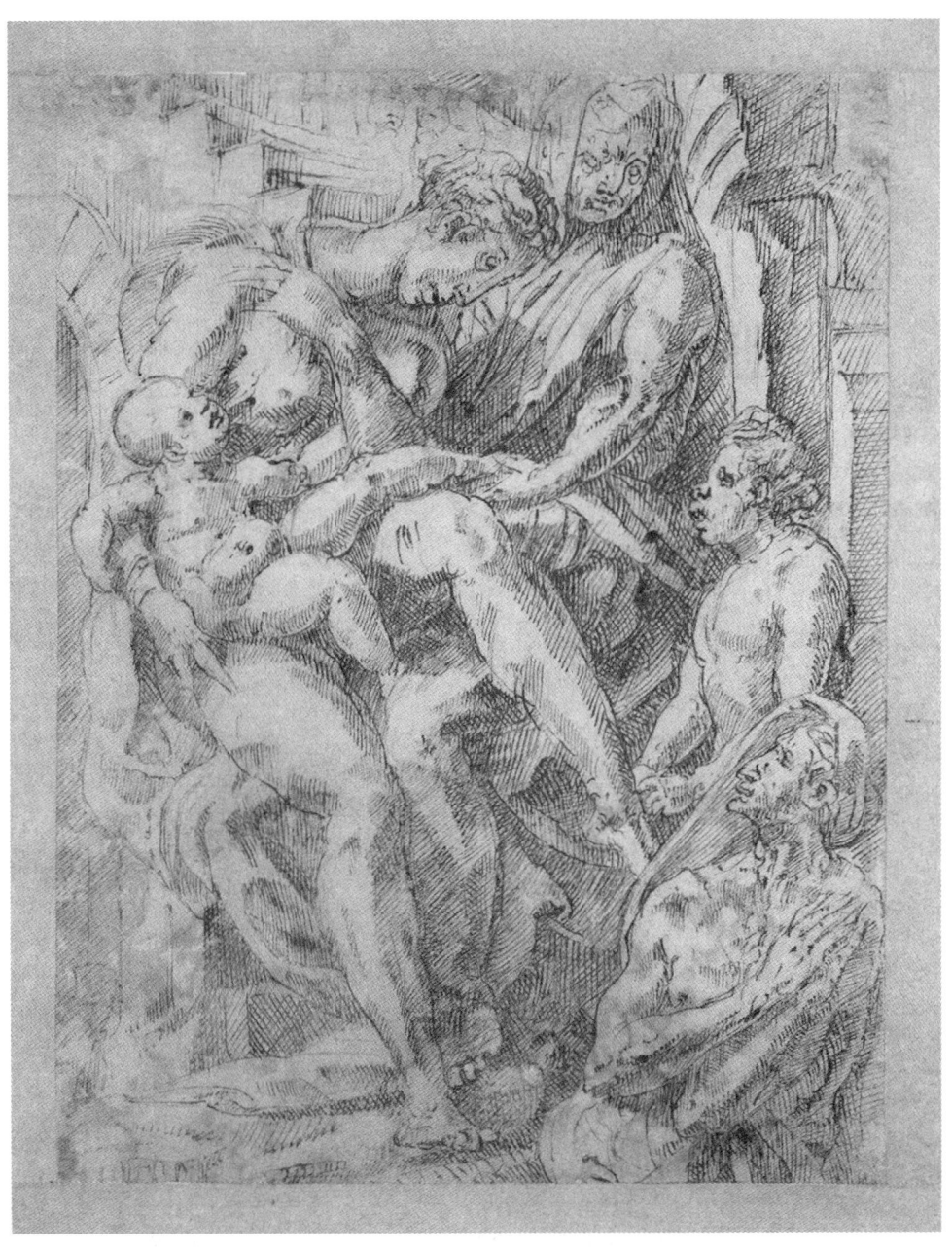

32. Jacone (Jacopo di Giovanni di Francesco), *Virgin and Child with St. Anne, Elizabeth, and St. John the Baptist*. Ca. 1527–30. Oxford, Christ Church Picture Gallery.

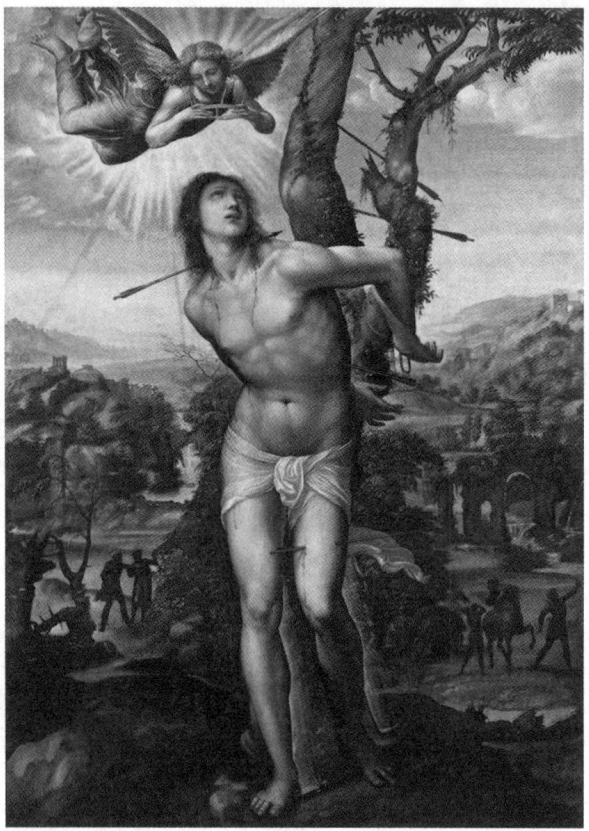

33. Sodoma, *St. Sebastian*. 1525. On canvas, 206 × 154 cm.
Florence, Palazzo Pitti, Galleria Palatina.

There were approaches to Leonardo in Tuscany that were less overtly dissident, but it is telling that we have to look to Siena to find these. Andrea del Brescianino's forays into Leonardism resulted in a Venus, now in the Galleria Borghese, modeled on the Leda, and two versions of the lost original composition of *The Virgin and Child with St. Anne*. Sodoma's *St. Sebastian*, painted in 1525 as a banner for a Confraternity of St. Sebastian by Siena's Porta Camollia, seems more like a textbook example of Leonardo imitation—and it is a stunning artistic performance (fig. 33). Although the work has been said to reflect Sodoma's study of the *Laocoön*, it far more directly reflects knowledge of Leonardo's drawings and hence a connection with his North Italian circle: a study of a bound captive for the Trivulzio

Monument, and related earlier black chalk study of a St. Sebastian now in the Musée Bonnat-Helleu, Bayonne (plate 43). Sodoma responds to Leonardo's counterpoint of the twisted body of the martyr with the curving limbs of the tree. He achieved a highly accomplished (and mostly underappreciated) version of Leonardo's sfumato and of the distinctive landscapes of *The Virgin and Child with St. Anne* and the *Mona Lisa*.

Sodoma's access to Leonardo in person remains unknown. This is also the case with another artist born near Vercelli within a couple of years of Sodoma, whose engagement with Leonardo's legacy demands that we rethink what it means to be a Leonardo "follower." Gaudenzio Ferrari was a painter and sculptor who spent much of his career working in the Alpine region northwest of Milan, and he is best known for the spectacular mixed media ensembles of the pilgrimage site known as the Sacro Monte or Holy Mountain of Varallo.

Gaudenzio has sometimes been regarded as unproblematically a Leonardo follower. He has been singled out for his virtuosic command of Leonardo's technique of chalk drawing with soft modeling, which has led some to suggest that he may have spent some time in the Milanese workshop.[89] He seems to have been aware that Leonardo's program of artistic training was aimed at an erasure of any stylistic resonance or citation of previous art. According to Lomazzo, Gaudenzio was frequently heard to say that, unlike himself, "every painter likes to steal the inventions of others, but they thus run a great risk of being found out and taken for a thief."[90] What might be most significant about his relationship to Leonardo is that it is based on ideas about art, and not finally on stylistic influence. There are even signs of an ironical or subversive relation to the Florentine painter, especially in the decades after Leonardo's departure from Lombardy.

In 1508, Ferrari began to sign his works "Vincius," "De Vincio," or "De Vince," clearly encouraging his patrons and viewers to connect him with the more famous artist.[91] One explanation is that "Vincio" was also his mother's surname, but that can hardly have served as the sole motivation for such a highly charged moniker. Gaudenzio's great 1510 polyptych for Arona, which conspicuously emulates Perugino's Sforza altarpiece for the Certosa di Pavia, is proudly inscribed GAUDETIUS VI[N]CIUS.

Above all, Gaudenzio responded to a dimension of Leonardo's work most evident in *The Virgin of the Rocks*, as it was finally installed in San Francesco Grande in 1508. The powerful pictorial simulation of depth and presence in the cavern-like space of the central panel would have presented the maximum contrast with the carved, gilt, and polychrome sculpture constituting most of the ensemble. The wood carver Giacomo del Maino had provided an imposing frame, now completely lost, with statues of the Virgin, seraphim, God the Father with angels, various "mountains" and "rocks," and figures of prophets and sibyls.[92] Leonardo, in response, had produced the maximum possible demonstration of the spatial and relief effects proper to painting—essentially staging the superiority of painting over sculpture, in the polemical writing that Melzi would include in the *Libro di pittura*.[93] Through its illusionistic resources, painting subsumes and surpasses what is possible in sculpture, commanding all the fleeting effects of luminosity, transparency, and reflection registered by the eye in a moment of experience, rendering them in permanent form. The works of the sculptor are merely what they appear to be, but "the major cause of wonder that arises in painting is the appearance of something detached from the wall or other flat surface, deceiving subtle judgements with this effect, as it is not separated from the surface of the wall."[94]

In a strikingly contrarian sense, Gaudenzio's mixed media chapels for the Sacro Monte of Varallo (1512–27) insist that sculpture extends the operations of painting, that a simulated third dimension is enhanced by figures that extend into the beholder's own space. In the *Chapel of the Magi*, sculpture can be seen to take over the role of painted foreshorten-ing, in spectacular fashion, where the head and foreparts of horses surge out of a painted ground, contravening Leonardo's principle that painting accomplishes tactile and spatial effects entirely by its own means (fig. 34). Ferrari's tableaux ask to be seen as "painting in the expanded field"—a defi-ance of frames or borders that integrates viewers and enables their tactile, dynamic, and visual involvement with the "image." Lomazzo appears to have recognized this. Commenting on Gaudenzio's accomplishments in painting, sculpture, and architecture in the Chapel of the Crucifixion, he asserts that "whoever had not seen did not know what painting was, nor in what its true excellence might lie." Painting, in other words, was the all-

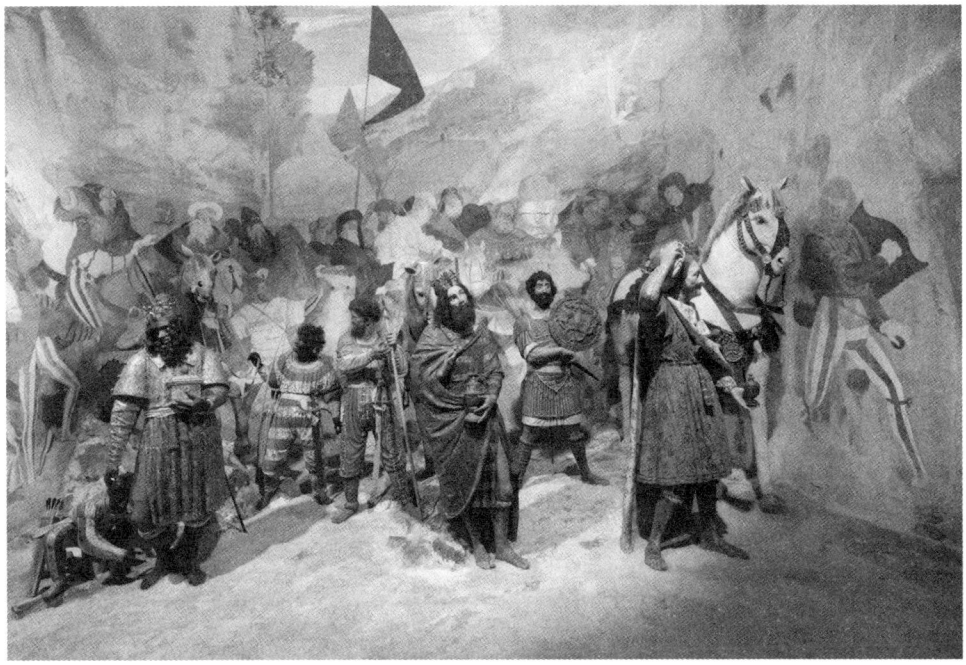

34. Gaudenzio Ferrari, *The Journey of the Magi*. 1520–23. Varallo, Sacro Monte, Chapel 38. Painted and sculptured figures.

inclusive category, and it accommodates the sculptural and the architectural. This was a kind of "painting" that physically enveloped its spectators. Late in life, as Gaudenzio in the 1540s became the senior painter in Milan with the death of Luini, he began to more consciously imitate works like Leonardo's *St. Jerome*, as if laying claim to the legacy of the Florentine.[95]

Leonardo, thereafter, seems to recede in the artistic culture of Renaissance Milan: even his heir Melzi, appointed as an adjudicator in commissions for public sites like the Duomo, seems to have favored more fashionable current mannerist styles based on the illusionistic pyrotechnics of Correggio and the *all'antica* orientations of Giulio Romano. Leonardo by the time of Melzi's death had receded from view—despite his best efforts, the Florentine had become the exemplar of a style, and all styles were destined to have their day.

This chapter has argued that any claim to explain Leonardo that isolates him from his milieu will be misguided and anachronistic. Seeing this figure in terms of his milieu means something more than what historians and art historians call "historical context." I have attempted to show that it means taking seriously ideas of personality or selfhood as co-inherence, as continuum. It means seeing even works held to be fully autograph as produced in relational or dialogic terms, as well as being more flexible in our understanding of where Leonardo's artistic contribution stops. It means looking closely at his art and his writing not for what they withhold—an imaginary person—but for what they do, whether to other artists or, indeed, to us. While technical analysis and connoisseurship can guide us in sorting out the differences between an artist working by himself or in collaboration, the cult of the timeless original masterpiece—the "is it or isn't it?" obsession of Da Vinci Worlds—does not serve us well in understanding historical objects or the individuals who brought them into being.

CONCLUSION

To write an anti-biography means to disrupt the illusion of familiarity and organic coherence that conventional biographies present. It means writing against the grain of received ideas through which the life of an individual is endowed with meaning in advance, before the life is written or written yet again. Anti-biography confronts the ways in which that life has been made to align with various grand narratives: the sense of history as in a unidirectional progress, with its Renaissances, its breakthroughs into modernity, and its exclusionist notions of "civilization." Anti-biography means demonstrating how the traces of a life—its documents and material legacy—already disrupt the shape that has been forced upon it. Instead of seeing artistic and literary remains as illustrations to a life mapped out in advance, the approach means letting them extend and complicate our idea of their maker in unforeseen and enlivening ways, especially in how this life enfolds the lives of others.

The problem, as I have said in a preceding chapter, is not with the practice or feasibility of life-writing.[1]

As a form of historical writing, biography has undergone intensive critique and self-scrutiny since the 1990s and even before, so that any number of biographers would see my characterization of anti-biography as fulfilled in their own rigorous and self-critical practice of life-writing.[2] Biography has been taken up as a medium of analysis in fields such as anthropology and political science as well as history.[3] What I have taken issue with in this book is a particular biographical attitude especially manifest in writing on Leonardo, that is, *the claim to know*, a claim called into question by the silence of historical sources; one arising from an absolute and unwarranted confidence in Leonardo's place in the scheme of things—whether the course of history, the meaning of "Europe,"[4] or something else.

Biographers who have given up on such claims do not do so simply because gaps in the documents make their subject unknowable; the problem was never just the lack of information. Credible experiments in life-writing have been produced for scantily documented and semi-legendary historical figures—among them Hatshepsut, Pontius Pilate, and Andrei Rublev—where the gaps and the unreliability of the record take center stage, and what is ultimately described is the lifeworld or habitus that such figures might have known.[5]

Leonardo biographies, and even some historical monographs, are written according to typology, where Leonardo comes to *stand for* or personify something larger than a localized historical experience, and even one larger than Italy around 1500; he becomes the proto-Newtonian, the genius polymath, the Renaissance Man, as we have seen. It is as if Leonardo existed just *for us* in the twenty-first century, to serve a certain image of ourselves. Such an instrumental or utilitarian view of history—that we study past lives as a legitimation of ourselves and the world we have made—seems particularly characteristic of mainstream biography. The words "instrumental" and "utilitarian" are used to describe a view of the natural world that arose in the scientific culture of the centuries after Leonardo, one associated with names sometimes questionably linked to his: Francis Bacon, Isaac Newton, René Descartes. Theirs is a world that exists as a seemingly inexhaustible quarry of resources to be put in the service of human beings, their technologies, and their markets. Certainly, there are moments in Leonardo's career, as we have seen, that would seem to anticipate such a worldview, such as his view of the city as an apparatus for maximizing and segregating human labor, the subordination of bodies to military apparatus (see plate 25).

The catastrophic consequences of the utilitarian worldview are all around us, and its ethos is depressingly persistent, in terminological disguise ("outcomes," "restructuring," "market expansion," "technology transfer," "socialization," etc.). Earlier, I referred to specialized knowledge of the past and its remnants as a fragile ecosystem, and the analogy can be sustained: an ethical approach to the past is endangered by an instrumentalist view of history that sees the object of its study in terms of use and of profit. Advocates of "learning from Leonardo" chose not to learn that he writes time and again against the instrumentalization of knowledge. In fact, he was openly dismissive of what he called "abbreviators"—writers who reduced the work of others to its usable content: "And you fancy you have wrought miracles when you spoil a work of some speculative mind, and do not perceive that you are falling into the same error as that of a man who strips a tree of the ornament of its branches covered with leaves mingled with the scented blossoms or fruit thereon in order to demonstrate that the tree is good for making planks."[6] While the technological achievement of Renaissance artisans is often characterized in terms of a desire to "master" or "dominate" nature, Leonardo never employed a rhetoric of domination. He saw the natural world not in terms of usefulness but in terms of its marvelous singularities—of a cloud, a rock, a tree, a blade of grass—as well as its patterns and deep structures.

Historical lives can be seen as characteristic or emblematic of their time, but such typicality, if considered attentively and not flattened into stereotypes, can be complex. Leonardo often seems like the fault line in competing paradigms: the artist legible in his civic milieu, "Leonardo the Florentine," is also the nomad constantly getting to grips with shattered states and broken societies. The philosopher with panoramic ideas of nature also speaks the artisanal language of the possessor of secret knowledge. In Leonardo the idea of *experience* as bodily encounter seems to coincide with experience as detached observation. The vehement polemicist against poets and men of letters is also a writer of fables, and allegories, and florid invective. (The passage on abbreviators quoted above is followed by an elaborate reference to the Roman historian Trogus Pompeius and his admirably ornate style, crudely "abbreviated" by Justinus Pompeius.)

The pursuit of the seamless life tends to smooth out such seeming paradoxes, regarding them as an inconvenience. The Windsor drawing of the old man with Botticellian braids (plate 19), with which we concluded the final chapter, seems precisely to present a degree of biographical inconvenience: so queer, in effect, that even partisans of a gay Leonardo can't find a place for it. That is because, as I have shown, its queerness does not lie in undiagnosable psychosexual motivations that have to be invented or assumed. Queerness here is relational: it lies in the anti-portrait's manifestation of attachment, a composite co-inherence of Leonardo/Sandro, which arises in the dynamics of artistic imitation and need have nothing to do with the actual personhood of Sandro Botticelli. Am I not here just "psychologizing" in the way that biographers often do? Yes and no. Yes, but then drawing psychological inferences was never the problem with biography. No, because I have sought to infer motivation from a chain of connections in the writings and the images, not in a set of a priori psychopathologies that have dominated biographies of Leonardo since Freud, and possibly as early as Pater, and that have become the mainstay of Da Vinci Worlds.

Archives can disorient historical inquiry given their own filtering mechanisms, their discriminations about what counts as documentation and whose documents count. Selective preservation and determining just what finally counts as evidence poses perennial challenges to scholars in the Leonardo archive, the copious but lacuna-riddled corpus dispersed in many libraries and museums. The very copiousness can produce an effect of splintering and dispersal. The notes and lists read like a relentless concrete poetics of the mundane through which the speaking voice atomizes into particularities: "Spectacles with case, firestick, fork, bistoury, charcoal, boards, sheets of paper, chalk, white, wax, forceps, pane of glass, fine-tooth bone saw, scalpel, inkhorn, pen-knife. Zerbi, and Agnolo Benedetti. Get hold of a skull. Nutmeg" (RCIN 919070, plate 30).

And here I find myself wondering whether the Leonardo archive itself registers an awareness of this plethoric character, its rain of references to and lists of persons and things. For instance, a piece of paper preserved at Windsor and catalogued as RCIN 912698 (plate 44): on one side, a list of household expenses; on the other, a tiny sketch, made by Leonardo ca. 1512–14, of an apocalyptic vision of a landscape with a cloudburst from which numerous domestic objects and workshop tools such as hammers, rakes, ladders, clocks, lanterns, bagpipes, compasses, shears, spectacles, bottles, and crockery rain upon the earth. The sketch may evoke the clamor and tumult of the Vatican workshops where Leonardo worked in 1514, but it seems—especially with its inscription—to give labor and production a larger eschatological dimension, even to conjoin the beginning with the end of time: "And here is Adam and there is Eve. Oh, human misery, to how many things are you enslaved just for money." It is a striking image of an Earth glutted to suffocation with the products and by-products of human industry and enterprise. Perhaps we can also allow ourselves a glimpse of a life experienced as a dispersal and fragmentation into its material attachments. In the clouds, a lion-like figure appears, and what may conjecturally be identified as tongues of flame: *il leone arde*. The lion burns. Or, the artist, as consumer, is consumed.

In concluding with these reflections, I wonder if we can find in them a way of thinking about and exhibiting Leonardo that might offer an alternative to twenty-first-century Da Vinci Worlds. A visualization of a life entangled with other lives, shaped by the clamor of the workshop as well as the performative poise of the court, of random encounters and serendipitous connections. An exhibition, for instance, of an extended Leonardo that would explore his own play of voices and personae, his connections with followers and disciples, without the usual fetishizing of the "original" and the "authentic." An entirely different enterprise could be an exhibition of modern and contemporary artistic responses to Leonardo that would seek to challenge rather than to reaffirm the gimmickry and cliché of Da Vinci World appropriations: from Malevich and Duchamp to Warhol to Mary Beth Edelson, Vivan Sundaram, and Jenny Saville. For me, two of the most powerful contemporary responses to Leonardo have been stage performances. In Jerron Herman's virtuosic dance solo *Vitruvian* (2022), a Black disabled performer strives with and against the vision of cosmic symmetry and balance represented by the famous Leonardo drawing. In Mary Zimmerman's theater work *The Notebooks of Leonardo da Vinci* (1993 and 2022), a multiracial team of actors perform Leonardo's words as a series of characters, kinetically visualizing his inventions and scientific demonstrations with their bodies.

Correlatively, and rather than canceling the biographical enterprise, we could call on it to be more conscious of what drives the inevitable fictionalizations at its heart. The drive toward normativity, for instance, that underlies the elaboration of a single name on a list, *la chermonese*, into the fantasy of a heterosexual Leonardo, as we saw in chapter 2. If we need to encounter Leonardo in the form of fiction, then we need fiction that is better informed. Outright fabulation might even be preferable in creating an empathetic and informative perspective on the past. The creative dimension and aesthetical logic would be emphasized rather than concealed: it has even been argued by Frank Ankersmit that the appeal of history is in an aesthetic experience of the Sublime, in the striving to find design and purpose in fragmentary and disorderly facts.[7] Given the partiality of archives—of their survival, of their criteria for inclusion and preservation—fiction could be a more favorable medium for visualizing the lifeworld of a premodern artist, as opposed to biographies with their claims of forensic procedure and discovery, their rhetoric of unmasking.[8] In this regard, Carlo Vecce's decision to cast documents that possibly but still deniably pertain to Catarina, Leonardo's mother, in fictional form, is of particular significance—it would constitute a critical fabulation, a thought experiment, by a rigorous scholar who understands the gray areas in the interpretation of documentary information.

I here think of Anna Banti's novel *Artemisia* (1947), which she wrote following the destruction during World War II of her doctoral research on Artemisia Gentileschi, or Amy Sackville's *Painter to the King* (2018), a minimalist and atmospheric imagining of Velázquez, or Ali Smith's conjuring of the figure of the Ferrarese painter Francesco del Cossa in *How to Be Both* (2014). Or I think of Álvaro Enrigue's *Muerte súbita* (2013, published in English as *Sudden Death*, 2016), which in connecting the rogue life of Caravaggio with indigenous artists living under violent colonization in New Spain wages war on archival authority, inventing both documents and historical objects along with fictionalized and semi-fictional situations. A. S. Byatt's *Biographer's Tale* (1988) and Catherine Lacey's *Biography of X* (2023) can be read as essays on the desires and illusions of biography but cast in the form of a novel. More importantly, in refusing complacency in the face of received ideas about their subjects, such books themselves constitute a kind of anti-biography, one that shares the ends if not the means from the historical anti-biography I conclude here.

Such authors work with a self-consciousness that steers clear of claims to know or discover; they concentrate on the everyday and the unsensational. They sometimes avoid empathetic or intelligible explications of character or motive, and generally allow their historical subjects to retain their pastness and their foreignness—their *singularity*—an ethical stance, in other words, or respect for the life of others, in their opacity and unknowability.

ACKNOWLEDGMENTS

I am indebted to the conversations and advice over many years of several colleagues, among them Luke Syson, who shared his thoughts on Leonardo while preparing the National Gallery exhibition of 2011, and in whose company I saw *The Virgin of the Rocks* in conservation and the *Salvator Mundi* during its first public exhibition. I learned a great deal from participating in a 2018 roundtable at the Denver Museum of Art, organized by Angelica Daneo, which involved Luke along with Claire Farago, Martin Clayton, and Sue Ann Chui. Since 2018, when I began this project, Monica Azzolini, Ellie Bernick, Michael Cole, Matthew Landrus, Dianne Dwyer Modestini, Mary Pardo, Jill Pederson, and Arielle Saiber all generously shared information and insights.

For careful readings of the manuscript at various stages, I am grateful to John Paul Clark, Max Hernandez, Frank Zöllner, and Rebecca Zorach, as well as one generous anonymous reader for Princeton University Press. It was truly helpful to receive editorial suggestions from Amanda Moon and Thomas LeBien.

Several chapters owe their final form to a series of invitations to present material at the University of Toronto (in 2021 and 2024), Villanova University, the University of Rochester, the Oklahoma Museum of Art, Indiana University, and Dartmouth College. On those occasions I benefited in particular from the responses of Tim McHall, Leslie Geddes, Rachel Haidu, Philip Sohm, Giancarla Periti, Ethan Matthew Kavaler, Christopher Heuer, and Eyal Sagie Pundik.

Needless to say, none of these individuals are to be held accountable for any errors or contestable opinions in this book.

The generous policy of several institutions who waive copyright fees should be noted, especially the Metropolitan Museum in New York and the National Gallery of Art in Washington, DC. I am particularly grateful for the cooperation of the Royal Library, Windsor Castle, whose holdings are obviously indispensable for any long publication on Leonardo.

I tried out some of my ideas on an undergraduate class in 2019, a freshman seminar in 2022, and a particularly lively seminar with graduates and undergraduates in the spring of 2024. Being able to teach and learn from intelligent and open-minded students for several decades has been the rarest gift: this book is dedicated to those students.

Last but not least, I am grateful to Michelle Komie for her confidence in this project.

NOTES

Introduction

1. The designation "Da Vinci" seems not to precede the 1800s; it can be found in the writings of, for instance, Théophile Gautier, which will concern us below.

2. Perhaps uniquely, Stefan Klein, *Leonardo's Legacy: How Da Vinci Reimagined the World*, trans. Shelley Frisch (Philadelphia: Da Capo Press, 2008), 9–13, conceives of the visit to the *Mona Lisa* as a pilgrimage-like experience, even corresponding to *Darshan*—a Hindu term for an encounter with the divine upon earth.

3. *Leonardo da Vinci: The Faces of the Genius in Madrid*, Post Online Media, November 26, 2018.

4. See the volume *A Second Mona Lisa? Challenges of Attribution and Authentication and Various Possibilities for Evaluating a Work of Art*, ed. Salvatore Lorusso and Andrea Natali (Rome: L'ErmArte, 2021).

5. Marc Gotlieb, "Our Monstrous Double: The Dream of Research in 'Outsider Art History,'" in *What Is Research in the Visual Arts? Obsession, Archive, Encounter*, ed. Michael Ann Holly and Marquard Smith (New Haven: Yale University Press, 2008), 86, which also characterizes peer review as a policing operation.

6. Nica Rieppi, principal investigator at Art Analysis & Research, on the authentication of the *Salvator Mundi*. Jennifer Calfas, "A Leonardo da Vinci Painting Just Sold for $450 Million; Here's How Experts Figured Out It Was Real," *Time*, November 17, 2017, https://time.com/5028341/leonardo-da-vinci-salvator-mundi-authentication/.

7. Quoted in Ben Lewis, *The Last Leonardo: The Secret Lives of the World's Most Expensive Painting* (London: Collins, 2019), 128.

8. Lewis, *The Last Leonardo*, 172. The jacket blurb refers to the *Salvator Mundi* as the "Holy Grail" of art history.

9. For an account of the controversies, as well as a consideration of the work's iconography and the typology of the "Christ-portrait," see Frank Zöllner, "Leonardo da Vinci's *Salvator Mundi*, Its Pictorial Tradition and Its Context as a Devotional Image," *Artibus et Historiae* 42 (2021): 53–84.

10. See the report by the conservator Dianne Modestini with full visual documentation: https://salvatormundirevisited.com/Condition-and-Restoration.

11. For instance, whether the painting is to be identified with a painting of Christ documented in the collection of King Charles I of England, and whether it is the source for a seventeenth-century engraving of a similar composition by Wenceslaus Hollar, who worked for much of his life in London. Countering the skepticism of Ben Lewis, *The Last Leonardo*, on these points, see Martin Kemp, Robert B. Simon, and Margaret Dalivalle, *Leonardo's Salvator Mundi and the Collecting of Leonardo in the Stuart Courts* (Oxford: Oxford University Press, 2020).

12. https://www.rtl.fr/culture/arts-spectacles/musee-du-louvre-le-salvator-mundi-de-de-vinci-expose-en-2019-7791205582; interview broadcast November 30, 2017.

13. *The Lost Leonardo* (2021), a documentary by Andreas Koefoed.

14. Vincent Delieuvin, Myriam Eveno, and Élisa-beth Ravaud, *Léonard de Vinci: Le Salvator Mundi* (Paris: Louvre editions/Hazan, 2019).

15. https://salvatormundirevisited.com/.

16. For a "review of a book that was never published," see Martin Kemp, "What the Science Says about the *Salvator Mundi*," *Art Newspaper* 334 (May 2021): 5.

Chapter 1: Da Vinci Worlds

1. On Leonardo and Melzi in Terracina, see Jan Sammer, *Leonardo da Vinci: The Untold Story of His Final Years* (independently published, 2019), 17–25.

2. For a comprehensive account of the painting, its reception, and the most recent conservation, see Pietro C. Marani and Pinin Brambilla Barcilon, *Leonardo: The Last Supper* (Chicago: University of Chicago Press, 2001 [original Italian edition: Milan, 1999]).

3. On the versions, see Marani and Barcilon, *Leonardo: The Last Supper*, 57–60, and the more detailed account in Leo Steinberg, *Leonardo's Incessant Last Supper* (New York: Zone Books, 2001), 219–72.

4. Federico Borromeo, *Sacred Painting/Museum*, ed. and trans. Kenneth S. Rothwell Jr. (Cambridge, MA: Harvard University Press, 2010), 189.

5. Francesco Scannelli, *Il microcosmo della pittura* (Cesena: Il Neri, 1657), 40–41.

6. Reported in 1777 by Venanzio de Pagave, a pioneering collector of biographical material on Leonardo, in a letter to Luigi Crespi. See Giovanna Perini Folesani, "Leonardo and His Eighteenth-Century Italian Biographies," in *The Lives of Leonardo*, ed. Thomas Frangenberg and Rodney Palmer (London: Warburg Institute, 2013), 112.

7. *Lettres historiques et critiques sur l'Italie, de Charles de Brosses, . . . avec des notes relatives à la situation actuelle de l'Italie*, 3 vols. (Paris: Ponthieu, 1798), 1:119.

8. "It is exceedingly ruined and all the Apostles on the Right-hand of Christ are entirely defaced and those on his Left-hand appear pretty plain, but the Colours are quite faded and in several places only the bare wall is left." Jonathan Richardson Sr. and Jr., *An account of some of the statues, bas-reliefs, drawings and pictures in Italy, &c.* (London: J. Knapton, 1722), 23. For the view that such reports gave rise to a "jolt of shame" on the part of the Milanese, see Marani and Barcilon, *Leonardo: The Last Supper*, 23.

9. Domenico Pino, *Storia genuina del Cenacolo insigne dipinto da Leonardo da Vinci nel refettorio de' padri domenicani di Santa Maria delle Grazie di Milano* (Milan: Cesare Orena, 1796).

10. A. Richard Turner, *Inventing Leonardo* (Berkeley: University of California Press, 1992), 93–94, on the surrogate nature of Bossi's replica, which he described as a "rinnovazione." See also Marani and Barcilon, *Leonardo: The Last Supper*, 26–27; Steinberg, *Leonardo's Incessant Last Supper*, 31–32.

11. Théophile Gautier, *Journeys in Italy* [1850], trans. Daniel B. Vermilye (London: Brentano's, 1902), 69–71.

12. Heinrich Wölfflin, *Die Klassische Kunst* (1898); English version, *Classic Art: An Introduction to the Art of the Italian Renaissance*, trans. Peter Murray and Linda Murray (London: Phaidon, 1952), 23.

13. Frances Kennedy, *The Independent*, May 19, 1999.

14. Ken Shulman, "ART; Monumental Toil to Restore the Magnificent," *New York Times*, July 2, 1995.

15. Nate Freeman, "Eataly Helping to Save Leonardo da Vinci's 'Last Supper' with 'Advanced Air Filtration System,'" *ArtNews*, April 12, 2017.

16. Marani in Marani and Barcilon, *Leonardo: The Last Supper*, 5, 39.

17. Steinberg, *Leonardo's Incessant Last Supper*, 15.

18. Key witnesses include Cardinal Federico Borromeo, as well as Leonardo's friend the mathematician Luca Pacioli, for whom the motions of the Apostles signified not just their horror at Christ's announcement of his betrayal but their *viva e afflicta admiratione*, their "lively and agitated sense of wonder," while the painting as a whole presents itself as the *prelibato simulacro de l'ardente desiderio de nostro salute*: "most precious image of our most ardently desired salvation." Steinberg, *Leonardo's Incessant Last Supper*, 31–33.

19. Martin Kemp, *Living with Leonardo: Fifty Years of Sanity and Insanity in the Art World and Beyond* (London: Thames and Hudson, 2018), 141, disparagingly referred to Steinberg as an "iconographer." Steinberg was one of numerous scholars who had disputed the attribution of the so-called *Bella Principessa* to Leonardo. Carmen C. Bambach's massive study, *Leonardo da Vinci Rediscovered*, 4 vols. (New Haven: Yale University Press, 2019), has a single reference to Steinberg's book and to a minor point about homiletic gesture (4:183n532).

20. Giorgio Vasari, *Lives of the Painters, Sculptors, and Architects*, trans. Gaston de Vere, 2 vols. (1927; London: Everyman's Library, 1996), 2:636.

21. Vasari/de Vere, 2:636.

22. Leonardo was by no means the first to enliven his figures with vivifying smiles: so too did Donatello, Luca della Robbia, and Desiderio da Settignano. On Antonello da Messina's portrait of an unknown man now in Cefalù, Donald Sassoon writes, "Few wonder why this handsome man is smiling or who is the sitter. . . . The portrait is regarded as outstanding, but men are more intrigued by the smiles of women, particularly if they hang in Paris and not in distant Sicily." See Sassoon, *Becoming Mona Lisa: The Making of a Global Icon* (New York: Harcourt, 2001), 11.

23. On the *Mona Lisa* in twentieth-century diplomacy, see Frank Zöllner, "John F. Kennedy and Leonardo's Mona Lisa: Art as the Continuation of Politics," in *Radical Art History: Internationale Anthologie*, ed. Wolfgang Kersten (Zurich: ZIP, 1997), 466–79.

24. See the exhibition catalog, *Leonardo y la copia de Mona Lisa del Museo del Prado* (Madrid: Museo del Prado, 2021).

25. On the 2019 sale, see Bendor Grosvenor, "Perhaps Even a Leonardo Copy Shows You're Rich and Cultured," *Art Newspaper*, March 13, 2019. Sold at Sotheby's as a seventeenth-century copy of Leonardo's original, its price soared past its estimate of $80,000–100,000 to sell for $1.69 million. On the 2021 Hekking sale, which broke the record set by the 2019 one, see *Art Newspaper*, June 20, 2021.

26. *Lives of Leonardo da Vinci*, ed. Charles Robertson (Los Angeles: J. Paul Getty Museum, 2019), 151–56.

27. Joanna Woods Marsden, "Leonardo da Vinci's *Mona Lisa*: A Portrait without a Commissioner?" in *Illuminating Leonardo: A Festschrift for Carlo Pedretti Celebrating His 70 Years of Scholarship (1944–2014)*, ed. Constance Moffatt and Sara Tagliagamba (Leiden: Brill, 2016), 169–83, argues that the picture came into being entirely at the behest of Leonardo himself, and that it was never commissioned by Giocondo.

28. Martin Kemp and Giuseppe Pallanti, *Mona Lisa: The People and the Painting* (Oxford: Oxford University Press, 2017).

29. For discussion of these identifications, see Carlo Vecce, *Leonardo* (Rome: Salerno, 2006), 324–26.

30. Armin Schlecter, "*Ita Leonardus Vincius facit in omnibus suis picturis*: Leonardo da Vincis Mona Lisa und die Cicero-Philologie von Angelo Poliziano bis Johann Georg Graevius," IASL, April 29, 2008, https://www.iaslonline.lmu .de/index.php?vorgang_id=2889. See also the summary by Jill Burke, "Agostino Vespucci's Marginal Note about Leonardo da Vinci in Hei-

delberg," *Leonardo da Vinci Society Newsletter* 30 (2008): 3–4.

31. James Fenton, "Portrait of a Lady," *The Guardian*, January 26, 2008.

32. Vincent Delieuvin, "Télématin," *Journal Télévisé*, France 2 Télévision, January 15, 2008.

33. Fiona Keating, "Secrets of the *Mona Lisa*: Forensic Examination Unlocks History's 'Most Enigmatic Work of Art,'" *International Business Times*, December 12, 2015.

34. *Il Fatto Quotidiano*, August 9, 2013.

35. For a photograph of the digital restoration, see Kemp and Pallanti, *Mona Lisa*, 222.

36. The documentary *Secrets of the Mona Lisa* was first broadcast in December 2015. Cotte's research is published in *Lumière sur Mona Lisa de Léonard de Vinci: Portraits multispectrales* (Rueil-Malmaison: Vinci, 2016).

37. Rab Hatfield, *The Three Mona Lisas* (Milan: Officina Libraria, 2014).

38. Timothy McCall, *Making the Renaissance Man: Masculinity in the Courts of Renaissance Italy* (London: Reaktion Books, 2023).

39. Hatfield, *The Three Mona Lisas*, 154–55.

40. Kemp and Pallanti, *Mona Lisa*, 225.

41. There are anticipations in the backgrounds of North Italian portraits and narrative paintings by Cosmè Tura, Francesco del Cossa, and Ercole de'Roberti, who worked at the courts of the Este of Ferrara and the Bentivoglio of Bologna. See Stephen J. Campbell, *The Endless Periphery: Towards a Geopolitics of Art in Lorenzo Lotto's Italy* (Chicago: University of Chicago Press, 2019), 32–33.

42. Quoted in Sassoon, *Becoming Mona Lisa*, 110–11.

43. Théophile Gautier, *The Louvre: Leonardo da Vinci, Esteban Bartolome Murillo, Sir Joshua Reynolds*, trans. Frederick Cesar de Sumichrast (New York: G. D. Sproul, 1901), 277.

44. On Leonardo and the French Empire, see Turner, *Inventing Leonardo*, 90–99. On the treatise, see Claire Farago, Janis Bell, and Carlo Vecce, eds., *The Fabrication of Leonardo da Vinci's Trattato della Pittura*, 2 vols. (Leiden: Brill, 2017), especially the essays by Claire Farago, Juliana Barone, and Janis Bell in volume 1. On Leonardo and the French academy, see Martin Kemp, "'A Chaos of Intelligence': Leonardo's *Traité* and the Perspective Wars at the Académie Royale," in *Re-reading Leonardo: The Treatise on Painting across Europe, 1550–1900*, ed. Claire Farago (Abingdon: Ashgate, 2009), 237–55; and Thomas Kirchner, "Between Academicism and Its Critics: Leonardo da Vinci's *Traité de la Peinture* and Eighteenth-Century French Art Theory," in *Re-reading Leonardo: The Treatise*

on Painting across Europe, 1550–1900, ed. Claire
Farago (Abingdon: Ashgate, 2009), 299–327, as
well as other essays in the same volume; Rebecca
Zorach, "Nature, Imagination, and Authority:
Leonardo in Seventeenth-Century France,"
in Leonardo in Dialogue: The Artist amid His
Contemporaries, ed. Francesca Borgo, Rodolfo
Maffeis, and Alessandro Nova (Venice: Marsilio,
2019), 335–51.

45. Perini Folesani, "Leonardo and His Eighteenth-
Century Italian Biographies," 89.

46. Stéphane Distinguin, "Et si on vendait la Joconde pour aider le secteur de la culture?" Usbek
& Rica, May 6, 2020.

47. For Jessica Beck, "a confession of the conflict he
felt between his faith and his sexuality, and ultimately a plea for salvation from the suffering to
which the homosexual community was subjected
during these years." Beck, "Warhol's Confession:
Love, Faith, and AIDs," in Andy Warhol: From
A to B and Back Again (New York: Whitney
Museum of American Art, 2018), 92.

48. Originally as an op-ed in Usbek & Rica, May 6,
2020. "Et si on vendait la Joconde pour aider
le secteur de la culture?" Remarks quoted here
are from Corriere della Sera, May 2020, in my
translation.

49. Salvatore Settis, If Venice Dies, trans. André
Naffis-Sahely (New York: New Vessel Press,
2016 [original Italian edition, 2014]), 56, citing
Maurice Lévy and Jean-Pierre Jouyet, L'économie
de l'immatériel: La croissance de demain (France,
Ministère de l'Economie, des Finances et de
l'Industrie, 2006), available online.

50. Luke Syson, "The Rewards of Service: Leonardo
da Vinci and the Duke of Milan," in Leonardo da
Vinci: Painter at the Court of Milan, ed. Luke
Syson with Larry Keith (London: National Gallery, 2011), 13.

51. https://www.nationalgallery.org.uk/exhibitions
/past/leonardo-experience-a-masterpiece.

52. The quotation is from a review of Leonardo:
Experience a Masterpiece by James Hall, Times
Literary Supplement, December 13, 2019.

53. Reported by John Yemma, "Leonardo on Tour:
The Good, the Bad . . . and the Phony?" Boston
Globe, February 23, 1997.

54. Henri Zerner, "The Vision of Leonardo," New
York Review of Books, September 25, 1997.

55. Melinda Henneberger, "The Leonardo Cover-
Up," New York Times Magazine, April 21, 2002.

56. For Seracini's own account of his findings, see
"Indagini diagnostiche sulla Adorazione dei
Magi di Leonardo da Vinci," in La mente di
Leonardo: Nel laboratorio del Genio Universale,
exhibition catalog, ed. Paolo Galuzzi (Florence:
Giunti, 2006), 94–101.

57. Maurizio Seracini, Oltre il visibile: Indagini
scientifiche sul disegno, in Leonardo da Vinci:
Studio per l'Adorazione dei Magi, ed. Francesco
Camerota (Roma: Argos, 2006), 33–107.

58. Grace Glueck, "Lost Da Vinci Mural Believed
Discovered," New York Times, November 2,
1979.

59. H. Travers Newton and John R. Spencer, "On
the Location of Leonardo's Battle of Anghiari,"
Art Bulletin 64 (1982): 45–52, concludes with
the words: "Many more square meters of [Vasa-
ri's Rout of the Pisans] mural have subsequently
been removed by the 'strappo' technique. We
recognize the informed decision of the Belle
Arti in Florence and Rome to remove sections
of the Vasari murals, and await the results of
their efforts with anticipation."

60. Massimiliano Pieraccini, Daniele Meccati,
Guido Luzi, Maurizio Seracini, Gianpaolo Pi-
nelli, and Carlo Atzeni, "Non-contact Intrawall
Penetrating Radar for Heritage Survey: The
Search of the Battle of Anghiari by Leonardo da
Vinci," NDT&E International 38 (2005): 151–57.

61. For a summary of the data and conclusions
about the structure of the counterwall, see Rab
Hatfield, Finding Leonardo: The Case for Recovering the Battle of Anghiari (Prato: Florentine
Press, 2007), 27–34.

62. Simone Siliani, quoted in Henneberger, "The
Leonardo Cover-Up," 48.

63. Daniel Williams, "Search for Missing Da Vinci
Work Hits Wall," Washington Post, July 29, 2005.

64. Michele Bocci, "Battaglia di Anghiari operazione
sbagliata," La Repubblica, February 9, 2012.

65. Stéphane Toussaint, "L'affaire de la Bataille
d'Anghiari," Tribune de l'art, June 12, 2012.
There is an English version published in the Art
Tribune, "The Affair of the Battle of Anghiari,"
but in the interests of readability I offer my own
translation here.

66. See the laconic report in Laura Rysman,
"Sleuths of the Artistic Kind," New York Times,
November 20, 2020: "A five-year rehabilitation
of Leonardo da Vinci's muddied Adoration of
the Magi revealed a painting teeming with 90
distinct figures and more than 30 animals."

67. Cecilia Frosinini with Roberto Bellucci and
Patrizia Riitano, "Il restauro dell' Adorazione
dei Magi di Leonardo da Vinci: Capire il non-
finito," Imagines 1 (2017), https://www.uffizi.it
/news/il-restauro-dell-adorazione-dei-magi-di
-leonardo-da-vinci-capire-il-non-finito; also,
The Restoration of Leonardo da Vinci's Adoration
of the Magi: Rediscovering a Masterpiece, ed.
Marco Ciatti and Cecilia Frosinini (Florence:
Edifir edizioni Firenze/Opificio delle pietre
dure, 2021).

68. See *La Sala Grande di Palazzo Vecchio e la "Battaglia di Anghiari" di Leonardo da Vinci: Dalla configurazione architettonica all'apparato decorativo*, ed. Roberta Barsanti, Gianluca Belli, Emanuela Ferretti, and Cecilia Frosinini (Florence: Olschki, 2019), in particular the contributions by Frosinini/Bellucci, Ferretti, Marco Ruffini, and Maurizio Pieraccini. Also, Francesca Fiorani, "Did Leonardo Ever Paint on the Walls of the Sala Grande?" https://uva .theopenscholar.com/files/francesca-fiorani /files/2022-did_leonardo_ever_paint_on_the _walls_of_the_sala_grande.pdf.

69. See Don Thompson, *The $12 Million Stuffed Shark: The Curious Economics of Contemporary Art* (New York: St. Martin's Press, 2008), especially 9–61. For art and finance capital, see Dave Beech, *Art and Value: Art's Economic Exceptionalism in Classical, Neoclassical, and Marxist Economics* (Leiden: Brill, 2015), 211–314.

70. See Iain Robertson, ed., *Understanding International Art Markets and Management* (London: Routledge, 2005), especially Robertson, "The Emerging Markets for Contemporary Art in East Asia," 146–71, and James Spencer, "World Taste in Chinese Art," 172–94.

71. Jean Baudrillard, *The Transparency of Evil: Essays on Extreme Phenomena*, trans. James Benedict (London: Verso, 2009 [original French edition, 1993]), 16.

72. Anna Brady, "Rolling with the Punches: How the Art Market Bounced Back," *Art Newspaper* (September 2018): 304.

73. Eileen Kinsella, "The Art Industry Is in Its Worst Recession since 2009, Art Basel's Latest Art Market Report Finds," *ArtNet News*, March 16, 2021, citing the 2021 annual Global Art Market Report sponsored by Art Basel and UBS and written by art economist Clare McAndrew.

74. Alexander Hope, "The Nature of Supply and Demand in the Old Master Picture Trade," in *Understanding International Art Markets and Management*, ed. Iain Robertson (London: Routledge, 2005), 195–213.

75. Simon Hewitt, *Leonardo da Vinci and the Book of Doom: Bianca Sforza, the Sforziada and Artful Propaganda in Renaissance Milan* (London: Unicorn Books, 2020); Alessandro Vezzosi, *Leonardo da Vinci: La pittura. Un nuovo sguardo* (Florence: Giunti, 2018); Martin Kemp, Pascal Cotte, et al., *Leonardo da Vinci "La Bella Principessa": The Profile Portrait of a Milanese Woman* (London: Hodder & Stoughton, 2010).

76. Kasia Pisarek, "*La Bella Principessa*— Arguments against the Attribution to Leonardo," *Artibus et Historiae* 36 (2015): 61–89; Carla

Glori, "La Sforziade e le miniature del Birago: L'epopea sforzesca e il destino tragico di Gian Galeazzo Sforza," *Fogli e parole d'arte— Rinascimento oggi* (May 2014; online), and "The Illumination by Birago in the Sforziad Incunabulum in Warsaw: In Defence of Horodyski's Thesis and a New Hypothesis," academia.edu.

77. *Leonardo da Vinci: Painter at the Court of Milan*, 88–89, entry by Arturo Galansino.

78. Pisarek, "*La Bella Principessa*—Arguments against the Attribution to Leonardo," 77.

79. Claude Phillips, "Verrocchio, or Leonardo da Vinci?" *Art Journal* [London], n.s. (1899): 33–39; Wilhelm Valentiner, "Leonardo and Desiderio," *Burlington Magazine* 61 (1932): 52–61; *Verrocchio: Master of Leonardo*, exhibition catalog, Florence: Palazzo Strozzi, ed. Andrea de'Marchi and Francesco Caglioti (Venice: Marsilio, 2019), cat. 9.9, 280–83, entry by Francesco Caglioti.

80. "The Ghent Altarpiece Reveals Its Greatest Secret: The Precise Contribution of Hubert and Jan van Eyck," *Artdependence*, October 13, 2021, https://artdependence.com/articles/the-ghent -altarpiece-reveals-its-greatest-secret-the-precise -contribution-of-hubert-and-jan-van-eyck/.

81. Claire Bishop, "Against Digital Art History," *International Journal for Digital Art History*, no. 3 (2018): 122–31 (127).

82. Sonia Drimmer, "How AI Is Hijacking Art History," *The Conversation*, November 1, 2021.

83. For instance, http://pieterbruegel.net/, a research database maintained by Dr. Elizabeth Honig of the University of Maryland.

84. For a cautionary investigation produced by computer scientists in collaboration with an art historian, see Alan Langmead, Christopher Nygren, Paul Rodriguez, and Alan Craig, "Leonardo, Morelli, and the Computational Mirror," *DHQ: Digital Humanities Quarterly* 15 (2021): 1, https://www.digitalhumanities.org /dhq/vol/15/1/000540/000540.html.

85. See also Paolo Galluzzi, "Leonardo//thek@ 1.0: A Digital Infrastructure to Avoid Shipwreck in the Ocean of Data of the Codex Atlanticus of Leonardo da Vinci," in *Decoding Leonardo's Codices: Compilation, Dispersal, and Reproduction Technologies*, ed. Paolo Galluzzi and Alessandro Nova (Venice: Marsilio, 2022), 289–99.

Chapter 2: "Now Unmade by Time . . ."

1. Codex Urbinas 12 r–v; translation in *Leonardo on Painting*, selected and edited by Martin Kemp and Margaret Walker (New Haven: Yale University Press, 1989), 29–32.

2. Martin Kemp, *Leonardo da Vinci: The 100 Milestones* (New York: Sterling Press, 2019), 5.

3. Walter Isaacson, *Leonardo da Vinci* (New York: Simon and Schuster, 2017), 47–48.

4. "Da Vinci may well be the first naturalist to have left us with a geologic history based on observations that, at the very least, were consistent with, if not the basis of, those used to construct a landscape." Gary D. Rosenberg, "An Artistic Perspective on the Continuity of Space and the Origin of Modern Geologic Thought," *Earth Sciences History* 20 (2001): 139.

5. Ernst Gombrich, "Light, Form, and Texture in Fifteenth-Century Painting North and South of the Alps," in *The Heritage of Apelles* (Oxford: Phaidon, 1976), 19–35. For a recent exploration of this view, with bibliography, see Geoff Lehman, "Leonardo, Van Eyck, and the Epistemology of Landscape," in *Leonardo in Dialogue: The Artist amid His Contemporaries*, ed. Francesca Borgo, Rodolfo Maffeis, and Alessandro Nova (Venice: Marsilio, 2019), 97–119.

6. "The Diagnostic Campaign of the Opificio delle Pietre Dure on the First Landscape by Leonardo," *Uffizi Online Magazine*, August 4, 2019, www.uffizi.it/en/magazine/diagnostic -campaign-first-landscape-leonardo-drawing -8p-opificio-pietre-dure. See also Roberta Barsanti, ed., *Leonardo a Vinci: Alle origini del genio* (Florence: Giunti, 2019).

7. Alessandro Nova, "'Addj 5 aghossto 1473': L'oggetto e le sue interpretazioni," in *Leonardo da Vinci on Nature: Knowledge and Representation*, ed. Fabio Frosini and Alessandro Nova (Venice: Marsilio, 2013), 285–303. David Alan Brown, *Leonardo da Vinci: Origins of a Genius* (New Haven: Yale University Press, 1998), 98, also argued that the drawing had a functional purpose "beyond that of seeking inspiration in nature."

8. Leonardo, as the evolutionary biologist Stephen Jay Gould reminds us, "was neither a spaceman or an angel—and we will never understand him if we insist on reading him as [Mark Twain's] Hank Morgan, a man truly out of time." Gould, *Leonardo's Mountain of Clams and the Diet of Worms: Essays on Natural History* (New York: Harmony Books, 1998), 22.

9. Julian Barnes, *The Man in the Red Coat* (London: Jonathan Cape, 2019), 167–68.

10. Codex Atlanticus (29v). *The Notebooks of Leonardo da Vinci*, ed. and trans. Irma A. Richter (Oxford: Oxford University Press, 2008), 275.

11. Barbara Newman, *The Permeable Self: Five Medieval Relationships* (Philadelphia: University of Pennsylvania Press, 2021), 6.

12. *Purgatorio* II.110–11: "l'anima mia, che, con la sua persona / venendo qui, è affannata tanto!"

13. On masks, "persona," and impersonation, see Denis J.-J. Robichaud, *Plato's Persona: Marsilio Ficino, Renaissance Humanism, and Platonic Traditions* (Philadelphia: University of Pennsylvania Press, 2018).

14. For an exploration of Cristoforo Landino's metaphor, see Stefano Cracolici, "Flirting with the Chameleon: Alberti on Love," *MLN* 121, *Italian Issue* (2006): 102–29. On the malleability of Renaissance selfhood, see Thomas M. Greene, "The Flexibility of the Self in Renaissance Literature," in *The Disciplines of Criticism: Essays in Literary Theory, Interpretations and History*, ed. Peter Demetz, Thomas M. Greene, and Lowry Silson Jr. (New Haven: Yale University Press, 1968), 241–64; John Martin, "Inventing Sincerity, Refashioning Prudence: The Discovery of the Individual in Renaissance Europe," *American Historical Review* 102 (1997): 1309–42.

15. Carmen C. Bambach, *Leonardo da Vinci Rediscovered*, 4 vols. (New Haven: Yale University Press, 2019), 1:29, repeated 2:291. Curiously Bambach attempts to reinstate the drawing as a portrait of Leonardo, even while redating it on technical grounds to 1500–1502.

16. Giorgio Vasari, *Lives of the Painters, Sculptors, and Architects*, trans. Gaston de Vere, 2 vols. (1927; London: Everyman's Library, 1996), 2:627.

17. *The Literary Works of Leonardo da Vinci*, ed. J. P. Richter, rev. ed. with Irma Richter, 2 vols. (1939; London: Phaidon, 1970), 2:364.

18. Some of this material is explored in Carlo Pedretti, "Il guardroba di Leonardo e Salaì," in *Leonardo da Vinci, L'angelo incarnato, e Salaì* (Foligno: CB Edizioni, 2009), 390–94.

19. Codex Forster 13r; translation in *Leonardo da Vinci: Notebooks*, ed. Irma A. Richter (Oxford: Oxford University Press, 2008), 333.

20. Windsor, Royal Library, RCIN 919145r; translation in *Leonardo da Vinci: Notebooks*, 343.

21. Madrid Codex 1r; translation in *Leonardo da Vinci: Notebooks*, 333.

22. Codex Urbinas 31v; translation in *Leonardo on Painting*, 205.

23. Codex Urbinas 37 r–v; translation in *Leonardo on Painting*, 205.

24. Codex Atlanticus 184v/505v; translation in *Leonardo on Painting*, 205.

25. *Leonardo da Vinci: La vera imagine. Documenti e testimonianze sulla vita e sull'opera*, ed. Vanna Arrighi, Anna Bellinazzi, and Edoardo Villata (Florence: Giunti, 2005), 152–54.

26. Carlo Vecce, "Per Caterina," *Leonardiana* 1 (2023): 11–48. For an earlier speculation that Catarina may have been a slave, see Francesco Cianchi, *La madre di Leonardo era una schiava? Ipotesi di studio di Renzo Cianchi* (Vinci: Museo Ideale Leonardo da Vinci, 2008).

27. Anne Leader, "'In the Tomb of Ser Piero': Death and Burial in the Family of Leonardo da Vinci," *Renaissance Studies* 31 (2016): 327.

28. Arrighi, Bellinazzi, and Villata, *Leonardo da Vinci: La vera imagine*, 202; Leader, "'In the Tomb of Ser Piero,'" 330.

29. Codex Atlanticus, c.a. 202 v. a.

30. Nino Smiraglia Scognamiglio, "Nuovi documenti su Leonardo da Vinci," *Archivio storico dell'arte* 2 (1896): 313–15.

31. Brown, *Leonardo da Vinci*, 8.

32. The catalog of the Florence exhibition *Verrocchio: Master of Leonardo*, Florence: Palazzo Strozzi, ed. Andrea de'Marchi and Francesco Cagliotti (Venice: Marsilio, 2019), 108, dates the David to ca. 1468–70; the exhibition catalog *Verrocchio: Sculptor and Painter of Renaissance Florence* (Washington, DC: National Gallery, 2019), 106–10, dates the work to ca. 1460, although with arguments that would support a dating to as late as 1471.

33. Brown, *Leonardo da Vinci*, 8.

34. Gary Radke in *Leonardo and the Art of Sculpture*, exhibition catalog, ed. Gary Radke (New Haven: Yale University Press, 2009), 36. Larry Feinberg, *The Young Leonardo: Art and Life in Fifteenth-Century Florence* (Cambridge: Cambridge University Press, 2011), 60–61, dissents from the identification of the David as a portrait of Leonardo; as he notes, "Verrocchio had many suitable young models from which to choose."

35. Bambach, *Leonardo da Vinci Rediscovered*, 1:196, identifies a perfunctory profile sketch on Windsor RCIN 91442r of a man wearing a *cappuccio* as Lorenzo based on similarities with the polychrome portrait bust in the National Gallery, Washington, DC, a replica dated 1513–20 of a lost wax original from the Verrocchio circle of ca. 1480–85.

36. F. W. Kent, "Patron-Client Networks in Renaissance Florence and the Emergence of Lorenzo as 'Maestro della Bottega,'" in *Lorenzo de' Medici: New Perspectives*, ed. Bernard Toscani (New York: Peter Lang, 1993), 279–81.

37. Dietrich Lohrmann, "The Date of Leonardo da Vinci's Letter to Ludovico Sforza (1489)," *Academia Letters*, May 2022, https://www.academia.edu/81183602/The_date_of_Leonardo_da_Vincis_letter_to_Ludovico_Sforza_1489_.

38. Ben Lewis, *The Last Leonardo: The Secret Lives of the World's Most Expensive Painting* (London: Collins, 2019), 35, writes, "Unlike every other picture Leonardo is widely recognized to have executed, there is no documentary evidence that his hand ever painted the Salvator. That is not in itself an unusual problem for a Renaissance painting." Citing Lewis but omitting the second sentence, Oxford professor of criminology Federico Varese adds, "We are expected to believe that Leonardo painted the greatest subject in Christian art and nobody ever mentioned it, including the author himself, who from time to time used to make an inventory of the paintings in his studio. Arguably, the more important the commission, the more letters and other documentation it would generate: ideally one might find a contract." Varese, "Asset Management: 'Salvator Mundi' and the Unreality of the Art Market," *Times Literary Supplement*, August 19, 2019.

39. The London panel preserves traces, visible in X-ray, of an even earlier composition, which corresponds more closely to the emerging Milanese iconography of the Immaculate Conception. See Francesca Fiorani, "Reflections on Leonardo da Vinci Exhibitions in London and Paris," *Studiolo* 10 (2013): 267–77. On the concealed image in the London panel, the modification of the figure of the angel in the Louvre version, and the indeterminacy of the written and material record, see Vincent Delieuvin in *Léonard de Vinci*, exhibition catalog (Paris: Louvre/Hazan, 2019), 134–35.

40. Scholarship on the workshop has tended to focus on copies and versions rather than membership or organization, and to concentrate on Milan. For a detailed treatment of Leonardo as a teacher, see Bambach, *Leonardo da Vinci Rediscovered*, 3:491–580.

41. See the classic study by Christiane Klapisch-Zuber, "*Parenti, amici, vicini*: Una famiglia mercantile del Quattrocento," *Quaderni storici* 33 (1976): 953–82; also Ronald F. E. Weissman, "The Importance of Being Ambiguous: Social Relations, Individualism, and Identity in Renaissance Florence," in *Urban Life in the Renaissance*, ed. Susan Zimmerman and Ronald F. E. Weissman (Newark: University of Delaware Press, 1989), 269–81.

42. Kathleen Wallace, "You Are a Network," *Aeon*, May 18, 2021; also Wallace, *The Network Self: Relation, Process, and Personal Identity* (New York: Routledge, 2019).

43. On Venturi's *Essai sur les ouvrages physico-mathématiques de Léonard de Vinci*, see Giovanna Perini Folesani, "Leonardo and His Eighteenth-Century Italian Biographies," in *The Lives of Leonardo*, ed. Thomas Frangenberg and Rodney Palmer (London: Warburg Institute, 2013), 106.

44. Margreta de Grazia, *Shakespeare without a Life* (Oxford: Oxford University Press, 2023), 4.

45. The texts by Giovio and the Anonimo are included with other sources including Vasari and Pietro da Novellara in *Lives of Leonardo da*

Vinci, ed. Charles Robertson (Los Angeles: J. Paul Getty Museum, 2019).

46. On the role of decorum, topoi, and received ideas in premodern lives of artists, see Ernst Kris and Otto Kurz, *Legend, Myth, and Magic in the Image of the Artist: A Historical Experiment* (1934; New Haven: Yale University Press, 1981), especially 30–60.

47. Translation in *Lives of Leonardo da Vinci*, ed. Robertson, 117–20. Original text in Carlo Vecce, *Leonardo* (Rome: Salerno, 2006), 555–57.

48. *Lives of Leonardo da Vinci*, ed. Robertson, 117–18.

49. Baldesar Castiglione, *The Book of the Courtier*, ed. and trans. George Bull (1967; London: Penguin, 1976), 149.

50. See the draft of a letter by Leonardo to Giuliano de'Medici, C.A. 182b, in *Literary Works*, 2:338, #1353.

51. These memos can be found among numerous others in *Literary Works*, 2:349ff.

52. Bambach, *Leonardo da Vinci Rediscovered*, 1:72.

53. Quotations from Ghiberti's Second Commentary are from *Italian Art: Sources and Documents, 1400–1500*, ed. Creighton E. Gilbert (Englewood Cliffs, NJ: Prentice Hall, 1980), 76–88.

54. Text and translation in John Pope-Hennessy, *Italian Gothic Sculpture*, 3rd ed. (New York: Phaidon, 1986), 236.

55. Pope-Hennessy, *Italian Gothic Sculpture*, 236.

56. Codex Atlanticus 66r. *Literary Works*, 2:342, #1363; see also the notes on context and dating in *The Literary Works of Leonardo da Vinci Compiled and Edited from the Original Manuscripts by Jean Paul Richter. Commentary* by Carlo Pedretti, 2 vols. (Berkeley: University of California Press, 1977), 2:311.

57. Jacobus de Voragine, *The Golden Legend: Readings on the Saints*, 2 vols., trans. William Granger Ryan (Princeton: Princeton University Press, 1993), 1:229.

58. On this point, see Meyer Schapiro, "Leonardo and Freud: An Art-Historical Study," *Journal of the History of Ideas* 17 (1956): 147–78.

59. Codex Arundel 156r. *Literary Works*, 2:257, #1217, although I am citing the more modern translation in *Leonardo da Vinci: Notebooks*, 257–58. Alberto Collareta, Marco Collareta, Annalisa Berta, and Giovanni Bianucci, "On Leonardo and a Fossil Whale: A Reappraisal with Implications for the Early History of Palaeontology," *Historical Biology* 33, no. 10 (2020): 2294: "Leonardo clearly states that an enormously lengthy period of time must be assumed for explaining the apparent translation of the vertebrate carcass from the seawater column

to its 'new and different habitation,' i.e. the emerged land. Such a consciousness of the depth of geological time, roughly two centuries before Stensen ([*De solido intra solidum naturaliter contento*] 1669) and three centuries before Hutton ([*Theory of the Earth*] 1788), is by all means astonishing."

60. Noted by André Chastel, *Art et humanisme à Florence au temps de Laurent le Magnifique* (Paris: Presses universitaires de France, 1961), 414–16. Although Leonardo never refers directly to Pythagoras, his self-image as a philosopher seems much beholden to Ovid's verse portrait, just as his physical appearance (as portrayed by Melzi) suggests that he sought to resemble images of the bearded philosopher he could have seen in Florence—for instance, in the campanile relief by Luca della Robbia, or in the frontispiece to Filippo Calandri's *Aritmetica* (Florence, 1491). Several books that Leonardo read or owned—by Giorgio Valla, Leon Battista Alberti, Luca Pacioli, Bartolomeo Platina—all evoke the authority of Pythagoras. On the interest in Pythagoras in fifteenth-century Italy, see Christiane L. Joost Gaugier, *Pythagoras and Renaissance Europe: Finding Heaven* (Cambridge: Cambridge University Press, 2009), especially 19–37, 55–123; Christopher S. Celenza, "Pythagoras in the Renaissance: The Case of Marsilio Ficino," *Renaissance Quarterly* 52 (1999): 667–711.

61. Collareta et al., "On Leonardo and a Fossil Whale." See also Kay Etheridge, "Leonardo and the Whale," in *Leonardo da Vinci: Nature and Architecture*, ed. Constance Moffatt and Sara Taglialagamba (Leiden: Brill, 2019), 89–106.

62. F. R. Ankersmit, *Sublime Historical Experience* (Stanford: Stanford University Press, 2005), 101.

63. Leonardo's contemporaries used the word *experimentare* to mean "make a trial of," as in Isabella d'Este's declaration in 1504, "havemo deliberato experimentare novi pictori" (we have decided to try out new painters). See Stephen J. Campbell, *The Cabinet of Eros: Renaissance Mythological Painting and the Studiolo of Isabella d'Este* (New Haven: Yale University Press, 2006), 293–94. For a contemporary philosophical approach calling into question the difference between experience and experiment with regard to the phenomenology of artistic process, see Alva Noë, "Experience and Experiment in Art," *Journal of Consciousness Studies* 7 (2000): 123–35.

64. Windsor, Royal Library, RCIN 919114v; translation from *Leonardo da Vinci: Notebooks*, 325–26.

65. Codex Atlanticus 145b; translation from *Leonardo da Vinci: Notebooks*, 249.

66. Translation in *Leonardo da Vinci: Notebooks*, 316.

67. Windsor, Royal Library 919119v; translation in *Leonardo da Vinci: Notebooks*, 347.

68. John Gagné, *Milan Undone: Contested Sovereignties in the Italian Wars*, I Tatti Studies in Italian Renaissance History (Cambridge, MA: Harvard University Press, 2021), 19.

69. For an account of the Cesare Borgia notebook, see Bambach, *Leonardo da Vinci Rediscovered*, 2:300–312; also Carlo Vecce, *Leonardo* (Rome: Salerno, 2006), 214–17.

70. Codex Atlanticus 247a; translation from *Leonardo da Vinci: Notebooks*, 314; more complete text in *Literary Works*, 2:349, #1379.

71. Gagné, *Milan Undone*, 234.

72. A. Richard Turner makes a similar observation in *Inventing Leonardo* (Berkeley: University of California Press, 1992), 57: "Leonardo did not have the advantage of the history and traditions of one proud place to perpetuate the facts and myths of his life and work."

73. The documents were published in 1896 by Scognamiglio, "Nuovi documenti su Leonardo da Vinci," but were clearly known to earlier scholars who referred obliquely to their contents. For instance, Charles Ravaisson-Mollien, *Les manuscrits de Léonard de Vinci*, 6 vols. (Paris: A. Quantin, 1881–91).

74. For a comprehensive discussion of the documents on Salaì, see Vecce, *Leonardo*, especially 129–34, 217–19.

75. Gian Paolo Lomazzo, *Scritti sulle arti*, ed. Roberto Paolo Ciardi, 2 vols. (Florence: Marchi and Bertolli, 1973–74), 1:104.

76. Lomazzo, *Scritti*, 1:19–21.

77. Carlo Pedretti and Margherita Melani, *Leonardo da Vinci: L'Angelo incarnato & Salaì* (Prato: CB Edizioni, 2011). The drawing, first attributed by Pedretti following its discovery in 1990, is not included in most monographs or catalogs, e.g., Brown, *Leonardo da Vinci*, Bambach, *Leonardo da Vinci Rediscovered*, or Frank Zöllner, *Leonardo da Vinci: The Complete Paintings and Drawings* (Cologne: Taschen, 2011), nor in various publications by Martin Kemp, nor in any of the major Leonardo exhibitions in London (2011), Milan (2015), and Paris (2019). Among biographers, it is accepted by Charles Nicholl, *Leonardo da Vinci: The Flights of the Mind* (London: Penguin, 2004), 469–71; while Isaacson, *Leonardo da Vinci*, 471–72, suggests that the drawing is by an assistant, perhaps Salaì himself, with corrections by Leonardo. Scholars outside the field of Leonardo studies regard the work as a document of Renaissance attitudes to homosexuality and androgyny; see, for instance, James Grantham Turner, *Eros Visible: Art, Sexuality and Antiquity in Renaissance Italy* (New Haven: Yale University Press, 2017), 40–45.

78. Even a scholar as scrupulous as Francesca Fiorani states, "Melzi became Leonardo's lover, replacing Salaì, the other Milanese apprentice, who had once filled that role and was ten years older than Melzi" (*The Shadow Drawing: How Science Taught Leonardo How to Paint* [New York: Farrar, Straus and Giroux, 2020], 233). Vecce, *Leonardo*, 290, posits a "rivalry" between Salaì and Melzi for Leonardo's favor. Bambach remarks, without explanation, "Leonardo's homosexuality can hardly be questioned given his long term friendships with men who never married" (*Leonardo da Vinci Rediscovered*, 1:89).

79. *Leonardo da Vinci: Notebooks*, 363–64.

80. On the poem by Leonico Tomeo, see Giovanni Agosti, *Un amore di Giovanni Bellini* (Milan: Officina Libraria, 2009).

81. John Pope-Hennessy, "Donatello's Bronze David," in *Scritti di storia dell'arte in onore di Federico Zeri* (Milan: Electa, 1984), 122–27. In a discussion that strikes a judicious balance between premodern sexual identities and the homoeroticism of the *David*, Adrian W. B. Randolph, *Engaging Symbols: Gender, Politics, and Public Art in Fifteenth-Century Florence* (New Haven: Yale University Press, 2002), 167, cites more recent instances of denial or refusal of the statue's sexual provocation.

82. Randolph Trumbach, "The Transformation of Sodomy from the Renaissance to the Modern World and Its General Sexual Consequences," *Signs: Journal of Women in Culture and Society* 37 (2012): 833. More recent research has called into question the assertions by Trumbach and others that premodern homosexual relations were exclusively intergenerational; see Umberto Grassi, *Bathhouses and Riverbanks: Sodomy in a Renaissance Republic* (Toronto: Center for Renaissance and Reformation Studies, 2021).

83. Michael Rocke, *Forbidden Friendships: Homosexuality and Male Culture in Renaissance Florence* (Oxford: Oxford University Press, 1996), 115.

84. See, for example, Trevor Dean, "Sodomy in Renaissance Bologna," *Renaissance Studies* 31 (2017): 426–43.

85. The homosexual activity of family members, friends, and their own adolescent selves is a recurring theme of the correspondence between Machiavelli and his friend Francesco Vettori. See Rocke, *Forbidden Friendships*, 114 and passim.

86. Isaacson, *Leonardo da Vinci*, 301.

87. Jules Michelet, *Histoire de France*, 19 vols. (Paris: C. Marpon et E. Flammarion, 1879), 10, *La*

Réforme, 349: "l'objet d'une telle idolatrie, qu'a son age de quatre-vingts ans il changea la mode, fut copie par le roi, et toute la court pour les habits, pour la coupe de barbe et les cheveux."

88. Antonella Campanini, "Vesti, colori, e onore: La scala del rosso," in *Identità cittadina e comportamenti socio-economici tra Medioevo ed Età Moderna*, ed. Paolo Prodi, Maria Giusipina Muzzarelli, and Stefano Simonetta (Bologna: CLUEB, 2001), 145–55. Regarding the Bologna sumptuary laws of 1453, the author points out that certain kinds of rose-colored cloth— depending on the quality—were regarded as less prestigious and allowed to families of craftsmen in the lesser guilds. On crimson and scarlet hues at court, see Timothy McCall, *Brilliant Bodies: Fashioning Courtly Men in Early Renaissance Italy* (University Park: Penn State University Press, 2022), 40–41.

89. Machiavelli, *Istorie fiorentine*, in *Opere*, ed. Mario Bonfantini (Milan: Ricciardi, 1963), 883; English translation, *Florentine Histories*, ed. and trans. Laura F. Banfield and Harvey C. Mansfield (Princeton: Princeton University Press, 1988), 283.

90. See Giorgione's portrait of a young man (Vienna, Kunsthistorisches Museum) and Giovanni Battista Moroni's full-length portrait of the Brescian noble Giovanni Girolamo Grumelli (Bergamo, Fondazione Moroni).

91. Nicholl, *Leonardo da Vinci*, 438–43. Bossi's attestation is however supported by Carlo Pedretti, "Li Medici mi crearono e destrussono," *Achademia Leonardi Vinci* 6 (1993): 174–84, Vecce, *Leonardo*, 317, and Valter Boggione, "Leonardo e il lessico erotico," in *Leonardo da Vinci e la lingua della pittura in Europa (secoli XIV–XVII)*, ed. Margherita Quaglino and Anna Sconza (Florence: Olschki, 2022), 87.

92. Paris MS H. Jean Paul Richter, *The Literary Works of Leonardo da Vinci*, 2 vols. (1883; London: Phaidon, 1970), 2:265, #1234: "The bat, owing to unbridled lust, observes no universal rule in pairing, but males with males and females with females pair promiscuously, as they chance to find themselves together."

93. Windsor RCIN 919009. See Kenneth D. Keele and Carlo Pedretti, *Leonardo da Vinci: Corpus of the Anatomical Drawings in the Collection of Her Majesty the Queen at Windsor Castle*, 2 vols. (London: Johnson Reprint Co., 1979–80), 143r; also Keele, *Leonardo da Vinci's Elements of the Science of Man* (New York: Academic Press, 1983), 350.

94. *Leonardo on Painting*, 228.

95. As proposed by Bambach, *Leonardo da Vinci Rediscovered*, 3:340. For the argument that

Leonardo's approach to science changed arising from a sense of the limits of human knowledge and the complexity of nature, leading him to confront a boundary between the knowledge of nature and knowledge of God and the soul, see Martin Kemp, "Dissection and Divinity in Leonardo's Late Anatomies," *Journal of the Warburg and Courtauld Institutes* 35 (1972): 200–225.

96. Richter, *Literary Works*, 2:168, #986.

97. Windsor, Royal Library, RCIN 919084. *The Notebooks of Leonardo da Vinci*, ed. and trans. Edward MacCurdy, 2 vols. (New York: Reynal and Hitchcock, 1938), 1:90.

98. Richter, *Literary Works*, 2:306, #1303. On iconophagy and its condemnation as idolatry by Eastern and Western religious authorities, see Jérémie Koering, *Les iconophages: Une histoire de l'ingestion des images* (Paris: Actes Sud, 2021), especially 177–80, referring to a 1507 prosecution for sorcery at Innsbruck of one Peter Wenbrenner for grinding and eating a statue of St. Christopher.

99. Kenneth Clark, *Leonardo da Vinci: An Account of His Development as an Artist* (Cambridge: Cambridge University Press, 1939), 83–84.

100. François Quiviger, *Leonardo da Vinci: Self, Art and Nature* (London: Reaktion, 2019), 64–68.

101. Ernst Gombrich, "Leonardo and the Magicians: Polemics and Rivalry" (1982), in *New Light on Old Masters* (London: Phaidon, 1986), 67.

102. See, for example, Giovanni Gioviano Pontano, *Dialogues: Volume I, Charon and Antonius*, ed. and trans. Julia Haig Gaisser (Cambridge, MA: Harvard University Press, 2012), 231.

103. *Leonardo on Painting*, 20.

104. See Marco Beretta, "Leonardo and Lucretius," *Rinascimento* 49 (2010): 341–72; Alison M. Brown, "*Natura Idest*? Leonardo, Lucretius, and Their Views of Nature," in *Leonardo da Vinci on Nature: Knowledge and Representation*, ed. Fabio Frosini and Alessandro Nova (Venice: Marsilio, 2013), 153–79.

105. Lucretius, *De rerum natura*, with a translation by W.H.D. Rouse (1975; Cambridge, MA: Harvard University Press, 1992), 143.

106. British Museum, Codex Arundel 155b; Richter, *Literary Works*, 2:257–58, #1218.

107. British Museum, Codex Arundel 155b; Richter, *Literary Works*, 2:257–58, #1218.

108. Codex Urbinas 38v; *Leonardo on Painting*, 195.

109. See the discussion in Christopher S. Celenza, "Orthodoxy: Lorenzo Valla and Marsilio Ficino," in *The Lost Italian Renaissance: Humanists, Historians, and Latin's Legacy* (Baltimore: Johns Hopkins University Press, 2004), 80–115.

110. Richter, *Literary Works*, 2:389–91, #1566.

111. Julia Vicioso, *Leonardo da Vinci e la Nazione Fiorentina a Roma* (Rome: GBE, 2019), 139. Jan Sammer, *Leonardo da Vinci: The Untold Story of His Final Years* (independently published, 2019), 57, points out that Leonardo, who never paid his membership fee and was suspended following a one-year grace period, was absent during his election and induction as a member: "The fact that Leonardo did not reapply within this grace period is consistent with the conclusion that he never intended to join the confraternity in the first place."

112. Vasari, *Vite*, 1550: "E tanti furono i suoi capricci, che filosofando de le cose naturali, attese a intendere la proprietà delle erbe, continuando et osservando il moto del cielo, il corso de la luna e gli andamenti del sole. Per il che fece ne l'animo un concetto sì eretico, che e' non si accostava a qualsivoglia religione, stimando per avventura assai più lo esser filosofo che cristiano."

113. As noted by Beretta, "Leonardo and Lucretius," 349.

114. Richter, *Literary Works*, 2:288, #1284.

115. Lettera di Andrea Corsali allo Illustrissimo Signore Duca Iuliano de Medici, Venuta dell'India del Mese di Octobre nel MDXVI, Stampato in Firenze per Io. Stephano di Carlo da Pavia adì XI di Dicembre nel MDXVI, ff. 6. Cited in *Literary Works*, 2:102n. and discussed in Carlo Vecce, "In margine alla prima lettera di Andrea Corsali (Leonardo in India)," in *Ai confini della letteratura: Atti della giornata in onore di Mario Pozzi*, ed. Jean Louis Fournel et al. (Turin: Nino Aragno, 2015), 67–81.

116. On Duarte Barbosa and Diego de Orta, see Edward Wilson-Lee, *A History of Water* (London: HarperCollins, 2022), 300. While *The Book of Duarte Barbosa* was only published in 1812, Wilson-Lee demonstrates its wide circulation among European travelers to Asia in the 1500s.

117. Richter, *Literary Works*, 2:383–85, #1544–50.

118. Windsor, Royal Library, RCIN 912613; see also RCIN 919077, a sheet dated January 9, 1513, for drawings made from the dissection of a dog.

119. Richter, *Literary Works*, 2:103–4, #844.

120. For the proposal that Leonardo is referring to the Spanish in the New World, see Joost Keizer, *Leonardo's Paradox: Word and Image in the Making of Renaissance Culture* (London: Reaktion, 2019), 70.

121. Amerigo Vespucci, quoted in Richter, *Literary Works*, 2:104n5–18.

122. Paula Findlen et al., *Leonardo's Library: The World of a Renaissance Reader* (Stanford: Stanford Libraries, 2019), 165.

123. Celenza, "Orthodoxy," 107–8; on Ficino and the consumption of human blood, see also Piero Camporesi, *Bread of Dreams: Food and Fantasy in Early Modern Europe* (Chicago: University of Chicago Press, 1989), 40–55.

124. Milan, Biblioteca Trivulziana, Codex Trivulzianus fols. 2–3. See Bambach, *Leonardo da Vinci Rediscovered*, 1:458–59; illustrated 2:11.

Chapter 3: Leonardo and the Biographers

1. Giorgio Vasari, *Lives of the Painters, Sculptors, and Architects*, trans. Gaston de Vere, 2 vols. (1927; London: Everyman's Library, 1996), 2:639.

2. Vasari, *Lives of the Painters*, 2:639.

3. See the entry on the painting—which was not the first treatment of the subject—by Paola Cordera, in *Leonardo da Vinci's Last Supper for Francois I: A Masterpiece in Gold and Silk*, ed. Pietro C. Marani (Milan: Skira, 2019), 214.

4. Giovanni Battista Venturi, *Essai sur les ouvrages physico-mathématiques de Léonard de Vinci* (1797); and the discussion in Giovanna Perini Folesani, "Leonardo and His Eighteenth-Century Italian Biographies," in *The Lives of Leonardo*, ed. Thomas Frangenberg and Rodney Palmer (London: Warburg Institute, 2013), 105–6.

5. Théophile Gautier, *Guide de l'amateur au musée du Louvre* [1867]; English version: *The Works of Théophile Gautier*, 21 vols., trans. Frederick Cesar de Sumichrast (London: Athenaeum Society, 1901), 9:255.

6. Jules Michelet, *Histoire de France*, 19 vols. (Paris: C. Marpon et E. Flammarion, 1879), 10, *La Réforme*, 90.

7. Edgar Quinet, *Les révolutions d'Italie* (Paris: Pagnerre, 1857), 350–51. For a useful account of Quinet and of nineteenth-century cultural politics around Leonardo, see A. Richard Turner, *Inventing Leonardo* (Berkeley: University of California Press, 1992), 102–13.

8. Jacob Burckhardt, *The Civilization of the Renaissance in Italy*, trans. S.G.C. Middlemore (London: Penguin Books, 1990), 104.

9. Théophile Gautier, *Italia* (Paris: Victor Lecou, 1852); English version: *Journeys in Italy*, trans. Daniel B. Vermilye (London: Brentano's, 1902), 71.

10. Michelet, *Histoire de France*, 9:88–89. On Michelet, Quinet, and Taine, see also Barrie Bullen, "Walter Pater's *Renaissance* and Leonardo da Vinci's Reputation in the Nineteenth Century," *Modern Language Review* 74 (1979): 268–80; and Turner, *Inventing Leonardo*, 102–13.

11. Hippolyte Taine, *Voyage en Italie* (1869; Paris: Hachette et Cie, 1874), 409.

12. Arsène Houssaye, *Histoire de Léonard de Vinci* (Paris: Libraire Académique Didier et

Cie, 1869), 96. See also Marc Gotlieb, "Our Monstrous Double: The Dream of Research in 'Outsider Art History,'" in *What Is Research in the Visual Arts? Obsession, Archive, Encounter*, ed. Michael Ann Holly and Marquard Smith (New Haven: Yale University Press, 2008), 85–102.

13. Houssaye, *Histoire de Léonard de Vinci*, 226: "Il avait toute l'étoffe d'un grand penseur, mais tout le Coeur d'un grand croyant. La nature en lui n'a pas masque les derniers symbols de la grandeur de Dieu. A force de s'éloigner de Dieu, on y revient. Les tableaux de Léonard sont des confessions. Son testament a eté pour Dieu. On a parler de son repentir, a l'heure dernièr. Je voudrai connaitre les péchés du Vinci."

14. Citation from the final edition of four. Walter Pater, *The Renaissance: Studies in Art and Poetry* (1893; Mineola, NY: Dover, 2005), 68. On Pater's Leonardo, see also Bullen, "Walter Pater's *Renaissance*," and Lene Østermark-Johansen, "The Power of an Intimate Presence: Walter Pater's Leonardo Essay (1869) and Its Influence at the *fin de siècle*," in *Leonardo in Britain: Collections and Historical Reception*, ed. Juliana Barone and Susanna Avery-Quash (Florence: Olschki, 2019), 303–23.

15. Pater, *The Renaissance*, 72.

16. Pater, *The Renaissance*, 78.

17. *Collected Works of Paul Valéry*, vol. 15: *Moi*, trans. Marthiel and Jackson Mathews (Princeton: Princeton University Press, 1975), 8.

18. The Leonardo MSS from the Bibliotheque de l'Institut de France were published in facsimile and transcriptions with translations by Charles Ravaisson-Mollien, *Les manuscrits de Léonard de Vinci*, 6 vols. (Paris: A. Quantin, 1881–91); the Codex Atlanticus was published as *Il Codice atlantico di Leonardo da Vinci nella Biblioteca ambrosiana di Milano* (Milan: U. Hoepli, 1894–1904).

19. *Collected Works of Paul Valéry*, vol. 8: *Leonardo, Poe, Mallarme*, trans. M. Cowley and James R. Lawler (Princeton: Princeton University Press, 2015), 48.

20. *Collected Works of Paul Valéry*, 8:21.

21. *Collected Works of Paul Valéry*, 8:7–8.

22. Dmitry Merezhkovsky, *Leonardo da Vinci: The Resurrection of the Gods*, trans. Ignat Avsey (London: Alma Classics, 2014 [original Russian edition, 1900]), 370.

23. Sigmund Freud, *Leonardo da Vinci and a Memory of His Childhood*, trans. Alan Tyson (New York: Norton, 1961), 30, 60.

24. Bernard Berenson, "Leonardo," in *The Study and Criticism of Italian Art*, 3rd ser. (London: Bell, 1916), 1–37.

25. On Berenson's artistic personalities, see Jeremy Melius, "Connoisseurship, Painting, and Personhood," *Art History* 34 (2011): 288–309.

26. Berenson, "Leonardo," 10.

27. Berenson, "Leonardo," 11.

28. Berenson, "Leonardo," 5.

29. Berenson, "Leonardo," 32.

30. Kenneth Clark, *Leonardo da Vinci: An Account of His Development as an Artist* (Cambridge: Cambridge University Press, 1939; edition cited Harmondsworth: Penguin Books, 1982), 18. See the illuminating essay by Francesca Fiorani, "Kenneth Clark and Leonardo: From Connoisseurship to Broadcasting to Digital Technologies," in *Leonardo in Britain: Collections and Historical Reception*, ed. Juliana Barone and Susanna Avery-Quash (Florence: Olschki, 2019), 353–77.

31. Clark, *Leonardo da Vinci*, 20.

32. Clark, *Leonardo da Vinci*, 58–59. He adds, "And those who wish, in the interest of morality, to reduce Leonardo, that inexhaustible source of creative power, to a neutral or sexless agency, have a strange idea of doing service to his reputation."

33. Clark, *Leonardo da Vinci*, 159.

34. Clark, *Leonardo da Vinci*, 159.

35. Exhibition program, *Mostra di Leonardo da Vinci e delle Invenzioni italiane* (Milan, 1939). See Claudio Giorgione, "The Birth of a Collection in Milan: From the Leonardo Exhibition of 1939 to the Opening of the National Museum of Science and Technology in 1953," *Science Museum Group Journal* 4 (2015), https://journal.sciencemuseum.ac.uk/article/leonardo-exhibition-of-1939/; Roberto Cara, "La mostra di Leonardo da Vinci a Milano tra arte, scienza e politica," in *All'origine delle grandi mostre in Italia (1933–1940)*, ed. Marcello Toffanello (Mantua: Il Rio Editore, 2017), 137–60.

36. V. P. Zubov, *Leonardo da Vinci*, trans. David H. Kraus, with a foreword by Myron P. Gilmore (Cambridge, MA: Harvard University Press, 1968). For the negative assessment of Leonardo's place in the history of science, see, for example, John Herman Randall Jr., "The Place of Leonardo Da Vinci in the Emergence of Modern Science," *Journal of the History of Ideas* 14 (1953): 193: "there is not discoverable, in Leonardo's Codici, a single theoretical scientific idea that is essentially new, or that was unknown in the organized scientific schools in Italy in his day. . . . Even if Leonardo had original ideas in scientific theory, he would still have no 'place' in and would have exerted no 'influence' on, the emergence of modern science."

37. The "Aristotelian Leonardo" had been most influentially analyzed by Pierre Duhem, *Études sur Léonard de Vinci*, 3 vols. (Paris: A. Hermann, 1906–13).

38. See the two essays in Ernst Gombrich, *The Heritage of Apelles: Studies in the Art of the Renaissance* (Ithaca: Cornell University Press, 1976) appearing under the heading "Leonardo da Vinci's Method of Analysis and Permutation": "The Grotesque Heads," 57–75, and "The Form of Movement in Water and Air," 39–56.

39. Martin Kemp, *Leonardo da Vinci: The Marvelous Works of Nature and Man* (London: J. M. Dent, 1981; rev. ed., Oxford: Oxford University Press, 2006), xvii.

40. Martin Kemp, *Leonardo* (Oxford: Oxford University Press, 2004).

41. Daniel Arasse, *Leonardo da Vinci: The Rhythm of the World* (Old Saybrook, CT: Konecky, 1998; original edition, Paris: Hazan, 1997), 14.

42. Arasse, *Leonardo da Vinci*, 88.

43. Matthew Landrus, "This Was the Most Prolific Year for Leonardo Scholarship in History—Here Is a Detailed Guide to the Best Books," *Art Newspaper*, December 20, 2019.

44. Based on a survey of titles published during 1994–2021 including books by Pascal Brioist, Martin Kemp, Carlo Vecce, Serge Bramly, Charles Nicholl, Ross King, Stefan Klein, Francesca Fiorani, Henning Klüver, Klaus-Rüdiger Mai, Sherwin B. Nuland, Jean-Pierre Isbouts and Christopher Heath Brown, Larry Feinberg, Antonio Forcellino, Valentina Fortichiari, Walter Isaacson, Michael White, Mike Lankford, Carmine Mastroiani, François Quiviger, Jan Sammer, Leonard Shlain, Bernd Roeck, Volker Reinhardt, Kia Vahland, Julia Vicioso, and Boris von Brauchitsch.

45. Respectively, Sherwin Nuland; Leonard Shlain; Antonio Forcellino; Michael White; Mark Lankford; Walter Isaacson.

46. Serge Bramly, *Léonard de Vinci* (Paris: éditions Lattès, 1988 [English edition trans. Sian Reynolds, London: HarperCollins, 1991]); Charles Nicholl, *Leonardo da Vinci: The Flights of the Mind* (London: Penguin, 2004).

47. Publisher's description of Mike Lankford, *Becoming Leonardo: An Exploded View of the Life of Leonardo da Vinci* (New York: Melville House, 2017).

48. Michael White, *Leonardo: The First Scientist* (New York: St. Martin's Press, 2001), jacket copy.

49. Christopher Heath Brown and Jean-Pierre Isbouts, *The Young Leonardo: The Evolution of a Revolutionary Artist, 1472–1499* (New York: St. Martin's Press, 2017).

50. Brown and Isbouts, *The Young Leonardo*, 19.

51. Brown and Isbouts, *The Young Leonardo*, 52–53.

52. Brown and Isbouts, *The Young Leonardo*, 67.

53. William St. Clair, "The Biographer as Archaeologist," in *Mapping Lives: The Uses of Biography*, ed. Peter Frane and William St. Clair (Oxford: Oxford University Press, 2002), 219–35 (223–24).

54. St. Clair, "The Biographer as Archaeologist," 225–26.

55. Scott E. Casper, *Constructing American Lives: Biography and Culture in Nineteenth-Century America* (Chapel Hill: University of North Carolina Press, 1999), 323.

56. Janet Malcolm, *The Silent Woman: Sylvia Plath and Ted Hughes* (New York: Vintage Books, 1993), 9.

57. Lankford, *Becoming Leonardo*, 57–58.

58. Walter Isaacson, *Leonardo da Vinci* (New York: Simon and Schuster, 2017), 6.

59. Isaacson, *Leonardo da Vinci*, 9.

60. On the corporate university and the appropriation of interdisciplinarity, see Jerry A. Jacobs, *In Defense of Disciplines: Interdisciplinarity and Specialization in the Research University* (Chicago: University of Chicago Press, 2013), as well as Jonathan Kramnick, "The Interdisciplinary Fallacy," *Representations* 140 (2017): 67–83.

61. Nancy C. Andreasen, *The Creating Brain: The Neuroscience of Genius* (New York: Dana Press, 2005).

62. Isaacson, *Leonardo da Vinci*, 2–5.

63. Isaacson, *Leonardo da Vinci*, 522.

64. Isaacson, *Leonardo da Vinci*, 4.

65. Isaacson, *Leonardo da Vinci*, 395.

Chapter 4: The Shape of Premodern Lives

1. For debates on the Renaissance self after Burckhardt, see Hans Baron, "The Limits of the Notion 'Renaissance Individualism': Burckhardt after a Century," in *In Search of Florentine Civic Humanism: Essays on the Transition from Medieval to Modern Thought* (Princeton: Princeton University Press, 1988), 2:155–81; Samuel Cohn, "Burckhardt Revisited from Social History," in *Language and Images of Renaissance Italy*, ed. Alison Brown (Oxford: Oxford University Press, 1995), 217–34. A key revisionist text on Renaissance selfhood is Natalie Zemon Davis, *The Return of Martin Guerre* (Cambridge, MA: Harvard University Press, 1982). Recent critiques of the individualist and modernist accounts of the Renaissance that locate themselves in Burckhardt's (far more dystopian) conception include Rebecca Zorach, *The Passionate Triangle* (Chicago: University of Chicago Press, 2011), 1–27, and Stephen J. Campbell, *The Cabinet of*

Eros: Renaissance Mythological Painting and the Studiolo of Isabella d'Este (New Haven: Yale University Press, 2006), 39–57.

2. On Restoro: Maria Monica Donato, "Un 'savio depentor' fra 'scienza de le stelle' e 'sutilità' dell'antico: Restoro d'Arezzo, le arti e il sarcofago romano di Cortona," *Annali della Scuola Normale Superiore di Pisa* 4 (1996): 51–78; Ivano del Prete, *On the Edge of Eternity: The Antiquity of the Earth in Medieval and Early Modern Europe* (Oxford: Oxford University Press, 2022), 69–76, with discussion on his influence in the 1400s.

3. Restoro d'Arezzo, *La composizione del mondo*, II.1.2.78. From the edition by Alberto Morino (Parma: Ugo Guanda, 1997), 78.

4. del Prete, *On the Edge of Eternity*, 72–73.

5. See James Amelang, *The Flight of Icarus: Artisan Autobiography in Early Modern Europe* (Stanford: Stanford University Press, 1998); Pamela H. Smith, *The Body of the Artisan: Art and Experience in the Scientific Revolution* (Chicago: University of Chicago Press, 2004), 95–129; Pamela O. Long, *Artisan/Practitioners and the Rise of the New Sciences, 1400–1600* (Corvallis: Oregon State University Press, 2011).

6. Francesca Fiorani, *The Shadow Drawing: How Science Taught Leonardo How to Paint* (New York: Farrar, Straus and Giroux, 2020), 47–50.

7. Fiorani, *The Shadow Drawing*, 44–47.

8. Angelo Poliziano, *Detti piacevoli*, ed. Tiziano Zanato (Rome: Istituto della Enciclopedia Italiana, 1983), 83, 84, 99.

9. Lauro Martines, *An Italian Renaissance Sextet: Six Tales in Historical Context*, with translations by Murtha Baca (New York: Marsilio, 1994), 171–72.

10. Adapted from translations with original texts in Rinaldina Russel, *Sonnet: The Very Rich and Varied World of the Italian Sonnet* (Bloomington, IN: Archway, 2017), 156–59. See also *Sonetti di Filippo Brunelleschi*, introduction by Giuliano Tanturli and notes by Domenico de Robertis (Florence: Accademia della Crusca, 1977), 21–22.

11. "Ha più inventione e sa bozzare più che finire, ordire più che essere paziente a tesserae." Francesco Caglioti, "Il David bronzeo di Donatello," in *Donatello: Il David restaurato*, exhibition catalog, ed. Beatrice Paolozzi Strozzi (Florence: Museo Nazionale del Bargello, 2008), 26–85 (83n2).

12. RCIN Windsor 919048; translation from *The Literary Works of Leonardo da Vinci*, ed. J. P. Richter, rev. ed. with Irma Richter, 2 vols. (1939; London: Phaidon, 1970), 2:252–53. See also Ernst Gombrich, "Leonardo and the

Magicians: Polemics and Rivalry" (1982), in *New Light on Old Masters* (London: Phaidon, 1986), 61–89.

13. *The Poetry of Burchiello: Deep-Fried Nouns, Hunchbacked Pumpkins, and Other Nonsense*, ed. and trans. Fabian Alfie and Aileen A. Feng (Tempe, AZ: ACMRS, 2017), 103–5.

14. Paula Findlen et al., *Leonardo's Library: The World of a Renaissance Reader* (Stanford: Stanford Libraries, 2019), 184. On Florentine artists and vernacular literature, see Christina Neilson, *Practice and Theory in the Italian Renaissance Workshop: Verrocchio and the Epistemology of Making Art* (Cambridge: Cambridge University Press, 2019), 25–34.

15. Full original text and translation of the letter in Alison M. Brown and Alessandro Parronchi, "The Language of Humanism and the Language of Sculpture: Bertoldo as Illustrator of the *Apologi* of Bartolomeo Scala," *Journal of the Warburg and Courtauld Institutes* 27 (1964): 130–31.

16. Luciano Patetta, "Bramante autore di sonetti burleschi," in *Bramante e la sua cerchia: A Milano e in Lombardia 1480–1500*, ed. Luciano Patetta (Milan: Electa, 2009), 77–81 (78).

17. Translation and original text of Alberti's *Vita* in Leon Battista Alberti, *Biographical and Autobiographical Writings*, trans. Martin McLaughlin (Cambridge, MA: Harvard University Press, 2023), 213–49. For analyses, see Michael Baxandall, "Alberti's Cast of Mind," in *Words for Pictures* (New Haven: Yale University Press, 2003), 27–39, and Anthony Grafton, *Leon Battista Alberti: Master Builder of the Italian Renaissance* (Cambridge, MA: Harvard University Press, 2002), 17–29.

18. Alberti, *Biographical and Autobiographical Writings*, 243.

19. Alberti, *Biographical and Autobiographical Writings*, 213, 215.

20. Alberti, *Biographical and Autobiographical Writings*, 215.

21. "Pinguiore idcirco, ut aiunt, Minerva scribendo utemur." Leon Battista Alberti, *On Painting and On Sculpture*, ed. and trans. Cecil Grayson (London: Phaidon, 1972), 36, 37, renders this "we [unlike mathematicians who contemplate form with the mind alone] will express ourselves in cruder terms."

22. Rebecca Zorach, "Fat Minerva: Recent Books on Perspective and *Perspectiva*, Medieval and Renaissance," *Exemplaria* 23 (2011): 415–25; also Zorach, *The Passionate Triangle*, 27–38, 134–38; and Franco Bacchelli, "Un frammento inedito di Leon Battista Alberti sul fuoco." *Noctua* 7 (2020):1–67.

23. Leon Battista Alberti, *Momus*, ed. Virginia Brown and Sarah Knight (Cambridge, MA: Harvard University Press, 2003), 309.

24. Richard Krautheimer, *Lorenzo Ghiberti* (Princeton: Princeton University Press, 1983), 230–31.

25. Alberti, *Momus*, 311.

26. Latin text of Pico's oration at https://www.brown.edu/Departments/Italian_Studies/pico/oratio.html, section 5. English translation by Elizabeth Gilmore Forbes in *The Renaissance Philosophy of Man*, ed. Ernst Cassirer, Paul Oskar Kristeller, and John Herman Randall Jr. (Chicago: University of Chicago Press, 1948), 223–57.

27. On melancholy and geometry: Zorach, *The Passionate Triangle*, 118–27; Mitchell B. Merback, *Perfection's Therapy: An Essay on Albrecht Dürer's Melancolia I* (New York: Zone Books, 2017), 53–62.

28. Codex Arundel 156r. *Literary Works*, 2:257, #1217.

29. Codex Atlanticus 76b. *Literary Works*, 2:105, #847; see also 104, #845; 245, #1178, #1179.

30. *The Literary Works of Leonardo da Vinci Compiled and Edited from the Original Manuscripts by Jean Paul Richter. Commentary* by Carlo Pedretti, 2 vols. (Berkeley: University of California Press, 1977), 2:113 (supplement to Richter's #843).

31. Codex Atlanticus 126v. Richter, *Literary Works*, 2:249, #1203. Translation cited here from *The Notebooks of Leonardo da Vinci*, ed. and trans. Edward MacCurdy, 2 vols. (New York: Reynal and Hitchcock, 1938), 2:418.

32. Richter, *Literary Works*, 1:362–64, #628, #630, #639.

33. Paris MS H. Translation modified from Richter, *Literary Works*, 2:258, #1219.

34. Codex Urbinas 22r–v. *Leonardo on Painting*, selected and edited by Martin Kemp and Margaret Walker (New Haven: Yale University Press, 1989), 38–39.

35. For the original and an Italian translation, see Pomponio Gaurico, *De sculptura*, ed. Paolo Cutolo (Naples: Edizioni Scientifiche Italiane, 1999), 226. The passage is briefly discussed by Smith, *The Body of the Artisan*, 81.

36. Smith, *The Body of the Artisan*, 82.

37. On the preoccupation with bodily experience in Pontormo's personal journal and its significance for an understanding of Pontormo's late painting, see Philip L. Sohm, *The Artist Grows Old: The Aging of Art and Artists in Early Modern Italy* (New Haven: Yale University Press, 2007), 105–30.

38. See Nancy Struever, "Petrarch's Invective *Contra Medicum*: An Early Confrontation of Rhetoric and Medicine," *MLN* 108 (1993): 659–79.

39. Further discussion in Stephen J. Campbell, *Cosmè Tura of Ferrara: Style, Politics and the Renaissance City* (New Haven: Yale University Press, 1996), 52–53.

40. Translation adapted from Cennino Andrea Cennini, *The Craftsman's Handbook: Il Libro dell'Arte*, trans. Daniel V. Thompson Jr. (New York: Dover, 1960), 1–2.

41. Text in Carlo Dionisotti, "Leonardo uomo di lettere," *Italia medioevale e umanistica* 5 (1962): 209.

42. See the account in Monica Azzolini, "Anatomy of a Dispute: Leonardo, Pacioli and Scientific Courtly Entertainment in Renaissance Milan," *Early Science and Medicine* 9 (2004): 115–35. On Pacioli as author and mathematician, see Arielle Saiber, *Measured Words: Computation and Writing in Renaissance Italy* (Toronto: University of Toronto Press, 2017), 49–107.

43. Michele Savonarola, *Libellus De magnificis ornamentis regie civitatis Padue Michaelis Savonarole*, ed. Arnaldo Segarizzi, Rerum Italicarum Scriptores, XXIV–XXV (Città di Castello, Editore S. Lapi, 1902).

44. Codex Urbinas 5r; translation in *Leonardo on Painting*, 13.

45. As noted by Azzolini, "Anatomy of a Dispute," 124.

46. Codex Urbinas 5r; translation in *Leonardo on Painting*, 20–21.

47. Codex Urbinas 9r; translation in *Leonardo on Painting*, 34.

48. Codex Urbinas 8r; translation in Richter, *Literary Works*, 1:57, #23.

49. Codex Urbinas 5or; translation in *Leonardo on Painting*, 16.

50. Codex Urbinas 12v; translation in *Leonardo on Painting*, 46.

51. Codex Urbinas 15v; translation in *Leonardo on Painting*, 46.

52. Codex Urbinas 21v; translation in Richter, *Literary Works*, 1:93, #38.

53. Leonardo da Vinci, *Trattato della pittura*, ed. Guglielmo Manzi and Giovanni Gherardo de Rossi (Rome: Nella Stamperia de Romanis, 1817).

54. James Beck, *Leonardo's Rules of Painting: An Unconventional Approach to Modern Art* (New York: Viking, 1979).

55. Codex Urbinas 12v; translation (modified) from Richter, *Literary Works*, 1:63.

56. Codex Urbinas 18v; *Leonardo on Painting*, 37–38.

57. Translation quoted here from Carmen C. Bambach, *Leonardo da Vinci Rediscovered*, 4 vols. (New Haven: Yale University Press, 2019), 3:307.

58. On Barbaro's *Orationes contra poetas*, see Stephen J. Campbell, *Andrea Mantegna: Humanist Aesthetics, Faith, and the Force of Images* (Turnhout: Brepols/Harvey Miller, 2020), 182–85.

59. William Marx, *The Hatred of Literature* (Cambridge, MA: Harvard University Press, 2018), 32.

60. Marx, *The Hatred of Literature*, 94.

61. Martin Kemp, "Mirror of His Mind: The Codex in Leonardo's Thought," in *Leonardo da Vinci's Codex Leicester: A New Edition*, ed. Domenico Laurenza and Martin Kemp, vol. 2: *Interpretive Essays and the History of the Codex Leicester* (Oxford: Oxford University Press, 2019), 21. The word list in Madrid Codex I, 71v–72r was also discussed in Ernst Gombrich, "The Form of Movement in Water and Air," in *The Heritage of Apelles* (Ithaca: Cornell University Press, 1976), 39–56.

62. Gombrich, "The Form of Movement," 44.

63. The "cascading" effect of Leonardo's language when writing about water is noted by Kemp, "Mirror of His Mind," 21.

64. Marx, *Hatred of Literature*, 37.

65. Petrarch, *On His Own Ignorance and That of Many Others*, in *Francesco Petrarca: Invectives*, ed. and trans. David Marsh (Cambridge, MA: Harvard University Press, 2003), 233.

66. On "low" style and authenticity, see Amelang, *The Flight of Icarus*, 155–64. On the artisanal rhetoric of witnessing, despite the frequent tendency to incorporate preexisting accounts, see 145–50.

67. Codex Atlanticus 119v; translation in Richter, *Literary Works*, 1:116–17.

68. Claire Farago, *Leonardo da Vinci's Paragone: A Critical Interpretation with a New Edition of the Text of the Codex Urbinas* (Leiden: Brill, 1992), 200–201, but incorporating revisions by Frank Fehrenbach, "The Cycle of Images," in *Leonardo and Nature*, ed. Fabio Frosini and Alessandro Nova (Venice: Marsilio, 2015), 208–9.

69. Fehrenbach, "The Cycle of Images," 213: "Leonardo's cohabitation of *sensus communis* and imagination . . . mirrors the general tendency of Renaissance psychology to reduce the sophisticated scholastic differentiations of the faculties of the soul." See also Martin Kemp, "From Mimesis to Fantasia: The Quattrocento Vocabulary of Creation, Inspiration and Genius in the Visual Arts," *Viator* 8 (1977): 347–98.

70. Codex Urbinas 31r–v; *Leonardo on Painting*, 197.

71. Bernard Berenson, "Leonardo," in *The Study and Criticism of Italian Art*, 3rd ser. (London: Bell, 1916), 15.

72. Paul Barolsky, "The Mysterious Meaning of Leonardo's *Saint John the Baptist*," *Source: Notes in the History of Art* 8 (1989): 11–15.

73. On the painting as a visual exegesis of the "Magi" passages in Isaiah, see Frank Fehrenbach, *Licht und Wasser: Zur Dynamik naturphiloso-phischer Leitbilder im Werk Leonardo da Vincis* (Tübingen: Wasmuth, 1997); see also Bambach, *Leonardo da Vinci Rediscovered*, 1:247.

74. On possible borrowings from Botticelli, see Michael W. Kwakkelstein, "Did Leonardo Always Practice What He Preached? Discrepancies between Leonardo's Didactic Views on Painting and His Artistic Practice," in *"Proxima Studia": Arte e letteratura a Firenze (1300–1600)*, ed. Stefano Ugo Baldassarri (Florence: Fabrizio Serra Editore, 2011), 107–36.

75. On symbolic or mystical geometry and its role in Renaissance religious pictures, see Zorach, *The Passionate Triangle*. On Leonardo and analogy, see Daniel Arasse, *Leonardo da Vinci: The Rhythm of the World* (Old Saybrook, CT: Konecky, 1998; original edition, Paris: Hazan, 1997), 73–98, especially 82.

76. Codex Atlanticus 203r. MacCurdy, *Notebooks*, 1:70.

77. Listed in Madrid Codex II, fol. 3r. See Findlen et al., *Leonardo's Library*, 186.

78. Codex Atlanticus 58r. First identified by Carlo Pedretti, "The Ravenna Monster," in *Leonardo da Vinci Codex Atlanticus: A Catalogue of Its Newly Restored Sheets* (Florence: Giunti, 1979), 307–17. See, however, Lorenzo Montemagno Cisneri, "Leonardo da Vinci, the Genius and the Monsters: Casual Encounters?" *Medicina nei Secoli, Arte e Scienza/Journal of History of Medicine* 26 (2014): 92–97. The author disputes the connection proposed by Pedretti with the "Monster of Ravenna," a monstrous birth held to predict the Battle of Ravenna in 1512, citing closer parallels with a Florentine abnormal birth recorded by the Venetian diarist Marin Sanudo in 1506, when Leonardo was in Florence. See also Joost Keizer, *Leonardo's Paradox: Word and Image in the Making of Renaissance Culture* (London: Reaktion, 2019), 176–79, proposing a parallel in Leonardo's thought between anomalous nature and his allegorical inventions. On the iconographic connection between the Monsters of 1506 and 1512, see also Lorraine Daston and Katharine Park, *Wonders and the Order of Nature, 1150–1750* (Cambridge, MA: Zone Books, 1998), 177–82.

79. Cisneri, "Leonardo da Vinci," 103–5.

80. For arguments about the earlier dating, based on evidence that the relationship began in 1485 when Cecilia was as young as twelve, see Timothy McCall, *Making the Renaissance Man: Masculinity in the Courts of Renaissance Italy* (London: Reaktion Books, 2023), 137–73.

81. This is the paradox at issue in the title of Keizer's *Leonardo's Paradox*.

82. Gombrich, "Leonardo and the Magicians," 65.

83. On the prophecies as an instance of the generative role of catastrophe in Leonardo's thought, see Gerard Passannante, *Catastrophizing: Materialism and the Making of Disaster* (Chicago: University of Chicago Press, 2019), 29–51.

84. *Leonardo da Vinci's Codex Leicester*, ed. Laurenza and Kemp, 4:268.

85. The "prophecies" are from Codex Atlanticus 370v and other sheets; the translations that follow can be found in *Leonardo da Vinci: Notebooks*, 230–39.

86. Codex Atlanticus 370v; translation in *Leonardo da Vinci: Notebooks*, 233.

87. See Michel Jeanneret, *Perpetual Motion: Transforming Shapes in the Renaissance from Da Vinci to Montaigne* (Baltimore: Johns Hopkins University Press, 2001), 50–79; Leslie Geddes, *Watermarks: Leonardo da Vinci and the Mastery of Nature* (Princeton: Princeton University Press, 2020), 107–17.

88. For a recent account of hands, mirroring, self-reflexivity, and embodiment in the case of one of Leonardo's younger contemporaries, see Michael Fried, *Painting with Demons: The Art of Gerolamo Savoldo* (London: Reaktion, 2021), especially 44–78.

89. Translation from Martin Clayton and Ron Philo, *Leonardo da Vinci, Anatomist* (London: Royal Collection Publications, 2012), 131.

90. "The writer exits only where the page is blank; everywhere that there are words, the writer has become a reader. Writers know (or at least seem to hope) that they are only the first readers of their works; others will follow. . . . And the blank page is not only the vanishing point of this gaze: it is its source." Shane Butler, *The Matter of the Page: Essays in Search of Ancient and Medieval Authors* (Madison: University of Wisconsin Press, 2011), 104.

Chapter 5: Leonardo, Extended

1. Codex Urbinas (Urb.lat.1270) 44r–v; *Leonardo on Painting*, selected and edited by Martin Kemp and Margaret Walker (New Haven: Yale University Press, 1989), 204.

2. Frank Zöllner, "*Ogni pittore dipinge se*: Leonardo da Vinci and 'Automimesis,'" in *Der Künstler über sich in seinem Werk: Internationales Symposium der Bibliotheca Hertziana*, ed. Matthias Winner (Weinheim: Wiley-VCH Verlag, 1992), 137–60.

3. Ernst Gombrich, "Leonardo da Vinci's Method of Analysis and Permutation: The Grotesque Heads," in *The Heritage of Apelles* (London: Phaidon, 1976), 57–75.

4. The contradiction is addressed in Frank Zöllner, "Leonardo da Vinci on Painting: From the Use of Types to the Criticism of Types," in *Leonardo da Vinci e la lingua della pittura in Europa (secoli XIV–XVII)*, ed. Margherita Quaglino and Anna Sconza (Florence: Olschki, 2022), 89–98. See also Michael W. Kwakkelstein, "Leonardo da Vinci's Recurrent Use of Patterns of Individual Limbs, Stock Poses and Facial Stereotypes," in *Artistic Innovations and Cultural Zones*, ed. Ingrid Ciulisova, Spectrum Slovakia series, vol. 7 (Frankfurt: Peter Lang Verlag, 2014), 45–61.

5. *New York Times*, January 28, 2010. On the "Kansas City Leonardo," possibly by a seventeenth-century French artist, see John Brewer, *The American Leonardo: A Tale of Obsession, Art, and Money* (Oxford: Oxford University Press, 2009).

6. Walter Pater, *The Renaissance: Studies in Art and Poetry*, 4th ed. (1893; Mineola, NY: Dover, 2005), 82.

7. J. P. Isbouts and C. H. Brown, "A Multidisciplinary Study of the Tongerlo *Last Supper* and Its Attribution to Leonardo da Vinci's Second Milanese Studio," *Conservation Science in Cultural Heritage* 20 (2020): 49–64. The authors rightly point to the close correspondence between the Tongerlo painting and the original, reasonably suggesting that the artist(s) had access to Leonardo's cartoons. Yet those cartoons were accessible to artists working in Milan long after Leonardo completed the fresco; their use cannot be taken as proof of production under Leonardo's supervision. There is no record of the painting before a 1542 inventory from the Château de Gaillon, or any basis for dating it within Leonardo's lifetime. The copy is sometimes attributed to Andrea Solario, who could have made it while working at Gaillon for d'Amboise in 1507 or after his return to Italy in 1515. Solario, however, has no documented connection with Leonardo's workshop.

8. For a detailed discussion of the dating of the three versions and the multiple versions from the 1500s, see *St. Anne: Leonardo da Vinci's Ultimate Masterpiece*, ed. Vincent Delieuvin, exhibition catalog (Milan: Officina Libraria, 2012).

9. Luke Syson, "Leonardo and Leonardism in Sforza Milan," in *Artists at Court: Image-making and Identity, 1300–1550*, ed. Stephen J. Campbell (Chicago: University of Chicago Press, 2004), 110.

10. For the correspondence, see *Lives of Leonardo da Vinci*, ed. Charles Robertson (Los Angeles: J. Paul Getty Museum, 2019), 141–46; Delieuvin in *St. Anne: Leonardo da Vinci's Ultimate Masterpiece*, 77–78.

11. Amoretti in his preface to *Disegni di Leonardo da Vinci: Incisi sugli originali de Carlo Giuseppe Gerli* (Milan: Giuseppe Vallardi, 1830), 4, lists *The Last Supper, il quadro detto della Concezione* (i.e., *The Virgin of the Rocks*), a Madonna in S. Celso, a half-length portrait (sitter unspecified by name or gender) in the house of Signor Sironi, an unfinished painting in the archbishop's palace and another in the Casa Belgioso representing the Virgin and Child, a portrait of the Chancellor Moroni in the Scotti household (the portrait by Cristoforo Solario; see fig. 2), although expressing some doubt as to the identity of the sitter or the reliability of the attribution to Leonardo, the *Leda* in the collection of the Conte di Firmian, an unfinished *Adam and Eve* in the possession of the Abbot Bianconi, and two half-length St. Johns, in the Ambrosiana and in the Litta household.

12. Megan Holmes, "Copying Practices and Marketing Strategies in a Fifteenth-Century Florentine Painter's Workshop," in *Artistic Exchange and Cultural Translation in the Italian Renaissance City*, ed. Stephen J. Cambell and Stephen J. Milner (New York: Cambridge University Press, 2004), 38–74.

13. I am grateful to Christopher Daly for sharing his expertise on Lorenzo di Credi's production and the Botticelli workshop. See Daly, "Dans l'atelier de Sandro Botticelli: L'exemple du Maître des bâtiments gothiques (Jacopo Foschi?)," in *Botticelli, artiste et designer*, exhibition catalog, Musée Jacquemart-André (Paris: Mercator, 2021).

14. On the problems of separating Raphael from his assistants, see Bette Talvacchia, "Raphael's Workshop and the Development of a Managerial Style," in *The Cambridge Companion to Raphael*, ed. Marcia B. Hall (Cambridge: Cambridge University Press, 2005), 167–85; Tom Henry and Paul Joannides, "Raphael and His Workshop between 1513 and 1525 'per la mano di maestro Rafaello e Joanne Francesco e Giulio sui discepoli,'" in *Late Raphael*, ed. Tom Henry and Paul Joannides, exhibition catalog (Madrid: Museo del Prado, 2012), 17–85.

15. See the discussion of Armenini and the transformation of pictorial labor after Raphael in Robert Williams, *Raphael and the Redefinition of Art in Renaissance Italy* (Cambridge: Cambridge University Press, 2017), 201–11.

16. Codex Atlanticus 141rb/387r; quoted here from *Leonardo on Painting*, 193.

17. Text quoted from Claire Farago, Janis Bell, and Carlo Vecce, eds., *The Fabrication of Leonardo da Vinci's Trattato della Pittura*, 2 vols. (Leiden: Brill, 2017), 2:612; controlled against digi.vatlib.it/view/MSS_Urb.lat.1270. The translation in

Leonardo on Painting, 197, omits the passage "poi dal naturale, per conformarsi la ragione la ragione dele cose imparate; poi vedere un tempo l'opere di mano di diverse maestri, per fare habito di mettere in praticha et operare l'arte."

18. *Leonardo on Painting*, 198.

19. As argued by Michael W. Kwakkelstein, "The Limited Impact of Leonardo da Vinci's Ideas on Painting in Sforza Milan," *Artibus et Historiae* 39 (2018): 77–98, and Kwakkelstein, "Did Leonardo Always Practice What He Preached? Discrepancies between Leonardo's Didactic Views on Painting and His Artistic Practice," in *"Proxima Studia": Arte e letteratura a Firenze (1300–1600)*, ed. Stefano Ugo Baldassarri (Florence: Fabrizio Serra Editore, 2011), 107–36. Regarding Boltraffio and Marco d'Oggiono: they were already mature painters when they came to work for Leonardo and were not trained by him. It is notable that Antonio Allegri, known as Correggio, who had no known contact with Leonardo, in his art achieves a highly independent application of Leonardesque principles (perspective, chiaroscuro, color, expression, landscape) without any sign of formulaic imitation or derivation. See also David Alan Brown, *Leonardo da Vinci: Art and Devotion in the Madonnas of His Pupils* (Milan: Silvana, 2003).

20. Farago, Bell, and Vecce, *Fabrication*, 2:622.

21. Urb.lat.1270, 39v. Farago, Bell, and Vecce, *Fabrication*, 2:624.

22. Rebecca Zorach, "Nature, Imagination, and Authority: Leonardo in Seventeenth-Century France," in *Leonardo in Dialogue: The Artist amid His Contemporaries*, ed. Francesca Borgo, Rodolfo Maffeis, and Alessandro Nova (Venice: Marsilio, 2019), 342.

23. Farago, Bell, and Vecce, *Fabrication*, 2:616. On Leonardo and Dante, see Carlo Vecce, "Old Friends: Leonardo's Books (before the Library)," in Paula Findlen et al., *Leonardo's Library: The World of a Renaissance Reader* (Stanford: Stanford Libraries, 2019), 128–41.

24. Farago, Bell, and Vecce, *Fabrication*, 2:633.

25. Farago, Bell, and Vecce, *Fabrication*, 2:635.

26. Farago, Bell, and Vecce, *Fabrication*, 2:631.

27. For a different approach to style and embodiment in Leonardo, see Catherine M. Soussloff, "Discourse/Figure/Love: The Location of Style in Early Modern Sources on Leonardo da Vinci," in *Leonardo da Vinci and the Ethics of Style*, ed. Claire Farago (Manchester: Manchester University Press, 2008), 37–58.

28. Christina Neilson, *Practice and Theory in the Italian Renaissance Workshop: Verrocchio and the Epistemology of Making Art* (Cambridge: Cambridge University Press, 2019), 152–56.

29. On line as a point of contention in Florentine art around 1500, with particular attention to the opposed artistic values of Leonardo and Michelangelo, see Michael W. Cole, *Leonardo, Michelangelo, and the Art of the Figure* (New Haven: Yale University Press, 2014), 31–83.

30. Even if he didn't engrave the plates himself, Mantegna's self-publicizing use of engraving probably precedes that of Antonio Pollaiuolo, despite what is commonly asserted. See Stephen J. Campbell, *Andrea Mantegna: Humanist Aesthetics, Faith, and the Force of Images* (Turnhout: Brepols/Harvey Miller, 2020), 224–29.

31. Codex Urbinas 46r–v, 50v; *Leonardo on Painting*, 210, 211.

32. *The Literary Works of Leonardo da Vinci*, ed. J. P. Richter, rev. ed. with Irma Richter, 2 vols. (1939; London: Phaidon, 1970); on the dating, see Richter/Pedretti, 1:127.

33. David Summers, "Chiaroscuro, or the Rhetoric of Realism," in *Leonardo da Vinci and Optics*, ed. Francesca Fiorani and Alessandro Nova (Venice: Marsilio, 2013), 29–55, shows that Leonardo's paintings are not simply a scientific demonstration of optical principles, a pedantic rendering of gradations of shadow. They show a process of adjustment governed by a principle of internal coherence, requiring that some elements receive emphasis over others, and a light form be placed against a dark form for compositional rather than optical reasons. The pursuit of emphasis can mean that the form will appear with dark borders.

34. On Leonardo and Botticelli, see Jonathan K. Nelson, "Leonardo contro Botticelli: Nuovi spunti su un'antica rivalità," in *Leonardo e Firenze: Fogli scelti dal Codice Atlantico*, ed. Cristina Acidini (Florence: Giunti, 2019), 125–33.

35. Codex Urbinas 33v–34r; the words "se un non li piace li paesi" (who does not care for landscapes) are altered in the 1651 published *Trattato* to "se ad uno piacciono li paesi" (one who likes landscapes). See Farago, Bell, and Vecce, *Fabrication*, 2:615–16.

36. *Leonardo on Painting*, 201–2.

37. Codex Urbinas 35v; quotation from the *Trattato* in Farago, Bell, and Vecce, *Fabrication*, 2:619. Leonardo is drawing on the procedure recorded in Pliny's *Natural History* XXXV.101, when the painter Protogenes flings a sponge at his painting in frustration at not being able to portray the foam on the jaws of a dog—and accidentally achieves the desired result.

38. On the literary and artistic tradition of the "potential image," see Stephen J. Campbell, "Cloud-poiesis: Perception, Allegory, Seeing the Other," in *Senses of Sight: Towards a Multisensorial Approach of the Image: Essays in Honor of Victor I. Stoichita*, ed. Henri de Reidmatten, Nicolas Galley, et al. (Rome: L'Erma di Bretschneider, 2015), 7–37.

39. Emanuele Lugli, "Leonardo and the Hair Makers," in *Leonardo in Dialogue: The Artist amid His Contemporaries*, ed. Francesca Borgo, Rodolfo Maffeis, and Alessandro Nova (Venice: Marsilio, 2019), 32–34, noting the similarities between the hairstyles of Jethro's daughters in Botticelli's Sistine fresco and Leonardo's study of a coiffure for his figure of Leda, in Windsor RL 12516. See also by the same author, *Knots, or the Violence of Desire in Renaissance Florence* (Chicago: University of Chicago Press, 2023).

40. Kwakkelstein, "Did Leonardo Always Practice What He Preached?"

41. London, British Museum 1895-9-15-482.

42. The male figure right-of-center in *The Bearers of Trophies and Bullion*. See the discussion in Martin Clayton, *Leonardo da Vinci: A Life in Drawing* (New York: Rizzoli Electa, 2019), 212.

43. See Nelson, "Leonardo contro Botticelli."

44. On the orality of Leonardo's writing, see Carlo Vecce, "Word and Image in Leonardo's Writings," in *Leonardo da Vinci Master Draftsman*, exhibition catalog, ed. Carmen C. Bambach (New York: Metropolitan Museum, 2003), 62–63. Joost Keizer, *Leonardo's Paradox: Word and Image in the Making of Renaissance Culture* (London: Reaktion, 2019), 32–43, also addresses Leonardo's script as an emulation of speech; I differ from his assessment of the aesthetic character of the right-to-left handwriting, as a form of pattern making.

45. British Library, Codex Arundel 245v. See Carlo Pedretti, *"Eccetera: Perché la minestra si fredda,"* Codice Arundel, fol. 245 recto, Lettura Vinciana 15 (Florence: Giunti Barbèra, 1975).

46. Jill Pederson, *Leonardo, Bramante, and the Academia: Art and Friendship in Fifteenth-Century Milan* (Turnhout: Brepols/Harvey Miller, 2020), 61–89.

47. On the paradox of geometrical truth and optical visibility in Leonardo, see Daniel Arasse, *Leonardo da Vinci: The Rhythm of the World* (New York: Konecky, 1998), 270–78.

48. Clayton, *Leonardo da Vinci: A Life in Drawing*, 206.

49. On Gallerani's hairstyle, see Timothy McCall, *Making the Renaissance Man: Masculinity in the Courts of Renaissance Italy* (London: Reaktion Books, 2023), 140–45.

50. Codex Urbinas 170 r/v0; *Leonardo on Painting*, 153.

51. Leonardo cites the passage in Paris BN 2037, 8b. See Richter, *Notebooks*, 2:373, #1492.

52. To draw on the analysis of Leonardo's theory and workshop practice in Claire Farago, "A Short Note on Artisanal Epistemology in Leonardo's *Treatise on Painting*," in *Illuminating Leonardo: A Festschrift for Carlo Pedretti (1944–2014)*, ed. Constance Moffatt and Sara Taglialagamba (Leiden: Brill, 2015), 51–68. On the possibility that the later (London) painting is actually based on the original design, modified in the Paris version, see Francesca Fiorani, "Reflections on Leonardo da Vinci Exhibitions in London and Paris," *Studiolo* 10 (2013): 267–74.

53. On the *leonardeschi*, see Pietro C. Marani et al., *The Legacy of Leonardo: Painters in Lombardy, 1490–1530* (Milan: Skira, 1998); Brown, *Leonardo da Vinci: Art and Devotion*; Furio Rinaldi, "The *Academia Leonardi Vinci*: Leonardo's Pupils, Followers and the Legacy of the Master's Works," in *Leonardo da Vinci, 1452–1519: The Design of the World*, ed. Pietro C. Marani and Maria Teresa Fiorio (Milan: Skira, 2015), 439–49.

54. These include the Chéramy *Virgin of the Rocks*, by an artist close to Giampietrino, in a Swiss private foundation; a Magdalene or Lucretia, also probably by Giampietrino, in a Swiss private foundation; a poor-quality painting of a crowned female martyr made from Leonardo's portrait drawing of Isabella d'Este in the Louvre, also in a Swiss private foundation; and a version of the Pitti *Virgin and Child with St. John* by Fernando Llanos or Fernando Yáñez, in a Russian private collection.

55. On Cesare's travels, see Stephen J. Campbell, *The Endless Periphery: Towards a Geopolitics of Art in Lorenzo Lotto's Italy* (Chicago: University of Chicago Press, 2019), 65–86.

56. Disputed in *Bernardino Luini e i suoi figli*, ed. Giovanni Agosti, Giovanni Stoppa, et al., exhibition catalog (Milan: Officina, 2014), 312–18, ascribing the painting in the Ambrosiana to "the heirs of Luini." The museum, rightly, maintains the attribution to Bernardino Luini.

57. On Melzi's hand in Leonardo's notes, see Carlo Vecce, "Dalla parte di Melzi," in *Decoding Leonardo's Codices: Compilation, Dispersal, and Reproduction Technologies*, ed. Paolo Galluzzi and Alessandro Nova (Venice: Marsilio, 2022), 89–110.

58. Gian Paolo Lomazzo, *Scritti sulle arti*, ed. Roberto Paolo Ciardi, 2 vols. (Florence: Marchi and Bertolli, 1973–74), 2:553.

59. Giorgio Vasari, *Lives of the Painters, Sculptors, and Architects*, trans. Gaston de Vere, 2 vols. (1927; London: Everyman's Library, 1996), 2:519.

60. The starting point is invariably Harold Bloom, *The Anxiety of Influence: A Theory of Poetry* (Oxford: Oxford University Press, 1977), with influence conceived as an adversarial strife with a creative precursor. For a reconceptualizing of influence that embraces authorial poetics as well as porous selfhood and trans-personal political subjectivity, see Jane Bennet, *Influx and Efflux: Writing Up with Walt Whitman* (Durham: Duke University Press, 2020), especially the discussion of Bloom at 75–92. For a perspective on quantum mechanics and its implications for thinking human/nonhuman relationality and "entanglement," see Carlo Rovelli, *Helgoland* (London: Allen Lane, 2020), 63–99.

61. Paris, MS A, 113v. See *The Literary Works of Leonardo da Vinci Compiled and Edited from the Original Manuscripts by Jean Paul Richter. Commentary* by Carlo Pedretti, 2 vols. (Berkeley: University of California Press, 1977), 1:350–51.

62. Codex Urbinas 130v; *Leonardo on Painting*, 195.

63. Vasari/de Vere, 1:629, 630.

64. To build on observations by Alexander Nagel, "Leonardo and Sfumato," *RES: Anthropology and Aesthetics* 24 (1993): 7–20.

65. Sigmund Freud, *Leonardo da Vinci and a Memory of His Childhood*, trans. Alan Tyson (New York: Norton, 1961), 73.

66. Arasse, *Leonardo da Vinci: The Rhythm of the World* (1998), 455.

67. Christopher Pye, "Leonardo's Hand: Mimesis, Sexuality, and Early Modern Political Aesthetics," *Representations* 111 (2010): 4–6.

68. David Summers, *The Judgment of Sense: Renaissance Naturalism and the Rise of Aesthetics* (Cambridge: Cambridge University Press, 1987), 8.

69. Fritjof Capra, *Learning from Leonardo: Decoding the Notebooks of a Genius* (San Francisco: BK, 2013), 20.

70. *The Dialogue of the Seraphic Virgin Catherine of Siena* [1370], trans. Algar Thorold (London: K. Paul, Trench, Trübner & Company, 1896), 359. For water and devotional literature, see Hetta Elizabeth Howes, *Transformative Waters in Late-Medieval Literature: From Aelred of Rievaulx to the Book of Margery Kempe* (Cambridge: D. S. Brewer, 2023); John Arblaster, "'Flowing from the Wild Sea and Back to the Sea': Water Metaphors and Mystical Union in the Late Medieval Low Countries," *Journal of Religion* 98 (2018): 169–91.

71. His library included works of more formal theology and patristic literature, like Augustine's *City of God* and the same author's Sermons. He owned Giacomo Campora's popular devotional tract *Dell'Immortalità dell'Anima*, probably of interest for its adaptation of Aristotle's *De anima* and its commentary on the motions of the soul;

see Carmen C. Bambach, *Leonardo da Vinci Re-discovered*, 4 vols. (New Haven: Yale University Press, 2019), 1:323–28, and Bernardo Pulci's poem *La Passione del Nostro Signore Gesù Cristo*, 421.

72. See the discussion in Cole, *Leonardo, Michelangelo*, 34–37.

73. On antique models for the Battle, see Frank Zöllner, *La Battaglia di Anghiari di Leonardo da Vinci fra mitologia e politica*, vol. 37 of *Lettura vinciana* (Florence: Giunti, 1998).

74. Here he was responding to a type apparently known to Michelangelo, who employed it for his Christ Child in the Burges Madonna of 1504, and even earlier, by Cosmè Tura in his personification of the planet Venus from the 1468 organ shutters for the cathedral of Ferrara (Tura's precocious anticipation of the Leda pose also includes the untwining strands of hair).

75. The dating of 1485 is that of Clayton, *Leonardo da Vinci: A Life in Drawing*, 38. Carmen C. Bambach, *Leonardo da Vinci Rediscovered*, 4 vols. (New Haven: Yale University Press, 2019), 1:141, dates the drawing between 1475 and 1482–83, on the basis of a similar pose in Lorenzo di Credi's heavily draped St. John in the *Madonna di Piazza* altarpiece in Pistoia cathedral, dated 1475–85. Yet other drawings with a blue wash do not appear in Leonardo's oeuvre until his move to Milan (e.g., the Windsor horse studies from ca. 1490).

76. Some years later Yáñez once again used the same pose for a figure of Christ but this time of more tender years in a more emphatically Leonardesque *Virgin and Child with St. Anne, St. Elizabeth, and St. John* (Prado).

77. Francesco Bocchi, *Le Bellezze della città di Fiorenza* (1591), ed. Giovanni Sannino (Florence: Fondazione Memofonte, 2019), 150; Antonio Natali, *Andrea del Sarto* (New York: Abbeville, 1999), 101–3.

78. "E nel vero si conosce in quel che si vede di suo uno spirito molto vario et astrattato dagli altri, et una certa sottilità nello investigare certe sottigliezze della natura che penetrano, senza guardare a tempo o fatiche, solo per suo diletto."

79. Vasari/de Vere, 1:650.

80. Vasari/de Vere, 1:675.

81. Vasari/de Vere, 1:684–85.

82. Claire Farago, "Who Abridged Leonardo da Vinci's *Treatise on Painting*?" in *Re-Reading Leonardo: The Treatise on Painting across Europe, 1550–1900*, ed. Claire Farago (London: Routledge, 2009), 77–107.

83. Robert Williams, "Leonardo and the Florentine Academy," in *Re-Reading Leonardo: The Treatise on Painting across Europe, 1550–1900*, ed. Claire Farago (London: Routledge, 2009), 67.

84. Elizabeth Pilliod, *Pontormo, Bronzino, and Allori: A Genealogy of Florentine Art* (New Haven: Yale University Press, 2001).

85. Stephen J. Campbell, "Bronzino's *Martyrdom of St. Lawrence*: Counter Reformation Polemic and Mannerist Counter Aesthetics," *RES 46: Polemical Objects* (2004): 99–121.

86. *Le Opere di Giorgio Vasari* VI, 277: "I quali disegni di Michelagnolo furono cagione che, considerando il Puntormo la maniera di quello artifice nobilissimo, se gli destasse l'animo, e si risolvesse per ogni modo a volere, second il suo sapere, imitarla e seguitarla."

87. Vasari/de Vere, 2:204–5.

88. Vasari/de Vere, 1:900.

89. On Gaudenzio, Bernardino Lanino, and their acquaintance with Leonardo's drawing technique, see Bambach, *Leonardo da Vinci Rediscovered*, 3:538; *Il Rinascimento di Gaudenzio Ferrari*, exhibition catalog, ed. Giovanni Agosti and Jacopo Stoppa (Milan: Officina Libraria, 2018), 408–14.

90. See discussion in Campbell, *Endless Periphery*, 103. On Gaudenzio's resistance to Leonardo, see also Eduoardo Villata, "Gaudenzio di fronte a Leonardo: Inclinazioni e resistenze verso il Cenacolo tra Piemonte e Lombardia," in *Il Genio e le Passioni: Leonardo e il Cenacolo; Precedenti, innovazioni, riflessi di un capolavoro*, ed. Pietro C. Marani (Milan: Rizzoli, 2001), 155–64.

91. Massimiliano Caldera, "Gaudenzio Ferrari fino al 1528," in *Fermo Stella e Sperindio Cagnoli seguaci di Gaudenzio Ferrari: Una bottega d'arte nel Cinquecento padano*, ed. Giovanni Romano (Milan: Silvana, 2006), 23–39 (24), and 111 in the same volume: Gaudenzio also goes by this name in the contract for the 1508 Vercelli commission: "Magister Gaudentius de Vincio de Varali pinctor."

92. See the entry by Luke Syson in the catalog *Leonardo da Vinci: Painter at the Court of Milan* (London: National Gallery, 2011), 168. For the pre-Leonardo tradition of combining painted panels with polychrome sculpture in an altarpiece, see Iris Wenderholm, *Bild und Berührung: Skulptur und Malerei auf dem Altar der italienischen Frührenaissance* (Berlin: Deutscher Kunstverlag, 2006).

93. Claire J. Farago, *Leonardo da Vinci's Paragone: A Critical Interpretation with a New Edition of the Text in the Codex Urbinas* (Leiden: Brill, 1992). For a cautionary perspective on the use of the term *paragone* before Benedetto Varchi's mid-century *lezioni*, see Charles Dempsey, "*Disegno* and Logos, *Paragone* and Academy," in *The Accademia Seminars: The Accademia di*

San Luca in Rome, c. 1590–1635, ed. Peter M. Lukehart (Washington, DC: National Gallery of Art, 2009), 43–53.

94. *Leonardo on Painting*, 44.

95. Campbell, *Endless Periphery*, 178–79.

Conclusion

1. My reservations are with a model of biography as described by an avowedly nonacademic professional biographer, Paula R. Backscheider, *Reflections on Biography* (Oxford: Oxford University Press, 1999), xviii–xix: "The genre biography assumes that what a person does expresses an inner life—personality, motives, aspirations, character. To some extent a military campaign, a symphony, and serial murders can be used to interpret a human being just as reliably as many novels. This is not to deny the life in the works; rather it is an emphasis on the common purposes and strategies that biographers share when their primary purpose is to tell the life of a fascinating person rather than, for instance, to commit an act of literary criticism."

2. There are historical methodologies for dealing with individual lives—notably the practice of microhistory—that can be put into critical dialogue with biography. According to Sigurður Gylfi Magnússon, the procedure of the microhistorian "differs from that of the conventional historian in that the choices and challenges of the research strategy are often made part of the narrative. There is candid discussion of the sources, the technique used in making a particular argument, and what it comprises." He earlier notes that "we actively seek out the contradictions and gaps in our knowledge about one person, and make these tensions and lacunae essential subjects of inquiry." Magnússon, "The Life Is Never Over: Biography as a Microhistorical Approach," in *The Biographical Turn: Lives in History*, ed. Hans Renders, Binne de Haan, and Jonne Harmisa (London: Routledge, 2017), 42–52 (45, 47). Microhistorians have thus made a point of pursuing the experiences of the nonfamous and the obscure, sometimes of people haplessly on the receiving end of political and religious scrutiny and coercion. A life like Leonardo's might seem overcelebrated, freighted with the distorting perceptions of contemporaries, and Leonardo himself just too exceptional or sui generis.

3. See the use of personal and family biography by the anthropologist Clara Han, *Seeing Like a Child: Inheriting the Korean War* (New York: Fordham University Press, 2021). The political scientist Bartholomew Sparrow writes, "Biography fulfills many of political science's disciplinary objectives, in fact: it speaks to important issues of political science, it offers thick description and facilitates the drawing of causal inferences, it addresses agency and structure, it is falsifiable, and it is able to communicate with a larger public." Sparrow, "Why Would a Political Scientist Write a Biography?" *Perspectives on Politics* 14 (2016): 1101–11.

4. See in this regard James J. Porter, *Homer: The Very Idea* (Chicago: University of Chicago Press, 2021), which addresses Homer's absence or even nonexistence, his very anonymity, as the precondition for a tradition.

5. For example, Kara Cooney, *The Woman Who Would Be King: Hatshepsut's Rise to Power in Ancient Egypt* (New York: Crown, 2014); Ann Wroe, *Pontius Pilate* (New York: Random House, 2000); Robin Milner-Gulland, *Andrey Rublev: The Artist and His World* (London: Reaktion, 2023).

6. Windsor RCIN 919084; Richter, *Notebooks*, #1210. On the ecological possibilities of Leonardo's thought and its distinctness from the utilitarianism of Baconian science, see Fritjof Capra, *The Science of Leonardo* (New York: Random House, 2008), especially 257–65.

7. F. R. Ankersmit, *Sublime Historical Experience* (Stanford: Stanford University Press, 2005), 112–33.

8. Fabulation here has an overlapping agenda with the "critical fabulation" of Saidiya Hartman, *Wayward Lives, Beautiful Experiments: Intimate Histories of Riotous Black Girls, Troublesome Women and Queer Radicals* (New York: Profile, 2019).

BIBLIOGRAPHY

EDITIONS AND FACSIMILES OF
LEONARDO'S WRITINGS

e-Leo: Archivio digitale di storia della tecnica e della scienza.

Leonardo da Vinci. *Trattato della pittura*. Ed. Guglielmo Manzi and Giovanni Gherardo de Rossi. Rome: Nella Stamperia de Romanis, 1817.

The Notebooks of Leonardo da Vinci. Ed. and trans. Edward MacCurdy. 2 vols. New York: Reynal and Hitchcock, 1938.

The Literary Works of Leonardo da Vinci. Ed. J. P. Richter, rev. ed. with Irma Richter. 2 vols. 1939. London: Phaidon, 1970.

The Literary Works of Leonardo da Vinci Compiled and Edited from the Original Manuscripts by Jean Paul Richter. Commentary by Carlo Pedretti. 2 vols. Berkeley: University of California Press, 1977.

Leonardo on Painting. Selected and edited by Martin Kemp and Margaret Walker. New Haven: Yale University Press, 1989.

Leonardo da Vinci's Paragone: A Critical Interpretation with a New Edition of the Text of the Codex Urbinas. Ed. Claire Farago. Leiden: Brill, 1992.

Leonardo da Vinci: I documenti e le testimonianze contemporanee. Ed. Edoardo Villata. Milan: Ente Raccolta Vinciana, 1999.

Leonardo da Vinci: La vera imagine. Documenti e testimonianze sulla vita e sull'opera. Ed. Vanna Arrighi, Anna Bellinazzi, and Edoardo Villata. Florence: Giunti, 2005.

The Notebooks of Leonardo da Vinci. Ed. and trans. Irma A. Richter. Oxford: Oxford University Press, 2008.

PRIMARY AND SECONDARY SOURCES

Agosti, Giovanni, Giovanni Stoppa, et al. *Bernardino Luini e i suoi figli*. Exhibition catalog. Milan: Officina, 2014.

Alberti, Leon Battista. *Biographical and Autobiographical Writings*. Trans. Martin McLaughlin. Cambridge, MA: Harvard University Press, 2023.

———. *Momus*. Ed. Virginia Brown and Sarah Knight. Cambridge, MA: Harvard University Press, 2003.

———. *On Painting and On Sculpture*. Ed. and trans. Cecil Grayson. London: Phaidon, 1972.

Amelang, James. *The Flight of Icarus: Artisan Autobiography in Early Modern Europe*. Stanford: Stanford University Press, 1998.

Ankersmit, F. R. *Sublime Historical Experience*. Stanford: Stanford University Press, 2005.

Arasse, Daniel. *Leonardo da Vinci: The Rhythm of the World*. Old Saybrook, CT: Konecky, 1998. Original edition, Paris: Hazan, 1997.

Arblaster, John. "'Flowing from the Wild Sea and Back to the Sea': Water Metaphors and Mystical Union in the Late Medieval Low Countries." *Journal of Religion* 98 (2018): 169–91.

Azzolini, Monica. "Anatomy of a Dispute: Leonardo, Pacioli and Scientific Courtly Entertainment in Renaissance Milan." *Early Science and Medicine* 9 (2004): 115–35.

Bacchelli, Franco. "Un frammento inedito di Leon Battista Alberti sul fuoco." *Noctua* 7 (2020): 1–67.

Bambach, Carmen C. *Leonardo da Vinci Rediscovered*. 4 vols. New Haven: Yale University Press, 2019.

Barnes, Julian. *The Man in the Red Coat*. London: Jonathan Cape, 2019.

Barolsky, Paul. "The Mysterious Meaning of Leonardo's *Saint John the Baptist*." *Source: Notes in the History of Art* 8 (1989): 11–15.

Baron, Hans. "The Limits of the Notion 'Renaissance Individualism': Burckhardt after a Century." In *In Search of Florentine Civic Humanism: Essays on the Transition from Medieval to Modern Thought*, 2:155–81. Princeton: Princeton University Press, 1988.

Barsanti, Roberta, ed. *Leonardo a Vinci: Alle origini del genio*. Florence: Giunti, 2019.

Baudrillard, Jean. *The Transparency of Evil: Essays on Extreme Phenomena*. Trans. James Benedict. London: Verso, 2009. Original French edition, 1993.

Baxandall, Michael. "Alberti's Cast of Mind." In *Words for Pictures*, 27–39. New Haven: Yale University Press, 2003.

Beck, James. *Leonardo's Rules of Painting: An Unconventional Approach to Modern Art*. New York: Viking, 1979.

Beck, Jessica. "Warhol's Confession: Love, Faith, and AIDs." In *Andy Warhol: From A to B and Back Again*, 84–94. New York: Whitney Museum of American Art, 2018.

Beech, Dave. *Art and Value: Art's Economic Exceptionalism in Classical, Neoclassical, and Marxist Economics*. Leiden: Brill, 2015.

Bennet, Jane. *Influx and Efflux: Writing Up with Walt Whitman*. Durham: Duke University Press, 2020.

Berenson, Bernard. "Leonardo." In *The Study and Criticism of Italian Art*, 1–37. 3rd ser. London: Bell, 1916.

Beretta, Marco. "Leonardo and Lucretius." *Rinascimento* 49 (2010): 341–72.

Bishop, Claire. "Against Digital Art History." *International Journal for Digital Art History*, no. 3 (2018): 122–31.

Bloom, Harold. *The Anxiety of Influence: A Theory of Poetry*. Oxford: Oxford University Press, 1977.

Boggione, Valter. "Leonardo e il lessico erotico." In *Leonardo da Vinci e la lingua della pittura in Europa (secoli XIV–XVII)*, ed. Margherita Quaglino and Anna Sconza, 75–88. Florence: Olschki, 2022.

Borromeo, Federico. *Sacred Painting/Museum*. Ed. and trans. Kenneth S. Rothwell Jr. Cambridge, MA: Harvard University Press, 2010.

Bourdieu, Pierre. "The Biographical Illusion." Trans. Yves Winkin and Wendy Leeds-Hurwitz. *Working Papers and Proceedings of the Center for Psychosocial Studies* (1987): 1–7.

Bramly, Serge. *Léonard de Vinci*. Paris: éditions Lattès, 1988. English edition trans. Sian Reynolds. London: HarperCollins, 1991.

Brewer, John. *The American Leonardo: A Tale of Obsession, Art, and Money*. Oxford: Oxford University Press, 2009.

Brown, Alison M. "*Natura Idest*? Leonardo, Lucretius, and Their Views of Nature." In *Leonardo da Vinci on Nature: Knowledge and Representation*, ed. Fabio Frosini and Alessandro Nova, 153–79. Venice: Marsilio, 2013.

Brown, Alison M., and Alessandro Parronchi. "The Language of Humanism and the Language of Sculpture: Bertoldo as Illustrator of the *Apologi*

of Bartolomeo Scala." *Journal of the Warburg and Courtauld Institutes* 27 (1964): 108–36.

Brown, David Alan. *Leonardo da Vinci: Art and Devotion in the Madonnas of His Pupils*. Milan: Silvana, 2003.

———. *Leonardo da Vinci: Origins of a Genius*. New Haven: Yale University Press, 1998.

Brunelleschi, Filippo. *Sonetti di Filippo Brunelleschi*. Introduction by Giuliano Tanturli and notes by Domenico de Robertis. Florence: Accademia della Crusca, 1977.

Bullen, Barrie. "Walter Pater's *Renaissance* and Leonardo da Vinci's Reputation in the Nineteenth Century." *Modern Language Review* 74 (1979): 268–80.

Burchiello (Domenico di Giovanni). *The Poetry of Burchiello: Deep-Fried Nouns, Hunchbacked Pumpkins, and Other Nonsense*. Ed. and trans. Fabian Alfie and Aileen A. Feng. Tempe, AZ: ACMRS, 2017.

Burckhardt, Jacob. *The Civilization of the Renaissance in Italy*. Trans S.G.C. Middlemore. 1860. London: Penguin Books, 1990.

Burke, Jill. "Agostino Vespucci's Marginal Note about Leonardo da Vinci in Heidelberg." *Leonardo da Vinci Society Newsletter* 30 (2008): 3–4.

Butler, Shane. *The Matter of the Page: Essays in Search of Ancient and Medieval Authors*. Madison: University of Wisconsin Press, 2011.

Campanini, Antonella. "Vesti, colori, e onore: La scala del rosso." In *Identità cittadina e comportamenti socio-economici tra Medioevo ed Età Moderna*, ed. Paolo Prodi, Maria Giusipina Muzzarelli, and Stefano Simonetta, 145–55. Bologna: CLUEB, 2001.

Campbell, Stephen J. *Andrea Mantegna: Humanist Aesthetics, Faith, and the Force of Images*. Turnhout: Brepols/Harvey Miller, 2020.

———. "Bronzino's *Martyrdom of St. Lawrence*: Counter Reformation Polemic and Mannerist Counter Aesthetics." *RES 46: Polemical Objects* (2004): 99–121.

———. *The Cabinet of Eros: Renaissance Mythological Painting and the Studiolo of Isabella d'Este*. New Haven: Yale University Press, 2006.

———. "Cloud-poiesis: Perception, Allegory, Seeing the Other." In *Senses of Sight: Towards a Multisensorial Approach of the Image: Essays in Honor of Victor I. Stoichita*, ed. Henri de Reidmatten, Nicolas Galley, et al., 7–37. Rome: L'Erma di Bretschneider, 2015.

———. *Cosmè Tura of Ferrara: Style, Politics and the Renaissance City*. New Haven: Yale University Press, 1996.

———. *The Endless Periphery: Towards a Geopolitics of Art in Lorenzo Lotto's Italy*. Chicago: University of Chicago Press, 2019.

Camporesi, Piero. *Bread of Dreams: Food and Fantasy in Early Modern Europe*. Chicago: University of Chicago Press, 1989.

Capra, Frijof. *Learning from Leonardo: Decoding the Notebooks of a Genius*. San Francisco: BK, 2013.

——. *The Science of Leonardo*. New York: Random House, 2008.

Cara, Roberto. "La mostra di Leonardo da Vinci a Milano tra arte, scienza e politica." In *All'origine delle grandi mostre in Italia (1933–1940)*, ed. Marcello Toffanello. Mantua: Il Rio Editore, 2017.

Castiglione, Baldesar. *The Book of the Courtier*. Ed. and trans. George Bull. 1967. London: Penguin, 1976.

Celenza, Christopher S. *The Lost Italian Renaissance: Humanists, Historians, and Latin's Legacy*. Baltimore: Johns Hopkins University Press, 2004.

——. "Pythagoras in the Renaissance: The Case of Marsilio Ficino." *Renaissance Quarterly* 52 (1999): 667–711.

Chastel, André. *Art et humanisme à Florence au temps de Laurent le Magnifique*. Paris: Presses universitaires de France, 1961.

Cianchi, Francesco. *La madre di Leonardo era una schiava? Ipotesi di studio di Renzo Cianchi*. Vinci: Museo Ideale Leonardo da Vinci, 2008.

Ciatti, Marco, and Cecilia Frosinini, eds. *The Restoration of Leonardo da Vinci's Adoration of the Magi: Rediscovering a Masterpiece*. Florence: Edifir edizioni Firenze/Opificio delle pietre dure, 2021.

Cisneri, Lorenzo Montemagno. "Leonardo da Vinci, the Genius and the Monsters: Casual Encounters?" *Medicina nei Secoli, Arte e Scienza/Journal of History of Medicine* 26 (2014): 69–116.

Clark, Kenneth. *Leonardo da Vinci: An Account of His Development as an Artist*. Cambridge: Cambridge University Press, 1939.

Clayton, Martin. *Leonardo da Vinci: A Life in Drawing*. New York: Rizzoli Electa, 2019.

Clayton, Martin, and Ron Philo, *Leonardo da Vinci, Anatomist*. London: Royal Collection Publications, 2012.

——. *Leonardo da Vinci: The Mechanics of Man*. Windsor: Royal Collection Trust, 2013.

Cohn, Samuel. "Burckhardt Revisited from Social History." In *Language and Images of Renaissance Italy*, ed. Alison Brown, 217–34. Oxford: Oxford University Press, 1995.

Cole, Michael W. *Leonardo, Michelangelo, and the Art of the Figure*. New Haven: Yale University Press, 2014.

Collareta, Alberto, Marco Collareta, Annalisa Berta, and Giovanni Bianucci. "On Leonardo and a Fossil Whale: A Reappraisal with Implications for the Early History of Palaeontology." *Historical Biology* 33, no. 10 (2020): 2289–98.

Cotte, Pascal. *Lumière sur Mona Lisa de Léonard de Vinci: Portraits multispectrales*. Rueil-Malmaison: Vinci, 2016.

Cracolici, Stefano. "Flirting with the Chameleon: Alberti on Love." *MLN* 121, *Italian Issue* (2006): 102–29.

Daly, Christopher. "Dans l'atelier de Sandro Botticelli: L'exemple du Maître des bâtiments gothiques (Jacopo Foschi?)." In *Botticelli, artiste et designer*. Exhibition catalog. Musée Jacquemart-André. Paris: Mercator, 2021.

Daston, Lorraine, and Katharine Park. *Wonders and the Order of Nature, 1150–1750*. Cambridge, MA: Zone Books, 1998.

Davis, Natalie Zemon. *The Return of Martin Guerre*. Cambridge, MA: Harvard University Press, 1982.

de Grazia, Margreta. *Shakespeare without a Life*. Oxford: Oxford University Press, 2023.

Dean, Trevor. "Sodomy in Renaissance Bologna." *Renaissance Studies* 31 (2017): 426–43.

del Prete, Ivano. *On the Edge of Eternity: The Antiquity of the Earth in Medieval and Early Modern Europe*. Oxford: Oxford University Press, 2022.

Delieuvin, Vincent, ed. *St. Anne: Leonardo da Vinci's Ultimate Masterpiece*. Exhibition catalog. Milan: Officina Libraria, 2012.

Delieuvin, Vincent, Myriam Eveno, and Élisabeth Ravaud. *Léonard de Vinci: Le Salvator Mundi*. Paris: Louvre editions/Hazan, 2019.

Dempsey, Charles. "*Disegno* and Logos, *Paragone* and Academy." In *The Accademia Seminars: The Accademia di San Luca in Rome, c. 1590–1635*, ed. Peter M. Lukehart, 43–53. Washington, DC: National Gallery of Art, 2009.

Dionisotti, Carlo. "Leonardo uomo di lettere." *Italia medioevale e umanistica* 5 (1962): 183–216.

Donato, Maria Monica. "Un 'savio depentor' fra 'scienza de le stelle' e 'sutilità' dell'antico: Restoro d'Arezzo, le arti e il sarcofago romano di Cortona." *Annali della Scuola Normale Superiore di Pisa* 4 (1996): 51–78.

Drimmer, Sonia. "How AI Is Hijacking Art History." *The Conversation*, November 1, 2021.

Duhem, Pierre. *Études sur Léonard de Vinci*. 3 vols. Paris: A. Hermann, 1906–13.

Etheridge, Kay. "Leonardo and the Whale." In *Leonardo da Vinci: Nature and Architecture*, ed. Constance Moffatt and Sara Taglialagamba, 89–106. Leiden: Brill, 2019.

Farago, Claire. "A Short Note on Artisanal Epistemology in Leonardo's *Treatise on Painting*." In *Illuminating Leonardo: A Festschrift for Carlo Pedretti (1944–2014)*, ed. Constance Moffatt and Sara Taglialagamba, 51–68. Leiden: Brill, 2015.

——. "Who Abridged Leonardo da Vinci's *Treatise on Painting*?" In *Re-Reading Leonardo: The Treatise on Painting across Europe, 1550–1900*, ed. Claire Farago, 77–107. London: Routledge, 2009.

Farago, Claire, Janis Bell, and Carlo Vecce, eds. *The Fabrication of Leonardo da Vinci's Trattato della Pittura*. 2 vols. Leiden: Brill, 2017.

Farago, Claire, and Matthew Landrus. "Leonardo da Vinci." *Oxford Bibliographies: Renaissance and Reformation*. Oxford: Oxford University Press, 2013.

Fehrenbach, Frank. "The Cycle of Images." In *Leonardo and Nature*, ed. Fabio Frosini and Alessandro Nova, 207–20. Venice: Marsilio, 2015.

———. *Licht und Wasser: Zur Dynamik naturphilosophischer Leitbilder im Werk Leonardo da Vincis*. Tübingen: Wasmuth, 1997.

Feinberg, Larry. *The Young Leonardo: Art and Life in Fifteenth-Century Florence*. Cambridge: Cambridge University Press, 2011.

Findlen, Paula, et al. *Leonardo's Library: The World of a Renaissance Reader*. Stanford: Stanford Libraries, 2019.

Fiorani, Francesca. "Kenneth Clark and Leonardo: From Connoisseurship to Broadcasting to Digital Technologies." In *Leonardo in Britain: Collections and Historical Reception*, ed. Juliana Barone and Susanna Avery-Quash, 353–77. Florence: Olschki, 2019.

———. "Reflections on Leonardo da Vinci Exhibitions in London and Paris." *Studiolo* 10 (2013): 267–77.

———. *The Shadow Drawing: How Science Taught Leonardo How to Paint*. New York: Farrar, Straus and Giroux, 2020.

Freud, Sigmund. *Leonardo da Vinci and a Memory of His Childhood*. Trans. Alan Tyson. New York: Norton, 1961.

Fried, Michael. *Painting with Demons: The Art of Gerolamo Savoldo*. London: Reaktion, 2021.

Frosinini, Cecilia, with Roberto Bellucci and Patrizia Riitano. "Il restauro dell' *Adorazione dei Magi* di Leonardo da Vinci: Capire il non-finito." *Imagines* 1 (2017). https://www.uffizi.it/news/il-restauro-dell-adorazione-dei-magi-di-leonardo-da-vinci-capire-il-non-finito.

Gagné, John. *Milan Undone: Contested Sovereignties in the Italian Wars*. I Tatti Studies in Italian Renaissance History. Cambridge, MA: Harvard University Press, 2021.

Galluzzi, Paolo. "Leonardo//thek@ 1.0: A Digital Infrastructure to Avoid Shipwreck in the Ocean of Data of the Codex Atlanticus of Leonardo da Vinci." In *Decoding Leonardo's Codices: Compilation, Dispersal, and Reproduction Technologies*, ed. Paolo Galluzzi and Alessandro Nova, 289–99. Venice: Marsilio, 2022.

Gaurico, Pomponio. *De sculptura*. Ed Paolo Cutolo. Naples: Edizioni Scientifiche Italiane, 1999.

Gautier, Théophile. *Guide de l'amateur au musée du Louvre* [1867]. English version: *The Works of Théophile Gautier*. 21 vols. Trans. Frederick Cesar de Sumichrast. London: Athenaeum Society, 1901.

———. *Journeys in Italy* [1850]. Trans. Daniel B. Vermilye. London: Brentano's, 1902.

———. *The Louvre: Leonardo da Vinci, Esteban Bartolome Murillo, Sir Joshua Reynolds*. Trans. Frederick C. de Sumichrast. New York: G. D. Sproul, 1901.

Geddes, Leslie. *Watermarks: Leonardo da Vinci and the Mastery of Nature*. Princeton: Princeton University Press, 2020.

Giorgione, Claudio. "The Birth of a Collection in Milan: From the Leonardo Exhibition of 1939 to the Opening of the National Museum of Science and Technology in 1953." *Science Museum Group Journal* 4 (2015). https://journal.sciencemuseum.ac.uk/article/leonardo-exhibition-of-1939/.

Gombrich, Ernst. "The Form of Movement in Water and Air." In *The Heritage of Apelles: Studies in the Art of the Renaissance*, 39–56. Ithaca: Cornell University Press, 1976.

———. "Leonardo and the Magicians: Polemics and Rivalry" (1982). In *New Light on Old Masters*, 61–89. London: Phaidon, 1986.

———. "Leonardo da Vinci's Method of Analysis and Permutation: The Grotesque Heads." In *The Heritage of Apelles*, 57–75. London: Phaidon, 1976.

———. "Light, Form, and Texture in Fifteenth Century Painting North and South of the Alps." In *The Heritage of Apelles*, 19–35. London: Phaidon, 1976.

Gotlieb, Marc. "Our Monstrous Double: The Dream of Research in 'Outsider Art History.'" In *What Is Research in the Visual Arts? Obsession, Archive, Encounter*, ed. Michael Ann Holly and Marquard Smith, 85–102. New Haven: Yale University Press, 2008.

Gould, Stephen Jay. *Leonardo's Mountain of Clams and the Diet of Worms: Essays on Natural History*. New York: Harmony Books, 1998.

Grafton, Anthony. *Leon Battista Alberti: Master Builder of the Italian Renaissance*. Cambridge, MA: Harvard University Press, 2002.

Grassi, Umberto. *Bathhouses and Riverbanks: Sodomy in a Renaissance Republic*. Toronto: Center for Renaissance and Reformation Studies, 2021.

Greene, Thomas M. "The Flexibility of the Self in Renaissance Literature." In *The Disciplines of Criticism: Essays in Literary Theory, Interpretations and History*, ed. Peter Demetz, Thomas M. Greene, and Lowry Silson Jr., 241–64. New Haven: Yale University Press, 1968.

Hatfield, Rab. *Finding Leonardo. The Case for Recovering the Battle of Anghiari*. Prato: Florentine Press, 2007.

———. *The Three Mona Lisas*. Milan: Officina Libraria, 2014.

Henneberger, Melinda. "The Leonardo Cover-Up." *New York Times Magazine*, April 21, 2002.

Henry, Tom, and Paul Joannides. *Late Raphael*. Exhibition catalog. Madrid: Museo del Prado, 2012.

Hewitt, Simon. *Leonardo da Vinci and the Book of Doom: Bianca Sforza, the Sforziada and Artful Propaganda in Renaissance Milan*. London: Unicorn Books, 2020.

Holmes, Megan. "Copying Practices and Marketing Strategies in a Fifteenth-Century Florentine Painter's Workshop." In *Artistic Exchange and Cultural Translation in the Italian Renaissance City*, ed. Stephen J. Campbell and Stephen J. Milner, 38–74. Cambridge: Cambridge University Press, 2004.

Hope, Charles. "The Biography of Leonardo in Vasari's *Vite*." In *The Lives of Leonardo*, ed. Thomas Frangenberg and Rodney Palmer, 11–28. London: Warburg Institute, 2013.

Houssaye, Arsène. *Histoire de Léonard de Vinci*. Paris: Libraire Académique Didier et Cie, 1869.

Howes, Hetta Elizabeth. *Transformative Waters in Late-Medieval Literature: From Aelred of Rievaulx to the Book of Margery Kempe*. Cambridge: D. S. Brewer, 2023.

Isaacson, Walter. *Leonardo da Vinci*. New York: Simon and Schuster, 2017.

Isbouts, J. P., and C. H. Brown. "A Multidisciplinary Study of the Tongerlo *Last Supper* and Its Attribution to Leonardo da Vinci's Second Milanese Studio." *Conservation Science in Cultural Heritage* 20 (2020): 49–64.

Jacobs, Jerry A. *In Defense of Disciplines: Interdisciplinarity and Specialization in the Research University*. Chicago: University of Chicago Press, 2013.

Jeanneret, Michel. *Perpetual Motion: Transforming Shapes in the Renaissance from Da Vinci to Montaigne*. Baltimore: Johns Hopkins University Press, 2001.

Joost Gaugier, Christiane L. *Pythagoras and Renaissance Europe: Finding Heaven*. Cambridge: Cambridge University Press, 2009.

Keele, Kenneth D. *Leonardo da Vinci's Elements of the Science of Man*. New York: Academic Press, 1983.

Keele, Kenneth D., and Carlo Pedretti. *Leonardo da Vinci: Corpus of the Anatomical Drawings in the Collection of Her Majesty the Queen at Windsor Castle*. 2 vols. London: Johnson Reprint Co., 1979–80.

Keizer, Joost. *Leonardo's Paradox: Word and Image in the Making of Renaissance Culture*. London: Reaktion, 2019.

Kemp, Martin. "'A Chaos of Intelligence': Leonardo's *Traité* and the Perspective Wars at the Académie Royale." In *Re-reading Leonardo: The Treatise on Painting across Europe, 1550–1900*, ed. Claire Farago, 237–55. Abingdon: Ashgate, 2009.

———. "From Mimesis to Fantasia: The Quattrocento Vocabulary of Creation, Inspiration and Genius in the Visual Arts." *Viator* 8 (1977): 347–98.

———. "'Il concetto dell'anima' in Leonardo's Early Skull Studies." *Journal of the Warburg and Courtauld Institutes* 34 (1971): 115–34.

———. *Leonardo*. Oxford: Oxford University Press, 2004.

———. *Leonardo da Vinci: The Marvelous Works of Nature and Man*. London: J. M. Dent, 1981. Rev. ed. Oxford: Oxford University Press, 2006.

———. *Leonardo da Vinci: The 100 Milestones*. New York: Sterling Press, 2019.

———. *Living with Leonardo. Fifty Years of Sanity and Insanity in the Art World and Beyond*. London: Thames and Hudson, 2018.

———. "Mirror of His Mind: The Codex in Leonardo's Thought." In *Leonardo da Vinci's Codex Leicester: A New Edition*, ed. Domenico Laurenza and Martin Kemp, vol. 2: *Interpretive Essays and the History of the Codex Leicester*, 19–74. Oxford: Oxford University Press, 2019.

———. "What the Science Says about the *Salvator Mundi*." *Art Newspaper* 334 (May 2021): 5.

Kemp, Martin, Pascal Cotte, et al. *Leonardo da Vinci "La Bella Principessa": The Profile Portrait of a Milanese Woman*. London: Hodder & Stoughton, 2010.

Kemp, Martin, and Giuseppe Pallanti. *Mona Lisa: The People and the Painting*. Oxford: Oxford University Press, 2017.

Kemp, Martin, Robert B. Simon, and Margaret Dalivalle. *Leonardo's Salvator Mundi and the Collecting of Leonardo in the Stuart Courts*. Oxford: Oxford University Press, 2020.

Kent, F. W. "Patron-Client Networks in Renaissance Florence and the Emergence of Lorenzo as 'Maestro della Bottega.'" In *Lorenzo de' Medici: New Perspectives*, ed. Bernard Toscani, 279–81. New York: Peter Lang, 1993.

Kirchner, Thomas. "Between Academicism and Its Critics: Leonardo da Vinci's *Traité de la Peinture* and Eighteenth-Century French Art Theory." In *Re-reading Leonardo: The Treatise on Painting across Europe, 1550–1900*, ed. Claire Farago, 299–327. Abingdon: Ashgate, 2009.

Klapisch-Zuber, Christiane. "*Parenti, amici, vicini*: Una famiglia mercantile del Quattrocento." *Quaderni storici* 33 (1976): 953–82.

Klein, Stefan. *Leonardo's Legacy: How Da Vinci Reimagined the World*. Trans. Shelley Frisch. Philadelphia: Da Capo Press, 2008.

Koering, Jérémie. *Les iconophages: Une histoire de l'ingestion des images*. Paris: Actes Sud, 2021.

Kramnick, Jonathan. "The Interdisciplinary Fallacy." *Representations* 140 (2017): 67–83.

Krautheimer, Richard. *Lorenzo Ghiberti*. Princeton: Princeton University Press, 1983.

Kris, Ernst, and Otto Kurz. *Legend, Myth, and Magic in the Image of the Artist: A Historical Experiment*. 1934. New Haven: Yale University Press, 1981.

Kwakkelstein, Michael W. "Did Leonardo Always Practice What He Preached? Discrepancies between Leonardo's Didactic Views on Painting and His Artistic Practice." In *"Proxima Studia": Arte e letteratura a Firenze (1300–1600)*, ed. Stefano Ugo Baldassarri, 107–36. Florence: Fabrizio Serra Editore, 2011.

———. *Leonardo da Vinci as a Physiognomist: Theory and Drawing Practice*. Leiden: Primavera Pers, 1994.

———. "Leonardo da Vinci's Recurrent Use of Patterns of Individual Limbs, Stock Poses and Facial Stereotypes." In *Artistic Innovations and Cultural Zones*, ed. Ingrid Ciulisova, 45–61. Spectrum Slovakia series, vol. 7. Frankfurt: Peter Lang Verlag, 2014.

———. "The Limited Impact of Leonardo da Vinci's Ideas on Painting in Sforza Milan." *Artibus et Historiae* 39 (2018): 77–98.

La Sala Grande di Palazzo Vecchio e la "Battaglia di Anghiari" di Leonardo da Vinci: Dalla configurazione architettonica all'apparato decorativo. Ed. Roberta Barsanti, Gianluca Belli, Emanuela Ferretti, and Cecilia Frosinini. Florence: Olschki, 2019.

Ladis, Andrew. "Giovanni Pisano: Unfinished Business in Siena." In *Studies in Italian Art*, 177–84. London: Pindar Press, 2001.

Langmead, Alan, Christopher Nygren, Paul Rodriguez, and Alan Craig. "Leonardo, Morelli, and the Computational Mirror." *DHQ: Digital Humanities Quarterly* 15 (2021): 1. https://www.digitalhumanities.org/dhq/vol/15/1/000540/000540.html.

Lankford, Mike. *Becoming Leonardo: An Exploded View of the Life of Leonardo da Vinci*. New York: Melville House, 2017.

Leader, Anne. "'In the Tomb of Ser Piero': Death and Burial in the Family of Leonardo da Vinci." *Renaissance Studies* 31 (2016): 324–45.

Lehman, Geoff. "Leonardo, Van Eyck, and the Epistemology of Landscape." In *Leonardo in Dialogue: The Artist amid His Contemporaries*, ed. Francesca Borgo, Rodolfo Maffeis, and Alessandro Nova, 97–119. Venice: Marsilio, 2019.

Leonardo y la copia de Mona Lisa del Museo del Prado. Madrid: Museo del Prado, 2021.

Lewis, Ben. *The Last Leonardo: The Secret Lives of the World's Most Expensive Painting*. London: Collins, 2019.

Lives of Leonardo da Vinci. Ed. Charles Robertson. Los Angeles: J. Paul Getty Museum, 2019.

Lohrmann, Dietrich. "The Date of Leonardo da Vinci's Letter to Ludovico Sforza (1489)." *Academia Letters*, May 2022. https://www.academia.edu/81183602/The_date_of_Leonardo_da_Vincis_letter_to_Ludovico_Sforza_1489_.

Lomazzo, Gian Paolo. *Scritti sulle arti*. Ed. Roberto Paolo Ciardi. 2 vols. Florence: Marchi and Bertolli, 1973–74.

Long, Pamela O. *Artisan/Practitioners and the Rise of the New Sciences, 1400–1600*. Corvallis: Oregon State University Press, 2011.

Lugli, Emanuele. *Knots, or the Violence of Desire in Renaissance Florence*. Chicago: University of Chicago Press, 2023.

———. "Leonardo and the Hair Makers." In *Leonardo in Dialogue: The Artist amid His Contemporaries*, ed. Francesca Borgo, Rodolfo Maffeis, and Alessandro Nova, 19–51. Venice: Marsilio, 2019.

Machiavelli, Niccolò. *Istorie fiorentine*, in *Opere*. Ed. Mario Bonfantini. Milan: Ricciardi, 1963.

Malcolm, Janet. *The Silent Woman: Sylvia Plath and Ted Hughes*. New York: Vintage Books, 1993.

Marani, Pietro C. *Leonardo da Vinci: The Complete Paintings*. New York: Abrams, 2000.

———, ed. *Leonardo da Vinci's Last Supper for Francois I: A Masterpiece in Gold and Silk*. Milan: Skira, 2019.

Marani, Pietro C., and Pinin Brambilla Barcilon. *Leonardo: The Last Supper*. Chicago: University of Chicago Press, 2001. Original Italian edition: Milan: Motta Editore, 1999.

Marani, Pietro C., et al. *The Legacy of Leonardo: Painters in Lombardy, 1490–1530*. Milan: Skira, 1998.

Marsden, Joanna Woods. "Leonardo da Vinci's *Mona Lisa*: A Portrait without a Commissioner?" In *Illuminating Leonardo: A Festschrift for Carlo Pedretti Celebrating His 70 Years of Scholarship (1944–2014)*, ed. Constance Moffatt and Sara Tagliagamba, 169–83. Leiden: Brill, 2016.

Martin, John. "Inventing Sincerity, Refashioning Prudence: The Discovery of the Individual in Renaissance Europe." *American Historical Review* 102 (1997): 1309–42.

Martines, Lauro. *An Italian Renaissance Sextet: Six Tales in Historical Context*. With translations by Murtha Baca. New York: Marsilio, 1994.

Marx, William. *The Hatred of Literature*. Cambridge, MA: Harvard University Press, 2018.

Melius, Jeremy. "Connoisseurship, Painting, and Personhood." *Art History* 34 (2011): 288–309.

Merback, Mitchell B. *Perfection's Therapy: An Essay on Albrecht Dürer's Melancolia I*. New York: Zone Books, 2017.

Merezhkovsky, Dmitry. *Leonardo da Vinci: The Resurrection of the Gods*. Trans. Ignat Avsey. London: Alma Classics, 2014. Original Russian edition, 1900.

Michelet, Jules. *Histoire de France*. 19 vols. Paris: C. Marpon et E. Flammarion, 1879.

McCall, Timothy. *Brilliant Bodies: Fashioning Courtly Men in Early Renaissance Italy*. University Park: Penn State University Press, 2022.

———. *Making the Renaissance Man: Masculinity in the Courts of Renaissance Italy*. London: Reaktion Books, 2023.

Nagel, Alexander. "Leonardo and Sfumato." *RES: Anthropology and Aesthetics* 24 (1993): 7–20.

Neilson, Christina. *Practice and Theory in the Italian Renaissance Workshop: Verrocchio and the Epistemology of Making Art*. Cambridge: Cambridge University Press, 2019.

Nelson, Jonathan K. "Leonardo contro Botticelli: Nuovi spunti su un'antica rivalità." In *Leonardo e Firenze: Fogli scelti dal Codice Atlantico*, ed. Cristina Acidini, 125–33. Florence: Giunti, 2019.

Newman, Barbara. *The Permeable Self: Five Medieval Relationships*. Philadelphia: University of Pennsylvania Press, 2021.

Newton, H. Travers, and John R. Spencer. "On the Location of Leonardo's *Battle of Anghiari*." *Art Bulletin* 64 (1982): 45–52.

Nicholl, Charles. *Leonardo da Vinci: The Flights of the Mind*. London: Penguin, 2004.

Noë, Alva. "Experience and Experiment in Art." *Journal of Consciousness Studies* 7 (2000): 123–35.

Nova, Alessandro. "'Addj 5 aghossto 1473': L'oggetto e le sue interpretazioni." In *Leonardo da Vinci on Nature: Knowledge and Representation*, ed. Fabio Frosini and Alessandro Nova, 285–303. Venice: Marsilio, 2013.

Østermark-Johansen, Lene. "The Power of an Intimate Presence: Walter Pater's Leonardo Essay (1869) and Its Influence at the *fin de siècle*." In *Leonardo in Britain: Collections and Historical Reception*, ed. Juliana Barone and Susanna Avery-Quash, 303–23. Florence: Olschki, 2019.

Pardo, Mary. "The Subject of Savoldo's Magdalene." *Art Bulletin* 71 (1989): 67–91.

Passannante, Gerard. *Catastrophizing: Materialism and the Making of Disaster*. Chicago: University of Chicago Press, 2019.

Pater, Walter. *The Renaissance: Studies in Art and Poetry*. 1893. 4th ed. Mineola, NY: Dover, 2005.

Patetta, Luciano. "Bramante autore di sonetti burleschi." In *Bramante e la sua cerchia: A Milano e in Lombardia 1480–1500*, ed. Luciano Patetta, 77–81. Milan: Electa, 2009.

Pederson, Jill. *Leonardo, Bramante, and the Academia: Art and Friendship in Fifteenth-Century Milan*. Turnhout: Brepols/Harvey Miller, 2020.

Pedretti, Carlo. "*Eccetera: Perché la minestra si fredda*." Codice Arundel, fol. 245 recto. Lettura Vinciana 15. Florence: Giunti Barbèra, 1975.

———. "Il guardaroba di Leonardo e Salaì." In *Leonardo da Vinci, L'angelo incarnato, e Salaì*, 390–94. Foligno: CB Edizioni, 2009.

———. "Li Medici mi crearono e destrussono." *Achademia Leonardi Vinci* 6 (1993): 174–84.

———. "The Ravenna Monster." In *Leonardo da Vinci Codex Atlanticus: A Catalogue of Its Newly Restored Sheets*, 307–17. Florence: Giunti, 1979.

Pedretti, Carlo, and Margherita Melani. *Leonardo da Vinci: L'Angelo incarnato & Salaì*. Prato: CB Edizioni, 2011.

Perini Folesani, Giovanna. "Leonardo and His Eighteenth-Century Italian Biographies." In *The Lives of Leonardo*, ed. Thomas Frangenberg and Rodney Palmer, 83–114. London: Warburg Institute, 2013.

[Petrarch]. *Francesco Petrarca: Invectives*. Ed. and trans. David Marsh. Cambridge, MA: Harvard University Press, 2003.

Phillips, Claude. "Verrocchio, or Leonardo da Vinci?" *Art Journal* [London], n.s. (1899): 33–39.

Pieraccini, Massimiliano, Daniele Meccati, Guido Luzi, Maurizio Seracini, Gianpaolo Pinelli, and Carlo Atzeni. "Non-contact Intrawall Penetrating Radar for Heritage Survey: The Search of the *Battle of Anghiari* by Leonardo da Vinci." *NDT&E International* 38 (2005): 151–57.

Pilliod, Elizabeth. *Pontormo, Bronzino, and Allori: A Genealogy of Florentine Art*. New Haven: Yale University Press, 2001.

Pino, Domenico. *Storia genuina del Cenacolo insigne dipinto da Leonardo da Vinci nel refettorio de' padri domenicani di Santa Maria delle Grazie di Milano*. Milan: Cesare Orena, 1796.

Pisarek, Kasia. "*La Bella Principessa*—Arguments against the Attribution to Leonardo." *Artibus et Historiae* 36 (2015): 61–89.

Poliziano, Angelo. *Detti piacevoli*. Ed. Tiziano Zanato. Rome: Istituto della Enciclopedia Italiana, 1983.

Pontano, Giovanni Gioviano. *Dialogues: Volume I, Charon and Antonius*. Ed. and trans. Julia Haig Gaisser. Cambridge, MA: Harvard University Press, 2012.

Pope-Hennessy, John. "Donatello's Bronze David." In *Scritti di storia dell'arte in onore di Federico Zeri*, 122–27. Milan: Electa, 1984.

———. *Italian Gothic Sculpture*. 3rd ed. New York: Phaidon, 1986.

Pye, Christopher. "Leonardo's Hand: Mimesis, Sexuality, and Early Modern Political Aesthetics." *Representations* 111 (2010): 1–32.

Quinet, Edgar. *Les révolutions d'Italie*. Paris: Pagnerre, 1857.

Quiviger, François. *Leonardo da Vinci: Self, Art and Nature*. London: Reaktion, 2019.

Radke, Gary, ed. *Leonardo and the Art of Sculpture*. Exhibition catalog. New Haven: Yale University Press, 2009.

Randall, John Herman, Jr. "The Place of Leonardo Da Vinci in the Emergence of Modern Science." *Journal of the History of Ideas* 14 (1953): 191–202.

Randolph, Adrian W. B. *Engaging Symbols: Gender, Politics, and Public Art in Fifteenth-Century Florence*. New Haven: Yale University Press, 2002.

Ravaisson-Mollien, Charles. *Les manuscrits de Léonard de Vinci*. 6 vols. Paris: A. Quantin, 1881–91.

Restoro d'Arezzo. *La composizione del mondo*. Ed. Alberto Morino. Parma: Ugo Guanda, 1997.

Rinaldi, Furio. "The *Academia Leonardi Vinci*: Leonardo's Pupils, Followers and the Legacy of the Master's Works." In *Leonardo da Vinci, 1452–1519: The Design of the World*, ed. Pietro C. Marani and Maria Teresa Fiorio, 439–49. Milan: Skira, 2015.

Robertson, Iain, ed. *Understanding International Art Markets and Management*. London: Routledge, 2005.

Robichaud, Denis J.-J. *Plato's Persona: Marsilio Ficino, Renaissance Humanism, and Platonic Traditions*. Philadelphia: University of Pennsylvania Press, 2018.

Rocke, Michael. *Forbidden Friendships: Homosexuality and Male Culture in Renaissance Florence*. Oxford: Oxford University Press, 1996.

Rosenberg, Gary D. "An Artistic Perspective on the Continuity of Space and the Origin of Modern Geologic Thought." *Earth Sciences History* 20 (2001): 127–55.

Russel, Rinaldina. *Sonnet: The Very Rich and Varied World of the Italian Sonnet*. Bloomington, IN: Archway, 2017.

Saiber, Arielle. *Measured Words: Computation and Writing in Renaissance Italy*. Toronto: University of Toronto Press, 2017.

Sammer, Jan. *Leonardo da Vinci: The Untold Story of His Final Years*. Independently published, 2019.

Sassoon, Donald. *Becoming Mona Lisa: The Making of a Global Icon*. New York: Harcourt, 2001.

Savonarola, Michele. *Libellus De magnificis ornamentis regie civitatis Padue Michaelis Savonarole*. Ed. Arnaldo Segarizzi. Rerum Italicarum Scriptores, XXIV–XXV. Città di Castello: Editore S. Lapi, 1902.

Scannelli, Francesco. *Il microcosmo della pittura*. Cesena: Il Neri, 1657.

Schapiro, Meyer. "Leonardo and Freud: An Art-Historical Study." *Journal of the History of Ideas* 17 (1956): 147–78.

Schlecter, Armin. "*Ita Leonardus Vincius facit in omnibus suis picturis*: Leonardo da Vincis Mona Lisa und die Cicero-Philologie von Angelo Poliziano bis Johann Georg Graevius." IASL, April 29, 2008. https://www.iaslonline.lmu.de/index.php?vorgang_id=2889.

Scognamiglio, Nino Smiraglia. "Nuovi documenti su Leonardo da Vinci." *Archivio storico dell'arte* 2 (1896): 313–15.

Seracini, Maurizio. "Indagini diagnostiche sulla Adorazione dei Magi di Leonardo da Vinci." In *La mente di Leonardo: Nel laboratorio del Genio Universale*, ed. Paolo Galuzzi, 94–101. Exhibition catalog. Florence: Giunti, 2006.

———. *Oltre il visibile: Indagini scientifiche sul disegno*. In *Leonardo da Vinci: Studio per l'Adorazione dei Magi*, ed. Francesco Camerota, 33–107. Roma: Argos, 2006.

Settis, Salvatore. *If Venice Dies*. Trans. André Naffis-Sahely. New York: New Vessel Press, 2016. Original Italian edition, 2014.

Smith, Pamela H. *The Body of the Artisan: Art and Experience in the Scientific Revolution*. Chicago: University of Chicago Press, 2004.

Sohm, Philip L. *The Artist Grows Old: The Aging of Art and Artists in Early Modern Italy*. New Haven: Yale University Press, 2007.

Soussloff, Catherine M. "Discourse/Figure/Love: The Location of Style in Early Modern Sources on Leonardo da Vinci." In *Leonardo da Vinci and the Ethics of Style*, ed. Claire Farago, 37–58. Manchester: Manchester University Press, 2008.

Steinberg, Leo. *Leonardo's Incessant Last Supper*. New York: Zone Books, 2001.

Struever, Nancy. "Petrarch's Invective *Contra Medicum*: An Early Confrontation of Rhetoric and Medicine." *MLN* 108 (1993): 659–79.

Summers, David. "Chiaroscuro, or the Rhetoric of Realism." In *Leonardo da Vinci and Optics*, ed. Francesca Fiorani and Alessandro Nova, 29–55. Venice: Marsilio, 2013.

———. *The Judgment of Sense: Renaissance Naturalism and the Rise of Aesthetics*. Cambridge: Cambridge University Press, 1987.

Syson, Luke. "Leonardo and Leonardism in Sforza Milan." In *Artists at Court: Image-making and Identity, 1300–1550*, ed. Stephen J. Campbell, 106–23. Chicago: University of Chicago Press, 2004.

———. "The Rewards of Service: Leonardo da Vinci and the Duke of Milan." In *Leonardo da Vinci: Painter at the Court of Milan*, ed. Luke Syson with Larry Keith, 13–53. London: National Gallery, 2011.

Taine, Hippolyte. *Voyage en Italie*. 1869. Paris: Hachette et Cie, 1874.

Talvacchia, Bette. "Raphael's Workshop and the Development of a Managerial Style." In *The Cambridge Companion to Raphael*, ed. Marcia B. Hall, 167–85. Cambridge: Cambridge University Press, 2005.

Trumbach, Randolph. "The Transformation of Sodomy from the Renaissance to the Modern World and Its General Sexual Consequences." *Signs: Journal of Women in Culture and Society* 37 (2012): 832–47.

Turner, A. Richard. *Inventing Leonardo*. Berkeley: University of California Press, 1992.

Turner, James Grantham. *Eros Visible: Art, Sexuality and Antiquity in Renaissance Italy*. New Haven: Yale University Press, 2017.

Valentiner, Wilhelm. "Leonardo and Desiderio." *Burlington Magazine* 61 (1932): 52–61.

Valéry, Paul. *Collected Works of Paul Valéry*. Vol. 8: *Leonardo, Poe, Mallarme*. Trans. M. Cowley and James R. Lawler. Princeton: Princeton University Press, 2015.

Varese, Federico, "Asset Management: 'Salvator Mundi' and the Unreality of the Art Market." *Times Literary Supplement*, August 19, 2019.

Vasari, Giorgio. *Lives of the Painters, Sculptors, and Architects*. Trans. Gaston de Vere. 2 vols. 1927. London: Everyman's Library, 1996.

Vecce, Carlo. "Dalla parte di Melzi." In *Decoding Leonardo's Codices: Compilation, Dispersal, and Reproduction Technologies*, ed. Paolo Galluzzi and Alessandro Nova, 89–110. Venice: Marsilio, 2022.

———. *Il sorriso di Caterina: la madre di Leonardo*. Florence: Giunti, 2023.

———. "In margine alla prima lettera di Andrea Corsali (Leonardo in India)." *Ai confini della letteratura: Atti della giornata in onore di Mario Pozzi*, ed. Jean Louis Fournel et al., 67–81. Turin: Nino Aragno, 2015.

———. "Le biografie antiche di Leonardo." In *Leonardo da Vinci: La vera immagine: Documenti e testimonianze sulla vita e sull'opera*, ed. Vanna Arrighi, Anna Bellinazzi, and Edoardo Villata, 62–71. Florence: Giunti, 2005.

———. *Leonardo*. Rome: Salerno, 2006.

———. "Per Caterina." *Leonardiana* 1 (2023): 11–48.

———. "Word and Image in Leonardo's Writings." In *Leonardo da Vinci Master Draftsman*, 59–77. Exhibition catalog, ed. Carmen C. Bambach. New York: Metropolitan Museum, 2003.

Venturi, Giovanni Battista. *Essai sur les ouvrages physico-mathématiques de Léonard de Vinci*. Paris : Chez Duprat, 1797.

Verrocchio: Master of Leonardo. Exhibition catalog. Florence: Palazzo Strozzi. Ed. Andrea de' Marchi and Francesco Cagliotti. Venice: Marsilio, 2019.

Verrocchio: Sculptor and Painter of Renaissance Florence. Washington, DC: National Gallery, 2019.

Vezzosi, Alessandro. *Leonardo da Vinci: La pittura. Un nuovo sguardo*. Florence: Giunti, 2018.

Vicioso, Julia. *Leonardo da Vinci e la Nazione Fiorentina a Roma*. Rome: GBE, 2019.

Villata, Eduoardo. "Gaudenzio di fronte a Leonardo: Inclinazioni e resistenze verso il Cenacolo tra Piemonte e Lombardia." In *Il Genio e le Passioni: Leonardo e il Cenacolo; Precedenti, innovazioni, riflessi di un capolavoro*, ed. Pietro C. Marani, 155–64. Milan: Skira, 2001.

Voragine, Jacobus de. *The Golden Legend: Readings on the Saints*. 2 vols. Trans. William Granger Ryan. Princeton: Princeton University Press, 1993.

Wallace, Kathleen. *The Network Self: Relation, Process, and Personal Identity*. New York: Routledge, 2019.

Weissman, Ronald F. E. "The Importance of Being Ambiguous: Social Relations, Individualism, and Identity in Renaissance Florence." In *Urban Life in the Renaissance*, ed. Susan Zimmerman and Ronald F. E. Weissman, 269–81. Newark: University of Delaware Press, 1989.

Wenderholm, Iris. *Bild und Berührung: Skulptur und Malerei auf dem Altar der italienischen Frührenaissance*. Berlin: Deutscher Kunstverlag, 2006.

White, Michael. *Leonardo: The First Scientist*. New York: St. Martin's Press, 2001.

Williams, Robert. "Leonardo and the Florentine Academy." In *Re-Reading Leonardo: The Treatise on Painting across Europe, 1550–1900*, ed. Claire Farago, 61–76. London: Routledge, 2009.

———. *Raphael and the Redefinition of Art in Renaissance Italy*. Cambridge: Cambridge University Press, 2017.

Wilson-Lee, Edward. *A History of Water*. London: HarperCollins, 2022.

Wölfflin, Heinrich. *Die Klassische Kunst* (1898). English version, *Classic Art: An Introduction to the Art of the Italian Renaissance*. Trans. Peter Murray and Linda Murray. London: Phaidon, 1952.

Zöllner, Frank. "John F. Kennedy and Leonardo's Mona Lisa: Art as the Continuation of Politics." In *Radical Art History: Internationale Anthologie*, ed. Wolfgang Kersten, 466–79. Zurich: ZIP, 1997.

———. *La Battaglia di Anghiari di Leonardo da Vinci fra mitologia e politica*. Vol. 37 of *Lettura vinciana*. Florence: Giunti, 1998.

———. *Leonardo da Vinci: The Complete Paintings and Drawings*. Cologne: Taschen, 2011.

———. "Leonardo da Vinci's *Salvator Mundi*, Its Pictorial Tradition and Its Context as a Devotional Image." *Artibus et Historiae* 42 (2021): 53–84.

———. "Leonardo da Vinci on Painting: From the Use of Types to the Criticism of Types." In *Leonardo da Vinci e la lingua della pittura in Europa (secoli XIV–XVII)*, ed. Margherita Quaglino and Anna Sconza, 89–98. Florence: Olschki, 2022.

———. "*Ogni pittore dipinge se*: Leonardo da Vinci and 'Automimesis.'" In *Der Künstler über sich in seinem Werk: Internationales Symposium der Bibliotheca Hertziana*, ed. Matthias Winner, 137–60. Weinheim: Wiley-VCH Verlag, 1992.

Zorach, Rebecca. "Fat Minerva: Recent Books on Perspective and *Perspectiva*, Medieval and Renaissance." *Exemplaria* 23 (2011): 415–25.

———. "Nature, Imagination, and Authority: Leonardo in Seventeenth-Century France." In *Leonardo in Dialogue: The Artist amid His Contemporaries*, ed. Francesca Borgo, Rodolfo Maffeis, and Alessandro Nova, 335–51. Venice: Marsilio, 2019.

———. *The Passionate Triangle*. Chicago: University of Chicago Press, 2011.

Zubov, V. P. *Leonardo da Vinci*. Trans. David H. Kraus. Foreword by Myron P. Gilmore. Cambridge, MA: Harvard University Press, 1968.

INDEX

Note: Page numbers in *italic* type indicate illustrations.

ILLUSTRATION CREDITS